DOMESTICITY AND DISSENT IN THE SEVENTEENTH CENTURY

In *Domesticity and Dissent* Katharine Gillespie examines writings by seventeenth-century English Puritan women who fought for religious freedom. Seeking the right to preach and prophesy, women such as Katherine Childley, Anna Trapnel, Elizabeth Poole, and Anne Wentworth envisioned the modern political principles of toleration, the separation of church from state, privacy, and individualism. Gillespie argues that their sermons, prophecies, and petitions illustrate the fact that these liberal theories did not originate only with such well-known male thinkers as John Locke and Thomas Hobbes. Rather, they emerged also from a group of determined female religious dissenters who used the Bible to reassess traditional definitions of womanhood, public speech, and religious and political authority. Gillespie takes the "pamphlet literatures" of the seventeenth century as important subjects for analysis, and her book contributes to the growing scholarship on the revolutionary writings that emerged during the volatile years of the mid-seventeenth-century civil war in England.

KATHARINE GILLESPIE is assistant professor of English and American literature at Miami University in Oxford, Ohio. She has published articles in *Genders*, *Bunyan Studies*, *Tulsa Studies in Women's Literature*, and *Symbiosis*.

DOMESTICITY AND DISSENT IN THE SEVENTEENTH CENTURY

English Women Writers and the Public Sphere

KATHARINE GILLESPIE

PUBLISHED BY THE PRESS SYNDICATE OF THE UNIVERSITY OF CAMBRIDGE
The Pitt Building, Trumpington Street, Cambridge, United Kingdom

CAMBRIDGE UNIVERSITY PRESS
The Edinburgh Building, Cambridge, CB2 2RU, UK
40 West 20th Street, New York, NY 10011–4211, USA
477 Williamstown Road, Port Melbourne, VIC 3207, Australia
Ruiz de Alarcón 13, 28014 Madrid, Spain
Dock House, The Waterfront, Cape Town 8001, South Africa

http://www.cambridge.org

© Katharine Gillespie 2004

This book is in copyright. Subject to statutory exception
and to the provisions of relevant collective licensing agreements,
no reproduction of any part may take place without
the written permission of Cambridge University Press.

First published 2004

Printed in the United Kingdom at the University Press, Cambridge

Typeface Adobe Garamond 11/12.5 pt.   *System* LATEX 2ε   [TB]

A catalogue record for this book is available from the British Library

Library of Congress Cataloging in Publication data
Gillespie, Katharine.
Domesticity and dissent in the seventeenth century: English women writers and the
public sphere / Katharine Gillespie.
p.   cm.
Includes bibliographical references and index.
ISBN 0 521 83063 X
1. English literature – Early modern, 1500–1700 – History and criticism.   2. Great
Britain – History – Civil War, 1642–1649 – Literature and the war.   3. Literature and
history – Great Britain – History – 17th century.   4. English literature – Puritan
authors – History and criticism.   5. English literature – Women authors – History and
criticism.   6. Dissenters, Religious – England – History – 17th century.   7. Women and
literature – England – History – 17th century.   8. Puritan women – England – Intellectual life.
9. Dissenters, Religious, in literature.   I. Title.
PR435.G55   2004
820.9′358 – dc21   2003053296

ISBN 0 521 83063 X hardback

For Nick

Do not you enact any law against any Saints exercising the gifts of the spirit that are given to them in Preaching or prophesying because the Lord hath promised in the latter dayes to power out his spirit more abundantly upon all flesh, & your sons and your daughters shall prophesie

Mary Cary, *A Word in Season To the Kingdom of England*
(1647), p. 15

Contents

Acknowledgments		*page* x
	Introduction: Sabrina versus the state	1
1	"Born of the mother's seed": liberalism, feminism, and religious separatism	25
2	A hammer in her hand: Katherine Chidley and Anna Trapnel separate church from state	62
3	Cure for a diseased head: divorce and contract in the prophecies of Elizabeth Poole	115
4	The unquenchable smoking flax: Sarah Wight, Anne Wentworth, and the "rise" of the sovereign individual	166
5	Improving God's estate: pastoral servitude and the free market in the writings of Mary Cary	215
	Conclusion	262
Index		267

Acknowledgments

This book began, I'm pretty sure, back when my grandmother, Eleanor Henry Walke, reassured the anxious kids who had gathered in her basement for one of her many private prayer meetings that, yes, had he lived in the late twentieth century, Jesus would have worn jeans. That interesting combination of independent religion, basements, freelance preaching women, and topical exegesis (not to mention the denim-clad Jesus) so indelibly forged in my mind at that moment, has continued to fuel my enjoyment of the ways in which ordinary individuals participate in the creation of new cultures and new ideas.

Since then, a whole lot of Beat literature and L*A*N*G*U*A*G*E poetry has come in between me and the study of seventeenth-century English Puritanism, and so my story picks up again several years later at Temple University, where I earned my master's degree. There, in a seminar in early American literature, Sharon Harris asked, why do so few people read Anne Bradstreet's early poetry? Intrigued, I began a quest that led me to learn that Bradstreet's sister, Sarah Keayne, had done a little street preaching during a trip to London. A woman? Street preaching? In the seventeenth century? I've never stopped being intrigued. I am grateful to Sharon for firing my imagination, and to the many faculty members who continued to stoke it both at Temple and at SUNY Buffalo, where I earned the Ph.D. In particular, Susan Eilenberg showed me how pleasurable it can be to read Milton late into the snowy Buffalo night. Mili Clark gave me actual course credit for reenacting almost all of the Putney Debates. And Susan Howe, whose *Eikon Basilike* first taught me to see the world upside down, took the time to teach me Du Bartas and to convince me that my obsession with a handful of blurry pamphlets by women named Anna Trapnel and Elizabeth Poole was worthwhile.

Finally there is my dissertation committee. Robert Daly, a fellow Ohioan, encouraged my interest in Puritan women and offered generous praise for my dissertation when it was needed most. Deidre Lynch and Stacy Hubbard represented enabling role models as feminist scholars and inspired me to use my work on female sectarians to engage larger critical questions. And the arrival of director James Holstun during my second year at Buffalo was somehow meant to be. Pleased (and somewhat startled) to learn that I had actually done a whole qualifying exam list on mid-seventeenth-century English prophetesses, Jim took me under his wing and shared with me his own vast expertise in the field and his enthusiasm for the enthusiasts. He has worked ever since to make me feel that a girl from small-town Ohio can be part of a larger transatlantic community of scholars working in the pamphlet literatures of seventeenth-century England. The warm encouragement that he and Joanna Tinker have given me over the years has made all the difference.

Speaking of which, I am extremely grateful to those in the field who, over the years, made it possible for me to present and publish my work. These include Vera Camden, Teresa Feroli, Carolyn Williams, Ann Kibbey, and Paul Stevenson. In this vein, I must also thank the Society for the Study of Early Modern Women for rewarding my essay on Katherine Chidley with an honorable mention prize. This recognition played no small part in making me feel that I might be doing something of interest and value to others. I treasure it. Many others – Arthur Marotti, Margaret Olof Thickstun, John Rogers, Nigel Smith, Diane Purkiss, Catharine Gray, Carola Scott-Luckens, David Norbrook, Sharon Achinstein, Sylvia Brown, Melissa Mowry, Jodi Mikalachki, Sara Rubenstein, and Laura Lungar Knoppers – posed thoughtful questions, floated useful comments, and/or shared their own work. Finally, two readers at Cambridge University Press offered extremely beneficial suggestions at that crucial, late stage of composition, when it is difficult to appraise one's own words with a cold eye. I am deeply indebted to all for influencing and educating me. And to Ray Ryan for his deft and pivotal stewardship.

By providing me with release time and summer research support, Sam Houston State University helped me to move beyond the dissertation. My senior colleagues in the English department, Gene Young and John Schwetman, deserve special thanks. Other "Sam" pals – Joe Thomas, Julie Hall, John Trombold, Susan Donahue, Peter Donahue, Rafael Saumell-Munoz, Helena Halmari, Chris Buttram, Paul Child, and Debbie Phelps – did their part by brewing up a rowdy and brilliant mix of intellectual and social camaraderie. I feel particularly grateful to Rafael for sharing with a life story that filled me with conviction. And to Julie and

Bob Donahoo for all they did to help me find my initial way into the profession.

By providing further release time and research monies, Miami University enabled me to take this book home. Diane Sadoff's intelligent advice was instrumental. Judith Zinsser, Ann Little (an honorary Redhawk), Heather Schell, and Laura Mandell provided additional writing support. Sally Lloyd arranged for me to present portions of my work at a Women's Studies Colloquium. Brit Harwood and Scott Shershow asked just the right questions. Gregg Crane guided me through the legalities. Keith Tuma saw me through the endgame. Finally, Frances Dolan cut across all categories and helped out with everything. An exemplary mentor, she is a major reason why I find myself in the exhilarating position of writing the acknowledgments page for a book.

For helping me to compile hundreds of pamphlets in the days before the internet, I owe a debt of gratitude to research librarians at the State University of New York at Buffalo in Amherst, New York; the Clark Library in Los Angeles, California; Texas A&M University in College Station, Texas; the Ransom Center in Austin, Texas; Miami University in Oxford, Ohio; and the Bodleian Library in Oxford, England. I hope I didn't break too many microfilm copiers along the way.

I cannot go without thanking Brenda Little, my family's babysitter and friend, because without her, there would be no end in sight. The same goes for the many friends who cheered me on at crucial junctures in the journey: Stephanie Theodorou, Tamara Carper, Carl Ragland, Lauren McKinney, Lisa Udel, Robert Rebein, Alyssa Chase, Mary Obropta, Trino Boix, Charlie Jones, and Kerry Maguire. I am deeply grateful to my father and mother, who know more than anyone how much I always wanted to be a writer. Each of the many times they encouraged me to realize a dream is inscribed in these pages, the final one in particular. My brother's beautiful paintings surrounded and inspired me as I wrote. Something of mine was needed to keep his many sports trophies and artistic creations company on the proverbial shelf of family pride. Nick Gillespie encouraged me, supported me, and sacrificed more than I can ever repay. My son, Jack, was born along with the dissertation and my son, Neal, with this book. These two most marvelous of all my creatures are alive in every word.

Introduction: Sabrina versus the state

> this I hold firm,
> Vertue may be assail'd, but never hurt,
> Surpriz'd by unjust force, but not enthralled
>
> John Milton, Comus

THE ADVENTURES OF THE POSSESSIVE SELF

In the anonymously published 1637 version of *A Maske Presented at Ludlow Castle,* Milton narrates the "birth" of the possessive individual.[1] Liberally paraphrased, the story goes something like this:

The Lady could take it no longer. She had been so determined to remain silent while Comus, the seductive Cavalier, plied her virgin ears with seductive sweet talk and such "false rules pranckt in reasons garb" (157) as the sophistical notion that virginity was fool's gold. True "good," he had cooed, "Consists in mutual and partak'n bliss," and then he had punned naughtily: "Beauty is natures coyn," therefore, it "must not be hoorded" but spent, if you know what I mean, if it wants to "be currant" (156).

But the Lady knew what he meant and so, betraying the mark of a true "democratic personality" – one who is compelled to speak even when it is not altogether convenient to do so – she unlocks her lips and lets her tongue fly: "It doesn't matter how much you "wave" your "wand" around, you can never "touch the freedom of my mind" (153).[2] And anyway, I know what "good" means – "Should I go on? Should I say more" – well then, if you need for me to explain "the sage and serious doctrine of Virginity" to you then think again because you're not "fit to hear thyself convinct" (158). And were I to even try, you'd be sorry because the "uncontrouled worth" of my "pure cause" would work my "spirits" up into such a lather that the earth itself would shake until "all your magick structures rear'd so high, Were shatter'd into heaps o're your false head" (158–159).

Comus was shocked. He hadn't even gotten to hear what the "sage and serious doctrine of Virginity" was! She'd found him unworthy of the very effort of explaining it, although her threat to do so was so forceful that it alone gave him the feeling that a "cold shuddring dew" had "dip[ped]" him "all o'r" (159). Still, while she'd unclasped her purse, the "coin" she'd "spent" was not quite what he'd had in mind and so he tried her again, but from a different angle. Come now, he retorted, "This is meer moral babble, and direct / Against the canon laws of our foundation" (159). Just take a sip o' this and you'll feel better.

Does she swallow his concoction? We never know because, at that moment, her brothers rushed in, toting a couple of swords. He'd had his fun, now it was time for the girl to go home.

So what was that "doctrine of virginity" anyway? As they were searching for their sister in the woods outside their estate, fearful that she would succumb to the charms of her wily seducer before they could recover her, the elder brother reassuringly explained it to the younger one thusly: Even if sister does, shall we say, sip the guy's sauce, she'll still be a virgin. For one thing the Attendant Spirit has given us this St. John's wort to give to her, a cleansing herb capable of undoing any, shall we say, damage, and for another, "true virginity" is that which "may be term'd her own," and it allows its bearer to "pass on" through dangers "with unblencht'd majesty" (142). In fact, he rhapsodized, "So dear to Heav'n is Saintly chastity / That when a soul is found sincerely so, / A thousand liveried Angels lacky her, / Driving far off each thing of sin and guilt, / And in cleer dream, and solemn vision / Tell her of things that no gross ear can hear, / Till oft convers with heav'nly habitants / Begin to cast a beam on th' outward shape, / The unpolluted temple of the mind, / And turns it by degrees to the souls essence, / Till all be made immortal" (144).

Oh okay, said little brother, now I (think I) get it.

And so do we. True or "saintly" virginity is not simply an unbroken hymen, rather it is a "divine property" one holds in one's "first self," regardless of who or what crosses its ultimately inviolable boundaries (144). It is not something that someone can "take" from someone else (although it does appear that one can give it away or "alienate" it through a desire all one's own) because one acquires it directly from heaven, through "visions" and "dreams" that one alone can see and hear. Whether or not one's body is chaste, one can always listen to the angels speaking within the "unpolluted temple of the mind," the seat of one's true immortal essence. One need not heed the call to become Comus's "Queen," rather, because of the entitlement that the individual holds by way of the soul, one already walks in an autonomous state of "unblencht'd majesty." The doctrine of virginity is, in short, the enunciation of a baseline "self" which one defines and possesses in defiance of all attempts by others to describe, prescribe, and circumscribe it on *their* terms. What is more, the very act of articulating the doctrine is a sign of its efficacy – one may "have intercourse" with public authority because one's self ultimately and already resides beyond any other's jurisdiction; the fact that one is speaking the doctrine is a sign that its mandate is already in place. (Still, sister had loosened her lips and may have exchanged some fluids with the slickster. So, just to be safe, before taking her home, her brothers rushed her off to the Severn to have her scrubbed – scraped? – clean of the "charmed band" that her vile enchanter had placed around her. It was worth the effort. Their servants, the Attendant Spirit and Sabrina, did the work and the procedure was finished before you could finish humming "By the rushy-fringed bank." The Lady was home and dancing in no time.)

And so, amidst the dews and drops of ambrosial oils from the servants' laboring ministrations, the Lady was returned to the spirit voices who were the original source of her purity; she was reintroduced to the world, her "grace" intact, and the liberal notion of the iconoclastic possessive or sovereign self – "her grace" – was reborn along with her. One could almost hear the "magical structures" of patriarchalism beginning to shatter, even as the Lady was escorted right back to her "father's residence."

THE LADY AND THE BAPTISTS

This is, of course, a much different ur-story of the possessive self's inscription than the usual one that positions Locke as "father" of the "bourgeois" idea that "no man can be subjected to the political power of another without his own consent."[3] For one thing, because this concept emerges in Milton's story from the need to argue that one possesses something "pure" and inalienable, no matter how "interpenetrated" one might be by the nefarious designs of others, Milton ironically identifies the already enclosed and premarital but imminently penetrable "lady," not the "man," as the emblematic possessive self.[4] For another, because, I suggest, the story continues beyond the parameters of Milton's text, it does not, contrary to appearances, position Milton as the newly triumphant patriarch of the idea that "the pre-eminent and supreme authority . . . is the authority of the Spirit, which is internal, and the individual possession of each man."[5] Instead it travels on to include actual events that, I contend, form an oblique but imaginable backdrop to Milton's fictional scene. I refer not to the increasingly controversial and Puritan-incensing revelries that traditionally accompanied Michaelmas – the time of year at which the masque was set and the official enforcement of which it purports to critique.[6] Nor do I mean the sex scandals that surrounded the extended clan of John Egerton, the Earl of Bridgewater, the inhabitants of the castle of Ludlow for whom this entertainment was written and by and for whom it was performed in 1634.[7] Rather, I gesture towards 1633, the year when Egerton kinswoman, Lady

Eleanor Davies, published yet another of her many infamous visions (this a particularly haunting, skull-filled one foretelling the death of Charles I), petitioned against the appointment of Archbishop Laud, and was called before the High Commission, who ordered the burning of her books and her imprisonment in the Gatehouse at Westminster.[8] As a woman who was literally placed in bondage by her interrogating Comus for believing that the true "fifth" monarch was Christ and that it was she, not Laud, who "sang" on his behalf, Davies forms one viable prototype for Milton's Lady.

And yet the set of "Fifth Monarchist" ideas to which Lady Eleanor "fell prey" points towards another important source for Milton's story about the true subject of sovereignty, a source that can be found in the clandestine meetings of outlawed separatist and semiseparatist churches who, throughout the first half or so of the seventeenth century, plied their trade in such "private" places as riversides, fields, barns, taverns, and homes.[9] For the "Anabaptists" among them, water was crucial to the eponymous and controversial rituals of "rebaptizing" those who had, "against their will," been baptized as infants.[10] At these Jack-and-Joan-the-Baptist gatherings, self-styled everyman and everywoman ministers and healers – real-life Attendant Spirits and Sabrinas – contravened the baptismal "scripts" issued by the Book of Common Prayer and perpetuated their own "extemporaneous" antirituals throughout the decades during and after which Milton penned *A Maske Presented at Ludlow Castle* in Buckinghamshire (itself an old Lollard haunt and site of a rising tide of Baptism).[11] And within these groups, a popular notion of self-sovereignty was practiced and preached as a philosophical foundation for the "Protestant tradition of voluntarism in the organization of church membership" which became one of the "interdependent influences on [Locke's] liberal use of consent theory": all individuals, including women and servants, could choose to be rebaptized (and to rebaptize others in turn) by virtue of the majestic Spirit that each person owned by virtue of the grace bestowed upon them by the one true king, the fifth and last monarch, Christ.[12] As the 1641 Baptist creed stated:

Those that have this pretious faith wrought in them by the Spirit, can never finally nor totally fall away; and though many stormes and floods do arise and beat against them, yet they shall never be able to take them off that foundation and rock which by faith they are fastened upon, but shall be kept by the power of God to salvation where they shall enjoy their purchased possession . . .[13]

These real-life Anabaptist rituals can be said to coincide with, inform, and ultimately supercede the subversive religious politics of Milton's own "reformed masque."[14] In 1632, just a couple of years before Milton staged

Comus, the independent Jacob Church, a "complete church in itself, offering the sacrament of the Lord's Supper to all members and baptism to those who wished it" – was uncovered and arrested.[15] The High Church and its officials, as well as more moderate Puritans of the day, were mortified at the inroads that this and other "conventicles" were making into their parish populations, especially their female affiliates, who would go on to comprise the bulk of private church membership.[16] Under Archbishop Laud's increasingly restrictive insistence upon uniformity, opposition stiffened against such "dangerous men" who formed a "scattered company sown in all the city" of London and an increasing number of other "different places."[17] As Patricia Crawford argues, the crackdown on such groups in 1632 illustrates the degree to which "sexuality, female insubordination and separatism were associated in the bishops' minds," as English society began to fear that more and more of its young women had succumbed to the enchanting wiles of those it viewed more as "mechanic" Comuses than Attendant Spirits.[18] At one point in the High Commission's proceedings against the Jacob church, Laud asked one of the group's ministers, John Lathrop, "how manie women sate crosse legged upon ye bedd, whilest you sat on one side & preached & prayed most devoutlie?" While, Lathrop denied that his female listeners were "such women," his sister congregants were arrested along with him.[19] Whereas the subversion represented by this group was, in this scenario, "contained," gathered churches gathered more momentum and bad press as the thirties and forties wore on.[20] Echoing Bishop Laud, indignant Presbyterians such as Thomas Edwards lodged universal complaints against separatist churches that were in large part based on the fact that their "lusty young" separatist ministers "traded chiefly with young women and young maids."[21] It is possible, then, to say that some of the most compelling drama of the age lay even further outside the Whitehall theatre than did the Earl of Bridgewater's Ludlow Castle. While Milton may have transferred the "ideal masque world" and its intrinsic project of religious "reformation" away from the stage-managed gambols of Charles I and his heavenly consort, Henrietta Maria, and on to the perilous pilgrimages of the Protestant elite, self-baptizing sectarians from the lower and middle orders widened this "disjunction" even further by assuming for themselves the elite aristocratic, religio-mythological, and "sovereign" roles of Heroic Virtue and Divine Grace.[22]

To be sure, Milton provides a devilishly ironic twist upon the heated debate that English society was just beginning to wage over the "new kind of talking Trade" being conducted within separatist groups.[23] His "anti-Laudian" script in part honors Egerton's resistance to Laud's policies by surrounding Comus and his midnight crew with the trappings not of radical sectarianism but of aristocratic (and latent Catholic) Anglicanism: the "treasonous offer" of the idolatrous Communion "cup" from which the Lady was to drink for her salvation; Comus's gallant invitation to escort her to courts, feasts, and other "high solemnities"; and the nervous defence of the "canon law" in the face of the Lady's disturbing disquisition of the individualist doctrine of unassailable self-possession and undivided loyalty to God alone.[24] In Milton's waggish equivalence (if not outright reversal), the "true apostles" might just as well be found alongside the "rushy-fringed banks" of the rivers and other nondescript places where an autonomous band of shepherds and their female helpmates "dipped" men and women alike in the cathartic dews of self-possession and choice, while it is the palace-bound "high priest," Comus, who is preaching in the proverbial wilderness.[25] At the same time, *Comus* arguably displays Milton's earlier, still moderate interest in resubmitting the liberated Lady to "a church government of Presbyters and Deacons."[26] True to masque form, Milton brings it all back "home" as a sign that male guardianship and domestic order have been restored.[27] As a procession, *Comus* climaxes with the reentry of the Lady, played by the earl's daughter, Alice, back "*into* [her father's] House."[28] While she was innately "pure," Milton hedges, that extra bit of cleansing and that hustled retreat back to the castle certainly couldn't hurt.

Within separatist circles, however, the "Ladies" who actually underwent Sabrina's dissevering cure are, as often as not, on record for refusing to cap off their own personal progresses with a return to the official venues of English patriarchy, either literally or figuratively, and for instead remaining committed to the private church with which they had affiliated and/or to its root Pauline ideal that God's grace endowed them with reason as a property of the soul that they alone could "alienate" to consume a church of their own.[29] Thus, for every story such as the one recounted in *The Brownist Haeresies Confuted* (London, 1641) wherein the unnamed author describes how a young "gentlewoman," Sarah Miller, had to be saved by a "reverend Divine" and friend of her father after being seduced and impregnated by the charismatic crown-offering "Comus" of a nearby Brownist church, there is an account such as Thomas Edwards's which concedes the fact that these self-styled Attendant Spirits had managed to attract many "young maids, Citizens daughter, about one and two a clock in the morning, tempting them out of their fathers' houses at midnight to be baptized, the parents asleep and knowing nothing."[30] The pastoral ideal of marriage, which was to end every social plot with the virginal woman's rupturing submission and

Introduction

reconsignment to the dictates of her father, brother, and husband, was both reified and frustrated through the separatist displacement of "marriage" on to the eternally "chaste" and enclosed relationship that every individual enjoyed with God as a self-sufficient "couple" of one.[31]

In fact, it was women's exercise of the prerogative of religious choice that they derived from this subversive appropriation of the cultural logic of "the thematics of pastoral eroticism" that amped up the volume on the iconoclastic rumblings that reverberated throughout England during the years of rising religious dissent, as patriarchy's "magical structures" clashed with "popular sovereignty."[32] Through pulpit and pen, the established clergy and other detractors tried to allay what Sharon Achinstein has identified as the old *charivari* fear that women had somehow gotten "on top" – embodied in this case in the possibility that women were capable of plotting their own paradises – by warning these would-be Eves that they had once again succumbed to self-destructive delusions of grandeur: those Attendant Spirits who promised salvation were in actuality Comus-like, sexually predacious "wolves in sheep's clothing" who had only salivation in mind.[33] As Edward Harris maintained:

> In the County of Monmouth in Wales, in divers parts a number of Non-conformists being assembled together, not regarding in what place they meet, whether in field, garden, orchard, barne, kitchen, or high waies, being (as they teach) available to their devotion as the Church: where by their doctrine they perswade their auditory to contemne the prayers of the Church, and the Preachers of the Gospell; also avowing their own zealous prayers to have such power with God, as that they dare challenge him *ex tempore*. By which lewd persuasion for theirs they have drawne diverse honest mens wives in the night times to frequent their Assembles, and to become of most loose and wicked conversation, and likewise many chaste Virgins to become harlots, and the mothers of bastards; holding it no sinne for a brother to lye with a brothers wife; as also a virgin gotten with childe by a brother not to be the worse, but by another, then by the wicked, and so consequently a sinne.[34]

To further spin the idea that this was a sexual rather than an intellectual seduction, Daniel Featley concluded, "the resort of great multitudes of men and women together in the evening, and going naked into rivers, there to be plunged and Dipt, cannot be done without scandall, especially where the State giveth no allowance to any such practice, nor appointed any order to prevent such fowl abuses as are likely at such disorderly meetings to be committed."[35]

Fathers all across the kingdom could relate as more and more young women became nonfictional "usurers' daughters" who borrowed against their property-in-self for the purpose of circulating their choice-based coinage *outside* the regulated parameters of the established church and the patriarchal home.³⁶ If it could happen to Lord Audley's daughter, Lady Eleanor, then it could happen to anybody. After all, these daughters reasoned, this "resort" was not the "state's" possession to "allow" or "order" and it was their souls, not their sex, for which they were loved. In 1645 there came the case of Mr. Robert Poole, a good citizen who quite literally lost his own daughter, Elizabeth, to a Baptist "jugler" – a low-born mechanic named William Kiffin who dared to call himself a minister.³⁷ After his entire household ran off to join Kiffin's congregation, Poole confronted this Comus and demanded an explanation. However, when asked "what warrant of the Word of God" he used to justify separating from the established church and forming new churches in which "sillie seduced Servants, Children, or People" were inducted into the "Anabaptisticall way," Kiffin replied as an Attendant Spirit, offering to cure the agitated father's "indigestion" of separatist principles with some of his trademark "ambrosial" ministrations and "adjuring verses":

> I see our separated Congregations sticks very hard upon your stomack, therefore as I laboured to help you to digest our separation, so I hope I shall give you something from the Word of Truth, that may remove your imbitternese of Spirit against our Congregations: and first know this, that that infinite Love which hath redeemed a people to God, out of all Nations, tongues, and kindred, hath also made them Kings and Priests unto God, to reigne with him in his spirituall kingdom here on earth, Rev. 9,10 . . .³⁸

In other words, alarmist warnings to the contrary, women and servants may have actually been attracted to the likes of Kiffin because he recognized them as equals, as prepossessing kings and priests – fathers even of a sort – in and of themselves. For the relatively disenfranchised, this was an irresistible call "home" to sovereign or possessive personhood, a courtship of the mind as much as if not more than the body.

SABRINA SPEAKS

Because of this, the tale of the birth of the possessive self, as well as other foundational concepts within liberal political philosophy, does not end with Kiffin or his fellow persuasionists. Instead, the plot moves on to comprehend the voices of actual separatist women, including Elizabeth Poole. One of the most scandalous features to emerge from the growing religious Independency movement was that many of its female constituents used a doctrine of virginity as a license to travel beyond the role of worshipful attendee, to take their own turns upon the makeshift pulpits that private congregations reportedly fashioned out of wash tubs, hayracks, and beer barrels.[39] As John Vicars lamented in *The Schismatick Sifted*, it was not only "saucie boyes" and "bold, botching taylors" but also "bold impudent huswives" who were taking it upon themselves to "prate an hour or more."[40] And as the anonymous author of *A Spirit Moving in the Women Preachers* contended, they were able to do this because the level of "insinuation" achieved by the "holy brothers" of "the separation" "with this Female Sex"

hath so prevailed with this poore ignorant sort of Creatures, that puffed up with pride, divers of them have lately advanced themselves with vain-glorious arrogance, to preach in mixt Congregations of men and women, in an insolent way of usurping authority over men, and assuming a calling unwarranted by the word of God for women to use: yet all under colour, that *they act as the Spirit moves them* . . .[41]

As Keith Thomas has documented, some three hundred female sectarian preachers and prophetesses were so moved from the 1630s through the 1670s, many of whom recorded their words through the virtual pulpit of print.[42] Publications by women attained a new high during these middle decades of the seventeenth century, due in no small measure to the prose genres published by female sectarians.[43]

In 1644, for example, one Sarah Jones published a "sermon" called *To Sions Lovers*.[44] Apparently a young girl (her cover quotes, "out of the mouthes of babes, *Jehovah* shall have praise"), Jones figures her text as a curative "golden egge to avoid infection" and structures it around a strategic collection of Scriptures that defend "shee preachers," "baptism," and the "doctrine of laying on of hands" (B2–B3). In her dedication, she plays the Lady to Dr. William Gouge's Comus, identifying him as an ordained minister (and a friend of her late father), who, to her way of thinking, had too long preached "the Doctrine of Repentance from dead workes" instead of relinquishing his "Eldership" to "the spouse of Christ," the Independent church or "Assemblie of the Saints" which have a "right" to "appoint" for themselves those who shall effect the cure (A2). Writing literally from outside the bounds of her dead father's house, Jones insists that she alone is the "father" of her own text, this "naked child without Scholasticke phrases, or School learning to dresse it and garnish it" (A2).

As did the example of Lady Eleanor, Jones's text showcases the century's newfangled logic: because Sabrina was a female "instrument of divine grace" and an "embodiment of the transformative power of song and poetry," then a free-spirited lady could sing for herself.[45] Even if she was forced to enact Revelation's captivity narrative of the woman in the wilderness (that is, to attend her assigned parish church and drink from Comus's communion cup), this unmoved mover did not need to be led home by another.[46] As the natural "source" of "truth," why would she need an Attendant Spirit's intervention into purifying something – her innately majestic ladyness – that was already, inherently, pure?[47] As a "goddess," was she not always and already "at home" in the house of God her father and husband, the ultimate Attendant Spirit whose spirit voice called her to move and purify others on his behalf?[48] As the Attendant Spirit says, "Goddess dear, / We implore thy powerful hand" (164). As Sabrina replies, "Shepherd 'tis my office best / To help insnared chastity; Brightest Lady look on me, / Thus I sprinkle on thy brest / Drops that from my fountain pure, / I have kept of pretious cure" (164).

As I shall show, there was a virtual living theatre of "Shepherd/Sabrina" dyads at work in the history of the separatist churches: Samuel Chidley and Katherine Chidley, Hugh Peter and Anna Trapnel, William Kiffin and Elizabeth Poole, Henry Jessey and Sarah Wight. In many of these cases, the men, playing out their deeply embedded mythological heritage as Orphic language-bearing Attendant Spirits, conjured up their goddesses to sing by serving as their amanuenses and penning their stories.[49] However, it also appears to have been a kind of Miltonic fantasy on the part of sectarian male preachers that they could command their watery muses when they wanted while counting upon them to lie dormant when they were of no apparent use, just as the Attendant Spirit did with Sabrina (and as Milton did with the sectarians whose power he invoked in his own battles against the tyrannical crown and then later decried when they dissented from his Protectorate as well: "Back Shepherds, back, anough your play" [167]). In practice, the "fixed" and "crypto-Catholic" logic of possessive individualism, with its ascetic emphasis upon enclosure and purity, provided even nonelite sectarian women with the mercurial wherewithal to speak through their own volition – and speak out they did against Presbyterian ministers, judges, members of Parliament, kings, and even their own ministers, who did not always anticipate the degree to which their "creatures" would apply the servant's "office" of securing imperiled liberties to "offices" of all sorts.[50]

As Lois Schwoerer has argued, "a growing number" of these "middle- and lower middle-class women in England" parlayed their self-sovereignty into a platform from which to "meddle with State Affairs."[51] Broadly speaking, sectarian women writers participated in the movement for religious toleration that was advanced by various separatist groups seeking protection for their unorthodox and illegal religious practices.[52] Separatist women were particularly concerned with envisioning a toleration settlement that would

Introduction

allow them, as widely caricatured members of the so-called "brazen-faced, strange, new *Feminine Brood*," to preach and prophesy.[53] Given the deeply entrenched prohibitions against the exercise of female religious authority, not to mention the emergent equation of religious toleration *with* the awful spectacle of women preachers (in 1641 Thomas Wilson warned the House of Commons that, "Christ will have no toleration: *I [saith he] have a few things against thee, because thou suffrest that woman Jezabel, which calleth herself a prophetesse, to teach and to seduce my servants*"), sectarian women were compelled to engage with larger questions about the anatomy of the individual and its relationship to government authority.[54] As Sarah Jones put it, "Let us hear here what hath beene done against the Saints, There have been councellors of state that have councelled for their hurt."[55] As did Jones's, sectarian women's liberal ideas emerge not, like Locke's, from within a well-stocked Earl of Shaftesbury's library; rather, their penny pamphlets dropped off the popular press to expose the price they paid for their struggles to preach, prophesy, and petition, and to publicize their nascent but growing sense of what sort of political order was necessary for them to continue practicing these markers of religious and (increasingly) political freedom.[56] To borrow a phrase used by Mary Ann Radzinowicz to characterize Milton, "the liberty of prophesying was [female sectarians'] paradigm for political liberty."[57]

Katherine Chidley was an original member of the Jacob church as well as the founder of several separatist congregations.[58] Her son, Samuel, appears to have served as her own personal "Attendant Spirit"; he transcribed the texts she dictated and the two of them became a dynamic mother-and-son Spirit–Sabrina team, both as "Brownists" and later as Levellers.[59] Chidley's protoleration tracts, first and foremost her *Justification of the Independent Churches of Christ* (1641), are as programmatic an argument on behalf of the separation of church from state as is Milton's *Reason of Church Government* or Locke's *Letter Concerning Toleration*.[60] The petitions she, along with other Leveller women, later presented, drew upon protoleration logic to insist that women be acknowledged as having "rights" that would also allow them to protest what they saw as illegitimate incursions by the magistrates into their homes and families.[61]

After hearing another Baptist minister, Hugh Peter, call for "saints" to enclose themselves in their "chambers" and prophesy, Anna Trapnel also turned herself into a one-woman Lady/Sabrina hybrid.[62] Like the Lady, she prophesied from her bed in a state of paralyzed enthrallment while sizable crowds gathered outside her window to be feel her "dew." Like Sabrina, she rose from her bed to publish visions as well as her *Report and*

Plea, a cathartic self-defense rationalizing the need for a zone of privacy which would simultaneously function as an Independent church as well as a "public sphere" that was critical of and oppositional to the state.[63] An everywoman's *Pilgrim's Progress*, Trapnel's text is as blistering a critique of her incarceration for exercising her "right" to freedom of expression and privacy as is John Lilburne's *Freeman's Freedom Vindicated*.[64]

Attendant Spirit William Kiffin's own "Lady," Elizabeth Poole, was sent to do Cromwell's bidding at an army general council meeting in Whitehall, where the fate of the captive king was to be determined.[65] In *A Vision Wherein is Manifested the Disease and Cure of the Kingdome* (1648/49), Poole, much to Kiffin's apparent chagrin, seized the moment to utilize the spiritual power of Sabrina's cure for constructing a prototypical (and female) individual who enjoyed the contractual right of exit for removing tyrannical and abusive kings from the throne as well as tyrannical and abusive husbands from the home.[66] Her appeal to consent rather than divine right as the basis for legitimate monarchy anticipates Locke and may surpass his gender politics by metaphorically locating the contractual right of exit within the prerogative enjoyed by the patriarch's wife to remove herself from an abusive marriage.

In *The Exceeding Riches of Grace Advanced by the Spirit of Grace, In an Empty Nothing Creature*, the young prophetess, Sarah Wight, was portrayed by her Attendant Spirit, Henry Jessey, as a veiled and bed-bound Lady/Sabrina who used her home as the basis for a restorative ministerial practice.[67] And in *A Wonderful Pleasant and Profitable Letter* (1656), Wight took hold of "the wand" for herself and carefully anatomized the "sovereign subject" as one who inherently enjoyed new liberties by virtue of the "true" royal authority of God that resided within.[68] Likewise, Anne Wentworth, another religious dissenter who played Sabrina to her own imperiled Lady, constructed her *True Account* (1676) and *A Vindication* (1677) as critiques of her husband's abuse, which developed a pre-Lockean articulation of possessive individualism.[69] While Wight's *A Wonderful Pleasant and Profitable Letter* and Anne Wentworth's *True Account* and *A Vindication* are written in the genres named by their titles – a letter, an account, a vindication – they are comparable to such works as Richard Overton's *An Arrow against all Tyrants* or, again, Locke's *Two Treatises* in their attempts to delineate a subject who, by virtue of *her* nature, enjoys a sphere of self-determination.[70]

Finally, while Mary Cary's works have been cited as a penultimate example of the manic rhetoric that allegedly defines Sabrina-speak, they should, in fact, be read alongside such "Grand Instauration" writers as Samuel Hartlib and Henry Jessey.[71] More like Jessey and less like Hartlib, Cary believed that the "path" to a just commonwealth lay within an enlarged sphere of religious and economic choice that, she argued, deserved state protection instead of intervention or dissolution.[72] In *A Word in Season to the Kingdom of England* (1648), she envisioned a free market in ministerial labor that promised to provide the lasting material conditions necessary for allowing all men and women to preach, especially those who, like Sabrina, labored as mere "servants."[73] In this and other works, she constructs a cultural paradigm in which women could "spend" their "currency" on "the new talking trade" without being considered ungodly.[74]

Given their concerns, these texts rightfully deserve to be included in "genealogies" of liberal political theory, even as these genealogies will (continue to) be redisciplined by the particular ways in which dissenting women articulated liberal precepts. As Hilary Hinds has pointed out, these texts frustrate received definitions of authorship and literary genre; much less, I would add, will they conform to a conventional understanding of political theory as, in Andrew Hacker's words, "a generalized description or explanation of the behavior of men" which is "dispassionate and disinterested" and which, therefore, can be "studied without attention to the particular conditions which surrounded [its authors] at the time they wrote."[75] Rather ensconcing liberalism's mothers alongside its fathers will entail moving "from politics conceived (anachronistically) as the business of institutions, bureaucracies, and officers to the broader politics of discourse and symbols, anxieties and aspirations, myths and memories."[76] It will mean viewing politics as "something done *by*" ordinary men and women rather than "to them" by rulers or for them by great thinkers.[77] It will further illustrate the fact that "the public–private divide" and other liberal ideas were themselves "the object of struggle . . . rhetorical construct[s] which [were] deployed in kaleidoscopically shifting ways to a variety of ends" and that, "in this process, moreover, women were participants as well as objects."[78] It will involve recognizing that, for "large masses of people," political theory takes the "exclamatory" form of "broadsides, sermons, newspapers, plays, poetry, and so on" and that it can even, if we're being truly generous, consist of virtually *anything* which serves as both the "ideological and intellectual criticism and justification of [political] domination."[79] It will offer further evidence that "democracy" has a "prehistory" that was as grounded in a "dynamic symbolic system of theater," a "popular voice," and a "personality" as it was "a dissenting and then revolutionary republicanism" articulated by a "civil and clerical elite."[80] And it will confirm the contention that a high concept such as "possessive individualism" emerged heteronomously – in the more situated and contingent process of "debating something else" for which the idea of property-in-self was said to function as "the real cause or precondition of whatever [that something else] was."[81] In this case, that "something else" was the desire experienced by a small but determined number of sectarian women to preach, prophesy, publish, and petition.

As a result, assimilating sectarian women's voices into a history of early liberalism will mean taking interpretive stock of the rhetorical devices these writers used to "open up" and "structure" "new potentially antipatriarchal conceptualizations of political and religious authority."[82] This will include the simultaneous toleration of unauthored and/or multiauthored texts and a willingness to "regain authorial intention," which, while "considered conservative in the current critical climate," is the "best way of understanding" the critique that popular theorists launched of their "political world."[83] It will consist of establishing "a field of potentially political reference, a texture of allusion," rather than always insisting upon the prefabricated presence of "a sustained political critique."[84] It will require the reconstruction of the "rich intertextuality" that infuses sectarian women's "constant recourse to biblical discourse," particularly for that discourse's ability to rewrite the social scripts that governed women's domestic identities.[85] At a time when the Bible "was central to all arts, sciences and literature," sectarian women also discovered that a "biblical metaphor" could function as a "programme in shorthand."[86] And last but not least, it will reveal the ways in which not just biblical discourse but "whole vocabularies of inherited allusion and contemporary associations" could "acquire polemical thrust" as "the proto-liberal language of contract, consent, and rational self-interest" also "intersected" with the vocabularies of home, childbirth, marriage, motherhood, servitude, myth, and romance.[87]

When subjected to just such a contextualized and interdisciplinary set of interpretive moves, sectarian women's texts emerge rewardingly as a modest but nonetheless important body of early heteronomous, multigeneric, performative, aspirational, allusive, religiomythological, exclamatory, and antinomian liberalism that intentionally critiqued its political world. In complexly constructed and impassioned but also rational voices, these writers made a case that all individuals are abstractly defined as the product of their "maker" and hence as formed for his rather than for one another's "pleasure"; that there should therefore be some sort of demarcation between the public political sphere of government and a private sphere of individual choice, voluntary association, and self-determination; that a government gains authority through the consent of the governed; that its people have the right to express dissent from as well as to remove rulers who transgress their prescribed bounds; that individuals have the right to retain the fruits of their labor as a form of property and that, as a result, they should not be coerced into handing over a portion of that property to the state. I will end by appropriating and reappraising a phrase that Attendant Spirit, Hugh Peter, used while in New England to criticize the fact that one of the Church of Boston's "Ladies," Anne Hutchinson, had, Sabrina-like, fashioned her own church of sorts within the spaces of her home and used it to judge her ministers. To learn more about the ways in which female sectarians contributed to the history of liberal ideas, we must examine the strategies they used to domesticate the privileged discourse of political theory and to make it their "table talk."[88]

NOTES

1. John Milton, "A Maske Presented at Ludlow Castle," in Roy Flannagan, ed., *The Riverside Milton* (Boston: Houghton Mifflin, 1998), pp. 109–172. For discussions of *Comus* and the possessive individual, see John Rogers, "The Enclosure of Virginity: The Poetics of Sexual Abstinence in the English Revolution," in Richard Burt and John Michael Archer, eds., *Enclosure Acts: Sexuality, Property, and Culture in Early Modern England* (Ithaca: Cornell University Press, 1994), pp. 229–250; Julie H. Kim, "The Lady's Unladylike Struggle: Redefining Patriarchal Boundaries in Milton's *Comus*," *Milton Studies* 35 (1997), 1–20; and Patrick Cook, "Eroticism and the Integral Self: Milton's Poems, 1645 and the Italian Pastoral Tradition," *Comparatist* 24 (May 2000), 123–45.
2. I borrow the phrase "democratic personality" from Nancy Ruttenburg, *Democratic Personality: Popular Voice and the Trial of American Authorship* (Stanford: Stanford University Press, 1998).
3. John Locke, *Two Treatises of Government*, rev. edn, ed. Peter Laslett (New York: Mentor, 1965), vol. II, p. 375. See especially C. B. Macpherson, *The Political Theory of Possessive Individualism* (Oxford: Oxford University Press, 1989).
4. Susan M. Felch, "The Intertextuality of Comus and Corinthians," *Milton Quarterly* 27, 2 (May 1993), 59–70, in particular p. 67.
5. John Milton, *De Doctrina* 6: 587. For other accounts of Milton's formation of "the individual," see William Haller, *Tracts on Liberty in the Puritan Revolution 1638–1647*, vol. I, *Commentary* (New York: Columbia University Press, 1934), pp. 6–8; Matthew Jordan, *Milton and Modernity: Politics, Masculinity, and Paradise Lost* (New York: Palgrave, 2001); Herman Rapaport, "Milton and the State," in *Milton and the Postmodern* (Lincoln: University of Nebraska Press, 1983), pp. 167–207; Nicholas von Maltzahn, "The Whig Milton, 1667–1700," in David Armitage, Armand Himy, and Quentin Skinner, eds., *Milton and Republicanism* (Cambridge: Cambridge University Press, 1995), pp. 229–253.
6. James G. Taaffe, "Michaelmas, the Lawless Hour, and the Occasion of *Comus*," *ELN* 6 (1968–1969), 257–262; M. S. Berkowitz, "An Earl's Michaelmas in Wales: Some Thoughts on the Original Presentation of *Comus*," *Milton Quarterly* 13

(October 1979), 122–125. For a discussion of Milton's "revelry," see William A. Sessions, "Milton and the Dance," in Albert C. Labriola and Edward Sichi, Jr., eds., *Milton's Legacy in the Arts* (University Park: Pennsylvania State University Press, 1988), pp. 181–203.
7. Barbara Breasted, "*Comus* and the Castlehaven Scandal," *Milton Studies* 3 (1971), 2001–2024; John D. Cox, "Poetry and History in Milton's Country Masque," *English Literary History* 44 (winter 1977), 622–640; John Creaser, "Milton's *Comus*: The Irrelevance of the Castlehaven Scandal," *Milton Quarterly* 21, 4 (December 1987), 24–34; Leah Marcus, "The Milieu of Milton's Comus," *Criticism* 25 (1983), 293–327 and "The Earl of Bridgewater's Legal Life: Notes Toward a Political Reading of *Comus*," *Milton Quarterly* 21, 4 (December 1987), 13–23.
8. Lady Eleanor Davies, "Given to the Elector Prince Charles of the Rhyne," in Esther S. Cope, ed., *Prophetic Writings of Lady Eleanor Davies* (Oxford: Oxford University Press, 1995), pp. 59–69. For biographical information on Davies, see Cope's introduction to this collection and her *Handmaid of the Holy Spirit: Dame Eleanor Davies, Never Soe Mad a Ladie* (Ann Arbor: University of Michigan Press, 1992). See also Stevie Davies, *Unbridled Spirits: Women of the English Revolution 1640–1660* (London: Women's Press, 1998), pp. 50–60; and Teresa Feroli, "The Sexual Politics of Mourning in the Prophecies of Eleanor Davies," *Criticism* 36, 3 (summer 1994), 359–382.
9. For contemporary complaints against these meetings, see especially Thomas Edwards, *Gangraena* (London, 1645), *The Second Part of Gangraena* (London, 1646), and *The Third Part of Gangraena* (London, 1646). For modern accounts of separatist churches, see Patrick Collinson's, "The English Conventicle,' *SCH* 23 (1986), 223–259, *The Religion of Protestants: The Church in English Society, 1559–1625* (Oxford: Clarendon Press, 1982), and *Godly People: Essays on English Protestantism and Puritanism* (Hambledon Press, 1983), pp. 527–562; Geoffrey Nuttall, *Visible Saints: The Congregational Way 1640–1660* (Oxford: Oxford University Press, 1957); Murray Tolmie, *The Triumph of the Saints: The Separate Churches of London, 1616–1649* (Cambridge: Cambridge University Press, 1977); George Huntston Williams, *The Radical Reformation* (Philadelphia, PA: Westminster Press, 1962); and B. R. White, *The English Separatist Tradition* (Oxford: Oxford University Press, 1971).
10. Louise Fargo Brown, *The Political Activities of the Baptists and Fifth Monarchy Men* (Washington, DC: American Historical Association, 1913); W. T. Whitley, *A History of British Baptists*, 2nd rev. edn (London: Kingsgate Press, 1932); B. R. White, *The English Baptists of the Seventeenth Century* (London Baptist Historical Society, 1983); J. F. McGregor, "The Baptists: Fount of All Heresy," in J. M. McGregor and Barry Reay, eds., *Radical Religion in the English Revolution* (Oxford: Oxford University Press, 1984); and Mark R. Bell, *Apocalypse How? Baptist Movements During the English Revolution* (Macon, GA: Mercer University Press, 2000).
11. Michael R. Watts, *The Dissenters: From the Reformation to the French Revolution* (Oxford: Clarendon Press, 1978), pp. 13–14.

12. Jules Steinberg, *Locke, Rousseau, and the Idea of Consent: An Inquiry into the Liberal-Democratic Theory of Political Obligation* (Westport, CT: Greenwood Press, 1978), p. 25. See also Alan Bullock and Maurice Schock, eds., *The Liberal Tradition: From Fox to Keynes* (Oxford: Clarendon Press, 1967); William Haller, *Liberty and Reformation in the Puritan Revolution* (New York: Columbia University Press, 1955); A. S. P. Woodhouse, ed., *Puritanism and Liberty* (London: J. M. Dent, 1992); Brian Manning, *Religion and Politics in the English Civil War* (London: Edward Arnold, 1975); William H. Brackney *et al.*, eds., *Pilgrim Pathways: Essays in Baptist History in Honour of B. R. White* (Macon, GA: Mercer University Press, 1999).
13. William Kiffin, *The Confession of Faith of those Churches which are Commonly (though falsely) called Anabaptists* (London: 1644), pp. B3–B4.
14. Barbara Lewalski, "Milton's *Comus* and the Politics of Masquing," in David Bevington and Peter Holbrook, eds., *The Politics of the Stuart Court Masque* (Cambridge: Cambridge University Press, 1998), pp. 296–320. See also Maryanne Cale McGuire, *Milton's Puritan Masque* (Athens, GA: University of Georgia Press, 1983); David Norbrook, *The Reformation of the Masque* (Manchester: Manchester University Press, 1984), pp. 94–110; Leah Marcus, *The Politics of Mirth* (Chicago: University of Chicago Press, 1986); Eugene R. Cunnar, "*The Shepherd* of Hermas and the Writing of the Puritan Masque," *Milton Studies* 23 (1987), 33–52; Stephen Kogan, *The Hieroglyphic King: Wisdom and Idolatry in the Seventeenth-Century Masque* (Rutherford, NJ: Fairleigh Dickinson University Press, 1986), pp. 229–265; Andrew J. Hubbell, "Milton's Re-Formation of the Masque," in Charles Durham and Kristin Pruitt McColgan, eds., *Spokesperson Milton: Voices in Contemporary Criticism* (Selinsgrove, PA: Susquehanna University Press, 1994), pp. 193–205.
15. Tolmie, *Triumph of the Saints*, p. 14. See also Bell, *Apocalypse How?*, pp. 55–62, and Watts, *Dissenters*, p. 71.
16. R. A. Knox, *Enthusiasm: A Chapter in the History of Religion with Special Reference to the XVII and XVIII Centuries* (Oxford: Oxford University Press, 1950), p. 20. Other discussions of women's role in the construction of "voluntary religion" include Keith Thomas, "Women and the Civil War Sects," *Past and Present* 13 (1958), 42–62; Claire Cross, " 'She-Goats before the Flocks': a Note on the Part Played by some Women in the Founding of some Civil War Churches," in G. J. Cuming and D. Baker, eds., *Popular Belief and Practice: Papers Read at the Ninth Summer Meeting and the Tenth Winter Meeting of The Ecclesiastical History Society* (Cambridge: Cambridge University Press, 1972), vol. VIII, pp. 195–202; Richard Greaves, *Triumph over Silence: Women in Protestant History* (Westport, CT: Greenwood Press, 1985); Patricia Crawford, *Women and Religion in England* (London: Routledge, 1993); Anne Laurence, "A Priesthood of She-Believers: Women and Congregations in Mid-Seventeenth-Century England," in W. J. Sheils and D. Wood, eds., *Women in the Church* (Oxford: Basil Blackwell, 1990).
17. Tolmie, *Triumph of the Saints*, p. 17.
18. Crawford, *Women and Religion*, p. 123.

19. Ibid.
20. Bell, *Apocalypse How?*, p. 48.
21. Edwards, *Gangraena*, p. 121.
22. Lewalski, "Milton's *Comus*," pp. 308–309; Marcus, *Politics of Mirth*, p. 171.
23. Anon., *New Preacher, N E W* (London, 1641).
24. Marcus, *Politics of Mirth*, pp. 69–112. See also Andrew Milner, *John Milton and the English Revolution* (Totawa, NJ: Barnes & Noble, 1981), p. 135; Michael Wilding, *Dragon's Teeth: Literature in the English Revolution* (Oxford: Clarendon Press, 1987), pp. 52–58; and Achsah Guibbory, *Ceremony and Community from Herbert to Milton* (Cambridge: Cambridge University Press, 1998), pp. 157–172.
25. David Gay, " 'Rapt Spirits': 2 Corinthians 12.2–5 and the Language of Milton's *Comus*," *Milton Quarterly* 29, 3 (October 1995), 76–85; Hubbell, "Milton's Re-Formation," p. 196.
26. Sylvia Brown, "Household Words and Rhetorical Seductions in Milton's *The Reason of Church-Government*," *Prose Studies* 23, 1 (April 2000), 63–80, quote from p. 68.
27. Cedric Brown, "Presidential Travels and Instructive Augury in Milton's Ludlow Masque," *Milton Quarterly* 21, 4 (December 1987), 1–12, quote from p. 1. See also Kim, "Lady's Unladylike Struggle," 1–20.
28. Mindele Anne Treip, "Comus as Progress," *Milton Quarterly* 20, 1 (March 1986), 1–13, quote from p. 4.
29. See Maggie Kilgour, "Comus's Wood of Allusion," *University of Toronto Quarterly* 61, 3 (spring 1992), 316–323, for a discussion of Milton's pun on "Severn" and "dissevering power" in *Comus* (p. 321).
30. Anon., *The Brownist Haeresies Confuted* (London, 1641), p. 2; Edwards, *Gangraena*, pp. 66–67.
31. John Demeray, "The Temple of the Mind: Cosmic Iconography in Milton's 'A Mask,' " *Milton Quarterly* 21, 4 (December 1987), 59–76.
32. For the "thematics of pastoral eroticism," see Cook, "Eroticism and the Integral Self," p. 123.
33. Sharon Achinstein, "Women on Top in the Pamphlet Literature of the English Revolution," in Lorna Hutson, ed., *Feminism and Renaissance Studies* (Oxford: Oxford University Press, 1999), pp. 339–372. In *A Spirit Moving in Women Preachers* (London, 1645), the anonymous author lambastes women in private churches for "wasting their estates, and furnishing their pretended holy brothers of the Separation, or Schisme, with whatever he pleases, not displeasing this man of God, as they call him, (though perhaps a wolf in sheeps cloathing)" (p. 3).
34. Edward Harris, *A True Relation of a Company of Brownists, Separatists, and Non-Conformists, in Monmouthshire in Wales* (London, 1641), p. A2.
35. Daniel Featley, *The Dippers Dipt* (London, 1644), p. 36.
36. I adapt the phrase "usurers' daughters" from Lorna Hutson, *The Usurer's Daughter: Male Friendship and Fictions of Women in Sixteenth-Century England* (London: Routledge, 1994), p. 8.

37. William Kiffin, *Certaine Observations upon Hosea the Second* (London, 1642). See also *The Life and Approaching Death of William Kiffin* (London, 1660).
38. William Kiffin, *A Brief Remonstrance of the Reasons and Grounds of those People commonly called Anabaptists* (London, 1645), pp. 3 and 11.
39. For contemporary objections to female preaching, see Anon., *A Discovery of Six Women Preachers in Middlesex, Kent, Cambridgeshire, and Salisbury* (London, 1641); Anon., *Spirit Moving in the Women Preachers*; Edwards, *Gangraena*; Anon., *Tub-Preachers Overturn'd* (London, 1647). For modern reevaluations, see Ethyn Morgan Williams, "Women Preachers in the Civil War," *Journal of Modern History* 1, 4 (December 1929), 561–569; Alfred Cohen, "Prophecy and Madness: Women Visionaries during the Puritan Revolution," *Journal of Psychohistory* 11, 3 (winter 1984), 411–430; Dorothy Ludlow, "'Arise and be doing': English 'Preaching' Women, 1640–1660" (unpublished dissertation, Indiana University, 1978), and "Shaking Patriarchy's Foundations: Sectarian Women in England, 1641–1700," in Greaves, *Triumph over Silence*, pp. 93–123; Christine Berg and Philippa Berry, "'Spiritual Whoredom': An Essay on Female Prophets in the Seventeenth Century," in Francis Barker, *et al.*, eds., *1642: Literature and Power in the Seventeenth Century* (Colchester: University of Essex Press, 1981), pp. 39–54; Phyllis Mack, "Women as Prophets during the English Civil War," *Feminist Studies* 8, 1 (1982); Phyllis Mack, *Visionary Women: Ecstatic Prophecy in Seventeenth-Century England* (Berkeley: University of California Press, 1992); Diane Purkiss, "Producing the Voice, Consuming the Body: Women Prophets of the Seventeenth Century," in Isobel Grundy and Susan Wiseman, eds., *Women, Writing, History 1640–1740* (Athens, GA: University of Georgia Press, 1992), pp. 139–158; Susan Wiseman, "Unsilent Instruments and the Devil's Cushions: Authority in Seventeenth-Century Women's Prophetic Discourse," in Isobel Armstrong, ed., *New Feminist Discourse* (London: Routledge, 1992), pp. 176–196; Elizabeth Sauer, "Maternity, Prophecy, and the Cultivation of the Private Sphere in Seventeenth-Century England," in *Explorations in Renaissance Culture* 24 (1998), 119–148; Hilary Hinds, *God's Englishwomen: Seventeenth-Century Radical Sectarian Writing and Feminist Criticism* (Manchester: Manchester University Press, 1996); Elaine Hobby, "The Politics of Women's Prophecy in the English Revolution," in Helen Wilcox, Richard Todd, and Alasdair MacDonald, eds., *Sacred and Profane: Secular and Devotional Interplay in Early Modern British Literature* (Amsterdam: VU University Press, 1996), pp. 295–306; Elaine Hobby, "'Come to live a preaching life': Female Community in Seventeenth-Century Radical Sects," in Rebecca D'Monte and Nicole Pohl, eds., *Female Communities, 1600–1800: Literary Visions and Cultural Realities* (New York: St. Martin's Press, 2000), pp. 76–92; and Elaine Hobby, "Prophecy, Enthusiasm and Female Pamphleteers," in N. H. Keeble, ed., *The Cambridge Companion to Writing of the English Revolution* (Cambridge: Cambridge University Press, 2001), pp. 162–178.
40. John Vicars, *The Schismatick Sifted: Or, A Picture of Independents Freshly and Fairly Washt Over Again* (London, 1646).
41. Anon., *Spirit Moving in the Women Preachers*, p. 3.

42. Thomas, "Women and the Civil War Sects," p. 42.
43. Patricia Crawford, "Women's Published Writings 1600–1700," in Mary Prior, ed., *Women in English Society, 1500–1800* (New York: Methuen, 1985), pp. 211–282.
44. Sarah Jones, *To Sions Lovers, Being a Golden Egge, to Avoide Infection* (London, 1644). See also her *This is Lights Appearance in the Truth* (London, 1650).
45. Lewalski, "Milton's *Comus*," p. 309.
46. See Guibbory, *Ceremony and Community*, p. 166, for the "Wandering Woman of Revelation 12" as a prototype of *Comus*'s Lady.
47. See William A. Oram, "The Invocation of Sabrina," *Studies in English Literature*, 24 (1984), 121–139, quote from p. 123.
48. Margaret Hoffman Kale, "Milton's 'Gums of Glutinous Heat': A Renaissance Theory of Movement," *Milton Quarterly* 29, 3 (October 1995), 86–91.
49. For the Attendant Spirit as Mercury, see Oram, "Invocation of Sabrina," p. 135, and Hubbell, "Milton's Re-Formation," p. 199.
50. The term "creatures" appears in Anon., *Spirit Moving in the Women Preachers*, p. 3. For the crypto-Catholicism in *Comus*, see Guibbory, *Ceremony and Community*, p. 169.
51. Lois G. Schwoerer, "Women's Public Political Voice in England: 1640–1740," in Hilda Smith, ed., *Women Writers and the Early Modern British Political Tradition* (Cambridge: Cambridge University Press, 1998), pp. 56–74, quote from p. 56. See also Patricia Crawford, "The Challenges to Patriarchalism: How did the Revolution affect Women?," in John Morrill, ed., *Revolution and Restoration: England in the 1650s* (London: Collins & Brown, 1992), pp. 112–128; also Davies, *Unbridled Spirits*.
52. See W. K. Jordan, *The Development of Religious Toleration*, four volumes (London: Allen & Unwin, 1932–1940); Henry Kamen, *The Rise of Toleration* (New York: McGraw-Hill, 1967); Jay Newman, *Foundations of Religious Tolerance* (Toronto: University of Toronto Press, 1982); Blair Worden, "Toleration and the Cromwellian Protectorate," in W. J. Sheils, ed., *Persecution and Toleration: Papers Read at the Twenty-Second Summer Meeting and the Twenty-Third Winter Meetings of the Ecclesiastical History Society* (Oxford: Basil Blackwell, 1984), pp. 199–235; Avihu Zakai, "Religious Toleration and its Enemies: The Independent Divines and the Issue of Toleration during the English Civil War," *Albion* 21:1 (1989), 1–33; O. P. Grell, J. I. Israel, and N. Tyacke, eds., *From Persecution to Toleration: The Glorious Revolution and Religion in England* (Oxford: Oxford University Press, 1991); and John Christian Laursen and Cary J. Nederman, eds., *Beyond the Persecuting Society: Religious Toleration before the Enlightenment* (Philadelphia, PA: University of Pennsylvania Press, 1998).
53. Anon., *Spirit Moving in the Women Preachers*, title page.
54. Thomas Wilson, *Davids Zeale for Zion. A Sermon Preached Before Sundry of the Honourable House of Commons* (London, 1641).
55. Jones, *Sions Lovers*, pp. A5–A6.
56. D. A. Lloyd Thomas, *Locke on Government* (London: Routledge, 1995), pp. 5–7.

57. Mary Ann Radzinowicz, " 'In those days there was no king in Israel': Milton's Politics and Biblical Narrative," *Yearbook of English Studies* 21 (1991), quote from p. 243, p. 248. See also David Norbrook, *Poetry and Politics in the English Renaissance* (London: Routledge & Kegan Paul, 1984), pp. 280–284.
58. Tolmie, *Triumph of the Saints*, pp. 21–22.
59. Ian Gentles, "London Levellers in the English Revolution: The Chidleys and their Circle," *Journal of Ecclesiastical History* 29, 3 (July 1978), 281–309.
60. Katherine Chidley's texts consist of *Justification of the Independent Churches of Christ Being an Answer to Mr. Edwards his Booke which he hath written against the government of Christ's Church* (London, 1641), *A New-Yeares Gift to Mr. Thomas Edwards* (London, 1645), and *Good Counsell to the Petitioners for Presbyterian Government* (London, 1645).
61. *To the Supreme Authority of this Nation, the Commons Assembled in Parliament: The humble Petitions of divers well-affected Women* . . . (London, 1649); *To the Supreme Authority of England the Commons assembled in Parliament. The humble petition of divers well-affected Women . . . Affecters and approvers of the Petition of Sept. 11. 1648* (London, May 5, 1649); *The Women's Petition to the Right Honourable, his Excellency, the most Noble and Victorious Lord General Cromwell* . . . (London: October 27, 1651); *To the Parliament of the Common-Wealth of England: The humble Petition of divers afflicted Women, in behalf of Mr. John Lilburne* . . . (London, July 29, 1653); *Unto every individual Member of Parliament: The humble Representation of divers afflicted women-Petitioners to the Parliament on the behalf of Mr. John Lilburne* (London, July 29, 1653). For critical discussions of these petitions, see John Higgins, "The Reactions of Women, with Special Reference to Women Petitioners," in Brian Manning, ed., *Politics, Religion, and the English Civil War* (London: Edward Arnold, 1973), pp. 179–222; Davies, *Unbridled Spirits*, pp. 61–90; Ann Marie McEntee, " 'The [un]civill-sisterhood of oranges and lemons': Female Petitioners and Demonstrators, 1642–53," in James Holstun, ed., *Pamphlet Wars: Prose in the English Revolution* (London: Frank Cass, 1992), pp. 92–111; and Ann Hughes, "Gender and Politics in Leveller Literature," in Susan D. Amussen and Mark A. Kishlansky, eds., *Political Culture and Cultural Politics in Early Modern England* (Manchester: Manchester University Press, 1995), pp. 162–88.
62. Anna Trapnel, *The Cry of a Stone, or a Relation of Something Spoken in Whitehall by Anna Trapnel, being in the Visions of God* (London, 1654). See Hilary Hinds's introduction to Trapnel's *Cry of a Stone* (Tempe, AZ: Arizona Center for Medieval and Renaissance Studies, 2000), pp. xiii–xlvii.
63. *Anna Trapnel's Report and Plea, or A Narrative of her Journey from London into Cornwall* (London, 1654). Trapnel's other publications are *A Legacy for Saints; Being Several Experiences of the dealings of God with Anna Trapnel, in, and after her Conversion* (London, 1654); *Strange and Wonderful News from Whitehall* (London, 1654); and an Untitled Volume of Verse in Bodleian Library (London, 1658). For discussions of Trapnel's career and writings, see C. Burrage, "Anna Trapnel's Prophecies," *English Historical Review* 26 (1911), 526–535; Nigel Smith, *Perfection Proclaimed: Language and Literature in English Radical*

Religion 1640–1660 (Oxford: Clarendon Press, 1989); Davies, *Unbridled Spirits*, pp. 150–180; Megan Matchinske, "Holy Hatred: Formations of the Gendered Subject in *English Apocalyptic Writing, 1625–1651*," *ELH* 60 (1993), 349–377; Susan Wiseman, "Unsilent Instruments and the Devil's Cushions: Authority in Seventeenth-Century Women's Prophetic Discourse," in Isobel Armstrong, ed., *New Feminist Discourses* (London: Routledge, 1992), pp. 176–196; Kate Chedgzoy, "Female Prophecy in the Seventeenth Century: The Instance of Anna Trapnel," in William Zunder and Suzanne Trill, eds., *Writing and the English Renaissance* (Harlome: Longman, 1996), pp. 238–254; James Holstun, *Ehud's Dagger: Class Struggle in the English Revolution* (London: Verso, 2000), pp. 257–304.

64. John Lilburne, *Freeman's Freedom Vindicated* (London, 1646); see also Pauline Gregg, *Free-born John: A Biography of John Lilburne* (London: Harrap, 1961).
65. For accounts of Poole's appearance in Whitehall, see Davies, *Unbridled Spirits*, pp. 136–149; Manfred Brod, "Politics and Prophecy in Seventeenth-Century England: The Case of Elizabeth Poole," *Albion* 31, 3 (fall 1999), 395–412; Brian Patton, "Revolution, Regicide, and Divorce: Elizabeth Poole's Advice to the Army," in Alvin Vos, ed., *Place and Displacement in the Renaissance* (Binghamton: SUNY Press, Medieval and Renaissance Texts and Studies, 1995), pp. 133–145; and Rachel Trubowitz, "Female Preachers and Male Wives," in Holstun, *Pamphlet Wars*, pp. 112–133.
66. Elizabeth Poole, *A Vision Wherein is Manifested the Disease and Cure of the Kingdome* (London, 1648). Her other publications are *An Alarum of War, given to the Army, and to their High Court of Justice (so called)* (London, 1649); and *An(other) Alarum of War* (London, 1649).
67. Henry Jessey, *The Exceeding Riches of Grace Advanced by the Spirit of Grace, in an Empty Nothing Creature, viz. Mrs. Sarah Wight Lately Hopeless and Restless* (London, 1652). For critical discussions of Wight, see Davies, *Unbridled Spirits*, pp. 123–135, Smith, *Perfection Proclaimed*, pp. 45–51, and Barbara Ritter Dailey, "The Visitation of Sarah Wight: Holy Carnival and the Revolution of the Saints in Civil War London," in *Church History* 55, 4 (December 1986), 438–455. Thanks also to Carola Scott-Luckens for sharing with me her essay-in-progress, "The Broken Tabernacle: Bodily and Cosmic Paradigms in Henry Jessey's 1647 Soul-Narrative of Sarah Wight."
68. Sarah Wight, *A Wonderful Pleasant and Profitable Letter . . . to a Friend* (London, 1656).
69. Anne Wentworth, *A True Account of Anne Wentworth being cruelly, unjustly and unchristianly dealt with* (London, 1676); *A Vindication of Anne Wentworth* (London, 1677); *The Revelation of Jesus Christ* (London, 1679). See Vera Camden, "Prophetic Discourse and the Voice of Protest: The Vindication of Anne Wentworth," *Man and Nature* (1989), 29–38.
70. Richard Overton, *An Arrow against all Tyrants* (London, 1646); Locke, *Two Treatises*, pp. 307–318.
71. See Clement Hawes, *Mania and Literary Style* (Cambridge: Cambridge University Press, 1996) for both a critique and a strategic exploitation of

the radical potential of the elitist view of Cary and other radical sectarians as "manic." For overviews of Cary's career, see Davies, *Unbridled Spirits*, pp. 136–149 and Jane Baston, "History, Prophecy, and Interpretation: Mary Cary and Fifth Monarchism," *Prose Studies* 21, 3 (December 1988), 1–18.

72. Laura Brace, *The Idea of Property in Seventeenth-Century England* (Manchester: Manchester University Press, 1998); Mark Jenner, " 'Another epocha?': Hartlib, John Lanyon and the Improvement of London in the 1650s," in Mark Greengrass et al., eds., *Samuel Hartlib and Universal Reformation* (Cambridge: Cambridge University Press, 1994), pp. 343–364.

73. Mary Cary, *A Word in Season to the Kingdom of England. Or, A Precious Cordial for a distempered Kingdom* (London, 1648).

74. Mary Cary, *A New and More Exact Mappe, Or, Description of New Jerusalems Glory when Jesus Christ and his Saints with him shall reign a thousand years* (London, 1651); *The Little Horns Doom & Downfall: A Scripture-Prophecie of King James and King Charles, and of this Present Parliament, unfolded* (London, 1647; published with *A New and More Exact Mappe*, 1651); *The Restitution of the Witnesses and Englands Fall from (the Mystical Babylon)*, 2nd edn, "corrected, and most enlarged, and all objections answered by the Author" (London, 1653); and *Twelve New Proposals to the Supreme Governours of the three Nations now assembled at Westminster* (London, 1653).

75. Hinds, *God's Englishwomen*; Andrew Hacker, *Political Theory: Philosophy, Ideology, Science* (New York: Macmillan, 1961), p. 12.

76. Kevin Sharpe, *Remapping Early Modern England: The Culture of Seventeenth-Century Politics* (Cambridge: Cambridge University Press, 2000), p. 3.

77. James Holstun, ed., *Pamphlet Wars*, p. 4; Laursen and Nederman, eds., *Beyond the Persecuting Society*, p. 3.

78. Rachel Weil, *Political Passions: Gender, the Family and Political Argument in England, 1680–1714* (Manchester: Manchester University Press, 1999), p. 11.

79. Richard Ashcraft, "The Two Treatises and the Exclusion Crisis," p. 40, and Gordon Schochet, "The Significant Sounds of Silence: The Absence of Women from the Political Thought of Sir Robert Filmer and John Locke (or, 'Why can't a woman be more like a man?')," in Smith, *Women Writers and the Early Modern British Political Tradition*, pp. 220–242, quote from p. 222. In "Women on Top," Achinstein also elucidates the rational quality of sectarian women's writings.

80. Ruttenburg, *Democratic Personality*, pp. 2–3.

81. Quentin Skinner and J. G. A. Pocock, "The Myth of John Locke and the Obsession with Liberalism," in J. G. A. Pocock and Richard Ashcraft, eds., *John Locke: Papers Read at a Clark Library Seminar, 10 December 1977* (Los Angeles: William Andrews Clark Memorial Library, 1980), pp. 12–13.

82. Wiseman, "Unsilent Instruments," pp. 176–196, quote from p. 193.

83. David Norbrook, "The Time Republican," *Times Literary Supplement*, 2 February 1996.

84. Michael Wilding, *Dragon's Teeth*, p. 2.

85. Wiseman, "Unsilent Instruments," p. 177.

86. Christopher Hill, *The English Bible and the Seventeenth-Century Revolution* (Harmondsworth: Penguin, 1993), pp. 31 and 125. See also Elizabeth Tuttle, "Biblical Reference in the Political Pamphlets," in Armitage, Himy, and Skinner, *Milton and Republicanism*, pp. 63–81.
87. Kevin Sharpe and Steven N. Zwicker, eds., *Politics of Discourse: The Literature and History of Seventeenth-Century England* (Berkeley: University of California Press, 1987), introduction, p. 2; Victoria Kahn, "Margaret Cavendish and the Romance of Contract," in Hutson, *Feminism and Renaissance Studies*, pp. 286–316, quote from p. 289.
88. "The Examination of Mrs. Anne Hutchinson at the Court at Newtown," in David D. Hall, ed., *The Antinomian Controversy, 1636–1638* (Durham, NC: Duke University Press, 1990), p. 320. For sustained discussions of Hutchinson, see Amy Schrager Lang, *Prophetic Woman: Anne Hutchinson and the Problem of Dissent in the Literature of New England* (Berkeley: University of California Press, 1987) and Selma R. Williams, *Divine Rebel: The Life of Anne Marbury Hutchinson* (New York: Holt, Rinehart & Winston, 1981). For another contemporary complaint that "religion is now become the common discourse and table talk" of the unordained in taverns and ale-houses, see John Taylor, *Religions Enemies* (London, 1641), p. 6.

I

"Born of the mother's seed": liberalism, feminism, and religious separatism

> But O my Virgin Lady, where is she?
> How chance she is not in your company?
> Attendant Spirit, *Comus*

It is perhaps an understatement to say that liberalism and contract theory have become anathematic terms within postmodern academic feminism.[1] As Carole Pateman most famously argues, because "republican" critiques by Locke (as well as Hobbes and Rousseau) liberated men from kingly rule in the political sphere by situating them as rulers over the domestic realm, then liberal political theory in general represents a "masculinist" tradition that contains little of value – and much of harm – for modern women.[2] Although writings by such seventeenth-century sectarian women as Katherine Chidley, Anna Trapnel, Elizabeth Poole, Sarah Wight, Anne Wentworth, and Mary Cary are but "dews and drops" in a much larger river of political thought, I will argue that they nonetheless represent an alternative source of liberal ideas that have the potential to complicate this powerful and still highly influential thesis.

As Rachel Weil puts it, Pateman's 1987 study, *The Sexual Contract: Aspects of Patriarchal Liberalism*, "provides a starting point for the anti-liberal feminist cause" by grounding its antipathy within what she sees as its genealogical origin in contract theory's critique of patriarchalism.[3] As it was reinvigorated in seventeenth-century England into a fully-fledged justification for divine right absolutism, patriarchal political theory was predicated upon the authority of the father.[4] In 1615, for example, James I decreed that all householders purchase a copy of *God and the King*, Richard Mocket's "justification of royal authority by means of the Fifth Commandment."[5] In this work, Mocket argued that "there is a stronger and higher bond of Duty between Children and the Father of their Country, than the Fathers of Private Families."[6] The King, he contended, received his authority from God and was therefore answerable to no one else. The people, as a result, were absolutely obligated to obey him as one would a father. The people's only remedy was that, if the King attempted to destroy the Church, then God would prevent him from doing so and punish him for the effort. Otherwise, if the King behaved tyrannically, then the people could only repent of whatever sins they must have committed to imperil their Church and country in such a way.

In such mid-seventeenth-century tracts as *The Anarchy of a Limited or Mixed Monarchy* (1648) and *Patriarcha: or the Natural Power of Kings* (1680), Sir Robert Filmer reconstructed defences of patriarchalist forms of government by reiterating Mocket's claim, arguing that the King's total and "absolute" power over his subjects extended vertically up to Adam's "Royal Authority" and down to the father's inherited position of "sovereignty" over his wife and children:

If God created only Adam, and of a piece of him made the Woman, and if by Generation from them two, as parts of them all Mankind be propagated: If also God gave to Adam not only the Dominion over the Woman and Children that should Issue from them, but also over the whole Earth to subdue it, and over all the Creature on it, so that as long as Adam lived, no Man could claim or enjoy any thing but by Donation, Assignation, or Permission from him.[7]

In other words, no human law or preexisting contract could limit the King's Adamic power. Laws functioned to govern the people, not the King, and Parliament was created not to act as an independent institution capable of making laws and/or providing a check upon and balance against the King's power, but to advise him and to create new laws at his request.

For Pateman, Locke's *Two Treatises of Civil Government* (1698) functions as liberalism's seminal but tragically flawed rejection of this patriarchalist creed. In this animadversion of Filmer's *Patriarcha*, Locke objected to the paternalistic basis for some men to rule over others on the grounds that individuals were not children and should not be constituted as such by a paternalistic state. To subvert the crown's patriarchalist claim to rule the subject as a father does a child, Locke drew a distinction between the "Political Power" of the "Magistrate over a Subject, from that of a Father over his Children, a Master over his Servant, a Husband over his wife, and a Lord over his Slave."[8] The latter were natural while the former was not because children, servants, slaves, and women were by nature less "able" and less "strong" than men. Because Locke's arguments removed the King's right to rule over his subjects as a father would a child and a husband would a wife, his subversion of "patriarchy" *could have had* far-reaching consequences for women. However, Pateman contends, because Locke models the individual after a particular and privileged "image" of masculinity, he was able to do away with the King's political authority over men only by retaining men's domestic authority over their wives and children. Thus, at the very moment when political relations among men were said to be founded on contract and consent, the ostensibly gender-neutral concept of "person" was invested with gender-based stereotypes that resubjected "weak" and "childish" women to male rule. Pateman's overall conclusion: republican contract theory is in and of itself a blighted "masculinist" system. The inevitability of female subordination is written into its very marrow and cannot be transcended by subsequent attempts to broaden (or further abstract) the definition of "person," for "person" in this context refers specifically to propertied white men such as Locke himself. As Pateman writes:

The conclusion is easy to draw that the denial of civil equality to women means that the feminist aspiration must be to win acknowledgement for women as "individuals." Such an aspiration can never be fulfilled. The "individual" is a patriarchal category. The individual is masculine and his sexuality is understood accordingly . . . The patriarchal construction of sexuality, what it means to be a sexual being, is to possess and to have access to sexual property.[9]

As a result, Pateman insists that modern women seeking new forms of empowerment and social justice must agitate for alternative political orders, more "democratic" ones that dissolve most (if not all) boundaries between public political and private spheres, that evolve from relatively free markets to socialistic economies, and that, in the end, provide an alternative, more communitarian portrait of the individual than that of a "sovereign man" who possesses self and women and who is fictitiously abstracted from a larger, overdetermining social, economic, or political matrix. As Pateman writes, "The civil individual has been constructed in opposition to women and all that our bodies symbolize, so how can we become full members of civil society or parties to the fraternal contract?"[10]

Influential feminists such as Zillah Eisenstein, Catherine MacKinnon, and Seyla Benhabib have offered comparable critiques.[11] Like Pateman, they attack liberalism for both "embodying" individualism in men and "abstracting" the individual so that the "essence of individuality appears transhistorical and as part of the nature of any individual within society."[12] Because liberalism defines the individual as "autonomous, atomistic, and distinct from the social relations of society," then "most of the time" we must "envision individual and social life as antagonistic to each other."[13] To redress this historical injustice, liberalism must first be recognized as a system invented by and for men, then it must be replaced by a different, more collectivist and symbiotic understanding of the relationship between something that is no longer the individual and the "private" on the one hand, and the more manifold state or the "public" on the other. Or as Benhabib puts it, we need to replace the "generalized" conception of the individual as a "rational being entitled to the same rights and duties we would want to ascribe to ourselves" with a "concrete" one which would draw upon the more "feminine" virtues of responsibility, sharing, and interrelatedness in order to acknowledge the differing needs and "moral identity of the concrete other."[14]

Some scholars soften or rebut these claims by pointing out that the principles forged by liberal thinkers did nonetheless (perhaps unintentionally, perhaps not) benefit women down the line. Pamela Grande Jensen, for example, suggests that "placing liberalism's treatment of the woman question in a context that takes into account friendly modifications and ancient alternatives can lead to a new feminism, one that alters both feminism's and liberalism's self-understanding in significant respects."[15] Gordon Schochet argues that, while Locke's theory did not explicitly enfranchise women into self-possessive subjectivity, it is nonetheless "precisely that Lockean voluntarism . . . that opens up the concept 'person' and makes possible political membership and significance beyond the narrow realm of white males."[16] Likewise, Jane S. Jacquette contends that, "when combined with a long tradition of anti-capitalist thought," contemporary feminism's attack upon the "male biases of liberalism" means that Enlightenment liberalism is "portrayed as a barrier to solving contemporary problems rather than as a basis upon which to build."[17] This is unfortunate she argues, because it is Hobbes's "stern gender egalitarianism" that has "proven foundationally critical to women's subsequent claims to equal rights in all spheres."[18] And Susan Wendell has maintained that "liberal ideas of political equality and individual liberty need not be derived from a view of human nature that includes abstract individualism and do not imply such a view."[19] Rather, as L. Susan Brown concurs, it is "not abstract to understand the human individual as not being socially constructed, but rather as capable of expressing free will within a social context."[20]

While clearly differing on the value of liberalism to postmodern feminism, both "sides" (revisionist antiliberal as well as neoliberal feminists) operate on two shared assumptions. The first is that contract theory, liberal individualism, and the division between a sphere that is understood to be private and conjugal on the one hand, and one that is understood to be public and statist on the other, are the product of male thinkers. As

Jensen argues, "we might say that [new liberal] feminist arguments extend the enlightenment that [male] liberalism began" and thus the essays in her collection return us to such thinkers as Machiavelli and Montesquieu.[21] This assumption is to some degree understandable given the result of long-standing gaps in the historical record; it is, after all, only relatively recently that religious and political writings by early modern women have gained the attention of historians and literary critics, and they continue to be unknown to political theorists, an omission that Pateman herself grants and begins to remedy in her conclusion to Hilda Smith's collection, *Women Writers and the Early Modern British Political Tradition*.[22] Pateman does not address the possibility that such gaps may have been exacerbated by the structural components of her own earlier work, heavily implying as it did that seventeenth-century women could not have gained a public voice because contract theory liberated men to political equality and possessive individualism by resubjecting women to the same silence and confinement within a private domestic sphere headed by men that they had (allegedly) endured under patriarchalism. However, after reviewing the burgeoning evidence of early modern women's literary activity produced by feminist historiography, Pateman has come to acknowledge that "women played a much greater part than we have been led to believe in the emergence of the popular press, the development of freedom of expression, and the 'public sphere' so important for democracy."[23] This makes Pateman a potentially powerful ally to have when it comes to contesting the "decontextualized" antiliberal postmodern feminist line which insists that the early feminist "foundational" notion of "woman" as an individual who possesses "natural rights" is "a reenactment of the sins of the fathers ... [an] ahistorical, partial, imperialist theor[y], masquerading as universalism, as 'the Enlightenment' " that must be eliminated on the road to true "democratization."[24]

And yet, because Pateman's work has been so influential in perpetuating the very hostility that postmodern feminism so often displays to liberal precepts, I will, at various points throughout this book, continue to put texts by female sectarians into dialogue with her original and still influential antiliberal analyses. Even as she now appears uncomfortable with postmodern feminism's lack of interest in the "feminist" category of "woman," Pateman still asserts that early modern women's political theory holds promise for postmodernism precisely because it anticipates the latter's critique of foundationalism. While Pateman is right that, like postmodernists, "Feminist writers before, during, and after the Enlightenment, challenged and criticized exclusion, attacked men's powers, interrogated 'man' as a 'foundation' of political theories, took issue with an 'essentialist' view of women and their alleged natural deficiencies, and showed unequivocally how power was implicated in claims about rights, freedom, and reason," I hasten to add that we cannot and should not conclude from this that all early modern women's political theory was, as a result, dedicated to subverting any notion whatsoever of "foundationalism," "essentialism," "rights," "freedom," and "reason."[25] Instead, as I will argue, we might take stock of the ways in which a group of seventeenth-century female Separatists helped to envision "the subject" in fundamental and universal terms, that is as an individual who possessed certain liberties precisely because she was essentially and foundationally grounded by something other than the earthly, embodied, and self-interested power of "man." These women insisted upon being recognized in equal and "general" terms as the product of their maker so as to gain the ability to perpetually melt and remix the "concrete" terms through which they had so long been constituted as morally different and other.

In short, sectarian women's writings will provide further evidence that liberalism can no longer be attributed solely to the "sins of the fathers." In fact, as I hope to illustrate in subsequent chapters, separatist women contended that basic liberal precepts were the necessary preconditions for women to perform such nontraditional acts as preaching, prophesying, petitioning, and publishing. There is, in other words, a much shorter distance than one might assume between the "I" that, as Nigel Smith has shown, utters prophecies for the purpose of achieving a climactic "communication with God," and the ostensibly Lockean "I" that draws upon a relationship with the "maker" in order to delineate a *suum* of one's own.[26] In the end, it is my hope that this book will lead to the conclusion that something called "feminism" should neither reject something called "liberalism" out of hand as an inherently sexist tradition, nor should it settle for seeking out the ways in which that male-authored body of thought may or may not have "trickled down" to benefit women down the line. To do so implies, ironically, that we accept the degree to which androcentric historiographies stake their genealogies on the plots of "great men." Instead, those interested in the intersections between gender and political systems might ask why and how it was that a handful of separatist women helped to publicize and agitate on behalf of some of the core ideas of what we now call liberalism; why and how it was that later male theorists excluded or even rejected as "antiliberal" those formulations penned earlier by women from their own domesticating and revisionist thought; and why and how it was that some strains within subsequent women's movements, even if they did not always know to whom they were indebted, must now work to *recover* what other women before them had already practised and preached: an individualistic claim to rights and property as opposed to a republican emphasis upon duty or a collectivist emphasis on the "responsibility" the individual has to the "community."

The second assumption shared by both antiliberal and some proliberal postmodern feminists is that the "conceptual orthodoxy of the West: the self-creating, autonomous subject of bourgeois liberal humanism" is as inherently sexist a notion as feminist detractors claim it is.[27] As is clear from the discussion above, even feminist defenders of liberalism still feel a need to point out that its conception of the individual "need not," as we have seen Susan Wendell put it, "be derived from a view of human nature that includes abstract individualism and does not imply such a view." However, separatist women writers both drew on and contributed to a radical religious and political milieu in which "liberty" was more inclined to comprehend women as well as men precisely because the free individual was envisioned in "abstract" ways. As Kristen Poole has demonstrated, "The phenomenon of religious nonconformity spurred English men and women to contemplate and interrogate the basis of their familial, parochial, and national communities, bringing questions concerning the organization of church and state into the alehouse and home" and "at stake" in their discussions were issues surrounding "the relationship of the individual to the community; the grounds for political authority; the autonomy of the individual conscience; the right to participate in public discourse; and the right to determine one's own religious society."[28] Thus Wendell is right to point out that, contrary to popular assertion, liberal concepts of the abstract individual are not devoid of any appreciation for social contexts. Indeed, in the case of separatist women, they agitated for abstract individualism in order to gain the right to associate on more equal terms with others (including men) in ways that had traditionally been forbidden by the "social context" of the state church. They actually forged definitions of abstract individualism from within a very specific set of social and political circumstances, ones that they refer to over and over again as the necessary starting point for their arguments. Indeed, they articulated their vision of an equality predicated on androgynous spirituality as opposed to embodied physicality precisely in order to liberate themselves from the age-old creed which said that their bodies rendered them susceptible to and in need of a patriarchal control that must, for the sake of the community, deny them such things as religious authority. What is more, as I shall show, Anne Wentworth codified her notion of abstract possessive individualism for the very purposes of rejecting the claim that she was her husband's sexual property.

Finally, it is also the case that the dichotomy that is so often drawn between the abstract individual, on the one hand, and the feminist "embodied" or collective one, on the other, is actually complicated *by* the specific historical context from which dissenting women's texts emerge. Drawing to various degrees on the Antinomian Controversy of 1637, in which the Puritan magistrates of the Massachusetts Bay Colony silenced self-styled preacher, Anne Hutchinson, and banished her and her followers from the community, scholars such as Lyle Koehler, Ben Barker-Bakersfield, and Margaret Olofson Thickstun have perhaps enabled Pateman's thesis by rejecting the possibility that what they see as Puritanism's patriarchal theology and its subordination of women could have served as an emancipatory force.[29] Amanda Porterfield has contested this line of thinking, arguing that, while feminized images of God as a nursing mother were "less prominent, frequent, and explicit than images of God as father, husband, and judge," they nonetheless "compose a significant leitmotif in Puritan theology that reflected and sanctioned the authority Puritan women exercised in their roles as mothers."[30] For Porterfield, the even more important fact that Puritanism led individuals to equate their "subjective experience with revelations from God" helps to explain the "considerable" appeal that "Puritan theology, and Puritan ministers" had held for women since the sixteenth century, when separatist women gave emotional and material forms of support, including going to jail, to their persecuted ministers (84). I would take Porterfield's useful analysis even further by suggesting that dissenting women could and did draw on a strain of highly "embodied" religious thought that constituted the actual mother's womb as the very ground and origin of the birth of the abstract individual and its claim to religious liberty. As the pro-toleration Presbyterian, Samuel Rutherford, stated it, "all jurisdiction of man over man is, as it were, artificial and positive, and inferreth some servitude whereof nature from the womb hath freed us."[31] Rutherford continued, "Every man by nature is a free man born, that is, by nature no man cometh out of the womb under any civil subjection to king, prince, or judge, to master, captain, conqueror, teacher, etc. What is from the womb, and so natural, is eternal and agreeth to all societies of men."[32] In this explicitly antipatriarchal formulation, every mother's womb is designated as the literal agent for a sociopolitical system of natural and "abstract" individual freedoms and voluntary association. As *The Ancient Bounds* – a 1645 pro-toleration pamphlet – puts it, the Christian Magistrate was no longer to view himself as the "begetting father" of the Church. That role was to go to Christ, the "everlasting father by the seed of the word" who would plant his seed in the maternalized receptacle of each individual believer.[33] Milton called "Christian Liberty" the "fundamental privilege of the Gospel, the new birthright of every true believer," and quoting 2 Corinthians 3.17 and Galatians 4.26, he intoned, "Where the Spirit of the Lord is, there is liberty. Jerusalem which is above is free; which is the mother of us all; and [verse 31]: We are not children of the bondwoman, but of the free."[34] William Dell wrote in *The Way of True Peace and Unity* (1649) that the "churches of men" were those in which members have "the government of them laid on [their] shoulders," while the "true Church hath its government laid only on Christ's shoulders."[35] While "the churches of men" were hierarchically defined "presbyteries" with internal and/or inter-congregational governing bodies, the "assembles" of the "true Churches" were "bodies" in which individual members of each congregation enjoyed "an equality among them all" (303). In keeping with this emphasis upon the necessary role of maternal agency in the production of individual liberty, Dell claimed that the false church of artificially imposed compliance with the intervening power of the "churches of men" was born of the "seed of the serpent," while the egalitarian "true church" of an individual's voluntary association unmediated by others, which he also referred to as the church of "love," was "born of the mother's seed" (303).

While a young "unfathered" woman like Sarah Jones wrote optimistically of a world in which just such an empowered "Congregation" consisted of a "body" of "Shee preachers to whom the command is given, to whom the promise is made, goe Preach and Baptize, observe and doe all I command you, and I will be with you to the end of the world," modern historians such as Keith Thomas caution modern readers to remember that these attractive-sounding statements did not always translate into the ability for women to exercise such institutional powers as serving as pastors, elders, or "messenger" to policy meetings (although, as Patricia Crawford points out, Independent and Baptist churches did implement the new position of "deaconess").[36] It is true that Rutherford and other dissenters expressed antipathy towards "civil subjection," except for when it determined the obedience of "children to parents, and the wife, to the husband."[37] At the same time, the emergence of the idea that choosing one's own religious affiliation was a bypassing of the earthly father in favor of following the spiritually free mother as both the "hiding space of strength" and the medium of plenitude for the production not just of "Puritanism" but also of a political system of religious liberty did, Thomas argues, coincide with a resurgence in popular forms of piety. This resurgence was defined in no small part by the participation of women and, in some cases, was translated into a political vocabulary as well as into actual instances of political action and even "rights." The basis for this was again an insistence on spiritual equality, meaning that all individuals alike were subordinate to – but only to – the will of God and that they were understood as such because of their "natural" passage through the free mother's womb. This simultaneously "abstract" and "embodied" principle of spiritual equality and individual "liberty of conscience" helped to underwrite the principle of voluntary association upon which the Independency movement was founded and by which it was perpetuated.[38] And this ostensibly Lockean principle was articulated and defended earlier on by women such as Katherine Chidley, who used it to claim various forms of social power for women.

Fundamentally, the new emphasis on voluntary association, consent, and persuasion meant that women, prophetess and nonprophetess alike, were deemed necessary components of Independent church formation, charter members who could help "gather" churches through friendship, family, and birth. This emphasis that separatist churches would place upon female participation provides a necessary counterpoint to the emphasis on social disorder that usually accompanies discussions of early modern women. As Catherine Gallagher observes, the figure of the mother especially generated anxiety due to her potential for "semiotic riot." The fear, as Gallagher explains it, was that

if the mother is not properly contained then semiotic riot is the result. One's name may mean nothing; one's property may have no natural relation to one's name. One's self-representations may prove to be mere mental constructions . . . if one's mother was capable of the biological equivalent of system-making, of generating an illegitimate and unprecedented progeny.[39]

This anxiety had social implications for, within this context, assertions of maternal agency were inevitably read as a transgression of the father's sole claim to authorship and generation. Historians such as Phyllis Mack and literary critics such as Diane Purkiss have tied seventeenth-century prophetesses into the history of this equation between maternal agency and transgression. They demonstrate how prophetesses were able to exploit the fine line between actual maternal reproduction and the literary production of the prophetic text, and to thereby authorize themselves as religious leaders.[40] As Purkiss lays it out,

The genre of prophecy . . . formed the basis for a metaphorization of female prophecy as a female reproduction which erased or occluded the mark of an earthly father or husband, raising the disturbing possibility that woman might not be a mere conduit for male words, truths, or self-replications, but an agent in producing them.[41]

At the same time, Purkiss reiterates the early modern conclusion that such erasures were inevitably read as transgression, for she concludes that "the management of this unsettling spectacle through the troping of women's brains and bodies as the makers of the monstrous, testifies to the power of such female self-representations to disrupt the homosocial order of rhetoric and property."[42]

This emphasis on disorder, while certainly merited and important, does have the unfortunate effect of eliding the ways in which the logic of voluntary association not only accepted but relied on new forms of female (even maternal) agency and new definitions of property (namely, property-in-self) as nontransgressive and necessary components for the orderly production of the Independent church and its foundation in the liberty of individual conscience. As Thomas argues, "women were essential to Nonconformity" and comprised a significant percentage of membership in gathered churches. I would suggest that this was in no small measure due to the fact that, as is implicitly recognized within such formulations as those of Dell and Rutherford, the role of "Mother" was both the fount for the principle of religious liberty and one of the primary means by which Independent congregations were not only metaphorically produced but also literally created and sustained.[43] According to Patricia Crawford, "Congregations depended upon the children of believers to continue the faith" and "mothers who taught their children on a daily basis about the importance of their faith ensured the perpetuation of Nonconformity."[44] Even as anti-Independents claimed them to be the children of devils, many sectarians represented themselves as the byproducts of holy parturition and the liberty of choice that was presumed to come with it. In *A Fiery Flying Roule* (1649), the Ranter, Abiezer Coppe, represented his conversion as a (re)birth scene. Though he writes that he was forsaken by his earthly family, he, nonetheless, intends for us to accept his call to deliver a "warning piece" to actual "gathered churches" as a reformation of the virtual and "true" church that occurs in and through a materially maternal body.[45] He writes:

I was utterly plagued, consumed, damned, rammed, and sunke into nothing, into the bowels of the still Eternity (my mother's wombe) out of which I came naked, and whetherto I returned again naked. And lying a while there, rapt up in silence, at length . . . I saw a great body of light, like the light of the Sun, and red as fire (in the forme of a drum as it were) whereupon with exceeding trembling and amazement on the flesh, and with joy unspeakable in the spirit, I clapt my hands and cryed out, Amen, Hallelujah, Hallelujah, Amen. (82)

After this dramatic moment, Coppe reports that he "lay trembling, sweating and smoaking (for the space of half an houre)" before the Lord tells him that before he receives salvation, he must travel to the "belly of hell" and dwell among the devils before being shown the spark of life at the end of a passageway and redeemed" (82).

In Henry Jessey's account of *The Exceeding Riches of Grace Advanced by the Spirit, in an Empty Nothing Creature, viz. Mris. Sarah Wight* (1647), Jessey represents the contentious but apparently generative relationship that the prophetess, Sarah Wight, had with her *actual mother* as playing a key role in the transformation of her social status from "empty nothing creature" to that of a minister. Wight's spiritual turmoil begins when she lies to her mother over the loss of her hood. Throughout the days that she subsequently spends in bed, her mother acts as her spiritual counselor and comforter, though both roles prove difficult to perform on behalf of the tortured Wight. Like the suffering Job, Sarah wishes at one point that she had never been born and asks, "Wherefore hast thou brought me forth of the womb?" Like Jeremy, she curses the fact that her mother's womb had not been her grave and her prolonged stay in bed becomes a symbolic reenactment of her desire to return to her mother and hence to death. But, like Coppe, she intends this death as a prelude to her rebirth, and she represents this renewal in material terms as a repetition of the passage through the mother. "There's a fountain open . . . A fountain not streames, but a fountaine: open, an open fountain: if a doore stand shelving, you cannot come in, but you must thrust to come in: but if it stand wide open, then there's freedome for you to goe, freedome for you to goe."[46] The fountain, Wight claims, is Jesus Christ, and yet the power of Christ is also conflated with the agency of the mother, whose forgiveness Sarah seeks for her earlier transgression. Wight's own salvation allows her, once again, to become a vehicle for the production of the autonomous religious community as she, in turn, ministers to others. In her spiritual autobiography, *The Cry of a Stone* (1653), Anna Trapnel directly credits her spiritual rebirth and the attendant acquisition of prophetic powers to a kind of spell her mother uttered on her death-bed nine years before: "The last words she uttered . . . were these to the Lord for her daughter. Lord! Double thy spirit upon my child; These words she uttered with much eagerness three times, and spoke no more."[47] As Purkiss forcefully observes, this moment in Trapnel's writing "represents the full subversive power of the woman prophet, for it inverts the most basic of all hierarchical relations, the relationship between God and the believer. The woman commands, and commands God."[48] But there is something else of interest at work in these formulations. Sectarians asserted that the right to choose one's own religious affiliation was, as I noted earlier, in and of itself a natural right; however, to illustrate the "natural" quality of this choice, Nonconformists often argued that the means by which they came to exercise it was not the result of what they called an artificial or man-made will, but that of God's acting directly upon them. Choice was ironically represented almost as its opposite: as submission to a persuasive call. As Michael Walzer has argued, a Calvinist notion of God as a demanding and controlling dictator underwrites the "revolution" that the "saints" launched against patriarchalism during this period: "A despot destroys the structure of intermediate powers and makes possible a politics based on individual interest."[49] But as I shall show, sectarians also identified the medium for the destruction of intermediate powers as the facilitating figure of the mother. Coming to one's calling or "individual interest" was as natural as being born or born again.

As these examples also illustrate, the idea that the passage through the mother provided the individual with the right to voluntarily affiliate with a church of his or her own choosing also placed the actual mother in a strategic position to quite literally produce at least the seeds of a church through the persuasive, at times ministerial effects of her own speech and, in an even more unmediated fashion, through the birth and care of her children.[50] The extension of the approved institution of "mother's council" to the realm of ministry was certainly to some degree enabled by the Protestant emphasis on plain speech. The pamphlet preacher Anne Wentworth located herself in a long line of plain speakers in Protestant rhetoric by persuading her readership that her pamphlets of prophecy and self-vindication "doth not come to the view of the World with eloquence of speech, nor any artificial dress, but in plainness of speech, in its own Mother's tongue, not set forth and adorned with the wisdom of men."[51] Such insistence on the unmediated, the plain, and the pure (not to mention the English as opposed to the Latin) in the artless art of persuasion interestingly enough results not in the idea that the mother's self-assertion wreaks semiotic havoc on the name of the father, but rather that the intervention of earthly fathers into the mother's coproduction with God only (the "mother's seed") wreaks semiotic riot with the maternal tongue. The Antinomian Controversy was sparked by the suspicion that Anne Hutchinson had used her roles as mother and midwife counselor to gain converts for her own church.[52] To be sure, detractors attempted to squelch this growing and "disorderly" phenomenon by linking it to popular tales of "monstrous births."[53] In his preface to Governor John Winthrop's account of the controversy, Thomas Welde claimed that the result of Hutchinson's approach to church building was that "afterwards you shall see a litter of fourescore and eleven of their brats hung up against the Sunne, besides many new ones of Mistris Hutchinson's, all which they hatched and dandled."[54] But often overlooked by the fact that

Hutchinson was silenced and banished by the Massachusetts Bay magistrates is the equally salient detail that widespread support for her activities was registered in the transcripts of her two trials by the civil and church courts of Boston respectively, specifically by her own sons and son-in-law, who underwent admonishment for adhering to their mother's religious counsel and who followed her into exile in Rhode Island to establish a new church.

Breast-feeding became another form of maternal agency positively associated not only metaphorically with the production of prophetesses' texts but also quite literally with the formation of the private and voluntary (as opposed to state-enforced) religious community.[55] Like the decision to affiliate one's self with a congregation through the mother's agency of birth, breast-feeding as a form of persuasion sought to represent religious freedom and the rational ability to choose for one's self as a "right" that emanated through the mother's body. *The Ancient Bounds* argued that even the so-called "heathen who impeached Paul for heresy" had "the natural principle of reason and justice that did glow in the hearts."[56] Because these heathen had "nothing [else] in them but what they sucked in with their mother's milk," the mother's milk is made the means by which the principle of religious liberty is transferred and sustained (255). It is true that some Puritan authors represented breast-feeding one's own child as a duty that called for female obedience, but even this signified the degree to which maternal functions were integrated as necessary components of the reproduction of the elect. The Lady Elizabeth Clinton in her *Countesse of Lincolnes Nurserie* argued that breast-feeding, like birth, was a materially reproductive means by which the religious community was to be produced, both in the example it set and in the actual materials it imparted. She writes,

Thinke againe how your Babe crying for your breast, sucking hartily the milke out of it, and growing by it, is the Lords owne instruction, every houre, and every day, that you are suckling it, instructing you to shew that you are his new borne Babes, by your earnest desire after his word, and the syncere doctrine thereof, and by your daily growing in grace and goodnesse thereby, so shall you reape and profit.[57]

Clinton's text helps to underscore a dynamic that is implicitly at work in much of the literatures that constitute the mother as the natural agency of religious liberty. While replacing earthly fathers with God meant that, to some degree, patriarchy was maintained even as maternal agency was recognized *and solicited*, it also resulted in a collapsing of the distance between God and woman, so that "natural" woman was practically coterminous with the Creator. Clinton, herself, makes the radical claim that women were "made as man in the image of God," thus nursing is concrete evidence of "the worke that God worketh in the very nature of mothers" (121–122). As a definition of the female self, this bears remarkable resemblance to the model of possessive individualism envisioned in Milton's *Comus*. God grants the individual property in himself and herself through visions and divine inspiration. But this selfhood is also to some degree "activated" or made fully manifest both when the individual is born through the mother and when the individual is reborn through the intervention of a Sabrina-like purgation. Divine sovereignty (God the father) and nature (the mother) commingle to produce an "abstract" definition of the individual.

The antipatriarchal formulations rehearsed above were accompanied by the actual generation of the innumerable and "unprecedented progeny" of separatist conventicles, autonomous "institutions" which antitolerationists inevitably demonized as monstrous and illegitimate because they were not headed by a properly ordained father. But as did Sarah Jones, sectarians themselves *propagated* and *celebrated* the idea that the gathered churches were institutional and holy products of a maternal agency expressly lacking in "elderships."[58] In the pamphlet, *The Brothers of the Separation. Or a True Relation of a Company of Brownists which kept their Conventicle at one Mr. Porter's in Goat Alley in Whitecrosse-street*, the said Mr. Porter was reported to have defended the practice of meeting in such unorthodox places as kitchens, barns, fields, and even highways on the grounds that the "Saviour chose a homely stable to be borne in."[59] This invocation of the Virgin Mary's immaculate conception and birth draws us to consider her semiotic riot with both the name and place of the father. As the maternal agent of the literal word made flesh, Mary's wandering disrupted a patriarchal emphasis on a fixed place and inheritance expressed most concretely in the laws of primogeniture. Joseph's displacement as father has an analogue in the displacement of the father's home as the site of the birth of the godhead. At the same time, such a displacement was conducted in the orderly name of God the father and the "property" he held within the individual soul.

Through the logic of spiritual equality and voluntary association, women claimed the prerogative of religious choice and spiritual consent. Because the independent church was formed through voluntary association rather than through enforced affiliation with the parish of one's abode, sectarians, including women, claimed the exercise of their "liberties" and "free wills" in determining their denominations. As Richard Mather wrote in *An Apology for Church Covenant* (1643), "nay, it implieth a contradiction in the very name of liberty or freedom that free men should take upon them authority or power over free men without their free consent and voluntary and mutual covenant or engagement."[60] Three years later John Saltmarsh wrote that established churches such as presbyteries are "set up by an alleged pattern of the eldership and presbytery of the Apostles and Elders."[61] These churches, he writes, are "parochial . . . as they are divided at first by the Romish prelates and the statute-laws of the state" (183). Independents and their more radical separatist offshoots, on the other hand, "are only a church when called by the Word and Spirit into consent or covenant" (183). Under the auspices of this principle, a woman might choose to leave her "father's house" and join a separatist congregation (as did Elizabeth Poole), or she might separate from the Church of England and form an alternative congregation within the confines of her home which included her family (as did Anne Hutchinson and Katherine Chidley), or she might set herself up as a minister through print, where she had no need for an actual congregation (as did Mary Cary).

In every instance, the traditional notion of the father and husband as arbiter of choice and decision was disrupted and this disturbance was believed to reverberate all the way up through the patriarchal hierarchy of father, minister, bishop, lord, and king. For example, in a tract entitled *The Copy of a Letter Written by Mr. Thomas Parker, Pastor of the Church of Newbury in New-England, to his Sister, Mrs. Elizabeth Avery*, Pastor Parker laments his sister's refusal to adhere to her earthly fathers by following her own persuasion. He writes,

You will not come to Ordinances, nor willingly joyn in private Prayer with your own Husband, but onely to condescend to his infirmities; for you say you are above Ordinances, above the Word and Sacraments, yea above the Blood of Christ himself, living as a glorified Saint, and taught *immediately* by the Spirit. Who would have thought or dreamed, that such expressions should have ever come out of the mouth of Sister Avery? (Emphasis added)[62]

But many groups not only differed from Elizabeth Avery's brother in not lamenting the woman's ability to choose, but rather they actively targeted women as their constituents. Mapping the Pauline analogy of the Church as the body or bride of Christ onto the logic of voluntary association meant that the feminized body or bride of Christ gained a significant measure of power and self-determination, including that of prophecy, which John Spenser described as that "gift" which "the Spirit giveth" for "the edifying of the body."[63]

Describing prophecy as a "gift" and spirit as a "possession" meant that one needed no formal training in order to speak in church. Members of the lower or "mechanic" classes who gained a great mastery of the Bible but who did not have an official degree in religion could not assume the position of minister within established churches. However, through the logic of voluntary association, they could form churches of their own where they could preach by being popularly accepted as one who "possessed" the spirit, as Samuel How so famously argued in 1640.[64] As the author of *The Brownist's Conventicle* complained, the sectaries "will endure no degrees in schools" because, to them, the idea that "all learning must be laid by Academies are to them abominable."[65] He especially complained of Samuel Eaton, newly returned from New England, who was preaching that "the very names of Parsons and Vicars were Antichristian" and that "Pastors and Teachers of particular Congregations must be chosen by the people," and this included "sisters" as well as "brothers" (5). This reveals the fact that in some congregations women did, in fact, exercise a vote.[66] It also reveals the degree to which preachers tailored their message and their medium to attract and persuade women. Ironically, one of the most infamous sectarian preachers *was* the tailor, Samuel How, and the antitolerationist writer, in Ipswich, New England, Nathaniel Ward, argued that allowing for religious choice was like allowing women to be overdressed by too many tailors pandering to their desires.[67] The pamphlet *The Brownists Synagogue* cast a wary eye at male sectarian preachers who consciously sought to court women. It reported that John Brumley in Chancery Lane, "*twice in a weeke* . . . teacheth, the women his holy & zealous sisters" who "well affect him" (emphasis mine) and, it noted that a coachman by the name of Greene who kept "no constant place" as a church but "[was] here, and every where" flatteringly likened the women of his congregation to self-determining queens, equal to their brethren, the self-proclaimed kings.[68] Elizabeth Avery's brother warns his sister away from ministers courting bodies to complete the social production of their congregation. "Your new Masters and Companions in Heresie," he writes, "speak fairly to you, and flatter you, and advance, and set you up on highs," all of which, he notes, plays to the "Pride of Women" and makes his sister feel as though she were "a goddess, and as if all should bow unto [her], as singularly beloved above others, yea as Christ himself, and as one with God."[69]

Reports of mechanic men preaching confirm Porterfield's contention that "Puritan preachers relied on the erotic responsiveness of women to establish and maintain their leadership in Puritan society" (92). A report of the aforementioned tailor, Samuel How, suggests that he drew directly on his flamboyant sex appeal to edify and "move" his female listeners: "His Text he clouted, and his Sermon welted, / His audience with devotion almost melted, / His speech was neither studied, chew'd or champ'd / Or ruminated, but most neatly vamp'd. / He ran beyond his latchet I assure ye, / As nimble as a Fairie or a Furie: / He fell courageously upon the Beast, / and very daintily the Text did wrest."[70] For developing what we might call advertising techniques designed to elicit the gaze of female consumers, male mechanic preachers were demonized by antisectarians such as Thomas Edwards for using the means of sexual seduction to gain converts, or correlatively, for using religious persuasion as a cover for their allegedly more basic goal of sexual seduction. The Presbyterian William Prynne called the practices of admitting women to preach and vote as members a "mere politic invention to engage that sex to their party."[71] But what is also noteworthy about these accounts are the scenarios they record wherein male sectarians worked to both argue rationally to female sectarians that they too mattered, and to develop styles of delivery and persuasion designed to activate rather than suppress a mode of female agency claimed *vis-à-vis* their passage through the liberated space of the womb, exercised through the liberty of choice, and, perhaps most significantly, deemed necessary for the very existence of the group. One implication was that male ministers had to compete for the attentions of potential female converts by convincing them that they possessed the true seed of Christ, which, when implanted in the willing listener, would help to conceive the true church. Another was that women who exercised choice within the logic of voluntary association did so, again, not on the grounds that they were disrupting the "homosocial" logic of property *per se*, but rather on the grounds that they were exercising a prerogative granted to them by the property-in-self and sovereign subjectivity that they possessed by virtue of their natural right to religious freedom. Like the Lady, they were, after all, "self-determining queens."

Finally, by claiming spiritual equality with men – and oftentimes by performatively "embodying" the figure of religious liberty so metonymically associated with femininity – actual women were also able to assume their own voices of authority within gathered churches.[72] In 1641 in England, *The Brownists Conventicle* records a male minister's enthusiastic praise for

> those blessed and fruit-bearing women, who are not only able to talk on any Text, but to search into the deep sense of the Scripture, and preach both in their own families and elsewhere. Whom though Saint Paul forbade to preach in the Church, yet he left them liberty to preach in the chambers: . . . we [are] all therefore, both brethren and sisters, to use our Talents together, that the brethren may be daily regenerate and new borne, and the sisters to labour in their severall vocations, that it may be the increase and multiplying of these thy Saints, Amen.[73]

Even women who were not mothers could exploit this power. Anna Trapnel imagined herself as the biblical Hannah, endowed with the right to prophesy through her petitioning of God for a child, in spite of the fact that she had no children.[74] By substituting symbolic or typological motherhood for actual maternity, the role of prophesying mother was available to her as a vehicle for gathering or procreating a church. Trapnel and Sarah Wight gained reputations as charismatic and persuasive speakers capable of gathering large crowds. The fact that they did so by staging spectacles of the female body in the throes of delivering the word in bed is significant for more than just its metaphoric value for authorizing the individual prophetess. Such scenes were again symbolic reenactments of maternal reproduction that resulted in the social production of a system: to gather a crowd *was* to produce a church and hence to conjure a counterculture into existence. Simulating the birth scene literally embodied this concept and it was a form of persuasive spectacle that would have appealed to men and women alike. For women, as Carola Scott-Luckens has pointed out, gathering around a supine sister in the throes of prophetic labor would have invoked the all-female community of the birthing bed, and for men it would have allowed them to participate in a ritual from which they were traditionally excluded.[75] The spectacle of birth demonstrated a public awareness of the procreative role of women in church formation and in the "right" to independent church formation that the church makes manifest. Congregating around the prophetess in her labors signified that men knowingly helped her as she brought a new free church into being just as the male mechanic's solicitation of the female gaze acknowledged the role of female desire in the coproduction of the separatist community. The degree to which Independents believed the delivery of the word and of the church to be synonymous works to dissolve the line between the metaphoric production used by individual prophetesses to authorize themselves and a perhaps even more semiotically riotous representation of maternal agency in the throes of actual social and political production. A concrete example of just such a dissolution occurs in the anonymous tract, *The Brownists Conventicle*, in which it was reported that "in some families the women catechize and preach, making the back side of [their] groaning Chaire the Pulpit."[76] As Thomas notes, "it was hardly surprising that women were attracted to those groups . . . which offered spiritual equality, the depreciation of educational advantages, and that opportunity to preach or even to hold priestly office which they were otherwise denied."[77]

As noted, the highly embodied figures used to compose these formulations paint a much different, much messier picture of liberalism's "abstract individual" than the one composed by antiliberal feminists. The individual is, to be sure, defined abstractly in that each individual was posited as a soul whose spirit was equal in God's eyes to everyone else's. At the same time, the individual dissolves into the "other" with which it chooses to associate and the very concept of religious freedom is feminized in that each individual by virtue of the nature received through the mother is equally endowed with the freedom to follow his/her own conscience. As Independent minister William Erbery preached, "O how happy is that man or woman that . . . have [Christ] for their head and husband, who hath all power in his hands, all heavenly blessings to bestow upon them, all spirituall graces to give unto them."[78] As a result, these texts also provide us with a much altered profile of the "private" sphere from the one perpetuated by much of postmodern feminism as an unremittingly repressive space for women. Sectarian women could often be found in their "chambers," however these "private" spaces of the home were the site of production for the "public" body of the church. And within them, women practiced a whole host of unorthodox social practices that defied patriarchal injunctions. In contrast to the modern assumption that women in the early modern period had no investment in defending the privacy of the home from any sort of tyrannical intrusion, Retha Warnicke has already argued that it was in fact the case that "private and public matters were organized somewhat differently from now but with distinctions that were just as obvious and definitive."[79] Separatist women worked to codify an important variation upon those distinctions. To defend and protect the innovative definition of the individual as well as the unconventional practices (such as refusing to baptize infants) that were being propagated within this sphere of voluntary association and religious Independency, Katherine Chidley, Anna Trapnel, Elizabeth Poole, Sarah Wight, Anne Wentworth, and Mary Cary wrote texts that translated their religious understanding of privacy, self-determination, and property-in-self into a set of political prerogatives. In doing so, they helped to construct a "public sphere" that more closely approximates the definition that Jürgen Habermas attaches to that term: a sphere that is public insofar as it is comprised of speakers/writers and audience members/readers and private insofar as it is separate from and oppositional to the state.[80]

At the same time, the terms upon which they constructed and defended this sphere significantly revise some of the key elements that comprise Habermas's famous account of this "ideal type."[81] Their religious affiliations confirm Habermas's underdeveloped and hence often overlooked claim that it was the "movement for a so-called freedom of religion which historically secured the first sphere of private autonomy," however, these affiliations also suggest that religious discourse was not as antithetical to the operations of instrumental reasoning as Habermas simultaneously holds it to be.[82] As David Zaret writes, "Faith and reason" may have come to be understood as "attributes of individuals, but they were defined, defended, and debated in arguments that appealed explicitly to public opinion" ("Religion, Science," 218). Sectarian women played an important role in this process of definition, defense, and debate; what is more, they grounded their ability to play this role within the property-in-self they claimed to enjoy as possessive individuals rather than, as Habermas does, within the specifically masculine prerogatives enjoyed by the property-owning bourgeois father. This means that their desire to break the clerical monopoly on religious discourse arose not simply in order to protect a commercial economy *per se*, but rather to safeguard their "right" to preach in part by attacking the economies that militated against it. A "free market" in ministerial authority was imagined as a superstructural outgrowth of separatist women's baseline push for the pulpit.

What is more, because separatist women writers helped to forge what Zaret describes as the "new democratic patterns of dissent" (218) that were circulating during the civil war period by speaking in their domestic capacities as mothers, wives, lovers, daughters, and servants, they offer a much different version of "liberal humanist discourse" than the one that is ostensibly committed "at once to the ideal of human freedom and to the wife's submission to the authority of the husband," and they provide an alternative perspective upon the sources of social agency that "the" seventeenth-century female subject is said to have required to mount a rational critique of absolutist forms of sociopolitical and religious authority. Traditionally, because husband and wife were considered to be one legal entity – the husband – by means of the husband's "subsumption" of his wife into himself, the wife was considered a *feme couvert*, meaning that she was "veiled, as it were, clouded and over-shadowed" to the point where she theoretically had no agency through which to criticize anything, much less the state.[83] This has led scholars such as Joy Wiltenburg and Frances E. Dolan to a large body of popular work in which women who achieved "power" beyond their prescribed roles were represented not only as "disorderly" but also as criminal.[84] As Dolan writes, "The wife emerged from this coverture into legal responsibility only when her husband ('her sterne, her primus motor, without whom she cannot doe much at home, and lesse abroad') died or deserted her, or when she committed a serious crime on her own."[85] As a result, it was "through transgression" that marginalized women such as wives of yeomen, shopkeepers, tradesmen, and small landowners . . . could command a place at the center of a popular narrative as the protagonist of the story in early modern England. Depictions of domestic "familiars" in popular accounts of crime were consistently associated with that which was "dangerous," that is, both "threatening" and "fraught with the particular early modern associations of 'difficult to deal with,' 'hard to please,' and 'reluctant to comply'" (4). When women and servants were represented as subjects and agents, they were shown to be "violent transgressors whose interiorities and voices [were] disruptive and destructive" (5). To recover or reconstruct "the processes by which the subjectivities of the socially marginalized, particularly women, were produced as resistant, criminal, and violent," Dolan, drawing upon Carlo Ginzburg, turned to the often "hostile testimonies, originating from or filtered by" the legal process that criminalized and executed them (5). As she cautions, in these documents "the voices of the accused reach us strangled, altered, distorted; in many cases, they haven't reached us at all" (5). Nonetheless, these remain "some of our richest resources for recovering those voices and for reflecting on the conditions under which the socially marginalized (for example, poor, unmarried women) could be constructed as subjects and their voices recorded" (5).

Perhaps these ostensible limitations on our ability to know about and "read" the dialogized voices of nonelite women in the early modern period, a category into which sectarian women have often been placed, have encouraged other feminist literary critics to join the opposition against liberalism by searching for "protofeminist attitudes" within such "deeply conservative political allegiances" as monarchy and Toryism rather than Puritanism.[86] Bridget Hill has nominated Mary Astell as "England's First Feminist," and Patricia Springborg follows suit, showing how Astell managed to combine a "self-conscious critique of the very institutions at the root of female oppression" with being a "commissioned Tory pamphleteer" by furnishing "one of the earliest and most percipient critiques of John Locke's political arguments."[87] Likewise, Carol Barash locates a search for the "Native Liberty... of the subject" within a militant Amazonian "feminist imperialism" that early eighteenth-century writers such as Astell, Mary Chudleigh, and Sarah Fyge Egerton derived through an "identification" with Queen Anne.[88] And in order to move beyond a concern with "women's rights" and into a larger, more inclusive concern with a "central theme of later feminist movements – namely, the understanding of women as a group with identifiable sociological characteristics," Hilda Smith also turns to "seventeenth-century English feminists" who were mostly "royalists and later Tories" and who "developed an independent criticism of their situation outside of the revolutionary and religious ideologies and groupings formed between 1640 and 1660."[89] While Rachel Weill's awareness of such feminist "Whigs" as Elizabeth Rowe and Susanna Centlivre leads her to argue that "Astell's achievement . . . was not just to appropriate Tory ideology for 'feminist' purposes, but to put her critique of gender relations and gender inequality to *use* in her Tory polemic," she too finds in Mary Astell a voice through which to contend that "rather than diminishing patriarchal authority, contract theory licensed its worst abuses."[90] And in a piece tellingly entitled "Embracing the Absolute," Catherine Gallagher insists that it was the royalist writer Margaret Cavendish who first gained the unique perspective necessary to criticize seventeenth-century women's exclusion from political subject-hood and citizenship.[91] Because she was a woman and hence excluded from any "public role" other than that of the monarch him/herself, and because she was an *aristocratic* woman who enjoyed a literal proximity to the crown, Cavendish was able to effect a "transition" from the "the ideology of absolute monarchy . . . to an ideology of the absolute self."[92]

But I suggest that sectarian women's writings offer another rich resource for reflecting on the condition under which socially marginalized women actually recorded their own voices and made the transition from "subject" to "absolute self." For female Separatists, it was not the king but God who provided an "authoritative metaphor" for their self-construction as sovereign subjects and a "foundation" for a "subjectivity that would make its own absolute claims."[93] Thus, far from requiring the analogic presence of an actual absolutist to anchor their critique of patriarchalism, sectarian women resisted absolutist tendencies whether on the part of the monarchy, Parliament, the New Model Army, and/or the new Commonwealth by embracing the spatial distance and social dislocation from the halls of power that their nonaristocratic identities and affiliations represented. They imagined "public roles" for women other than that of king or queen by imagining alternative "private-publics" in which popular sovereign subjects could stage their own "theatre of the person."[94] They defined themselves as "domestic familiars" – wives, mothers, and servants – who nonetheless enjoyed a "native liberty" due to a "contract" they enjoyed with God, which inducted them into new forms of equality rather than simply resubordinating them to fathers, husbands and masters, and they just as often portrayed the exercise of their own domestic agency as positive, nontransgressive, conducive to order, disruptive to some forms of property but protective of others, obedient (to God anyway), endowed with communal sanction, and respectful of the self-sovereignty of others. They may have been *femes couvert* but they were "veiled," so they will argue over and over again, ultimately by God alone and they emerged from couverture to protest not only their own persecution and imprisonment but that of fellow Separatists and, in the case of Leveller women, their husbands' as well. Without a doubt, detractors attempted to remand almost every one of the women that I will discuss here back into the familiar role of deviant. At the same time, their countervailing voices survive in the pages of pamphlets that bear their own names as authors to tell "other stories" about "other possibilities" for women to be accepted as both orderly and free in theretofore unprecedented ways.[95] To account for their practices, I propose that we think about "female subjects" rather "the female subject," that we look to sectarian women for a moment in which some women desired nothing less than to move from being considered as subjects to being understood as "individuals," and that we (re)"embrace" the "liberal" as well as the "absolute" in our search for philosophical "traditions" that might enjoy a "deep affinity" with "protofeminisms."[96]

As may now be clear from the above, it is an unfortunate irony of scholarship that we often find ourselves in disagreement with those to whom we are most indebted and by whom we are most inspired. This continues to hold true for the fact that, whereas many scholars in a variety of relevant disciplines remain unaware of the contribution that sectarian women's writings make to the development of political ideas, the ground-breaking historians and feminist literary scholars who deserve credit for initiating the relatively young but already challenging and high-level conversation about sectarian women's writings have tended to argue that they subvert rather than valorize or even complicate "Whig" narratives of history, either because they fail to develop the kinds of categories associated with later Anglo-American feminist movements or because they present modern readers with the postmodern feminist ideal of a decentered self or "subject," one whose interpenetration by God actually represents an antibourgeois and antihumanist model of subjectivity and authorship. In the former camp are those who, unlike antiliberal postmodern feminists, actually celebrate feminism's liberal past and its identification with "equality" but who exclude sectarian women from that legacy. While the work of Keith Thomas helped to first invoke the possibility of an intersection between sectarian women's writings and the history of liberal feminism, he ultimately denies it by insisting that "the sectarian insistence on women's spiritual equality" was "of very little importance in the later history of female emancipation in general" because "future feminist movements were to base their arguments less upon any renewed assertion of women's spiritual equality than upon natural right and the denial of any intellectual differences between the sexes."[97] Likewise, Patricia Crawford contends that "the really radical political ideas expressed by [sectarian] women owe more to religious beliefs than to political theory about patriarchalism."[98] Dorothy Ludlow urges us to focus on "the ambiguities of female religiosity and its *socially* disruptive potential [in the seventeenth century]."[99] And, while Phyllis Mack usefully claims that "we can trace a direct line" from dissenting women "to the nineteenth-century movements of abolition and women's suffrage and to twentieth-century feminism and peace activism," she locates the starting point for that line with "the earliest Quaker women leaders" later in the seventeenth century.[100]

My arguments – clearly intended as they are to assimilate at least some texts by dissenting women into such constructed, deconstructed, and at least partially reconstructed traditions as Puritanism's influence on the notion of the individual in later liberal thought, an Anglo-American feminist emphasis on rights and liberty, and a "humanist feminist critical approach" to social and literary history, will assert that these challenging theses cannot fully account for the particular contributions made by the women I discuss here.[101] With the exception of Anne Wentworth, they preceded the Quaker movement and so undercut the claim that seventeenth-century feminism becomes truly "radical" only with the advent of Quaker women. Furthermore, their writings challenge the very dichotomy that Thomas and Crawford establish between "religious beliefs" and "political theory about patriarchalism," or, as Crawford restates it, between "women's ideas and activities" and "liberal theory."[102] In fact, as stated, sectarian women's insistence upon as well as their enactment of spiritual equality for all formed the basis for their early feminist political theories about patriarchalism and natural rights just as it would for Locke with men. As David Wootton argues, Locke's argument for sovereign individualism is based on a "divinely ordained moral law."[103] Likewise, dissenting women took the idea that every individual was spiritually equal because he/she was constituted as a subject through the God within and used it to underpin a system in which all individuals held property within themselves and enjoyed a set of rights based on that sovereign self-possession. They drew on biblical precedents for strong maternal and marital roles as rationales for their insistence that the "public" sphere of the independent church was in essence private and hence protected from the censure of both the crown and the "sovereign" Parliament. They took the notion of consent derived from the principle of voluntary association in the church and transferred it to the public political sphere as a means by which to limit the power of the state. And they used the idea that every individual was a sovereign self whose "nature" was coterminous with that of God to argue that the market in religious labor, among other market-based activities, should be a free one.

In terms of the second camp, the literary critic Elizabeth Sauer speaks as a representative voice on behalf of those who find within sectarian women's texts the postmodern feminist ideal of a decentered self or "subject." She writes: "The absence of a unified sense of self does a good job . . . of summing up the current thinking on sectarian women's writings . . . "[104] Sauer is quite right that this has emerged as a dominant and important line of inquiry in the field, but it does not tell the whole story. Vera Camden has noted the fierceness with which Anne Wentworth sought to articulate the notion of an "autonomous authorized self."[105] Diane Purkiss observes that prophetesses represented their bodies "not as open" but as "closed to everything except God," even as she maintains that this "conditional autonomy" "disrupt[s] the homosocial order of rhetoric and property."[106] And Judith Kegan Gardiner has argued that the Quaker writer Margaret Fell Fox "re-gendered" individualism by shaping "an affective familialism that did not divide the individual from her community."[107] These arguments comport with my own very strong sense that, once discovered and "read," sectarian women's writings do something more complex than simply provide us with a vehicle through which to deconstruct the "myth" of the individual; they ask us, in fact, to ponder their role in establishing that "myth." What is more, the very opposition we sometimes draw between the "interpellated" or dialogic self versus the possessive self are called into question by sectarian women's writings. They do not deny the claim that the individual is subject to interpellation and revision by external or even internal forces, but rather reject the conclusion that this ostensible "weakness" or indeterminacy means that all are and must be subordinated to the communal will. They claim that God is the sole "known" overdetermining force because this provides them with the quasilegal protection or "centeredness" needed to perform various types of multiple and contingent subjectivities that transgress or decenter rather than buttress received social determinants. By developing a notion of sovereign subjectivity, sectarian women forge the philosophical foundation for their prophetic practices, but they also use it to erect a core defense against the various forms of oppression and slander they encounter for enacting the very sorts of nontraditional liberties that their tracts demand. The "insnared chastity" that these women in the wilderness are called upon to save is oftentimes their own; as a result, their claim to individualism necessarily extends beyond the parameters of the socioreligious context from which it first emerges – even that of "affective familialism" – and segues into a critique of that and, in some cases, nearly all collectivities. Finally, their formulations of "autonomy" are predicated on a notion of property-in-self that does not "disrupt" the "homosocial order of property" so much as ground it in such a way that it includes women.

This should, I contend, give us pause when it comes to arguing that feminism has always been and must continue to be synonymous with something called a "communally organized society," absolutist or otherwise.[108] The list is long of those who tell us that women want and need the state, that they benefit from a communitarian ethos of "care" rather than an individualistic ethos of "right" in society and government, and that this can only come about through the large-scale implementation of "socialism." As Jacquette argues, "Pateman's [actual] quarry is *capitalistic* social relations and contract connects capitalism and liberal theory."[109] As Pateman herself concludes, only "co-operative socialism" can "bring an end to the 'secrecy of domestic wrongs.'"[110] Interestingly enough, there is an older school of thought that does equate female sectarian writings with the evolution of socialism. To the small extent that prophetesses were visible in scholarship prior to the last couple of decades, it was in the work of early to mid 1900s historians of religion such as Norman Cohn and J. L. Talmon. These scholars argued that twentieth-century totalitarianism was not a "break with Western tradition, but an outgrowth – if a perversion – of very substantial elements in that tradition," and that those elements consisted specifically of "revolutionary eschatology" dating back to Luther and even earlier.[111] Later in the century, Alfred Cohen reiterated this argument by first characterizing revolutionary prophetesses as "mad" and then concluding that Mary Cary, like other members of the millenarian group, the Fifth Monarchists, had actually been a "totalitarian" fountainhead for the ideologies that ultimately resulted in the various genocidal regimes of the twentieth century.[112] For Cohen, the fact that Cary propagated the idea that a select group of saints should be in the "vanguard," as he puts it, of not merely advocating but enforcing new models of social justice, including the movement for universal preaching, should render her millenarianism suspect for modern readers all too familiar with the heinous crimes of twentieth-century fascist, national socialist, and communist orders (205).

As Cohen observes (and dismisses), in the wake of Cohn's and Talmon's claims, scholars such as Louise Brown and A. S. P. Woodhouse attempted to "rehabilitate [the] image" of such revolutionary eschatological groups as the Fifth Monarchists by arguing that, while these groups were in fact members of the "Puritans of the Left," this resulted not in totalitarianism but rather in the libertarian "demand for liberty, and above all for liberty of conscience" (205). Thus they deserve to be celebrated rather than condemned. One of the more prominent and important members of this school of thought is Christopher Hill, who famously argued that many "Left Puritans," including primitive communists, comprised a more radical and plebeian revolution that unfortunately gave way to the more "bourgeois" one championed by proponents of capitalism and private property. As Hill writes,

There were, we may oversimplify, two revolutions in mid-seventeenth-century England. The one which succeeded established the sacred rights of property (abolition of feudal tenures, no arbitrary taxation), gave political power to the propertied (sovereignty of Parliament and common law, abolition of prerogative courts), and removed all impediments to the triumph of the ideology of the men of property – the protestant ethic. There was, however, another revolution which never happened, though from time to time it threatened. This might have established communal property, a far wider democracy in political and legal institutions, might have disestablished the state church and rejected the protestant ethic.[113]

Following Hill, this failure has become a source of lament for many critics as well as a productive site for further efforts to recover, analyze, and restore the various types of rhetorics or discourses through which this lost cause was voiced. Clement Hawes has analyzed the class-based use of millenarian "mania" that characterized texts written by the proponents of "far more egalitarian social orders that could have emerged – but did not – from the revolution."[114] Margaret George observes that "in the popular revolt... one is constantly aware of the omnipresence of women, and of the centrality of their cooperation and contributions."[115] And Jane Baston holds Mary Cary up as a particularly elegiac monument to a lost "utopian socialism."[116]

As is obvious, what appears to be a disagreement between the Cohen camp and the Hill camp is predicated on a shared assumption that the more radical groups who emerged during the seventeenth-century civil war period in England, including sectarian women, offer a "leftist" perspective on issues and that the empowerment of women goes hand in hand with something called "socialism," whether that "fact" is touted or denigrated. I would certainly agree that the women I discuss here were among those who tried to implement a "far wider democracy" and that they exhibit elements in their thought that we might today recognize or label as left-wing (if "freedom of conscience" can be characterized as such, which is, I think, arguable) or "socialistic" (Mary Cary supports poor relief). But, along with the difficulties involved in mapping today's understanding of political "wings" on to seventeenth-century England, I would also point out that there is a consistent concern in sectarian women's writings – even as this concern varies somewhat in degree and kind across different authors and texts – for minimizing the relationship between the individual and/or the voluntary association on the one hand and the state on the other, and this was often true even when the women themselves were allied (however tenuously) with or hoped to be allied with men who had greater access to government power in the wake of the civil war and the execution of Charles I. Thus, sectarian women's writings ensnarl some of the criteria upon which Hill's influential "two revolutions" model is or is now commonly understood to be structured. As Elaine Hobby and James Holstun have demonstrated, sectarian women writers engaged in various sorts of collective or communal enterprises within voluntary associations that consisted sometimes of other women or "sisters" ("female petitioners," "communities of women") and sometimes of both sisters and brothers.[117] At the same time, as I will demonstrate, they also consistently (and often with hostility) imagined the individual as a nodal point in and of him/herself, one who could affiliate (or disaffiliate) freely with a chosen community because of the inward "right" that he/she possessed independent of any community or institution, be it familial, religious, or even governmental. They wished to disestablish the state church, including the "property" and the "right to work" that ordained clergy were said to have under its auspices, but they also invoked a work ethic to argue that all were entitled to form and attend the church of their choice, as well as to perform the "labor" of preaching, because all possessed forms of property-in-self which "entitled" them to do so. While Cary endorses such quasi- or perhaps protosocialist "Grand Instauration" initiatives as poor relief, she, along with Chidley, also protested tithes and other taxes that were levied on trade and commerce, and Chidley ventured that the private church should tend its own and not the nation's poor. Writers like Poole and Cary practiced an "ethos of care" when it came to their own approach to and metaphors for "curing" England's ills, but they did so in order to secure women's "right" to engage in such "secret domestic wrongs" as refusing to baptize one's children on the grounds that it would deny them free will, or refusing to be "churched" after childbirth on the grounds that God had already made the mother pure, or refusing to stay married to an "unregenerate" man on the grounds that a woman possessed and controlled her own separate religious "estate." In short, I suggest that their works are just as – perhaps even more so – defined by the rhetorics of privacy, individualism, property, the work ethic, and capitalism as they are those of community and the commons.

NOTES

1. By way of example, the collection, *Feminism and Philosophy: Essential Readings in Theory, Reinterpretation, and Application*, edited by Nancy Tuana and Rosemarie Tong (Boulder, CO: Westview Press, 1995) contains sections on the following "feminist perspectives": "Liberal," "Marxist," "Radical," "Psychoanalytic," "Socialist," "Anarcha and Ecological," "Phenomenological," "Postmodern," and "Race, Class, Gender." All, including "liberal," position themselves as revisionary critiques of "liberalism" in its "classical" (conservative) rather than its modern (anticonservative) iteration.
2. Carole Pateman, *The Sexual Contract* (Stanford: Stanford University Press, 1987), p. 8. See also her follow-up, *The Disorder of Women: Democracy, Feminism, and Political Theory* (Stanford: Stanford University Press, 1989).
3. Rachel Weil, *Political Passions: Gender, the Family and Political Argument in England, 1680–1714* (Manchester: Manchester University Press, 1999), p. 9.
4. J. P. Somerville, *Politics and Ideology in England, 1603–1640*, vol. 1, *1603–1644* (London: Longman, 1986); Perez Zagorin, *A History of Political Thought in the English Revolution* (London: Routledge & Kegan Paul, 1954); J. G. A. Pocock, *The Ancient Constitution and the Feudal Law: A Study in English Historical Thought in the Seventeenth Century* (Cambridge: Cambridge University Press, 1957) and *The Machiavellian Moment: Florentine Political Thought and the Atlantic Republican Tradition* (Princeton: Princeton University Press, 1975); Gordon Schochet, *Patriarchalism in Political Thought: The Authoritarian Family and Political Speculation and Attitudes, Especially in Seventeenth-Century England* (New York: Basic Books, 1975); Quentin Skinner, *The Foundations of Modern Political Thought*, vol. II (Cambridge: Cambridge University Press, 1978); James Daly, *Sir Robert Filmer and English Political Thought* (Toronto: University of Toronto Press, 1979).
5. Susan Amussen, *An Ordered Society: Gender and Class in Early Modern England* (Oxford: Basil Blackwell, 1988), p. 55.
6. Richard Mocket, *God and the King: or a Dialogue shewing that our sovereign Lord King James, being immediate under God within his DOMINIONS, Doth rightfully claime whatsoever is required by the Oath of Allegiance* (London, 1615), pp. 1–2.
7. Sir Robert Filmer, *Patriarcha and Other Political Works*, ed. Peter Laslett (Oxford: Oxford University Press, 1949), p. 241.
8. John Locke, *Two Treatises of Government*, rev. edn, ed. Peter Laslett (New York: Mentor, 1965), p. 308.
9. Pateman, *Sexual Contract*, pp. 184–185.
10. Ibid., p. 52.
11. Zillah Eisenstein, *The Radical Future of Liberal Feminism* (New York: Longman, 1981), and Zillah Eisenstein, *Feminism and Sexual Equality: Crisis*

in Liberal America (Berkeley: University of California Press, 1988); Catharine MacKinnon, *Toward a Feminist Theory of the State* (Cambridge, MA: Harvard University Press, 1989); Seyla Benhabib, "The Generalization and the Concrete Other: The Kohlberg-Gilligan Controversy and Feminist Theory," in Seyla Benhabib and Drucilla Cornell, eds., *Feminism as Critique: On the Politics of Gender* (Minneapolis: University of Minnesota Press, 1987).

12. Eisenstein, *Radical Future*, pp. 116–117; MacKinnon, *Toward a Feminist Theory*, pp. 45–46.
13. Eisenstein, *Radical Future*, pp. 116–117.
14. Benhabib, "Generalization and the Concrete Other," pp. 87 and 92.
15. Pamela Grande Jensen, *Finding A New Feminism: Rethinking the Woman Question for Liberal Democracy* (Lanham, MD: Rowman & Littlefield, 1996), p. 2.
16. Gordon Schochet, "The Significant Sounds of Silence: The Absence of Women from the Political Thought of Sir Robert Filmer and John Locke (or, 'Why can't a woman be more like a man?')," in Hilda Smith, ed., *Women Writers and the Early Modern British Political Tradition* (Cambridge: Cambridge University Press, 1998), pp. 220–242, quote from p. 223.
17. Jane S. Jacquette, "Contract and Coercion: Power and Gender in *Leviathan*," in Smith, ed., *Women Writers and the Early Modern British Political Tradition*, pp. 200–219, quote from p. 200.
18. Ibid., p. 219.
19. Susan Wendell, "A (Qualified) Defence of Liberal Feminism," in *Hypatia* 2, 2 (summer 1987), 75.
20. L. Susan Brown, *The Politics of Individualism* (Montreal: Black Rose Books, 1993), pp. 17–18.
21. Jensen, *Finding a New Feminism*, p. 7; Catherine H. Zuckert, "Fortune is a Woman – but so is Prudence: Machiavelli's *Clizia*," in Jensen, *Finding a New Feminism*, pp. 23–37; Diana J. Schaub, "Montesquieu on 'The Woman Problem,'" in Jensen, *Finding a New Feminism*, pp. 39–66.
22. Carole Pateman, "Women's Writing, Women's Standing: Theory and Politics in the Early Modern Period," in Smith, ed., *Women Writers and the Early Modern British Political Tradition*, pp. 365–382.
23. Ibid., p. 371.
24. Ibid., pp. 374–375.
25. Ibid., p. 375.
26. Nigel Smith, *Perfection Proclaimed: Language and Literature in English Radical Religion 1640–1660* (Oxford: Clarendon Press, 1989), p. 72.
27. Anita Pacheco, ed., *Early Women Writers: 1600–1720* (Harlow: Longman, 1998), intro., p. 13. See also Catherine Belsey, *The Subject of Tragedy: Identity and Difference in Renaissance Drama* (London: Routledge, 1985), pp. 149–160, pp. 192–221.
28. Kristen Poole, *Radical Religion from Shakespeare to Milton: Figures of Nonconformity in Early Modern England* (Cambridge: Cambridge University Press, 2000), p. 13.

29. Lyle Koehler, *A Search for Power: The Weaker Sex in Seventeenth-Century New England* (Urbana: University of Illinois Press, 1980; Ben Barker Bakersfield, "Anne Hutchinson and the Puritan Attitude Towards Women," *Feminist Studies* 1 (1973), 65–96; Margaret Olofson Thickstun, *Fictions of the Feminine: Puritan Doctrine and the Representation of Women* (Ithaca: Cornell University Press, 1988).
30. Amanda Porterfield, *Female Piety in New England* (Oxford: Oxford University Press, 1992), p. 80.
31. Samuel Rutherford, "Lex, Rex," in A. S. P. Woodhouse, *Puritanism and Liberty* (London: J. M. Dent, 1974), p. 201.
32. Ibid.
33. Anon., "The Ancient Bounds," in Woodhouse, *Puritanism and Liberty*, p. 253.
34. John Milton, "Of Civil Power in Ecclesiastical Causes" (1659), in Woodhouse, *Puritanism and Liberty*, p. 226.
35. William Dell, "The Way of True Peace and Unity," in Woodhouse, *Puritanism and Liberty*, pp. 305–306. Dell continues:

> The most honourable members cannot say thus to the most mean – not the Apostles themselves to believers among the Gentiles; for we are the body of Christ as well as they... Wherefore no member, for diversity of office, is to lift up himself above another member who is as necessary as itself to the making up the body, and also is every whit as useful in its place.

36. Sarah Jones, *To Sions Lovers, Being a Golden Egge, to Avoide Infection* (London, 1644), p. B3; Keith Thomas, "Women and the Civil War Sects," *Past and Present* 13 (1958), 42–62; and Patricia Crawford, *Women and Religion in England, 1500–1720* (London: Routledge, 1993), p. 144. See also Anne Laurence, "A Priesthood of She-Believers: Women and Congregations in Mid-Seventeenth-Century England," *Studies in Church History* 27 (1990), 345–363.
37. Rutherford, "Lex Rex," p. 201.
38. Gordon J. Schochet, "John Locke and Religious Toleration," in Lois G. Schwoerer, ed., *The Revolution of 1688–1689: Changing Perspectives* (Cambridge: Cambridge University Press, 1992), pp. 148–150.
39. Catherine Gallagher, "More About 'Medusa's Head,'" *Representations* 4 (fall 1983), 56.
40. Diane Purkiss, "Producing the Voice, Consuming the Body: Women Prophets of the Seventeenth Century," in Isobel Grundy and Susan Wiseman, eds., *Women, Writing, History 1640–1740* (Athens, GA: University of Georgia Press, 1992), pp. 139–158; Phyllis Mack, *Visionary Women: Ecstatic Prophecy in Seventeenth-Century England* (Berkeley: University of California Press, 1992).
41. Purkiss, "Producing the Voice," p. 158.
42. Ibid.
43. Thomas, "Women and the Civil War Sects," p. 42.
44. Patricia Crawford, "The Challenges to Patriarchalism: How did the Revolution affect Women?," in John Morrill, ed., *Revolution and Restoration: England in the 1650s* (London: Collins & Brown, 1992), pp. 112–128, quote from p. 123.

45. Abiezer Coppe, *A Fiery Flying Roule* (London, 1649), title page.
46. Henry Jessey, *The Exceeding Riches of Grace Advanced by the Spirit of Grace, in an Empty Nothing Creature, viz. Mrs. Sarah Wight Lately Hopeless and Restless* (London, 1652), p. 17.
47. Anna Trapnel, *The Cry of a Stone, or a Relation of Something Spoken in Whitehall by Anna Trapnel, being in the Visions of God* (London, 1654), p. 3.
48. Purkiss, "Producing the Voice," p. 143.
49. Michael Walzer, *The Revolution of the Saints* (Cambridge, MA: Harvard University Press, 1982), p. 240.
50. Porterfield, *Female Piety*, p. 94.
51. Anne Wentworth, *A True Account of Anne Wentworth being cruelly, unjustly and unchristianly dealth with* (London, 1676), pp. 21–22.
52. "A Report of the Trial of Mrs. Anne Hutchinson before the Church in Boston," in David D. Hall, ed., *The Antinomian Controversy, 1636–1638* (Durham, NC: Duke University Press, 1990), pp. 349–388, reference to pp. 368–369, and John Winthrop, "A Short Story of the Rise, Reign, and Ruine of the Antinomians, Familists and Libertines," in Hall, ed., *Antinomian Controversy* pp. 199–310, reference to pp. 262–263.
53. Ann Jacobson Schutte, " 'Such Monstrous Births': A Neglected Aspect of the Antinomian Controversy," *Renaissance Quarterly* 38, 1 (spring 1988), 85–106.
54. Thomas Welde, "Preface to a Short Story of the Rise, Reigne and Ruine of the Antinomians, Familists, and Libertines," in Hall, ed., *Antinomian Controversy*, p. 202.
55. Porterfield, *Female Piety*, pp. 94–95.
56. Anon., "The Ancient Bounds," in Woodhouse, *Puritanism and Liberty*, p. 256.
57. Lady Elizabeth Clinton, *The Countess of Lincolnes Nurserie* (1622), in Suzanne Trill, Kate Chedgzoy, and Melanie Osborne, eds., *Lay by Your Needles Ladies, take the Pen: Writing Women in England, 1500–1700* (London: Edward Arnold, 1997), pp. 119–124, quote from p. 124.
58. Jones, *Sions Lovers*, p. B1.
59. Anon., *The Brothers of the Separation. Or a True Relation of a Company of Brownists which kept their Conventicle at one Mr. Porter's in Goat Alley in Whitecrossestreet* (London, 1641), p. A4v.
60. Richard Mather, *An Apology for Church Covenant* (1643), in Woodhouse, *Puritanism and Liberty*, p. 299.
61. John Saltmarsh, "Smoke in the Temple," in Woodhouse, *Puritanism and Liberty*, p. 183.
62. Thomas Parker, *The Copy of a Letter Written by Mr. Thomas Parker, Pastor of the Church of Newbury in New-England, to his Sister, Mrs. Elizabeth Avery, Sometimes of Newbury in the County of Berks, Touching Sundry Opinions by her Professed and Maintained* (London, 1650), p. 5.
63. John Spenser, *A Short Treatise Concerning the Awe-fullnesse of Every Mans Exercising his Gift as God Shall call him thereunto* (London, 1641), p. 1.
64. Samuel How, *The Sufficiencie of the Spirits Teaching without Humane Learning* (London, 1640).

65. Anon., *The Brownists Conventicle, Or an assembly of Brownists, Separatists, and Non-Conformists* (London, 1641), p. 5.
66. Crawford argues that "The issue of voting marks the limits of radicalism in the sects. Either voting was on the basis of church membership, and all were to share in calling church officers and in discipline, or women's rights to vote were denied, and they were not full church members" (*Women and Religion*, p. 144).
67. Nathaniel Ward, *A Simple Cobler of Aggawam* (London, 1647).
68. Anon., *The Brownists Synagogue, or a Late Discovery of their Conventicles, Assemblies, and places of meeting* (London, 1641), p. 5.
69. Parker, *Copy of a Letter*, p. 13.
70. John Taylor, *A Swarm of Sectaries, and Schismatiques* (London, 1641), p. 9.
71. William Prynne, *Discovery of some Prodigious New Wandring Blazing Stars and Firebrands Styling Themselves New-Lights* (London, 1646). In "A true Relation of a Company of Brownists, Separatists, and Non-Conformists, in Monmouthshire in Wales" (London, 1641), Edward Harris argued that mechanic men styled themselves as "Teachers" in order to conceal the acts of fraud and seduction they were committing against undiscerning women.
72. For an account of the new fluidity between gender roles that arose during this time, see Rachel Trubowitz's "Female Preachers and Male Wives," in James Holstun, ed., *Pamphlet Wars: Prose in the English Revolution* (London: Frank Cass, 1992), pp. 112–133.
73. Anon., *Brownist Conventicle*, p. 6.
74. *Anna Trapnel's Report and Plea, or A Narrative of her Journey from London into Cornwall* (London, 1654), pp. A3–A4.
75. Carola Scott-Luckens, "The Broken Tabernacle: Bodily and Cosmic Paradigms in Henry Jessey's 1647 Soul-Narrative of Sarah Wight," unpublished essay, pp. 5–7.
76. Anon., *Brownist Conventicle*, p. 5.
77. Thomas, "Women of the Civil War Sects," p. 42.
78. William Erbery, *The Great Mystery of Godliness Jesus Christ our Lord God and man, and man with God; one in Jesus Christ Our Lord* (London, 1640).
79. Retha Warnicke, "Private and Public: The Boundaries of Women's Lives in Early Stuart England," in Jean R. Brink, ed., *Privileging Gender in Early Modern England* (Kirksville, MO: Sixteenth-Century Journal Publishers, 1993), pp. 123–140, quote from p. 140. For an account of contemporary discussions as to whether or not baptism was a private or public matter, see Crawford, *Women and Religion*, pp. 122–123.
80. Jürgen Habermas, *The Structural Transformation of the Public Sphere*, trans. Thomas Burger and Frederick Lawrence (Cambridge, MA: MIT Press, 1991).
81. Jürgen Habermas, "Further Reflections on the Public Sphere," in Craig Calhoun, *Habermas and the Public Sphere* (Cambridge, MA: MIT Press, 1992), pp. 421–461, quote from p. 422. For reflections on the public sphere as an "ideal type" in seventeenth-century England, see David Zaret, "Religion, Science, and

Printing in the Public Spheres in Seventeenth-Century England," in Calhoun, ed., *Habermas and the Public Sphere*, pp. 212–235.
82. Habermas, *Structural Transformation*, pp. 11–12.
83. Peter Laslett, *The World we have Lost: England before the Industrial Age – Further Explored*, 3rd edn (New York: Scribners, 1984), p. 20.
84. Joy Wiltenburg, *Disorderly Women and Female Power in the Street Literature of Early Modern England and Germany* (Charlottesville: University Press of Virginia, 1992); Frances E. Dolan, *Dangerous Familiars: Representations of Domestic Crime in England, 1550–1700* (Ithaca: Cornell University Press, 1994).
85. Dolan, *Dangerous Familiars*, p. 27.
86. Pacheco, ed., *Early Women Writers*, intro., p. 11.
87. Bridget Hill, *The First English Feminist: "Reflections Upon Marriage" and Other Writings by Mary Astell* (Aldershot: Gower Publishing, 1986); Patricia Springborg, "Mary Astell and John Locke," in N. H. Keeble, ed., *The Cambridge Companion to Writing of the English Revolution* (Cambridge: Cambridge University Press, 2001), pp. 276–303, quotes from pp. 277 and 279. See also Ruth Perry, *The Celebrated Mary Astell: An Early English Feminist* (Chicago: University of Chicago Press, 1986).
88. Carol Barash, "'The native liberty . . . of the subject': Configurations of gender and authority in the works of Mary Chudleigh, Sarah Fyge Egerton, and Mary Astell," in Grundy and Wiseman, eds., *Women, Writing, History*, pp. 55–69, quotes from p. 57 and p. 56.
89. Hilda Smith, *Reason's Disciples: Seventeenth-Century Feminists* (Urbana: University of Illinois Press, 1982), p. x.
90. Weil, *Political Passions*, p. 142 and p. 157.
91. Catherine Gallagher, "Embracing the Absolute: The Politics of the Female Subject in Seventeenth-Century England," in Pacheco, *Early Women Writers*, pp. 133–146.
92. Ibid., p. 25.
93. Pacheco, *Early Women Writers*, intro., p. 12; Gallagher, "Embracing the Absolute," pp. 136–137.
94. Reid Barbour, *Literature and Religious Culture in Seventeenth-Century England* (Cambridge: Cambridge University Press, 2002), pp. 151–175.
95. Dolan, *Dangerous Familiars*, p. 88.
96. The phrase "deep affinity" is taken from Gallagher, "Embracing the Absolute," p. 134.
97. Keith Thomas quoted in Crawford, "Challenges to Patriarchalism," pp. 112–113. Crawford notes that "Thomas's conclusion has been broadly repeated subsequently by other historians, whose interests, admittedly, were more in the family than in women" (pp. 112–113).
98. Ibid., p. 127.
99. Dorothy P. Ludlow, "Shaking Patriarchy's Foundations: Sectarian Women in England, 1641–1700," in *Triumph over Silence: Women in Protestant History*, ed. Richard L. Greaves (Westport, CT: Greenwood Press, 1985), pp. 95–96.
100. Mack, *Visionary Women*, p. 9.

101. See David Zaret, "Religion and the Rise of Liberal-Democratic Ideology in Seventeenth-Century England," *American Sociological Review* 54 (1989), 163–179, and Nicholas Tyacke, "The Legalizing of Dissent, 1571–1719," in Ole Peter Grell, Jonathan I. Israel, and Nicholas Tyacke, eds., *From Persecution to Toleration: The Glorious Revolution and Religion in England* (Oxford: Clarendon Press, 1991), p. 18, for claims that the pendulum has swung so far in the direction of seeing liberalism as something other than a simple extension of Puritanism's emphasis upon spiritual equality that, as Tyacke says, "the time has come to restore Puritanism to its rightful place of political and religious importance" in the "legalizing of dissent." Milestone works in that original genealogy include C. Burrage, *The Early English Dissenters* (Cambridge: Cambridge University Press, 1912); D. B. Robertson, *The Religious Foundations of Leveller Democracy* (New York: King's Crown Press, 1951); and Brian Manning, ed., *Politics, Religion, and the English Civil War* (London: Edward Arnold, 1973).
102. Crawford, "Challenges to Patriarchalism," p. 128.
103. David Wootton, ed., introduction to *Divine Right and Democracy: An Anthology of Political Writing in Stuart England* (Harmondsworth: Penguin, 1986), p. 41.
104. Elizabeth Sauer, "Maternity, Prophecy, and the Cultivation of the Private Sphere in Seventeenth-Century England," in *Explorations in Renaissance Culture* 24 (1998), 119–148.
105. Vera Camden, "Prophetic Discourse and the Voice of Protest: The Vindication of Anne Wentworth," *Man and Nature* (1989), 29–38, quote from p. 35.
106. Purkiss, "Producing the Voice," pp. 157, 158.
107. Judith Kegan Gardiner, "Re-Gendering Individualism: Margaret Fell Fox and Quaker Rhetoric," in Brink, ed., *Privileging Gender*, pp. 205–224, quote from p. 224.
108. Valerie Bryson, *Feminist Political Theory: An Introduction* (New York: Paragon House, 1992), p. 176.
109. Jacquette, "Contract and Coercion," p. 214.
110. Pateman, *Sexual Contract*, p. 156.
111. Norman Cohn, *The Pursuit of the Millennium* (London: Secker & Warburg, 1957), pp. xiii–xvi.
112. Alfred Cohen, "The Fifth Monarchy Mind: Mary Cary," *Social Research* 31, 1 (spring 1964), 195–213.
113. Christopher Hill, *The World Turned Upside Down* (Harmondsworth: Penguin, 1972), p. 15.
114. Clement Hawes, *Mania and Literary Style* (Cambridge: Cambridge University Press, 1996), p. 3.
115. Margaret George, *Women in the First Capitalist Society: Experiences in Seventeenth-Century England* (Urbana: University of Illinois Press, 1988), p. 53.

116. Jane Baston, "History, Prophecy, and Interpretation: Mary Cary and Fifth Monarchism," *Prose Studies* 21, 3 (December 1998), 1–18, reference to p. 6.
117. Elaine Hobby, "'Come to Live a Preaching Life': Female Community in Seventeenth-Century Radical Sects," in Rebecca D'Monte and Nicole Pohl, eds., *Female Communities 1600–1800* (London: Macmillan, 2000), pp. 76–92; James Holstun, *Ehud's Dagger: Class Struggle in the English Revolution* (London: Verso, 2000), pp. 257–304.

2

A hammer in her hand: Katherine Chidley and Anna Trapnel separate church from state

> Before the starry threshold of Joves Court
> My mansion is
> From *Comus* (The first Scene discovers a wilde Wood)

> and walking in a curious garden . . . I began to sing forth his praises, and continued while it was so late in the evening, that my friends that walked with me thought it convenient to lead me into the house
> Anna Trapnel, *Report and Plea*

> But while I was singing praises to the Lord for his love to me, the Justices sent their Constable to fetch me
> Anna Trapnel, *Report and Plea*

In the "revelatory" conclusion to Thomas Carew's Stuart masque, *Coelum Britannicum* (1634), King Charles I and Henrietta Maria are deified.[1] Mercury plays their Attendant Spirit, conducting his Lady, the actual Queen, and her king into the hallowed halls of sanctified sovereignty: "Then shall you see / The sacred hand of bright eternity; Mould you to stars, and fix you in the sphere / To you your royal half, to them she'll join / Such of this train as with industrious steps / In the fair prints your virtuous feet have made, / Though with unequal paces, follow you" (186). Here Carew even grants Henrietta and Charles, the royal twins, "CARLOMARIA," a virtual monopoly over this Platonic realm of representation and visibility, of personhood, perfection, and power. It was, the masque proclaimed, *these two alone* who were graceful and "formed fit for heaven" (189) enough to "dispense to th' world a pure refined influence" (168). In *Comus*, however, Milton defiantly divorces the royal from the divine, arguing that the true "servants" of "Joves Court" are all those members of the elect who, after death, live "insphear'd" with God well "above the smoak and stirr of this dim spot, which men call Earth."[2] The true heaven, in other words, *is heaven* and no earthly monarch can claim to serve as the exclusive embodiment of its power and mystique. At the same time, Milton argues, there is a little bit of the divine in everybody – even while still alive – and so the Lady is depicted as a perpetual work "in progress," one who "moves" or "influences" while always "insphere'd" in a fixed state of "unblench't majesty" (142).

As Milton's text suggests, even as Charles and Henrietta Maria lay absolute claim to their exclusive ability to embody "virtue" within a heavenly court, someone else was busy making a "somewhere else." This elsewhere was said to be a new "somewhere," a sphere equally if not more crowned by virtue than was the court. In *Comus*, this oppositional realm was established within the home of the Earl of Bridgewater, a man held up by Milton as an "entirely new type of leader: reformist, bourgeois, meritocratic."[3] But as my second epigraph suggests, a host of historical "Sabrinas" such as Anna Trapnel can also be found in these middle decades of the seventeenth century, holding their own court in the "house" of the separatist conventicle, virtual churches that nonaristocratic sectarians constructed out of family and friends as alternative havens for the representative embodiment of virtue, merit, and reform. These churches were "public," Separatists argued, in that they were composed of speakers and audiences and held together through what James Holstun, in a sustained analysis of Anna Trapnel, refers to as "public spiritedness" – the "public testimony to acts of indwelling divine grace which help to culture a new collective existence."[4] But these churches were also private, their constituents insisted, to the degree that they were (or should be) immune from government oversight and control because, as a result of their affiliation with the realm of godly protection, each one of their members enjoyed the right to "religious individualism."[5]

A recent mainstay of modern feminist thought has been to challenge the liberal association of privacy with "freedom," that is with a hedge against interference by other persons or the state. As Joan Landes writes, for women, the domestic sphere has long consisted of "sexual inequality, unremunerated work, and seething discontent" rather than rights and protection; thus, "among modern oppositional movements, feminism is unrivalled in its contribution to a deepening understanding of the historical, symbolic, and practical effects of the organization of public and private life."[6] And as Paula Backscheider observes, the private sphere is, in practice, infused with government oversight (marriage, for example, is subject to licensed controls over who can marry whom, when, and how); therefore, it is important to recognize the ongoing degree to which terms such as "public" and "private" rest on contingent, alterable definitions that are overdetermined by state power.[7] To so do, we must continually ask, "Who has the power to define the boundaries that seem to exist? To move them? To invade them? And for what ends?," and to remind ourselves that those boundaries have often been drawn in ways that "oppress women and restrict their opportunities, even their identities" (9). Backscheider notes that this position reflects the thinking of any number of feminists who have used the public–private paradigm as a productive framework within which to rethink women's history and/or as a precedent upon which to insist that some parameters dividing the public from the private be redrawn so that, for example, men are no longer protected from prosecution for marital rape or domestic abuse while, at the same time, women may still gain reproductive control over their own bodies.[8] As Jean Bethke Elshtain writes, feminists who come to the issue from radically different perspectives – psychoanalytic, Marxist, and even liberal – "share at least one overriding imperative: they would redefine the boundaries of the public and the private, the personal and the political, in a way that opens up certain questions for inquiry."[9]

However, even as attacks upon domestic abuse and demands for abortion arguably represent a beneficial "privatization" of the female individual, the malleability and historicity of private–public dichotomies have led a number of feminists to conclude that drawing any distinction whatsoever between private and public spheres perpetuates a dark "fairy tale" that has a decidedly unhappy ending for the female protagonist.[10] Joan Kelly maintains that "The conception of two social spheres" (both in the "liberal/radical" and the "socialist" models) functions merely to "legitimate" such "bourgeois patriarchal practices" as the "subordination of bourgeois women to the property and personal interests of the men of their class."[11] Nancy Fraser describes the domestic realm as a place of "egocentric, strategic, and instrumental calculation" and "usually exploitative exchanges of service, labor, cash, and sex, not to mention sites, frequently, of coercion and violence."[12] She argues that we need to "fight for a more egalitarian and democratic society" than our current "late capitalist" one, which, she contends, remains a product of those "bourgeois originators and current Eastern European proponents" who see public–private categories as ongoing "supports for and challenges to state power exclusively." Catherine MacKinnon insists that the private–public distinction is in and of itself a patriarchal tool of female subordination with which white propertied men dominate all others.[13] To end this domination, we must do away with the very notion of a private sphere and concomitantly expand the sphere of a "feminist" state so that it enjoys a near absolute power to "protect" all of its citizens. And Paula Backscheider offers: "The binary public–private model may be our past and even our present, but it, like so many other early modern, perhaps specifically Enlightenment formulations, may have generated more evils, more oppression and exclusion, more blindness and misconceptions, than illuminations."[14] As Timothy Dykstal concludes, a nuanced feminist critique of the terms upon which the public and private are divided within a liberal-individualist order often devolves into viewing "any vision of the public sphere that insists on keeping it distinct from the private one as an apology for a pre-feminist, patriarchal order that oppresses women and others who do not meet a narrow definition of citizenship."[15]

Carole Pateman traces the rise of the repressive "classical liberal" division between the private and the public back to seventeenth-century contract theories and their neopatriarchal separation between the home and the state.[16] However, in what follows I will argue that two seventeenth-century sectarian women, Katherine Chidley and Anna Trapnel, can be counted among the "originators" of a liberal theory that erects a boundary between the public realm of government and a private sphere of guaranteed protection (or "rights") against interference by authorities. As I hope to demonstrate, these religious separatists agitated for a "hedge" not because they wished to be enclosed within a site of "sexual inequality, unremunerated work, and seething discontent," but because they wished to be freed from just such a "public sphere" of mandatory church attendance (and the many forms of social and economic oversight that it encompassed) to which they already had by law been confined. They did so not in order to capitulate to new forms of male domination, but rather to overcome old ones, particularly as they pertained to the enforced economic maintenance of a state religion and its monopoly over the (male) ministry. And they did so not because they wanted to be "protected" from their husbands, but because they wished to be freed from an institution that claimed on the one hand that English society needed to be protected from the damage wrought by the spectacle of female preaching (a spectacle that, Holstun observes, was often staged in conjunction with the female sectarian's supportive husband, sons, and/or fellow congregationalists within "the domestic sphere"), and on the other that would-be women preachers themselves needed to be "protected" from their opportunistic exploiters – the "mechanic" "Comuses" who "lured" them from their homes and into private churches.[17] In short, history shows us that it was not only the sons of Locke who are on record as having "jealously protected [the private sphere] as unaccountable to the law, even common law, precedence, and community standards."[18]

In "A Woman's Place is in the Home-Based Church," I will briefly revisit the ways in which certain definitions of femininity were used to maintain a "private" domestic sphere that was subject to magisterial oversight long before Locke. (As I will argue later, dissenting women laid claims to privacy in order to liberate themselves from these particular – and legally enforced – definitions of womanhood and of home, so that they could engage in new forms of "public" speech and writing.) I will then detail the ways in which religious Separatists facilitated these forms of female religious speech and writing by turning their homes and even their own bodies into churches, thereby converting traditional gender hierarchies into a mode of sexual egalitarianism that was predicated on the Protestant understanding of spiritual equality. In the final three sections – "The Separation of Home from State," "A Woman's Home is her Castle," and "A Public Sphere of One's Own" – I will discuss the specific writings and practices of Katherine Chidley, the female Leveller petitioner, and Anna Trapnel, respectively, arguing that their texts express a woman's interest in safeguarding the home against intrusive attempts by authorities to subvert the new forms of female religious and political authority that were rising from within the ranks of the "private." These women, it might be said, began the process of building a "feminist theory of the state" which, in order to "recognize" a woman's "right" to preach and prophesy, rested on a necessary separation of a private sphere of individual and group-based self-determination from a public government sphere of patriarchal domination.

A WOMAN'S PLACE IS IN THE HOME-BASED CHURCH

Authors of early modern conduct manuals represented the house as the appropriate and effective site for containing and disciplining naturally wayward and eminently promiscuous women.[19] In *A Preparative to Marriage* (1591), conduct manualist Henrie Smith wrote: "we call the Wife, Huswife, that is house wife, not a street wife . . . but a housewife, to shew that a good wife keepes her house: & therefore Paule biddeth Titus to exhort women that they be chast, & keeping at home: presently after Chast, he saith keeping at home, as though Home were Chastities keeper."[20] And William Gouge's *Of Domestic Duties* (1622) cited Proverbs 7.11 to note that one sure sign of the strumpet was that "her feet cannot abide in the house."[21] Even at home women were to monitor their behavior with an eye towards the possible consequences that might befall them if they failed to obey social, cultural, and legal norms. As the character Lucretia says in Edmund Tilney's domestic dialogue *The Flower of Friendship* (1573), "As the wife must be thus wary in going abroade: so must she be as carefull what is done at home, on hir part not to sit ydlely . . . To be briefe, not only in chastitite of bodie, but in honestie of behaviour and talke, doth the womans honour, and good name consist, and is also mainteyned."[22] And Edward Reyner's *Considerations Concerning Marriage* (1657) details the domestic "duties" that were to occupy women's time: "To build a godly family; not onely by the procreation and religious education of children (which is a pillar of the house) but by a wise and godly Government and ordering of the house, in which the wife ought to act her part."[23]

In "Patriarchal Territories: The Body Enclosed," Peter Stallybrass carefully reconstructs this "production" of a "normative 'Woman'" by conduct manuals and other forms of high and popular culture: "The signs of the 'harlot' are her linguistic 'fulness' and her frequenting of public space" while the normative woman is "rigidly 'finished'" and her "signs" are "the enclosed body, the closed mouth, the locked home."[24] Noting the persistent equation that male theorists of female conduct drew between domestic enclosure, chastity, and female silence, Stallybrass elucidates the ways in which the early modern surveillance of women concentrated on these three patriarchal territories: the mouth, a woman's chastity, and the threshold of the house. Even when women were "gadding out and about," they were exhorted to emulate *emblematum liber*, that is the image of the tortoise or snail who carried its home on its back. Through a continuous meditation on this mental image, the housewife could maintain the demeanor and restraints of enclosure, even when she was beyond the walls of the house.

Stallybrass acknowledges that "We are not of course addressing here . . . women's resistances . . . both collectively and individually, but the production of normative 'Woman' within the discursive practices of the ruling elite" (127). When he does analyze an act of resistance, Stallybrass turns to the fictional Emilia from Shakespeare's *Othello* who, Stallybrass argues, "subverts the enclosed body" (142). But his invocation of the idea of resistance (Tilney's *Flowers of Friendship* does, after all, consist of a "dialogue *contesting* marriage") inspires us to look for the actual, oftentimes nonnormative social and political practices through which nonfictional women represented a less than obedient relationship to the body enclosed. Conduct manual writers themselves were all too aware of the potential vulnerability in their "solution" of sequestration to the "woman problem" and they characterized this weakness in architectural terms. In *The English Gentlewoman*, Richard Braithwaite paraphrased the solution of "surveillance" as "[Women] may bee in security, so long as [they] are sequestered from society," but he also detected a "structural flaw": "What an excellent impregnable fortresse were *Woman*, did not her *Windowes* betray her to her enemy?"[25] Henrie Smith also portrayed the "windowes" as the potential point of entry for the disruption of an otherwise secure domestic fortress for women: "And therefore Salomon depainting the Whore, setteth her at the doore, now sitting upon her stalls, now walking in the streetes, now looking out of the windowes, like curled Jezabel, as if she held forth the glasse of temptation, for vanitie to gaze upon."[26] Braithwaite even described a woman's eyes as "the Windowes by which death enters; [her] inward house cannot shine unlesse these be shut" for the eyes are a "catalogue of wandring phrenzie or wanton Fancy."[27] As Sara Mendelson and Patricia Crawford argue, "Both the flexibility and liminal ambiguity of feminized household boundaries were embodied in women's habit of posting themselves at their door . . . The liminal stance of the doorway connected women in their economic role as overseers of the household to their social role as participants in village life."[28]

Perhaps, then, it is not surprising to find that in the 1640s tracts which object to religious Separatism on the grounds that it gives rise to the woman preacher, there is a fair amount of talk about doors and windows. As the anonymous author of *Tub-preachers Overturn'd* (1647) announced, something had come along to shine "New Lights" through the windows of the normative woman's house.[29] "New Lights" was a widely used term for the small but disproportionately influential number of Separatists who challenged state control over religion in England throughout the seventeenth century. Their "independency," wrote the author of *Tub-preachers Overturn'd*, was to be "abandon'd and abhor'd as destructive to the Majesty and Ministry, of the Church and Common-wealth of England," because it brought into existence a whole new group of "lay illiterate men and women" who "usurp the Ministry, and Audaciously vent their own heretical opinions, in their house-(alias Tub) – Preachings" (1). Decrying the fact that lower- and middle-class men and (even more shockingly) women had begun to separate themselves from official churches, to form in the most extreme cases alternative "private conventicles" within such "secret" spaces as their own homes, and to themselves become ministers of the Bible, the author tries to neutralize this subversive new phenomenon by equating it with the old nemesis of the conduct manual: "Sathan may be truly said to have his Throne there; where ye have crept into widdows houses and have bewitched or deceived silly women, men and women, servants, children; and since your entrance ye have like Jezabel, painted your brazen fac'd pretences, and look out of those uppermost windows." But, as the anonymous author warns, "your New-Lights [only] makes him behold you the clearer; you, Sir are Arrians, Antinomians, Libertines, Soul-keepers, Anti baptists, Socinians, Pelagians, Self-seekers" (5–6).

These names were the slanderous terms for such groups as the Brownists, the Duppas, the General Baptists, and the Particular Baptists – "New Lights" which cropped up in the mid seventeenth century in England and which helped to build a movement for the separation of church from state. Separatist groups communicated their autonomy through the ironically "visible" act of enclosing themselves within "invisible" spaces – both in order to demarcate their separateness and to protect themselves against detection by angry authorities. Thus, as Murray Tolmie observes, while many Puritan groups pursued an aura of legitimacy by eschewing actual physical separation and utilizing actual parish church buildings for off-hours meetings of their own "congregations," more radically separatist "lay preachers" moved their meetings "from private house to private house or from fields to woods and back again."[30] This extreme form of nonconformity emerged as one of the most threatening social and political phenomena of the era, because its emphasis upon "separate" church government within "separate" spheres gave rise to two troubling notions. One was that religious "Independency" challenged various forms of "Absolutism," despite claims to the contrary. Another, perhaps even more controversial one for Puritan and non-Puritan alike, was that, as Patricia Crawford details, it was conducive to the rise of new and unprecedented forms of public female authority, both *viva voce* and in print.[31] As the author of *A Spirit Moving in the Women Preachers* opined, Separatists were able to "discredit" Paul's injunction for women to "keep silence in your Churches" by using "Houses in place of the Church."[32]

In terms of the former, Tolmie recounts that, in the wake of Queen Elizabeth's executions and silencing of Separatist Puritan clergy in 1593, Henry Jacob first petitioned King James in 1605 for permission to "assemble together somewhere publicly to the service and worship of God, to use and enjoy peaceably among ourselves alone the whole exercise of Gods worship and of church government."[33] In exile, Jacob petitioned the King again in 1609 for toleration of "some churches to be gathered by your majesty's special grace in some parts of this kingdom" (8). These churches were to be free from episcopal oversight but subject to "your subordinate civil magistrates"; however, this "limited and temporary" notion of the gathered church was soon replaced by a notion of the nonparochial gathered church as "a true visible church in its own right" when Jacob's congregational theory began to stress the "kingly office of Christ as the immediate head of each individual congregation" (8–9). When the "kingly office" of Christ was labeled the "immediate head," all sorts of traditionally placed heads in English social hierarchies were bypassed by implication, including that of the King himself, although Separatists denied the charge that they opposed the monarchy as an institution. As Tolmie continues, Jacob realized the potential for the concept of the "kingly office of Christ" to "liberate the gathered church from its subordination to the magistrate's consent for its very existence" when he wrote that congregations were to be formed through the "joining by willing consent into a visible church" rather than through mandatory or assumed membership within the church of one's local parish (9). In 1609, Jacob himself returned to London to form such a church, which he described in his *Confession and Protestations of the Faith of Certaine Christians* as consisting of dissenters from the Church of England and as "meeting in private for the exercise of our religion."[34]

Pamphlets raging against the subversive political implications of using private houses as alternative churches reached a crescendo in the early 1640s, when a number of separatist groups were detected in and around London. The temporary suspension of laws against private churches during the 1640s and 1650s appears to have enabled some growth in new separatist groups. However, these groups reportedly maintained a defensive aura of secrecy against those who wished to expose and control them, especially since crackdowns did still occur. An anonymous pamphlet entitled *The Brothers of the Separation* was subtitled, *A true Relation of a company of Brownists, which kept their Conventicle at one Mr. Porters in Goat Alley in Whitecrosse Street, where they were apprehended on Sunday, August 14, 1641, As also, A Sermon preached afterwards in the same house by John Rogers a Glover, wherein is shewed their wicked rancorous minds at full.*[35] This is an account of a group of Separatists who held weekly gatherings at the said Mr. Porter's house, meetings that were held "so covertly, that they there had meetings Sunday after Sunday for a great while to gather undiscerned." As the title states, they were arrested and released on Sunday, the 14th of August; nonetheless, to the outraged author's chagrin, they continued to meet. Similarly, the indignant author of *The Brownist's Synagogue or a Late Discovery of their Conventicles, Assemblies; and places of meeting, Where they Preach, and the manner of their praying and preaching* (1641) describes how a group of Separatists would decide on a house of meeting and would then appoint one member to "keep the door, for the intent to give notice if there should be any intrusion." Fear of detection, he maintained, also required them to refrain from "flock[ing]" in all together and to instead "come

2 or 3" at a time. After all had arrived, "the man appointed to teach, stands in the midst of the Room, and his audience gather about him." The man prayed for about half an hour and part of his prayers was that "those who come thither to scoff and laugh" be discovered by God. He then delivered a sermon, also half an hour in length, after which he asked the group to depart in twos or threes, just as they had arrived, again to insure that the group survived to congregate again.

Separatists justified what their detractors derisively referred to as "House-preaching" on both practical and theological grounds.[36] Complaining about another group of Separatists who held meetings in one Richard Rogers's "own house," *The Brownist's Synagogue* also registers the justifications that one of their ministers, a chandler called Edward Johnson, provided for their cause. Reversing the dominant claim that it was Separatists who practiced an objectionable form of worship, he explained that "the house, field, or Wood, wherein their Congregation meets, is the Church of God," whereas the Church of England is not "because the good and bad come both thither, neither is it lawful to have any Society with the wicked." Separatists also rationalized their actions by extending the concept of idolatry to include the "idol" of the architectural church itself. John Goodwin argued that "the Church is a spiritual building, framed of such lively stones as are not of the world . . . without any assistance from the kingdomes of the world."[37] And Katherine Chidley's son, Samuel, wrote in *Thunder from the Throne of God against the Temple of Idols* (1653) that the idea that a congregation's sanctity was dependent on "brick and mortar" was "popish" heresy.[38] What is more, the Bible is populated with figures such as Samuel, David, Luke, and John who use the architectural rhetoric of the "house" to define lineage, family, offspring, and even "heaven" as sites where God resides, as opposed to actual churches. This language sat well with groups of people who sought to wrest the power of religious authority away from an ordained clergy and to locate it within their own homes (or other private places of gathering), families, and social circles.

As stated above, it has been Carol Pateman's contention that the seventeenth century was a period when men were defined as equal individuals within the public sphere of rights and contract, while women were reassigned an apolitical, silent, and publicly ineffectual private sphere. However, the use of actual houses, among other more "private" and "domestic" spaces, as sites for audience-centered gatherings created an environment that was conducive to women's entry into public speech and print. As Dorothy Ludlow observes, the "distinction between women teaching at home and their preaching in public" became "blurred" during this period.[39] And as

Crawford reminds us, "the presence and participation of women" had been a "common feature" of these separatist groups and of 'enthusiastic religion' generally" since the Elizabethan period, when a significant female presence in such groups as the Brownists, the Barrowists, and the Family of Love led Miles Hogarde to complain that "in all ages at any tyme when one had devised some foolishe errour or other, straight way woemen were readye to apply to their fancies."[40] Given that women are said to have been heavily represented among the original supporters of Wycliff and Hus, it is possible to trace this phenomenon back even further and to ally it not simply with "Protestantism" but with (dissident) Catholicism as well. Once again, however, unavoidably loud alarms were sounded (even within Separatism) when, in the 1640s, it was feared that women were moving from congregant to preacher.[41] Tolmie recounts that one of the "most significant arrangements" of Separatist congregations from very early on was that, as Jacob wrote, "any understanding member of the church (but women)" could participate in "the sober, discreet, orderly, and well-governed exercise of expounding and applying the Scripture to the congregation."[42] However, by 1619 tensions had also formed *within* Congregationalism when early founders such as Richard Mansell left the church over the "matter of prophecy," that is, the "right extended to laymen," as Tolmie puts it, "to 'exercise' or preach." This was because "voluntary association" was drawing not only householders (or property owners) who could take a turn holding meetings at their houses, but those who were in "want" of houses as well, including "women without their husbands and servants without their masters' consent."[43] The tract entitled *A Discovery of Six Women Preachers* (1641) blames the apparently growing trend on a shortage of male preachers and argues that the only reason that so many women have "of late" become preachers is because "there was a deficiency of good men" (3). However, the women preachers featured in this tract reportedly argue that male preachers have been "good for nothing" anyway because they have been "expounding the language of the beast," whereas they, women preachers, would "preach nothing, but such things as the spirit should move them" (3). The author concedes the fact that women were filling a "Sacerdoticall function" and he goes on to name six women guilty of daring to take on the masculine role of preacher (3). The title page is prefaced with 1 Corinthians 14.34, 35: "Let your women keep silence in the Churches, for it is not permitted unto them to speak, but they are commanded to be under obedience, as also saith the Law. And if they will learn anything, let them ask their husbands at home: for it is a shame for women to speak in the Church." Nonetheless, as the tract notes, such patriarchal strictures were being violated in private practice. One of the six discovered women preachers discussed at length is Anne Hempstall (living, as the tract tells us, in the "Parish of Saint Andrews Holborne, neare London, and in the County of Middlesex"). Hempstall is reported to have "called an assembly of her bibbing Gossips together" to her own house and to have preached to them while standing on a stool. To authorize herself as a prophetess, Hempstall told her audience that she had had a "strange Dream" the previous night in which "Anna [Hannah] the Prophetess was presented unto [her] view." The "splendour" of Anna's countenance cast Hempstall into a trance and, when she awoke the next morning, she argued that she could "conceive no interpretation of my Dream but this, that I should imitate godly Anna, by preaching unto you, as shee prophesied to others."

The tract describes a series of spatial displacements and replacements: the officially recognized parish – that bearing the name of "Saint Andrews Holborne" – has been replaced with a private house – "the house of this Anne Hempstall." The name of a male (and hence ordained) saint, Andrew, has been changed to that of an unofficially sanctioned and self-titled female plebeian saint, Anne Hempstall (interestingly, the initials A. H. remain the same even as the gender is changed). The home – wherein women were to regulate their speech – has given way to a new definition of the house as a "church," one in which enclosed female residents could point to Hannah as a biblical precedent for a "public" female ministry. And, finally, the official prop of the minister – the pulpit – has been replaced by, of all things, a "stool, or a tub," as the dismayed author tells us. This suggests that the tools of domesticity, the very accoutrements of female silence and submission, have been literally turned on their heads and used as the foundation for public speech – the true tale of a tub. Mary Bilbrowe, the wife of a bricklayer, went so far as to use some of her husband's bricks to build a pulpit for herself in her parlour, as well as three bricks apiece for each of her audience members to sit on, her reason being, "she thought they would not sit much, because women to good instructions love standing." (The author, it should be noted, was especially disturbed that she built her brick pulpit "so high, that scarce any thing, but her standing up tippet could be seen.")

As stated, the use of the home as a gathering site meant that this "patriarchal territory" was being exploited for the very unpatriarchal purposes of generating female speech, which was felt to be "public" for the fact that it gathered an audience. Sometimes, as was the case with Anne Hutchinson as well as the Baptist radical known simply as Mrs. Attaway, other participants congregated inside the home and sat on chairs encircling a table or pulpit. Or, as the case of Anna Trapnel will show, crowds gathered just outside while she appeared – Juliet-like – through the open window. Or, as with both Trapnel and Sarah Wight, audiences entered deep into the patriarchal territory of the bedchamber, enraptured by the sight of a prostrate, entranced, and fasting prophetess delivering spontaneously composed prophecies recorded by an amanuensis. In fact, it was just as often these alternative social practices that prompted opposition as it was the "blasphemies" preached. Or rather, the alternative social practices *were* the religious and political blasphemies. Vicars's *The Schismatick Sifted* singled out the spectacle of "bold impudent huswives to take upon them to prate an hour or more" as one of his main objections to the implementation of toleration, as did the author of *The Brothers of the Separation* who saw the rise of "mechanic" and female preachers within dissenting groups as a threat to sermon standards.[44] These unordained and uneducated men and women, he complained, were preaching *ex tempore* sermons that were "without division, or any such matter." In his *Discovery of Some Prodigious New Wandring Blazing Stars and Firebrands Styling Themselves New-Lights* (1646), William Prynne claimed that disregarding Paul's edict against women preachers was a mere ploy by male sectarians to win feminine support for subversive political activities. He also attacked the preaching of women and other "mechanics" as in and of itself dangerous to traditional forms of social and political hierarchy.

Such denunciations were accompanied by new attempts at state suppression. As Crawford argues, "Religious policy was influenced by the interaction between men and women in 'private' houses seeking the worship of God. Neither ministers nor members of Parliament could, or would have wished to, separate religion from its family and household meaning. They wanted women to obey, not to initiate reform."[45] In 1641 the Presbyterian minister, Thomas Edwards, whose *Gangraena* was replete with examples of how the sectarian alteration of the patriarchal household would lead structurally and inevitably to the dissolution of the English state, petitioned Parliament to disregard separatist petitions for legitimacy in large part because they allowed women to preach and prophesy.[46] In response, the House of Commons resolved on June 7 to reprove "lay preachers."[47] In 1645 another Presbyterian, Thomas Coleman, a member of the Westminster Assembly, appeared before the House of Commons to condemn the "lowering of standards which permitted women as well as mere 'mechanics'" to preach.[48] And on January 16, 1646 the London Aldermen and Common Council successfully petitioned the House of Commons for an end to the Independent forms of church government responsible for allowing "private Meetings of Women Preachers."[49] Later that month several women preachers were arrested and others were called before the Committee of Examinations in the House of Commons. In December 1646 the House voted against allowing any person who was not ordained to preach in any church, chapel, or public place, or even *to write* against church government.[50] As Edith M. Williams points out, no penalty for violating this resolution was imposed, although a committee was appointed to enforce the new law.[51] Thus, while separatist churches continued to exist and women to preach and publish, they were continually in jeopardy for doing so until the law was changed. This appeared unlikely given the number of voices arrayed against "toleration" in no small part for its perpetuation of a radical new doctrine of gender equality. As Woodhouse reports, on May 17, 1647, Thomas Case warned the House of Commons that if they allowed "liberty of conscience," then "see . . . how long your civil peace will secure you when religion is destroyed . . . Liberty of conscience (falsely so called) may in time improve itself into liberty of estates and . . . houses and . . . wives, and in a word liberty of perdition of souls and bodies."[52]

To combat such claims, separatist women themselves went into print to protest the state's intrusions into what they insisted was a *private* sphere of religious independency. In the following three sections I will discuss a few such writings by Katherine Chidley, a founder of separatist churches and a pamphlet writer who issued a direct challenge to Thomas Edwards; the female Levellers, sponsors of several significant political petitions to Parliament that drew upon Independent definitions of privacy to extend a set of public political "rights" or prerogatives to women; and Anna Trapnel, a Fifth Monarchist prophetess and prolific author whose account of her own trial and arrest for Independent preaching actively constructs the home-based church as an early instance of a "public sphere," as Jürgen Habermas describes it, that is as a "private" site that was capable of critiquing, appropriating, and dispersing the "representative publicness" that was traditionally reserved for the sovereign.

THE SEPARATION OF HOME FROM STATE: THE WRITINGS OF KATHERINE CHIDLEY

The brief but significant literary career of Katherine Chidley, a seamstress and religious radical, provides an important basis for rethinking assumptions about the history of feminism's relationship to the separation of public from private spheres, especially as it impinged on and intersected the call for a separation of church from state. Between 1641 and 1645, Chidley published *The Justification of the Independent Churches of Christ Being an Answer* to Mr. Edwards his Booke, A New-Yeares-Gift to Mr. Thomas Edwards and *Good Counsell to the Petitioners for Presbyterian Government.* In these works she exhorts Parliament to institute religious "Independency" rather than replace the dissolved Anglican Church with a new Presbyterian form of state religion.[53] In *The Justification of the Independent Churches of Christ* she also develops a notion of spiritual equality within an autonomous sphere of religious dissent that later petitions by Leveller women translate into the earliest notion of female political equality grounded in contract and consent.

Katherine Chidley's birth and death dates are not known; it is reported, however, that she and her husband, Daniel, were members of persecuted separatist congregations in Shrewsbury in the 1620s and in London in the 1630s and 1640s. Katherine and Daniel were admonished for "nonattendance" at Peter Studley's rectory of St. Chad's in 1626. Katherine was also cited for refusing to be "churched after childbirth."[54] The Chidleys left Shrewsbury sometime around 1629 and moved to London, where both Daniel and the family's eldest son, Samuel, became members of the Haberdashers' Company; there Samuel eventually met the future Leveller, John Lilburne. In 1630, Daniel founded a separatist congregation along with John Duppa and Thomas Dyer. He escaped arrest in a sweep that landed twenty-six members of the Duppa church in prison in 1632, and, by 1639, the church was part of a federation of seven separatist churches in London. Daniel eventually disappears from the historical record, but Katherine and Samuel went on to establish separatist churches at Stepney and throughout the provinces and to form a mother–son writing and publishing team, with Samuel serving as his mother's amanuensis. From the mid 1640s through the early 1650s, both Katherine and Samuel were "Levellers," that is, members of a loose confederation of individuals, such as John Lilburne and Richard Overton, who agitated for a series of democratic reforms during the civil war era. Samuel Chidley became treasurer of this group in 1647 and between 1643 and 1657 published over a dozen pamphlets of his own on subjects ranging from infant baptism to kingship.[55] Katherine is reported as having become involved with other Leveller women who, throughout the 1640s and 1650s, petitioned Parliament on issues ranging from the loss of trade to what they saw as an unwarranted colonial war in Ireland, and to the imprisonment of their husbands and other male Levellers.

The early publication dates of Chidley's pamphlets locate her at the vanguard of two mid-seventeenth-century movements: the separation of church from state and sectarian women's entry into print. Chidley's *Justification of the Independent Churches of Christ* was a systematic refutation in plain

Puritan prose of Thomas Edwards's theological and political arguments in *Reasons against the Independent Government of Particular Congregations*.[56] The fact that both were published in 1641 means that Chidley's work came out after such landmark separatist and Baptist pleas for religious liberty as John Smyth's *Parallels, Censures, Observations* (1609), Henry Jacob's *A Confession and Protestation of the Faith of Certaine Christians in England* (1616), and John Robinson's *A Justification of Separation from the Church of England* (1639; a work which Chidley quotes extensively in her own), but before such noteworthy examples of the genre as John Goodwin's *Imputatio Fidei* (1642) and Roger Williams's *Bloody Tenent of Persecution* (1644).[57] As Ludlow observes, Chidley was "the first woman to take up her pen as the climactic middle decades [of the seventeenth century] opened."[58] In her writings, Chidley used social and rhetorical strategies simultaneously to justify the existence of private churches and her own early entry into print. Indeed, her work presents these two phenomena as interrelated and interdependent. The toleration of private religion was a necessary condition for her authorship as a nonelite woman.

Chidley was not an aristocrat like other, more prominent seventeenth-century women writers, such as Anne Clifford or Margaret Cavendish. Thus, she did not have access to their strategies for going public. Clifford and Cavendish, for example, invoked their fathers' or husbands' aristocratic credentials in order to legitimate their texts. Clifford signed her *Diary* (1616–17) "Anne, Countess of Dorset, Pembroke and Montgomery, daughter and heiress of George Clifford, Earl of Cumberland," and Cavendish signed her *True Relation of my Birth, Breeding, and Life* "Written by the thrice noble, illustrious and excellent Princess, the Lady Marchioness of Newcastle."[59] In contrast, Chidley derived her authority to write not from the aristocratic sphere of institutional privilege, but from the spiritual equality she enjoyed in what she constructed as the private and independent sphere of the separatist congregation. She prefaced *The Justification of the Independent Churches of Christ* not with noble titles, but with a set of biblical verses that refer to tools from the workaday world. For Chidley, the hammer and tent stake wielded by the biblical figure, Jael, symbolized the way in which her own literary authority was grounded in her separation from state institutions.

As a woman writer and preacher, Chidley had a vested interest in creating and protecting the sphere of Independent churches as a private one separate from and immune to state control. Her radical activities brought her to the attention of anti-Separatists very early on. She had, after all, assumed the authority of the preacher, a proactive role even more associated with masculine authority than that of the female prophetess, which was usually figured as an empty vessel waiting to be filled with God's word. Indeed, word-of-mouth reports of her public preaching influenced Edwards's 1641 petition. But Edwards's protest merely prompted Chidley to assume the even more "phallic" power of the pen in defense of Independency. As noted above, she composed *The Justification of the Independent Churches of Christ* as a rebuttal to Edwards's vituperative *Reasons*. Striking back once again, Edwards attacked her by name in *Gangraena*, his "catalog" of separatist "errors": "There is," he wrote, "one Katherine Chidley an old Brownist, and her sonne a young Brownist . . . who not content with spreading their poyson in and about London, goe down into the Country to gather people to them . . . Katherine Chidley and her sons Books (for the mother and the son made them together, one inditing, and the other writing) are highly magnified, and the brasen-faced audacious old woman resembled unto Jael."[60]

Chidley's *The Justification of the Independent Churches of Christ* is an attempt to protect the sphere that recognized her spiritual authority. At eighty-one pages, it is her longest and most comprehensive argument on behalf of the idea that "the Churches of Christ may be truely constituted according to the Scripture, and subsist a certaine time without Pastor and Teacher, and enjoy the power of Christ amongst themselves, having no dependencie upon any other Church or Churches which shall claim Authority or superiority over them."[61] Critics have characterized the text as one that does not offer overtly "feminist" or woman-centered arguments in favor of toleration. Rachel Trubowitz notes that Chidley "wrest[ed] the authority of the press and pulpit away from men like [Thomas] Edwards" and used it to "create a public record of herself and her vision of the world." But she also observes that Chidley used this power to "correct and counter Edwards's anti-female efforts to defame her ministerial authority by systematically proving his paternalistic arguments for centralized church government to be ungodly."[62] Phyllis Mack has claimed that Chidley "made no systematic attempt to counter . . . Edwards's attacks on women although she was tireless in her arguments in every other respect."[63] But Chidley's writings do articulate an explicit connection between the separation of church from state and her own status as a woman writer and religious authority. However, deciphering her rhetorical strategies for making these connections requires the kind of Bible-based hermeneutic that Susan Wiseman advocates. As Wiseman notes, one must identify the ways in which sectarian writers used "biblical precedents" as typologies for authorship and "biblical discourse" as a "structuring rhetoric" in their texts.[64] Utilizing these strategies, Chidley provided meaningful information about herself as a female religious leader of an autonomous community within the two sets of Scripture that she placed on the title page of *The Justification* as a gloss on her main argument.

The first of Chidley's glosses is from 1 Samuel, a text that both records Israelite history from the last years of the era of self-selecting Judges to the establishment of David's kingdom and that details Samuel's own personal history as a prophet-judge. The other is from the Book of Judges, a history of the period preceding the restoration of kingly authority when judges in the persons of faithful men and women were permitted by God to act as agents of divine will. Appearing before Chidley's text, these scriptural passages structure her arguments as a discourse emanating from a politically liberated sphere, for her readers – like Milton's – would recognize that both books were set against a historical backdrop of limited civil government and greater local congregational rule by collectively acknowledged "judges."[65] For instance, the author of Judges describes a period when "there was no king in Israel, but every man did that which was right in his own eyes."[66] Such a vision prepares us for the separatist notion of religious freedom and spiritual equality that Chidley articulates in the section of *The Justification* entitled "An Answer to Mr. Edwards his Booke": "all the Lords people, that are made Kings and Priests to God, have a free voyce in the Ordinance of Election, therefore they must freely consent before there can be any Ordination; and having so consented they may proceed to Ordination."[67] (The book of Samuel was also used as a basis for challenging absolutism in *England's Petition to their King* [1643].[68] The petition notes that "besides nature," there are frequent precedents in the Bible for "even more then defensive resistance of Transcendent Monarcke" in 1 Samuel 14.44, 45 and 23.11 and 12.2.) By alluding to these biblical texts, Chidley implies that England too is at a point in history when absolutism should give way to diffused, autonomous self-rule and consent. Interestingly, the order of her glosses – from 1 Samuel to Judges – reverses the biblical order and suggests that, in 1640s England, the era of judges will succeed the era of kings. Furthermore, both books couch Chidley's arguments in specifically gendered terms, for they discuss Hannah and Deborah, women who acted as judges in a society where kings were not in a position to silence them.

Through Scripture, Chidley not only creates analogues between her Separatism and her authorship, she also enacts the belief that Edwards's attacks on Independency could and must be countered specifically by a woman armed with the new, more public forms of female religious authority arising out of the Independent sphere of the separatist conventicle. In the first gloss, Chidley speaks through a quote by David from 1 Samuel 17.45.[69] As the smaller and weaker David said to Goliath before defeating him with a mere stone, so Chidley, the weaker woman writer and protector of her sphere says to the "philistine" Edwards: "Thou commest unto me with a Sword, and with a Speare, and with a Shield, but I come unto thee in the name of the Lord of Hoasts the God of the armies of Israel, whom thou hast defied."[70] Because the "weakness" of a woman writer is first buttressed by the words of a young and physically "weak" but spiritually mighty male predecessor from the Old Testament, Chidley's readers could understand that when she ends her preface by asking her "Christian Reader" to attribute her un-"Scholerlik" and "plain" style to the "ignorance and unskilfulnesse of the weake Instrument" rather than to any want of "truth" in "the cause" (2), they are intended to comprehend two things. First, while Chidley uses the adjective "weak," as in "weaker vessel," she uses it to modify "instrument" rather than "vessel." This emphasizes a more active image of a female user of tools as opposed to the more passive one of a vessel waiting to be filled. Second, Chidley wishes her audience to understand that the recent attacks on Independent churches, because they empowered weak instruments or women, may be viewed in the context of her allusion to the weak but ultimately triumphant David. In other words, the Bible itself provides a precedent for "weak instruments" to triumph over mightier foes.

But Chidley's use of 1 Samuel refracts in another direction as well. Mack has noted that one of the features that distinguished female "visionaries" from male clergymen in the seventeenth century was women's "location of spiritual transformation and creativity in the mother–child relationship." Chidley's use of this text reminds us that Samuel Chidley had recorded these very words for his mother; and it suggests that Katherine Chidley had consciously authorized herself as a preacher and writer within a private sphere separate from kingly rule by modeling her identity and her relationship with her own son, Samuel, after the biblical Hannah and Samuel. Katherine and Daniel Chidley named their first-born son Samuel rather than Daniel – the name of the father being reserved for Chidley's second-born son. As mentioned earlier, Chidley's first public protest against the state church was her refusal, along with that of six other women, to be "churched" by her minister after childbirth.[71] The biblical Samuel was born as a result of Hannah's prayer for a son and was dedicated by her to a life of religious service; however, Hannah also refused to perform the official church's obligatory postpartum religious rituals until after her baby was weaned. The biblical Hannah drew connections between maternity and speech. She believed that the conception of her son came as a result of her own "petition": "For this child I prayed; and the Lord hath given me my petition which I asked of him" (1 Sam. 1.27). And she associated God's gift of a child with the ability to prophesy what we might call a true "Leveller" vision of future social relations:

my mouth is enlarged over mine enemies ... The LORD maketh poor, and maketh rich: he bringeth low, and lifteth up. He raiseth up the poor out of the dust, and lifteth up the beggar from the dunghill, to set them among princes, and to make them inherit the throne of glory: for the pillars of the earth are the Lord's, and he hath set the world upon them. (I Samuel 2.1, 7, 8)

Both Katherine and Samuel Chidley were officially active in the Leveller party by the 1650s and wrote pamphlets and petitions on its behalf. As early as *The Justification*, Chidley echoes Hannah's Leveller-like messages of spiritual equality and religious self-determination for all:

It is fitter for well-meaning Christians than for ill-meaning Christians [to form churches] for well-meaning Christians be the fittest on the earth to make Churches, and to choose their Officers; whether they be Taylors, Felt-makers, Button-makers, Tent-makers, Shepherds, or Ploughmen, or what honest Trade soever, if they are well-meaning Christians; but ill-meaning Priests are very unfit men to make Churches; because what they build up with one hand, they pull downe with the other. (22–23)

The biblical Samuel was brought to the metropolis of Shiloh and given over to Eli for service to God. As a sign of his profession, his mother presented him annually with an ankle-length mantle such as was worn only by social superiors and by women, over another dress. He was made a prophet, received revelations from God, and issued proclamations exposing the sin of idolatry and urging reformation. Samuel Chidley, too, followed in his parents' footsteps and undertook the pastorship of their separatist Duppa church twenty years after its formation. He assumed his mother's "mantle" by inscribing her words for publication and later by writing pamphlets urging reformation and vigorously opposing all forms of "idolatry" in the churches of England, including the physical edifices of the buildings themselves. In his 1652 tract, *The Dissembling Scot Set Forth in his Colours*, he wrote that God had made his mother an "instrument" to "totally rout all the forces of Mr. Edwards, that great Champion for the Church of England, as may appear by her workes extant in print."[72] In *A Cry against a Crying Sinne* (1652), Samuel signed himself as having written "from [his] mother's house," and he glosses his *The Separatists Answer to the Anabaptists Arguments Concerning Baptism* with a quote from Psalm 116: "Oh Jehovah, surely I am thy servant, I am thy servant, and the son of thine handmaid."[73] Samuel Chidley's lifelong performance of the typological identity bestowed on him by his mother makes it clear that Katherine Chidley's use of 1 Samuel was intended to demonstrate the fact that her authority as a writer was inextricably bound with her authority as a mother-prophetess within a separatist church. Giving birth to Samuel simultaneously licensed her as a religious authority, a writer, and as the maternal wellspring of an autonomous religious community.

The second gloss on the title page of Katherine Chidley's *The Justification* is from the Book of Judges, another book in which a woman is ordained to throw off tyrannical rule. Here Edwards is cast as Sisera, general to the troops of King Jabin, who headed a twenty-year regime of oppression and violence over the Canaanites in Israel, while Chidley takes the part of Jael, the wife of Heber and murderer of Sisera. We might remember that in *Gangraena*, Edwards calls Chidley an "audacious old Jael." Mack has noted the "vilification" of the culturally precarious role of female preacher at work in Edwards's slur upon a woman who was among the "most rational and assertive of all preaching women, who organized debates with ministers, led her own Independent congregation, and wrote extensively on political and social issues."[74] But this was a "vilification" that, as Edwards well knew, Chidley had used to her own ends in its original context of heroism. In the Book of Judges, the prophetess and judge Deborah sent an inspired message to another Israelite, Barak, asking him to assemble a large army and to draw Sisera into captivity. Barak requested that Deborah accompany him, but Deborah consented only with the assurance that Sisera would meet his fate at the hands of a woman. Comprehending his imminent capture, Sisera hid in the tent of Heber and threw himself into the protection of Heber's wife, Jael, but this seeming ally turned out to be Deborah's chosen instrument of liberation. Jael lured Sisera into her tent and into a false sense of security by offering customary acts of hospitality, such as something to drink. Jael also provided the even greater maternal comfort of milk when Sisera asked for mere water. And just before Sisera dropped off to sleep, Jael covered him (in a curious echo of Hannah and Samuel) with a mantle. This was a mantle, however, not of religious authorization but of denunciation and "separation," for she murdered him in his sleep.

Chidley's second gloss reads: "Then Jael, Hebers wife, tooke a naile of the tent, And tooke an hammer in her hand, and went softly unto him, and smote the naile into his temples and fastened it into the ground, (for he was fast asleepe and weary) and so he died" (Judges 4.21). Chidley's quotation of this passage simultaneously suggests two typological scenarios.

In one, she is both Deborah, elected judge by members of her own congregation, and Jael, used by Deborah as her tool. Similarly Chidley converts her authority as a separatist preacher – the private sphere of the "tent" – into the public power of authorship in order to hammer the linchpin of Separation through the paternalistic "head" of a champion for some form of centralized religion. In the other scenario she is a Jael/Hannah-like converter of her son into an amanuensis who will be her phallic, pen-like tool for vanquishing Sisera/Edwards. Through these typologies, Chidley uses the Separatists' license for the physically "weak" but spiritually equal to preach within the private realm of the gathered church as a point of entry into the public sphere of print and debate. Her glosses may not qualify as "systematic" arguments for female empowerment and political theory, but they do make her feminism "readable," as Wiseman would put it. They also structure Chidley's entire argument by framing it as a discourse that is authorized to emerge specifically from a woman through her affiliation with the self-legitimating realm of Separatism. Chidley certainly intended for her biblically literate audience to make the allegorical connections between the biblical history contained in her glosses and the sociopolitical situation of her day. In fact, it was her goal to prove to a skeptical Presbyterian audience that both she and her allegedly illiterate separatist or "mechanic" readers were capable of constructing and deciphering typological and referential systems, and therefore of self-government within an autonomous community. Indeed, her tract was intended to demonstrate that this community was already in place and that it was the private source of her own legitimacy as its authorized public spokesperson. In short, Chidley's writings work to construct that sphere as a "public" but nongovernment-regulated sphere of religious debate in which women were authorized to represent private interests through publication.

Chidley's gendered interest in protecting this sphere is not confined to the title page of *The Justification*. Within the body of her text, she also asserts that a separatist church is the necessary ground for securing one's right to represent private interests in public through the even more overtly political act of petitioning. While she does not mention women *per se*, her arguments have a decidedly antipatriarchal thrust. In his *Reasons against the Independent Government of Particular Congregations*, Edwards claimed that he was first "moved" to write his tract "both against Independent Government" and "against the Toleration of it" when he discovered "Messengers" were being sent from Independent congregations to petition the "honourable House of Commons for a Toleration of some Congregations, to enjoy an Independent Government, and to be exempt from the Government which shall be established by Law" (17). Edwards exhorts the House to "put to [their] hands for the early and timely compounding of this great Controversie about the Church and Church Government." To justify his own attempt to "move and stirre" the Parliament to this task, Edwards distances himself from such self-selected "messengers" by instead assuming the patriarchal authority of the "Father of Families, and the Citizens" (5). These paternalistic figures, he argues, are the only ones licensed to petition or to act as "messengers" to Parliament (5).

In the section of *The Justification of the Independent Churches of Christ* entitled "The Answer to Mr. Edwards his Introduction," Chidley demonstrates that members of Independent congregations have the right to petition because it is granted to them by God, not by government (and hence government cannot revoke it). Developing an early version of contract theory, Chidley claims that citizens recognize and confer legitimacy upon governments; governments do not have the power to recognize and confer legitimacy upon citizens. She criticizes Edwards because he "leaveth it to the Magistrate, not undertaking to determine of himselfe what government shall be set over the Nation, for the bringing of men to God but leaveth it to the consideration of them that have Authority" (3). For this, she compares Edwards to "Amaziah, who bid the prophet Amos to flee away into the Land of Judah, and not to Prophesie at Bethel, the Kings Chappell, and the House of the Kingdome" (3). In other words, Edwards is the idolatrous king who refused to recognize the prophecies of Amos as legitimate, and the Independent petitioners are Amos, the man of low birth who, while not ordained, was still designated a divine prophet. The House of Parliament is compared to the "the King's chappell, and the house of the Kingdome" (3) of Bethlehem, from which Amos was driven by Amaziah in the latter's refusal to hear Amos's petition. The petitioners, Chidley claims, do not need official notice by Parliament to be recognized as legitimate any more than Amaziah's refusal to hear Amos's prophecy did not render that prophecy any less divine. The Separatists' legitimacy is sanctioned by God, and, if Parliament rejects it, then they too will have taken on the identity of Amaziah, the idolatrous king who refuses to hear God's "messenger."

Where Edwards conflates the power of the "House of Parliament" with what Chidley calls the "House of the Kingdome" in order to join church and state, Chidley plays on multiply refracting scriptural uses of the term *house* in order to redraw the lines that shaped social spheres. The state church may be the "King's chappell," but it is not the "Lord's house"; instead, the "house of the Lord" consists of the "seyled houses" of the private churches, many of which gathered in actual homes (4). The Lord's house is to be built outside the sphere of state control and within the privacy of the freely choosing congregation; from within these walls the public voices of women and petitioning messengers will issue – and, as Chidley's own tract illustrates – are issuing. In this way, Chidley makes the right to petition a God-given one that is equally available, if not more so, to the weak and unordained than the strong and mighty.

A WOMAN'S HOME IS HER CASTLE: THE FEMALE LEVELLER PETITIONS

As I noted in the introductory chapter, several scholars have asserted that the spiritual equality between genders practiced by many radical religious sects of the seventeenth century did not develop into a theory of female political equality. To complicate this claim, I will examine a series of later petitions written and presented to Parliament in the late 1640s and early 1650s by Leveller women. Authorship of these petitions is uncertain, yet as both Ludlow and Ian Gentles note, there is strong evidence to suggest that at least one and most likely several were penned either by Chidley herself or at least by someone directly influenced by Chidley's early writings.[75] These petitions take the separatist belief in spiritual equality between genders within the autonomous, self-legitimating sphere of religious choice, as it was developed by Chidley and elaborated later on by Trapnel, to create an early theory of women's rights.

Through their involvement in Leveller politics, Chidley and her son were aligned with individuals who protested the Presbyterians' dominance of Parliament. Leveller activity in this arena was a direct outgrowth of the Independency movement. Presbyterian pleas for state religion, argued the Levellers, were a betrayal of the principle of complete religious toleration. Woodhouse has also called the Levellers "the only genuinely democratic party thrown up by the Puritan revolution," in part for their 1647 *The Agreement of the People*, which argued that power should be transferred from the victorious Parliament and its army to the hands of the people.[76] Ralph Barton Perry has argued that the Levellers "translat[ed] spiritual into political rights," although he did not discuss the degree to which the Levellers may have begun the process of doing so for women as well as for men.[77] More recently, Ann Marie McEntee has argued that democratic Leveller principles were claimed by male and female members alike, even to the point of establishing female Levellers as an effective political collective in their own right.[78] Ann Hughes has identified the ways in which the Levellers pioneered new forms of "identity and agency ... by which a new political movement was imagined, or called into being."⁷⁹ Their strategies for imagining this new movement involved the delineation of a public–private divide that both carved out a private zone of oppositional political autonomy and populated that zone with publicly empowered women. As Hughes writes, "the Leveller image [of the household] does not share the conduct books' assumption that the wife is somehow 'confined' to her home, like a snail, while the 'wider world' was a male preserve."⁸⁰ Instead, in their pamphlets of 1649, Leveller men portrayed themselves as victims of Parliamentary tyranny who were ripped indiscriminately from their wives and children and sent to jail. Their "honest households" were imagined as a "refuge from oppression, yet households were clearly also embedded in a public world" as Leveller women were "forced" to petition Parliament for their husbands' release" (181). Thus, as Hughes concludes, "In these stories, an active public role for women, and a defiant public female voice, was a vital, even essential element" (181).

John Lilburne's *The Free-man's Freedome Vindicated* is a case in point.⁸¹ Written in 1646 to publicize the way in which Lilburne was, as he saw it, "arbitrarily and illegally committed" to prison "by the House of Peeres," Lilburne begins his long tale of government persecution by detailing how he was called out of his bed at 6 o'clock in the morning by an officer who read him a warrant (3). Arguing that there was in fact no "warrant" for the House of Peers to arrest a commoner in a "Criminal cause," Lilburne contended:

I would not in the present case, obey their warrant, nor twenty more of the like nature, but would defend my selfe in my own house (which is my Castle) against all that in such cases they should send unto me, to the death, because they have by the Law, no authority at all to make me dance attendance upon them . . . (3)

Lilburne is, of course, drawing on the legal theories of Sir Edward Coke, whose *Institutes* configured the house as a man's "castle" in order to secure it against "illegal search and seizure."⁸² While representative of a push towards new rights and freedoms, the figure of the home as a man's castle is, without a doubt, permeated by a neopatriarchal notion of the woman as secondary and subordinate. However, in what follows I will discuss the strong possibility that we might trace Leveller petitions designed to maintain the status of these "castles" as a private domain that secured certain "rights" for both men and women back to the writings of Katherine Chidley. As the previous section has shown, Chidley's tracts demonstrated the interest she had in "fortifying" a sphere that was both a "refuge from oppression" and a sponsor of a "defiant public female" voice. And while Hughes doubts that such Leveller wives as Elizabeth Lilburne or Mary

Overton actually penned the petitions attributed to Leveller women, I hope to show that some of the key language and concepts used by Chidley to imagine this space crop up again in these documents.[83]

On May 5, 1649 the so-called "female Leveller petitioners" protested to Parliament the imprisonment of four prominent Leveller men. First, however, the women had had to justify themselves as political agents in the public sphere, just as Chidley had had to justify her own presence as a woman in print. They did so by claiming that they had been legitimated by God.

> Sheweth, that since we are assured of our creation in the image of God, and of an interest in Christ equal unto men, as also of a proportionable share in the freedoms of this commonwealth, we cannot but wonder and grieve that we should appear so despicable in your eyes as to be thought unworthy to petition or represent our grievances to this honourable House. Have we not an equal interest with the men of this nation in those liberties and securities contained in the Petition of Right, and other the good laws of the land? Are any of our lives, limbs, liberties, or goods to be taken from us more than from men, but by due process of law and conviction of twelve sworn men of the neighbourhood? And can you imagine us to be so sottish or stupid as not to perceive, or not to be sensible when daily those strong defenses of our peace and welfare are broken down and trod underfoot by force and arbitrary power?
>
> Would you have us keep in our houses, when men of such faithfulness and integrity as the four prisoners, our friends in the Tower, are fetched out of their beds and forced from their houses by soldiers, to the affrighting and undoing of themselves, their wives, children, and families?[84]

This petition argues that spiritual equality entails "natural" political equality and extends the privilege to women. The right to petition is represented as a further extension of this spiritual equality "within the interest of Christ." Representing themselves as needing to defy conventional conduct manual style codes in order to defend themselves and their families against state intrusion and persecution, the female petitioners claim their right as wives and mothers to leave the violated private sphere of the house and enter the public sphere of debate. These arguments link Leveller writings to Chidley's earlier separatist writings. She too had claimed a right to represent the interests of Independency based on a Hannah-like right to petition, which arose out of her role as mother. She too represented petitioning as a necessary public undertaking for the protection of the private sphere of the "house [of the Lord]."[85] And she too predicated her power to enter into this public political activity on the spiritual equality she enjoyed in the private sphere whose autonomy she sought to defend.

Ludlow and Gentles note, in particular, that a petition circulated on Sunday, April 22, 1649, and printed two days later, bears the signs of having been composed by Chidley. As Gentles speculates, "the petition's preface, emotively egalitarian and richly larded with Biblical allusion, points to Katherine Chidley as its author" ("London Levellers," 292). Although Gentles and Ludlow do not suggest as much, *The Humble Petition of Divers Wel-affected Women* (April 24, 1649) also reflects Chidley's logic. It is addressed "To the Supream authority of this Nation, the Commons assembled in Parliament," and it blasts Parliament for bringing upon itself "those very particulars of tyranny that were complained of in former Rulers, and were the just cause of Gods displeasure against them, and so of their destruction."[86] The petition asks Parliament, "That laying all self-respect and vain affectations of wealth or Greatness aside (wherein true happinesse indeed consists not) you would be pleased to set your selves cordially and sensibly to remove the burthens of the people and settle this common-wealth upon foundations of true freedom" (6). The collective voice of the authors – "Women inhabiting the City of London, Westminster, the Borough of Southwark, Hamlets, and places adjacent" – assumes the subject position of grievously afflicted and sorrowful women who have so little power that they must take steps to secure certain rights: they can no longer "sit in silence, for our oppressions are too many and great for us, we are not able to bear them and live" (3).

The women cannot keep silent because they are "distracted in [their] selves" and they "know not which way to turn." In other words, they portray themselves as conventionally female, with a proclivity to wander. "If oppression makes a wise man mad," they ask, "how is it better to be expected from . . . the weaker vessel?" (4). They are "so over-prest, so over whelmed in affliction," that they cannot "keep to [their] compass, to be bounded" in the "custom" of their "sex." Instead, they must cross the circumference defining that compass, and "address [them]selves to the Publick behalf" (4). But whereas the rhetoric of conduct manuals represented women's "wanderlust" as the reason why they should be confined to their compasses, the petitioners represent it as the reason why they should leave that sphere and enter into public political activity. Furthermore, they represent that wanderlust as originating not in their own "natural" selves but rather in an unnatural political tyranny over the private sphere. Interestingly, the petitioners say that "it is not our custom to address ourselves to this House in the publick behalf," but the next phrase justifies such an address by arguing that "yet considering that we have an equal share and interest with men in the Commonwealth, [then] it cannot be laid waste (as it now is), and not we be the greatest and most helpless sufferers therein" (4). In effect, the petitioners are saying that in spite of the fact that they do not normally address Parliament, they can claim "an equal share and interest with men in the Commonwealth." The implication is that this equal share and interest derives from their customary sphere of the domestic compass and not from Parliament. So while, on the one hand, the act of petitioning Parliament is the public political forum for expressing an equal share and interest, on the other hand, the representation of that naturalized equality links it to the preexisting sphere of the compass. This creates yet another strong connection to Chidley's rationale for petitioning in her *Justification of the Independent Churches of Christ*, where its legitimacy was linked to the preexisting sphere of the separatist church and not to the authority of Parliament's recognition. In keeping, once again, with the doctrine of virginity, the presence of the women in the "public sphere" of oppositional political speech is a result of their prior possession of parity within the "private" sphere of the home and, even more fundamentally, of the self.

Another, even more explicit connection with Chidley's tract follows. The petition contains a lengthy compound sentence describing the many reasons why suffering women must cross the line dividing the compasses. All have to do with some aspect of women's collective position as "weak." Because their children are hungry and the petitions of their husbands, children, brethren, and servants for "upholding the cause of the people in their native freedom and right" have not only gone unanswered, but were met with imprisonment for treason and libel, the women are "resolved in our weak endeavours for the same ends to suffer and perish with them" (4). But, they say, while their endeavors may be "weak," "this we know that for our encouragement and example, God hath wrought many deliverances for severall nations, from age to age by the weake-hand of women" (4). And, as Gentles observes, the examples that the petitioners use to sustain this justification are the very ones that Chidley used to justify the emergence of the weak instrument into authorship ("London Levellers," 292). The petitioners write that "By the counsell and presence of Deborah, and the hand of Jaell, Israel was delivered from the King of Canaan, Sisera, and his mighty Host, Judges 4" (5). The authorizing epigraph from the title page of Chidley's *Justification* is used in the petition to direct the labor of the petitioners. "She," either as the actual author or as the source of literary and political inspiration, becomes the "counsell and presence of Deborah" as an already authorized "judge," while the petitioners become the "hand of Jaell," literally "delivering" the petition that will act as the agent of deliverance for the oppressed groaning under Edwards's old Parliament of Sisera.

Furthermore, in the petition's next sentence, this example of the separatist and specifically religious authorization of the female judge devolves into a second, secular example of how nations were delivered by the "weake-hand of women." This example is specifically Leveller in its focus on the history of usurpation and tyranny by foreign invaders of Britain: "And by the British women this land was delivered from the tyranny of the Danes [who then held the same under the sword, as now is endeavoured by some Officers of the Army]" (5). A third example follows from both the first and the second. It is religious but it also focuses on oppression in the specifically larger sense of British rather than English sufferings under the Church of England: "And the overthrow of Episcopall tyranny in Scotland was first begun by the women of that Nation" (5). (Chidley's last tract, a one-page broadside entitled *Good Counsell to the Petitioners for Presbyterian Government* [1645], urged that Scotland be converted through forms of persuasion offered in missionary work rather than by military conquest.) In the Leveller petition, the religious authorization of the female Separatist is equated with the ability of Scottish women to resist episcopal control. The rationale for Separatism offered by Chidley's tract leads directly to the Leveller petition's rationale for the establishment of "civil society" throughout Britain: each is predicated on precedents of female resistance that should be recognized as legitimate under both biblical *and* secular law.

The petition ends with the lament that the Leveller men who languish in the Tower are in a position where their "enemies" are "absolute Judges over them, masters of all power [who] answer hitherto of all petitions, and directors of all things concerning their tryall" (8). In essence, their judges function in a system with no due process, with no separation of power between prosecutor and jury. Thus, the petitioners close by calling for the true judgment of God to bestow upon them the self-regulating power of the separatist judge. "[W]e trust God will be pleased to deliver from amongst you, in preserving of whom you will preserve your selves, your wives, children and the whole Nation from bondage and misery" (8). Finally, the closing signature of this Leveller women's petition signals the construction of a new kind of political community for women arising out of concepts of spiritual equality: a democratic organization with self-elected representatives in which "all those Women that are Approvers hereof, are desired to subscribe it, and to deliver in their Subscriptions to the women which will be appointed in every Ward and Division to receive the same;

and to meet at Westminster Hall upon Monday the 28th of this instant April 1649, betwixt 8 and 9 o'clock in the fore noon" (8).

As Ludlow has lamented, much scholarship "focusing on the emergence of feminist tracts in the later decades [of the seventeenth century], suggests that female independence of thought and action during this period owes more to Anglican women than to Nonconformists and that sectarian attitudes over the long run were less conducive to changes in women's religious roles than were those of the *laissez-faire* Established Church."[87] In the wake of Ludlow's claim, impressive work on Nonconformist women has been done, such as Mack's extensive study of prophetesses, mentioned previously, and Hilary Hinds's *God's Englishwomen: Seventeenth-Century Radical Sectarian Writing and Feminist Criticisms* (1996), an important study in which she discusses the dialogism that characterizes the writings of sectarian women who derive the authority to write from God. I intend my discussion of Chidley to build on the observations of other critics by focusing more intensively on the set of theological and political ideas with which Chidley was engaged, specifically as they pertain to the construction and regulation of social spaces. Reading Chidley's writings in conjunction with the female Levellers' petitions illustrates how seventeenth-century ideas of spiritual equality and the separation of church from state evolved into more modern feminist concepts of political equality. Whether or not the Leveller petitions I have discussed were composed by Chidley (which is at least a strong possibility) or by someone who drew upon her allusions to Deborah and Jael for a similar purpose, they embody the idea that women could emerge as political agents in a free public sphere of publication and debate, from a private sphere associated with separatist principles of spiritual equality. Because this sphere recognized women as authorities, it faced regulation and suppression; this prompted women to demand that their governors acknowledge the political rights they held by virtue of their status as spiritual equals in the private sphere, not by virtue of the governors themselves. By formulating such concepts, these writings begin to elaborate a feminist theory that, like liberal political theory by men, moves from spiritual to political equality.

Perry writes: "To those [in the seventeenth century] who thought of the church as 'composed of believers all equally privileged,' it seemed evident that 'the state should be composed of men all equally privileged.' The moral law – the law of nature; the covenant of believers – the social compact: thus to reason by analogy from the sphere of religion to the sphere of civil polity was inevitable."[88] In fact, Locke based his liberal concept of natural rights on the idea that men enjoyed spiritual equality. In the second of his *Two Treatises of Government*, he wrote:

Men being all the Workmanship of one Omnipotent, and infinitely wise Maker; All the Servants of one Sovereign Master, sent into the World by his order and about his business, they are his Property, whose Workmanship they are, made to last during his, not one another's pleasure. And being furnished with like Faculties, sharing all in one Community of Nature, there cannot be supposed any such Subordination among us, that may Authorize us to destroy one another, as if we were made for one another uses, as the inferior ranks of Creatures are for ours.[89]

Because he posited that men were God's "property" rather than "one another's," Locke rejected the notion that institutionalized forms of hierarchy were natural. Jeremy Waldron argues: "Locke accorded basic equality the strongest grounding that a principle could have: it was an axiom of theology, understood as perhaps the most important truth about God's way with the world."[90] As Locke himself put it, "all of us lords, all of us kings" (II, 123). Like Puritans, he believed that "the religious judgement of common men remains as a check upon the ruler. Conscience takes precedence of kings and magistrates" (II, 4). Directly echoing Chidley's separatist rhetoric, Locke concludes his second treatise by asserting that "*every Man is Judge for himself*" (476). According to Perry, "it is not necessary . . . that the later historian should build a bridge from puritanism to democracy" because "the puritans themselves built such a bridge, and many of them crossed it, some decades before John Locke."[91] Chidley was an early envisioner of a world "without Kings" present to determine matters of conscience, a world in which women typed as Deborah and Hannah could function as religious equals with men and as popularly recognized "judges." In so doing, she demonstrated that spiritual equality, occurring in a fortified religious sphere that was both separate from the state and conducive to political equality, contributed as much to movements for the liberation of women from the tyranny of gender discrimination as it did to theories about the liberation of men from the hegemony of aristocratic class bias.

A *SUUM* OF ONE'S OWN: THE FORMATION OF A PUBLIC SPHERE IN ANNA TRAPNEL'S *REPORT AND PLEA*

If Katherine Chidley's writings theorize the formation of a private sphere which is said to exist prior to a government's ability to grant or deny access to the "rights" housed within it, and which functions in part as a site from which to critique public political power, then Anna Trapnel tells a vivid story about how she went to jail for her attempts to define and maintain just such a "private" sphere, one that sanctioned and protected voluntarily gathered and politically oppositional "publics." Trapnel was a member of the "Fifth Monarchist" offshoot of the radical Baptist congregation who published several major versions of her prophesies in generically "hybrid" blends of autobiography, songs, prayers, letters, factual narrative, and politically visionary poetry throughout the 1650s.[92] *The Cry of a Stone* came first, in 1654, followed by *A Legacy for Saints* (1654), *Strange and Wonderful Newes from Whitehall* (1654), *Anna Trapnel's Report and Plea* (1654), *A Voice for the King of Saints and Nations* (1658), and an untitled 990-page manuscript reputedly published in 1659.[93] Trapnel's *Report and Plea* is an especially compelling and highly accessible story about a woman's attempt to make a space for herself that is both conducive to public speech and off-limits to the authorities – in short, a "public sphere" as we have come to understand such a concept today through the work of Jürgen Habermas.

While, as Rachel Weil points out, "Habermas has provided a vehicle whereby the narrative of social historians about women's exclusion from the economic sphere has been transformed into a narrative about women's exclusion from the 'public sphere' of political debate and action," it is my argument here that Habermas's interest in a sphere that was both "public" and nonstatist actually provides a highly productive "third way" for understanding the complex and "liminal" space that Trapnel narrates into being in her *Report and Plea*.[94] In *The Structural Transformation of the Public Sphere*, Habermas describes the emergence of a new category of social life, one wherein private people gain the capacity to step forward and to participate in (and create new forms of) cultural representation.[95] Habermas differentiates this new public sphere from both the "representation of courtly-knightly publicity" (9) which preceded it and from the "state that in the meantime had developed, under absolutism, into an entity having an objective existence over against the person of the ruler" (11). The earlier "carriers of representative publicness" had been the church, the prince, and the nobility. But in the eighteenth century a process of disintegration occurred when a series of specific private sites – the table societies in Germany, the salons in France, and the coffeehouses in England – began to serve as sites for critical conversation and debate. In these places, "the coming together of private people into a public was therefore anticipated in secret, as a public sphere still existing largely behind closed doors," but this began the process that would eventually result in the emergence of a free and oppositional public sphere of opinion-sharing and criticism, a sphere wherein "private citizens" could debate public issues (35).

Scholars such as Gordon Schochet have rightly warned against anachronistic impositions of Habermas's terms on earlier eras, however a number of scholars who work in the seventeenth century have demonstrated that Habermas's basic idea proves to be remarkably useful for apprehending the core dynamics of seventeenth-century religious dissent, especially since, by Habermas's own estimation, the eighteenth-century public sphere was anticipated when "religion, as a result of the Reformation's assault on ecclesiastical authority, became a private matter" and "the so-called freedom of religion historically secured the first sphere of private autonomy."[96] As I showed earlier in this chapter, and as Habermas predicted, an "audience-oriented [*publikumsbezogen*] subjectivity" born within "the conjugal family's intimate domain [*Intimitsphaere*]" also "guided" an "understanding of the public use of reason" within this "first sphere" of the private church and, as would salons and coffeehouses, the house-bound conventicle likewise "turned the reproduction of life into something transcending the confines of private domestic authority and becoming a subject of public interest" (24). And finally, the nay-saying chorus that greeted the rise of separatist conventicles in general and their female preachers in particular valorize Habermas's commitment to preserving an historical interest in the formation and defense of a "private" realm defined by its "exclusion from the sphere of the state apparatus" (11).

At the same time, applying Habermas's scheme to the phenomena of independent religion revises as much of Habermas's criteria as it confirms. Because Habermas equates literary production in the seventeenth century with the court aristocracy and its system of court patronage, rather than with the significant numbers of prose pamphlets that were produced by small presses in mid-seventeenth-century England (38), he overlooks the fact that sectarians such as Chidley and Anna Trapnel also fashioned reading audiences through print. And because he argues that it was only the late "seventeenth-century British gentry" who began the process of gravitating towards the "permanent intimacy of the new family life" that extended "the line between the private and public sphere . . . right through the home," he misses the fact that women such as Chidley and Trapnel achieved an "audience-oriented intimacy" within the home-based church not by defining the father as the true "human being" whose "double role" as commodity-exchanger and head of the household conjoined the "private" economic sphere and the "private" realm of the domestic (44–48), but rather by defining both men and women as possessors of a property-in-self *vis-à-vis* the headship of Christ. Thus, while Habermas focuses on the degree to which certain types of actual physical spaces served as the "seedbeds" for a virtual public sphere of discussion and debate in which "privatized individuals" could come together and "censure and defame the proceedings of the State" (59), the overall thrust of Trapnel's *Report and Plea* is to remind her readers that the true "first sphere" "begins" and coheres most fundamentally within the "public sphere" of the private self and its embodiment of a portable, God-given right to religious freedom and oppositional political speech.

Trapnel, like Chidley, founded her arguments on the transformation of the normative wife's private piety into a basis for public speech. In *A Legacy for Saints* she portrays her religious commitment to the Fifth Monarchist sect in "new light" terms as a marriage to Christ: "Christ was mine and I was his."[97] This representation cast her in the role of pious wife in accordance with conduct manual strictures regarding chastity; however, insofar as she used it to segue into the role of Christ himself, it became an alternative version of the "one flesh" doctrine that allowed her to assume the nontraditional role of itinerant prophetess. As Trapnel explains, she was first inspired to prophesy when she heard the minister, Hugh Peter, deliver a sermon on Isaiah 26.20: "Come my people, enter then into thy chambers, and shut thy doors about thee, hide thy self as it were for a little moment, until the indignation be overpast" (2). Peter's sermon referred to the need for outlawed dissenting congregations to escape detection by the government until the "indignation" of persecution be "overpast," but it also conveniently dovetailed with conduct manual instructions for women to "keep to their chambers." After patriarchally "obeying" Peter's sermon, Trapnel began enclosing herself in various chambers – prophesying and fasting while lying in a trance in bed, at one point for twelve days straight.

The "publicness" of Trapnel's "private" performances resulted from the fact that she drew a crowd. In one of the first of her many appearances, she accompanied the Welsh Separatist, Vavasour Powell, to his trial in Whitehall.[98] While waiting in an antechamber, she developed her trademark of going into a trance in order to "sing" such visionary pronouncements as denunciations of Cromwell for being as tyrannical as the monarchical predecessor he had helped to displace. So many people gathered to hear her that she moved to an "ordinary" across the street, enclosed herself in a chamber, retired to her bed, and continued to chant as a "relator" took down her words. Sizable groups are recorded as both gathering at her bedside and congregating outside the chamber's windows, quite literally blurring the distinction between the private and the public. Soon after, she published the recorded version of her songs in the pamphlet, *Strange and*

Wonderful Newes from White-Hall. Trapnel had become a "public" figure even as she inhabited "private" spaces, thus very quickly coming under official scrutiny. Because Cromwell, who had been installed two months earlier as Lord Protector, was a target of Trapnel's criticism, he began to seek "intelligence" about her activities, through Marchamont Needham.[99] Needham reported back as follows:

> There is a twofold [Fifth Monarchist] design about the prophetess Hannah, who played her part lately at Whitehall at the ordinary; one to print her discourses and hymns, which are desperate against your person, family, children, friends and the government; the other to send her all over England, to proclaim them *viva voce*. She is much visited, and does a world of mischief in London, and would do in the country. The vulgar dote on vain prophesies. I saw hers in the hands of a man who was in the room when she uttered them day by day in her trance, as they call it. He promised to lend me them; if he does, I will show you them. They would make 14 or 15 sheets in print.[100]

This information likely contributed to the fact that, after Trapnel took her "show" on the road, she was tried for witchcraft and "aspersing the government" in Cornwall and transported by boat back to London for a stint in Bridewell prison. However, in *Anna Trapnel's Report and Plea*, her self-published version of this trial and her subsequent imprisonment, she turns to the printing press to defend her right to speak within the *public* sphere of the *private* house-bound conventicle, a right which emanated not simply from that sphere but from the individual who enjoyed an even more fundamental "audience-oriented" intimacy with God the father.

Written, as her subtitle indicates, in protest of the "harsh, rough, boisterous, rugged, inhumane and uncivil usage of Anna Trapnel by the justices and people in Cornwall," Trapnel's *Report and Plea* continues the Leveller project of constructing the household as a refuge from the forms of "public" tyrannies exercised by the magistrates while simultaneously embedding that household within a public world constituted through voluntary association. In Trapnel's narrative, however, she assumes the double role of the persecuted political actor and the woman-at-home who is forced to engage authority, thereby creating a complex rhetorical identity to match the complex hybridity of the private–public sphere that her work is composed to defend. What is more, because Trapnel is a female protagonist, her public practice exposes her to the additional charges of witchcraft and whoredom. This added complication, however, inspires her to be even more diligent in her defense of the privacy of the Independent church and to structure that defense around a "doctrine of virginity" whereby she can reclaim the property of her self in the wake of her encounter with the Comus-like corruptions of government authority. To achieve these ends, Trapnel fashions herself in the image of a female Christ, a rhetorical move that endows her private practices with the transcendent patina of public interest and which constructs her own body as a "public sphere" that accompanies her wherever she goes. As she writes,

And though I am a poor inferiour, unworthy to be compared with any of the holy men or women reported of in the Scripture, yet I can say with *Paul*, Through grace I am what I am; and I live, yet not I, but Christ lives in me, and the life that I live, is by the faith of the Son of God, who died and gave himself for a weak handmaid, as well as for a strong *Paul*. (A3)

Trapnel continues her Christological and Pauline argument for privacy by claiming that she was invited to come to Cornwall by friends who wished her to go there in order to "do good to poor souls" (1). Reluctant at first, Trapnel consented after receiving word from the Lord that he "goeth with thee" (2). Along the way, she visited two fellow Fifth Monarchists ("the Lord's Embassadours"), Henry Simpson and Christopher Feake, who had been imprisoned in Windsor Castle for their own itinerant preaching. While walking alone in a field two days after this visit, she reports that she was nearly made hoarse by Satan as he tempted her in the "wilderness." She survived this attempt to silence her after the Lord "refreshed" her with "many Scriptures" as she slept that night.

And [after] hearing the birds cherup in the morning early, about my chamber-window; I had this saying given into my heart, *Thou hearest those birds in their notes and notion which pleaseth thy ear: And doth the great Creator take care of birds, still maintaining them with a supply of food suitable for them, that so they may live, and be lively in their service to man?* (4)

Here, Trapnel sets the stage for recasting preaching as "singing" but she also, like Separatists in general, establishes the understanding that her "church" is one that resides not within a specific locale but within her, even as she roams through fields, homes, and chambers. As she opines, those who attempt to build actual churches out of earthly materials such as "hay, or wood, or gold, or silver" shall live to see their "tottering" "towers and Babels" "shaking and ready to fall" (5). The true "foundation" of Christ's ministry resides not within the "corruptible stuff" of buildings or materials, but within the "servants that build upon him" (5).

Carrying her church on her back, like the tortoise its shell, Trapnel travels, as she puts it, the same "Christ's Circuit" as he did while "taking the earth" (8). As she makes her way across England, moving closer and closer to Cornwall by hopping from one friend's house to another, she is seized with many visions, including one that, like the writings of Chidley, project a world without kings in which, by implication, individuals and voluntarily assembled communities govern themselves. As she writes, Christ's "Kingdom" needs to be "restored to this old Israel, which was the first married wife, as it's recorded in Scripture. And that Judges and Rulers might be as at the beginning, as Moses, and Joshua, and as Samuel, and Gideon, and other faithful ones, as is made mention of in Scripture" (14–15). Trapnel's call for self-governance becomes even more prescient when she next recounts how, in Truro, her popular self-based ministry alerted the local clergy, who, as she tells it, were scared of the threat she posed to their government-sanctioned hold over the ministerial franchise. (Or, as she puts it, they feared "they should lose their fleece.") To shut her down, the constables were brought in to post "listeners at the window," to (unsuccessfully) mount a "Bill of Indictment" against those who housed her, and finally, to call Trapnel to attend the sessions court that next day, so that they could "cast [her] into the Gaol" on the age-old charge of witchcraft (23).

As Christ had been, Trapnel recounts how, the next day, she was followed by "an abundance of all manner of people, men and women, boys and girls" who "mocked and derided" her as she walked towards the courthouse. And when she arrives, amidst crowds, she reiterates her analysis of the ways in which state power colluded with the church to rid the ordained clergy of, as she sees it, their new competition by noting how the clergyman in attendance had violated his Fast Day to be in the court so that he "might keep close to the work of Accusation." Whereas the ordained clergymen who witnessed against Trapnel felt that they were entitled to control access to the pulpit, Trapnel countered that her private preaching was a result of the fact that "The Lord moved me, and gave me leave" (26). The authorities have trouble combating this antinomian claim and find themselves in the position of trying to determine whether or not her activities constitute a public (and hence actionable) crime. As she records the conversation:

Justice Lobb told me I made a disturbance in the town. I asked wherein. He said by drawing so many people after me. I said "How did I draw them?" He said I set open my chamber doors and my windows for people to hear.

A.T. "That's a very unlikely thing, that I should do so, for I prayed the maid to lock my chamber door when I went to bed, and I did not rise in the night sure to open it." I said, "Why may not I pray with many people in the room, as well as your professing woman that prays before men and women, she knowing them to be there; but I know not that there is anybody in the room when I pray. And if you indict one for praying, why not another? Why are you so partial in your doings?"

Justice Lobb. "But you don't pray so, as others."
A. T. "I pray in my chamber."
Justice Trevill. "Your chamber!"
A. T. "Yea, that it's my chamber while I am there, through the pleasure of my friends." (83)

As did the anonymous author of *Tub-Preachers Overturn'd* and the Antinomian Controversy trial transcripts and histories, the Truro magistrates use the conventional language of conduct manuals to express their fear that Anna Trapnel's bed-generated prophesies had exceeded their confinement to her chamber and become public. Yet, what is significant is the fact that, while obviously utilizing the space of the house for its radical public potential, Trapnel nonetheless continues to claim the space of the chamber as her own "private" sphere, even when it was not in actuality her own. She at first denies knowledge that there were even other people in the room, and then defends her right to have them there. In order to both speak "publicly" and to protect her "privacy," Trapnel divorces the notion of a "chamber" from an actual site and relocates it in that "space" of wherever she happens to be. This "space" is a nonspace, a moving "locus" that is not dependent on confinement to an actual piece of property for its claim to chaste and godly female speech. Instead, it is both a *property* and a *practice* which is enclosed within Trapnel herself and which, as a result, allows her to "gad about" and to take on the "public" persona of the religious authority under the guise of the traditional feminine identity as the spatially "enclosed" woman.

Separatists from the state church in this period wanted to dislodge the congregation from its actual location in a physical object or place and relocate it in the home or wherever the members could gather. Trapnel similarly blurs the distinction between home and church by arguing – in keeping with the logic of the tortoise emblem – that one's home/church was wherever one was, hence the protection of privacy could be invoked even when one was outside the home. She asks her judges: "is it a breaking the good behavior to pray and sing?" She tells us that they answered: "no, so [long as] I did at the habitation where I abode." But, as I have shown, Trapnel synthesizes "normative" definitions of woman and home with separatist definitions of the church-within-the-self to redefine "abode" as wherever she happens to be. In this way, Trapnel, like Chidley, articulates a creed whereby sectarian women create alternative norms of femininity, piety, and privacy for the purpose of gaining "public" power that was nonetheless intended to remain immune from state intervention: through alliances with dissenting religious groups and beliefs, female Independents converted the private spaces of the home and their attendant domestic subject positions and discourses into sites for the production of a female public voice. At the same time, they drew upon a doctrine of virginity in order to define that space as private and individualized in order to defend it and its concomitant production of female public speech from state suppression. The "first sphere" secured through the movement for religious freedom turns out to reside ultimately not within houses, fields, barns, or taverns, but within the Marian "house" that the individual provides for the "moving" spirit of Christ.

Although ultimately freed from Truro, Trapnel's continued "singing" resulted in new confrontations with threatened local clergy who had, she claimed, "made [her] their Table and Pulpit Talk" (25). This time, however, the "Governours Troop" were sent on orders from Whitehall to have Trapnel arrested before she could travel on to her next destination. Thus, Trapnel's rhetorical quest at this point in her narrative is to inform her readers that her public preaching never ceased or desisted, even when she was locked into a series of increasingly correctional and juridical (and at times solitary) spaces. After enjoying a kind of "last supper" with her friends in the garden, a "half a Troop of Horse" arrived to arrest her (26–27). She was first carried by horseback to Foy-Town; there, while a prisoner consigned to a chair, she was nonetheless "moved" to convey "Scripture-language" to the "many people" who had come to gaze upon her over a separating wall (28). The next morning, she was placed in a boat but was nonetheless accompanied by "many men and women" who followed her into the room "where she lodged" to hear her prophesy. When she was soon after thrown into a "mans prison" at the military fort of Plymouth, she once again prayed and sang in "her" chamber while attended by the few friends who remained with her. When put on board a ship for Portsmouth, she enclosed herself within her cabin and "prayed and sang" where "she lay" while "the Sea-men were much affected" (35). Indeed, Trapnel contends that she continued her mobile ministry right to London, proclaiming all the while that she wished the "great Councel, and their Protectour" (Cromwell) could "receive a Present sent from the [true] great Protectour, [God] which is indeed, a Protectour of the faithfull, who makes use of silly handmaids to carry his present sometimes" (57). Whereas Cromwell and his men professed themselves to be "builders" of the nation, the great God had presented to them a "cornerstone elect and precious, a sure foundation, an excellent platform for those that are willing to build to purpose" (37–38), and that structure consisted not of actual churches, nor of Whitehall, or of any other edifice of state power. Instead, it was comprised of the ideal of religious freedom as it was enclosed and embodied within the liberated handmaid. Thus, even at

Bridewell, where Trapnel was "shut in alone" in a rat-infested cell, she drew upon the "audience-oriented intimacy" provided for her by her "father," Christ, and lay down upon her "hard damp bed" and commenced singing "the allelujahs song of thanksgiving" (40).

These spaces, watched over as they were by soldiers, still manage to serve as "seedbeds" for a Habermasian public sphere because Trapnel models them on the "home" that every individual is said to inhabit with (and to be inhabited by) God's fatherhood. Even for a woman who was single and hence outside the parameters of the "bourgeois" family, Trapnel's relationship with "God the father" was used to form what Habermas describes as a public sphere of a rational-critical debate in the world of letters within which the subjectivity originating in the interiority of the conjugal family, by communicating with itself, attained clarity about itself.[101] However, as stated, Trapnel's was a notion of "privatized individuals" that did not assume, in Habermas's words, "institutional form in the enclosed space of the patriarchal conjugal family" (46). Instead, it took the noninstitutional form of the enclosed space of the heavenly "family," thereby articulating an additional space for individual female participation.

As part of their critique of the public–private divide, some feminists caution against an "uncritical" "mingling of Habermas with the dominant Anglo-American model": "In academic hands," it is argued, the "political dimensions that [Michel] Foucault relentlessly revealed to us" within the Habermasian public sphere "became attractive, even utopian, and . . . not just masculine . . . but also middle class, white, and stripped of the discipline-and-punish kind of politics that Foucault tirelessly showed us."[102] But I suggest that, in Trapnel's hands, the "public sphere" of the home-based church is strategically represented as a much more "attractive" sphere than the overtly threatening discipline-and-punish kind of politics practiced against her by government authorities. In fact, as her appendix addressed, the authorities try to bring this sphere under their disciplinary and punitive control in part because it was female (and thus bewitched) as well as, in their eyes, "vagabondish."[103] Trapnel counters by uncovering what she sees as the true impetus behind this will to protection. Whereas the governors claimed that they sought to bring the "private" under their punitive control in order to guard the "common good" – Trapnel was a witch who was creating a "disturbance" in the towns she visited and so, to protect citizens from the threat she posed, she had to be silenced – Trapnel retorted that the true motive was to "protect" the monopoly that a privileged elite maintained over a particular service (preaching within a state-sponsored religious sphere, in which ordained clergy were to function as the sole purveyors of "representative publicity") from unregulated competition. Her claim that she could function as a public sphere of one – even in prison, when only God was there to witness her singing – is a repudiation of those who believed that by removing her from the actual spaces of the conventicle, they had succeeded in shutting down her church.

This reading marks a significant departure from Megan Matchinske's contention that 1640s "apocalyptic" writings such as Trapnel's evince a "holy hatred" or "marked aggression toward a perceived enemy" which "appears at a moment when . . . puritanism is helping to model a growing British population into more easily governable state subjects."[104] For Matchinske, this historical "moment" is defined by a "shift" in the "technologies" of religion "from the visible coercion of Church courts and public penance to internalized disciplines of conscience and sect." In order to exist, the secular state came to rely on a population who "internalized" the "power economies" that previously existed outside of them "through 'personal guilt, resistance to perceived authority, etc.'" (352). And to perpetuate this process of "internalization," the state had to "focus the development of powers around these two separate poles" of the "total" and the "singular and private" – the "one, globalizing and quantitative, concerning the population; the other, analytical, concerning the individual" (353). Puritanism, Matchinske argues, aided in this dual effort. While Puritan preachers "were demanding that people look inward for direction, to the particular and the individual, they were also calling for uniformity and sameness in church doctrine, for a broad and national outlook" (353). In this way, they contributed to the "embourgeoisment" of social relations and identities (353). Matchinske points to the minister, Edward Boughen, as a Puritan writer who insisted on "spiritual uniformity" in a global sense; what is more, she cites Anna Trapnel as an example of an apocalyptic writer who in "reiterating God's message to English sinners, emphasizes the singular and private" (353). Matchinske cites the following words from Trapnel's *Cry of a Stone* (1653) as evidence for her claim that apocalyptic writings perpetrated the "dividing practices" needed to maintain order through calls for individual acts of self-regulation:

I will not judge what you doe, when you meet, and speak and pray together . . . but I will follow you into your secret places, your Houses, your callings . . . those that breath after thee Lord, they are searching their secret sins . . . they cannot prosper that cover their secret sins, there is such a covering of secret sins. (353)

By calling for her audience to examine and correct their "secret sins," Matchinske implies, Trapnel forces them to internalize state power by disciplining and punishing themselves.

But Matchinske isolates Trapnel's quote from its larger context to reach this conclusion. The words she quotes from *The Cry of a Stone* are taken from the section subtitled "Here followes some short account of some things she uttered the 14th day, as the Relator could take them in some scattered expressions," and they do not consist of a "singular and personal" recitation of God's disciplinary injunction to a private reading audience. Rather, the subtitle's reference to "scattered" refers to the fact that this section consists of a "mixture" of two messages: the first addressed *from* Trapnel *to* God and the second addressed *from* Trapnel *to* the public head of state, Oliver Cromwell.[105] The readers *overhear* both of these messages but are not their intended audience. What is more, these messages are delivered at a point when Trapnel is defending independent preaching and worship by "mechanics" from attacks by Cromwell, the implied "Lord Protector" of a state-mandated religion. Thus they are intended as a warning to the government to stop disciplining sectarians rather than as an admonition to all individuals to begin disciplining themselves.

Trapnel begins by telling God that she is writing at a time when "the waters are brought so high, that thy poor children are ready to be overwhelmed by them" (36). This refers to the state of affairs under Cromwell's Protectorate when relatively nonelite sectarian critics of the government were imprisoned by higher-ups, just as they had been under Charles I. Trapnel asks God if she may "plead with thee concerning thy saints" who are, she says, "Thine inheritance" (36). Here we can see that she does not constitute the "bourgeois" class as the class of "secular" power. Instead, she describes the "poor" as the politically persecuted – and hence chosen – people. Then Trapnel shifts her subject of address from the "thou" of God to another "thou," an unnamed adversary (Cromwell) to whom she must explain God's ways. She does this by claiming that the "poor man" who God designates as his true elect is not being recognized as such by "thou," Cromwell and his government. While there is, she writes, "a great deale of provision for a poore man," yet "hee will wither and come to nothing; certainly folly will be writ upon his labour," since "Thou [Cromwell] wilt not commend it as a peece or wisdome, Thou wilt not give it a badge of honour, Thou wilt rather put a blot upon it" (36). In other words, rather than allowing sectarians to continue holding their conventicles in peace, Cromwell places them under surveillance and jails them for acts he deems seditious. Cromwell may *claim* that he is "coming to write faire concerning the Palace of the Lord Jesus, and the Glory of that Kingdome," but he and his men "have a veil over their eyes that they cannot see" the fact that God's true saints, "a *Jacob*, a dew, a Lyon [Micah 5.7–8]," are the actual "writer[s]" of the Glory of the Kingdome" (36). Now speaking in God's voice, Trapnel warns Cromwell, "I have but a few names among you, in whom any Name is found, though I have a great many soules" (36). In other words, only a few will come to be recognized as the "true elect" (and Cromwell need not consider himself one of them). Then she shifts again, to speak in her own voice and remind God (the *true* "Lord") that "the poor" are the "Saints" of his "Inheritance" rather than Cromwell – that pretender to the "palace of the Lord" – and the ordained clergymen: "Thou wilt find; Lord, but a few that have kept themselves undefiled from the world, that are pure Religious ones" (36). While there are "many fleshly, nationall, formall religious ones," it is "the poore, fatherlesse and widow" who are the "companions of the pure religious ones" (36). While the "formall religious ones" "think it scorne if one should tell them they are not Religious, they will say you are censorious," but God will tell them, "that they doe not doe that which is pure Religion, that is so before God" (36). And here Trapnel concludes that it is easy to "speak large and high things of Jesus Christ" when one is "in prosperity," however, "to hold out in time of temptation, *that* hath a good report with God" (36; emphasis added).

God saith, *I will judge righteous Judgement*, I will not judge what you doe, when you meet, and speake and pray together, but I will follow you into your secret places, your Houses, your Callings, your Offices, &c. those that breath after thee Lord, they are searching after their secret sins, for thou commest into the heart; they cannot prosper that cover their secret sins; there is such a covering of secret sins, that prosperity flyes from us, and takes wings and flies away. (36)

In other words, God does not bestow sanctification upon one because of one's mode of worship or one's station in life, but because of the state of one's soul. Matchinske reads this as Trapnel "dismissing communal repentance" in favor of a "Puritan" emphasis upon the "singular and private." But put in context, Trapnel's words reveal a tension between two different "Puritan" communities: the ordained clergy and the independent churches. It is her argument that, while the national and formal churches believe that their adherence to a "uniformity" of religious belief across the national spectrum guaranteed them righteousness, it is in actuality those in the state of poverty (the meek) who have as much a chance – even more – of earning God's "inheritance." Trapnel thereby links Protestantism's belief that one's inner state matters more than outward pomp and ceremony to sectarians' religious (and in some cases economic) disenfranchisement, not merely to individual acts of "self-regulation." In fact, she defends people's right to act in ways that were traditionally deemed "unregulated" and is insisting that these actions are in accordance with rather than in defiance of God's will. In conclusion, her words represent a *critique* of the more "bourgeois" or state-enforced champions of Presbyterian Puritanism and other forms of centralized or "uniform" religion. In Trapnel's scheme, God's entry into one's "house" and his ability to judge one as a "private" individual is meant to replace a "state" of affairs wherein, as she knew all too well, soldiers could enter one's house to judge one as a witch who had offended the "national and formal" religion. But more importantly, for Trapnel, those who are trying to "cover their secret sins" do not comprise the readership that she intends to discipline with her holy wrath, rather it consists of the governors who, according to Trapnel, are trying to cover their will to power beneath a veil of care and righteousness. Trapnel certainly does invoke a world of individual "self-regulating judges," but her idea, like Chidley's, of "regulation" is a world in which women are licensed to act in ways that radically depart from standard norms. In this deregulated world, all citizens, including women and members of other subordinate groups, would gain access to that which, they argue, they are legally entitled – to religious forms of authority traditionally denied them on the grounds that they were not capable of the self-regulation needed to council others in the ways of God.

If Foucauldians see the private subjectivities produced by (and in turn producing) the separation of church and state as one point of origin for a new Enlightenment-based model of internalized coercion, Anne Phillips offers an entirely different critique, viewing the privatization of something that was previously public as the cause of its ensuing irrelevance.[106] She argues that liberalism's emphasis upon "private spaces within which people can get on with their own chosen affairs and a public realm ordered around a set of minimum shared presumptions" means that "difference" gets "relegated" to a "private world" in which "variations" and "peculiarities" are kept "secret" and hence neutralized (480). As her primary example, she cites religious separatism, arguing that "The separation of church from state has long been considered the solution to the problems of religious difference, but it achieves this by requiring all religions to adopt a similarly self-denying ordinance that will limit the relevance of religious precepts to practices in the private sphere" (480). In other words, where Matchinske understands the "private" and the "individual" to be just another, even more virulent form of state-sponsored control which the individual delusionally experiences as freedom, Phillips views it as an all too autonomous realm that ceases to be significant since "no one else" can "see" it. Whereas Matchinske fails to question whether or not Trapnel's own flamboyant performances really constitute the actions of a self-regulating individual, Phillips fails to ask, "secret from whom?" and "what is the alternative?" Trapnel's text provides implicit answers to those questions. It reveals its protagonist to be involved in social networks that provided her with new modes of "publicity" and a sense of "relevance" in spite of or precisely because of her customary "difference" as a social nobody. As she represents them, Trapnel's performances were "public" and "relevant" to those who wished them to be. If the public ministers felt that they had become less relevant because fewer people were looking at them, the alternative is represented as being one in which someone is granted the force-backed means by which to compel the public's gaze. "Secrecy" was not tantamount to being hidden from a social world – even a world of one was deemed "relevant" – anymore than it was synonymous with self-suppression. Rather, "secrecy" meant invisibility from an official instrument that itself wanted to see, regulate, and suppress that which departed from its standardizing codes and hence threatened its hegemony.

This did not mean that women did not seek publicity within spheres other than the private church. Indeed, as we saw earlier, Chidley and the Leveller petitioners argued that their worth lay not within their public selves but within their status as "individuals" who were endowed with certain public rights and a sense of "relevance," which devolved from a prior and independent realm of privacy. This was an argument made by the nonelite, the implication being that waiting on the powerful to recognize and legitimize the "relevance" of the weak might have meant waiting for an awfully long time. In the next chapter Elizabeth Poole will enter and exit the political sphere of Whitehall with her "self" intact only because, in the end, she was one of the few willing to grant herself any sense of relevance at all.

NOTES

1. Thomas Carew, "Coelum Britannicum," in David Lindley, ed., *Court Masques* (Oxford: Oxford University Press, 1995), pp. 166–193.
2. John Milton, "Comus," in Roy Flannagan, ed., *The Riverside Milton* (Boston: Houghton Mifflin, 1998), pp. 109–171, quote from pp. 123–124.
3. J. Andrew Hubbell, "Milton's Re-Formation of the Masque," in Charles W. Durham and Kristin Pruitt McColgan, eds., *Spokesperson Milton: Voices in Contemporary Criticism* (Selinsgrove, PA: Susquehanna University Press, 1994), pp. 193–205, quote from p. 198.
4. James Holstun, *Ehud's Dagger: Class Struggle in the English Revolution* (London: Verso, 2000), p. 270.
5. Murray Tolmie, *The Triumph of the Saints: The Separate Churches of London, 1616–1649* (Cambridge: Cambridge University Press, 1977), p. 33.

6. Joan B. Landes, "Introduction," in Joan B. Landes, ed., *Feminism: The Public and the Private* (Oxford: Oxford University Press, 1998), pp. 1 and 2.
7. Paula Backscheider, "Introduction," in Paula Backscheider and Timothy Dykstal, eds., "The Intersections of the Public and Private Spheres in Early Modern England," *Prose Studies* 18, 3 (December 1995), 1–32.
8. See, for example, Gerda Lerner, *The Creation of Patriarchy* (Oxford: Oxford University Press, 1986); Seyla Benhabib and Drucilla Cornell, eds., *Feminism as Critique: On the Politics of Gender* (Minneapolis: University of Minnesota Press, 1987); Joan Scott, *Gender and the Politics of History* (New York: Columbia University Press, 1988); Susan Staves, *Married Women's Separate Property in England, 1660–1833* (Cambridge: Harvard University Press, 1990); Susan M. Reverby and Dorothy O. Helly, ed., *Gendered Domains* (Ithaca: Cornell University Press, 1992); Dena Goodman, "Public Sphere and Private Life," *History and Theory* 31 (1992); Linda Kerber, "Separate Spheres, Female Worlds, Woman's Place," and Amanda Vickery, "Shaking the Separate Spheres: did Women really descend into graceful Indolence?," in *Times Literary Supplement* (March 12, 1996).
9. Jean Bethke Elshtain, *Public Man, Private Woman: Women in Social and Political Thought* (Princeton: Princeton University Press, 1981), p. 202.
10. H. Radest, "The Public and the Private: An American Fairy Tale," *Ethics* 89 (1979), 289–291.
11. Joan Kelly, "The Doubled Vision of Feminist Theory," in *Women, History, and Theory: The Essays of Joan Kelly* (Chicago: University of Chicago Press, 1984), p. 59.
12. Nancy Fraser, "What's Critical about Critical Theory?: The Case of Habermas and Gender," in Benhabib and Cornell, eds., *Feminism as Critique*, pp. 40–56, and quoted in the "Introduction," p. 7.
13. Catherine MacKinnon, *Toward a Feminist Theory of the State* (Cambridge, MA: Harvard University Press, 1989).
14. Backscheider, "Introduction," p. 17.
15. Timothy Dykstal in Backscheider and Dykstal, "Intersections of the Public and Private Spheres," p. 32.
16. Carole Pateman, *The Disorder of Women: Democracy, Feminism and Political Theory* (Stanford, CA: Stanford University Press, 1989).
17. Holstun, *Ehud's Dagger*, pp. 288 and 279.
18. Backscheider, "Introduction," p. 12.
19. See Suzanne W. Hull's *Chaste, Silent and Obedient: English Books for Women: 1475–1640* (San Marino: Huntington Library, 1982); Leonard Tennenhouse and Nancy Armstrong, eds., *The Ideology of Conduct Manuals: Essays in Literature and the History of Sexuality* (London: Methuen, 1987); Suzanne Trill, Kate Chedgzoy, and Melanie Osborne, eds., *Lay by your Needles Ladies, take the Pen: Writing Women in England, 1500–1700* (London: Edward Arnold, 1997).
20. Henrie Smith, *A Preparative to Marriage* (London, 1591), p. 79.
21. William Gouge, *Of Domestic Duties*, rev. edn (London, 1634), pp. 289–291.

22. Edmund Tilney, *The Flower of Friendship: A Renaissance Dialogue Contesting Marriage* (Ithaca: Cornell University Press, 1992), p. 137.
23. Edward Reyner, *Consideration Concerning Marriage* (London, 1657), p. 7.
24. Peter Stallybrass, "Patriarchal Territories: The Body Enclosed," in Margaret Ferguson *et al.*, eds., *Rewriting the Renaissance* (Chicago: University of Chicago Press, 1986), p. 127.
25. Richard Braithwaite, *The Englishman and English Gentlewoman: Both in One Volume Couched*, third volume (1641), p. 294.
26. Smith, *Preparative to Marriage*, p. 79.
27. Braithwaite, *Englishman and English Gentlewoman*, p. 349. Henry Wotton's *Elements of Architecture* (first published in 1624, reissued in 1650, and included in *Reliquiae Wottonianae*) lists "doors, windowes, stair-cases, chymnies, or other *conducts*" as "in-lets, or outlets" of "men and light" to which "belong two generall cautions." The first was "that they be as few in number and as moderate in dimension, as may possibly consist with other due respects: for in a word, all *openings* are *weaknings*" (pp. 244–245). This treatise also describes the house as "Mans proper Mansion House and Home" and his own "private Princedom" (p. 271).
28. Sara Mendelson and Patricia Crawford, *Women in Early Modern England* (Oxford: Clarendon Press, 1998), p. 208.
29. Anon., *Tub-Preachers Overturn'd* (London, 1647), p. 1.
30. Tolmie, *Triumph of the Saints*, pp. 28–49. See also Geoffrey F. Nuttall's *Visible Saints: The Congregational Way, 1640–1660* (Oxford: Basil Blackwell, 1957); Benjamin Hanbury's *Historical Memorials relating to the Independents, or Congregationalists: from their rise to the restoration of the Monarchy, AD MDCLX*, 3 vols. (London: Fisher, Son, & Co., and Jackson & Walford, 1841); Patrick Collinson's *The Religion of Protestants: The Church in English Society, 1559–1625* (Oxford: Clarendon Press, 1982); and John Brown's *History of Congregationalism and Memorials of the Churches in Norfolk and Suffolk* (London: Jarrold & Sons, 1877).
31. Patricia Crawford, *Women and Religion in England, 1500–1720* (London: Routledge, 1993), pp. 119–159.
32. Anon., *A Spirit Moving in the Women Preachers* (London, 1645), p. 5.
33. Tolmie, *Triumph of the Saints*, p. 8.
34. Henry Jacob, *Confessions and Protestations of the Faith of Certaine Christians* (London, 1616), quoted in Tolmie, *Triumph of the Saints*, p. 14.
35. Published London, 1641.
36. Anon., *Spirit Moving in the Women Preachers*, p. 5.
37. John Goodwin, *Independencie Gods Veritie* (London, 1647), pp. 7–8.
38. Samuel Chidley, *Thunder from the Throne of God against the Temples of Idols* (London, 1653). Thomas Edwards's *Gangraena* (London, 1645) reports that Katherine Chidley herself voiced this opinion in a debate with William Greenhill in Stepney (p. 79).
39. Dorothy P. Ludlow, "'Arise and be doing': English 'Preaching' Women 1640–1660," unpublished dissertation, Indiana University, 1978. Hence, she

notes, "the indiscriminate sneers at 'catechizing women' in the family and 'prattling hus-wives' in the pulpit" (95–96) in such tracts as the anonymously written *Spirit Moving in the Women Preachers* (pp. 3–5), John Taylor's *The Brownists Conventicle* (London, 1641, pp. 2–3), and John Vickers's *The Schismatick Sifted* (London, 1646, p. 34).

40. Crawford, *Women and Religion in England*, pp. 119–120.
41. Anon., *A Discovery of Six Women Preachers* (London, 1641).
42. Tolmie, *Triumph of the Saints*, p. 14.
43. Ibid., p. 15.
44. Ethyn Morgan Williams, "Women Preachers in the Civil War," *Journal of Modern History* 1, 4 (December 1929), 561–579, quote from p. 563.
45. Crawford, *Women and Religion in England*, pp. 126–127.
46. Thomas Edwards, *Reasons against the Independent Government of Particular Congregations* (London, 1641).
47. Williams, "Women Preachers in the Civil War," p. 563.
48. Ibid.
49. Dorothy Ludlow, "Shaking Patriarchy's Foundations: Sectarian Women in England, 1641–1700," in Richard L. Greaves, ed., *Triumph Over Silence: Women in Protestant History* (Westport, CT: Greenwood Press, 1985), pp. 93–123, quote from p. 97.
50. Williams, "Women Preachers in the Civil War," p. 564.
51. Ibid.
52. Thomas Case, *Spiritual Whoredom Discovered in a sermon before the House of Commons, 26th May 1647* (London, 1647), p. 34.
53. Katherine Chidley, *The Justification of the Independent Churches of Christ Being an Answer to Mr. Edwards his Booke which he hath written against the government of Christ's Church* (London: William Larner, 1641); *A New-Yeares Gift to Mr. Thomas Edwards; That he may breake off his old sins, in the old yeare, and begin the New Yeare, with new fruits of Love, first to God, and then to his Brethren* (London, January 2, 1645); and *Good Counsell to the Petitioners for Presbyterian Government. That they may declare faith before they build their Church* (London, 1645).
54. Lichfield Joint Record Office, Lichfield Diocesan Records, Visitation Reports (1626). For information on "churching," see Louis Schwartz, "'Spot of child-bed taint': Seventeenth-Century Obstetrics in Milton's Sonnet 23 and Paradise Lost 8.462–78," *Milton Quarterly* 27, 3 (October 1993), 98–109, with special reference to pp. 101–102.
55. Samuel Chidley, *A Christian Plea for Christians Baptisme* (London, 1643); *A Christian Plea for Infants Baptisme* (London, 1644); *The Evening-Star Appearing to the Saints, directing them to celebrate their Holy Rest* (London, 1650); *The Separatists Answer to the Anabaptists Arguments Concerning Baptism* (London, 1651); *A Cry Against a Crying Sinne* (London, 1652); *The Dissembling Scot Set Forth in his Colours* (London, 1652); *Clothing for the Naked Woman, or the Second Part of the Dissembling Scot Set Forth in His Colours* (London, 1652); *Thunder from the Throne of God* (London, 1653); *Bells Founder Confounded*

(London, 1653); *A Remonstrance to the Valiant and Well Deserving Souldier* (London, 1653); *An Additional Remonstrance* (London, 1653); *A Remonstrance to the Creditors of the Common-Wealth of England* (London, 1653); *A Christian Plea against Christmass* (London, 1656); *To the Parliament of the Commonwealth of England* (London, 1657).

56. Thomas Edwards, *Reasons against the Independent Government of Particular Congregations* (London, 1641).
57. John Smyth, *Parallels, Censures, Observations Aperteyning to Three Several Writings* (Amsterdam, 1609); Henry Jacob, *A Confession and Protestation of the Faith of Certaine Christians in England* (Amsterdam, 1616); John Robinson's *A Justification of Separation from the Church of England* (London, 1639); John Goodwin, *Imputatio Fidei* (London, 1642); Roger Williams, *Bloody Tenent of Persecution* (London, 1644). Other protoleration tracts from this period include the anonymous *The Ancient Bounds* (London, 1644); *A Paranetic for not loose but Christian Liberty* (London, 1644); *The Arraignment of Persecution* (London, 1644); Samuel Richardson, *Necessity of Toleration* (London, 1644); and John Robinson's *Liberty of Conscience* (London, 1644).
58. Ludlow, "'Arise and be doing,'" p. 82.
59. See the title pages to Anne Clifford, *The Diary of the Lady Anne Clifford 1590–1676* (Boulder, CO: Aardvark Press, 1997), p. i, and Margaret Cavendish, *True Relation of My Birth, Breeding, and Life*, in Elspeth Graham *et al.*, eds., *Margaret Cavendish: Her Own Life* (London: Routledge, 1989), p. 87.
60. Edwards, *Gangraena*, p. 170.
61. Chidley, *Justification*, pp. 3–4.
62. Rachel Trubowitz, "Female Preachers and Male Wives," in *Pamphlet Wars: Prose in the English Revolution*, ed. James Holstun (London: Frank Cass, 1992), p. 116.
63. Phyllis Mack, *Visionary Women: Ecstatic Prophecy in Seventeenth-Century England* (Berkeley: University of California Press, 1992), p. 112 n.
64. Susan Wiseman, "Unsilent Instruments and the Devil's Cushions: Authority in Seventeenth-Century Women's Prophetic Discourse," in *New Feminist Discourses*, ed. Isobel Armstrong (London: Routledge, 1992), p. 177. Wiseman writes to rebut the idea that female prophets spoke "the semiotic," as claimed by Christine Berg and Phillipa Berry in "'Spiritual Whoredom': An Essay on Female Prophets in the Seventeenth Century," in Francis Barker *et al.*, eds., *1642: Literature and Power in the Seventeenth Century* (Colchester: University of Essex Press, 1981), pp. 39–54.
65. Mary Ann Radzinowicz, "'In those days there was no king in Israel': Milton's Politics and Biblical Narrative," *Yearbook of English Studies* 21 (1991), 242.
66. Judges 17.6 (King James Bible, New York: Meridian, 1974).
67. Presbyterians used the Book of Judges to argue against religious Independency, because in this book the people living without kings had difficulty understanding the concept of an *invisible* king (God) and hence became vulnerable to idolatry. For example, Jeremy Taylor's *A Collection of Offices on Forms of Prayers in Cases Ordinary and Extraordinary* (London, 1658)

quotes Judges 17.6 and 21.25 along with Deuteronomy 12.8 to argue that "When Judges were instead of Kings," then "every man did what was right in his own eyes, but few did what was pleasing in the eyes of the Lord" (p. 2).
68. Anon., *England's Petition to their King* (London, 1643).
69. This quote from I Samuel appears on the title page of Katherine Chidley's *Justification of the Independent Churches of Christ*.
70. This analogy between Chidley and Edwards and David and Goliath is invoked even more explicitly by Chidley in the main section of *The Justification*, "An Answer to Mr. Edwards his Booke":

> "Mr. Edwards," she writes, "understanding that you are a mighty Champion, and now mustering up your mighty forces (as you say) and I apprehending they must come against the Hoast of Israel, and hearing the Armies of the Living God so defied by you, could not be withheld, but that I [like David] (in stead of a better) must needs give you the meeting." (1)

For a discussion of Chidley within the larger context of sectarian women's use of tropes of weakness to denote strength, see Hilary Hinds, *God's Englishwomen: Seventeenth-Century Radical Sectarian Writing and Feminist Criticisms* (Manchester: Manchester University Press, 1996), pp. 71, 90, 95–96, and 159–161.

71. Ludlow, "Arise and be Doing," p. 85.
72. Chidley, *Dissembling Scot*, p. 6. Samuel Chidley's ideas about baptism oppose the Baptist claim that voluntary association is best expressed through an adult's right to choose to be baptized, as opposed to the parent's right to impose affiliation on a child through infant baptism. In other words, he exercises his own religious authority by accepting his mother's religious authority and the "mantle" of Separatism that she placed upon him.
73. Chidley, *Cry Against a Crying Sinne*, title page and p. 24.
74. Mack, *Visionary Women*, p. 120.
75. Ludlow, "Arise and be Doing," pp. 120–121; Ian Gentles, "London Levellers in the English Revolution: The Chidleys and their Circle," *Journal of Ecclesiastical History* 29, 3 (1978), quote from p. 292.
76. A. S. P. Woodhouse, *Puritanism and Liberty* (London: J. M. Dent, 1974), p. 17. Woodhouse also reprints the Levellers' first *Agreement of the People*, dated November 3, 1647, on pp. 443–445.
77. Ralph Barton Perry, *Puritanism and Democracy* (New York: Vanguard Press, 1944), p. 358.
78. Ann Marie McEntee, "'The [un]civill-sisterhood of oranges and lemons': Female Petitioners and Demonstrators, 1642–53," in Holstun, ed., *Pamphlet Wars*, pp. 92–111.
79. Ann Hughes, "Gender and Politics in Leveller Literature," in Susan D. Amussen and Mark A. Kishlansky, eds., *Political Culture and Cultural Politics in Early Modern England* (Manchester: Manchester University Press, 1995), pp. 162–188, quote from p. 165. See also Margaret George, "Leveller Husband/Leveller

Wife," in her *Women in the First Capitalist Society: Experiences in Seventeenth-Century England* (Urbana: University of Illinois Press, 1988), pp. 69–91.
80. Hughes, "Gender and Politics in Leveller Literature," p. 181.
81. London, 1646.
82. See Elizabeth Tuttle, "Biblical Reference in the Political Pamphlets," in David Armitage, Armand Himy, and Quentin Skinner, eds., *Milton and Republicanism* (Cambridge: Cambridge University Press, 1995), pp. 63–81, and William Haller and Geoffrey Davies's introduction to *Leveller Tracts 1647–1653*, vol. 1 (New York: Columbia University Press, 1944), pp. 43–47.
83. Hughes, "Gender and Politics in Leveller Literature," pp. 170–171.
84. *A Petition of Women, Affecters and Approvers of the Petition of Sept. 11, 1648* (London, 1649).
85. Chidley, *Justification*, p. 6.
86. *The Humble Petition of Divers Wel-affected Women* (London, 1649), p. 5.
87. Dorothy P. Ludlow, "Shaking Patriarchy's Foundations: Sectarian Women in England, 1641–1700," in *Triumph over Silence Women in Protestant History*, ed. Richard L. Greaves (Westport, CT: Greenwood Press, 1985), pp. 94–95. In her footnote to this claim, Ludlow cites Catherine Smith, "Jane Lead: The Feminist Mind and Art of a Seventeenth-Century Protestant Mystic," in Rosemary Ruether and Eleanor McLaughlin, eds., *Women of Spirit: Female Leadership in the Jewish and Christian Traditions* (New York: Simon & Schuster, 1979), pp. 184–203, the entirety of Hilda Smith, *Reason's Disciples: Seventeenth-Century Feminists* (Urbana; University of Illinois Press, 1982), and Joan K. Kinnaird, "Mary Astell and the Conservative Contribution to English Feminism," *Journal of British Studies* 19 (1979), 53–75.
88. Perry, *Puritanism and Democracy*, p. 67. For his quotes, Perry relies on Woodhouse, *Puritanism and Liberty*, intro., pp. 64, 69, 75, 76, 88 and *The Solemn Engagement of the Army* (June 5, 1647) contained in Woodhouse's appendix, pp. 401–403. He also relies on William Ames's *Conscience* (1639) in which, as he claims, Ames "identified natural law with the moral law implanted in every man, discernible by reason or 'natural light,' and defining the principles of civil welfare" (p. 67).
89. John Locke, *Two Treatises of Government* (New York: New American Library, 1960), vol. II, p. 4.
90. Jeremy Waldron, *God, Locke, and Equality: Christian Foundations in Locke's Political Thought* (Cambridge: Cambridge University Press, 2002), p. 6.
91. Perry, *Puritanism and Democracy*, pp. 358–359.
92. For a useful overview of Trapnel's life, see Hilary Hinds's introduction to Trapnel's *Cry of a Stone* (London, 1654; Tempe: Arizona Center for Medieval and Renaissance Studies, 2000), pp. xiii–xlvii.
93. Anna Trapnel, *Anna Trapnel's Report and Plea* (London, 1654); *Cry of a Stone; A Legacy for Saints* (London, 1654); *Strange and Wonderful Newes from White-Hall* (London, 1654); *A Voice for the King of Saints and Nations* (London, 1658); "Untitled" (1659) (see *English Historical Review* 26 [1911] for bibliographical notes on this manuscript). For critical discussions of Trapnel, see C. Burrage,

"Anna Trapnel's Prophecies," *English Historical Review* 26, 5; Nigel Smith, *Perfection Proclaimed: Language and Literature in English Radical Religion 1640–1660* (Oxford: Clarendon Press, 1989), pp. 45–47, 49–53, 86–90; Stevie Davies, *Unbridled Spirits: Women of the English Revolution, 1640–1660* (London: Women's Press, 1988), pp. 150–180; Elaine Hobby, *Virtue of Necessity* (London: Virago, 1988); Megan Matchinske, "Holy Hatred: Formations of the Gendered Subject in *English Apocalyptic Writing, 1625–1651*," *ELH* 60 (1993), 349–377; Susan Wiseman, "Unsilent Instruments and the Devil's Cushions: Authority in Seventeenth-Century Women's Prophetic Discourse," in Isobel Armstrong, ed., *New Feminist Discourses* (London: Routledge, 1992), pp. 176–196; Kate Chedgzoy, "Female Prophecy in the Seventeenth-Century: The Instance of Anna Trapnel," in William Zunder and Suzanne Trill, eds., *Writing and the English Renaissance* (London: Longman, 1996), pp. 238–254; Holstun, *Ehud's Dagger*, pp. 257–304.

94. Rachel Weil, *Political Passions: Gender, the Family and Political Argument in England, 1680–1714* (Manchester: Manchester University Press, 1999), p. 10. Weil has in mind Joan Landes, *Women in the Public Sphere in the Age of the French Revolution* (Ithaca: Cornell University Press, 1988); Dorinda Outram, "Le Langage male de la vertu: Women and the Discourse of the French Revolution," in Peter Burke and Roy Porter, eds., *The Social History of Language* (Cambridge: Cambridge University Press, 1987); and Dena Goodman, *Republic of Letters: A Cultural History of the French Enlightenment* (Ithaca: Cornell University Press, 1994). See also *Feminists Read Habermas: Gendering the Subject of Discourse*, ed. Johanna Meehan (New York: Routledge, 1995) for essays that are both critical and appreciative.

95. Jürgen Habermas, *The Structural Transformation of the Public Sphere*, trans. Thomas Burger and Frederick Lawrence (Cambridge, MA: MIT Press, 1991).

96. Gordon Schochet, "Vices, Benefits, and Civil Society: Mandevelle, Habermas, and the Distinction between Public and Private," in Backscheider and Dykstal, "Intersections of the Public and Private Spheres," pp. 245–269; Habermas, *Structural Transformation*, p. 11. For scholars who address the idea of a public sphere in mid-seventeenth-century England, see David Zaret, "Religion, Science, and Printing in the Public Spheres in Seventeenth-Century England," in Craig Calhoun, ed., *Habermas and the Public Sphere* (Cambridge, MA: MIT Press, 1992), pp. 212–235; Joad Raymond, "Introduction: Newspapers, Forgeries, and Histories" and "The Newspaper, Public Opinion, and the Public Sphere in the Seventeenth Century," *Prose Studies* 21, 2 (August 1998); David Norbrook, "*Areopagitica*, Censorship, and the Early Modern Public Sphere," in Richard Burt, ed., *The Administration of Aesthetics: Censorship, Political Criticism, and the Public Sphere* (Minneapolis: University of Minnesota Press, 1994), pp. 3–33; Sharon Achinstein, "Woman on Top in the Pamphlet Literature of the English Revolution," *Women's Studies* 24 (1994), 131–163 and *Milton and the Revolutionary Reader* (Princeton: Princeton University Press, 1994); Holstun, *Ehud's Dagger*, pp. 269–270; and Arthur F. Marotti and Michael D. Bristol,

eds., *Print, Manuscript and Performance: The Changing Relations of the Media in Early Modern England* (Columbus: Ohio State University Press, 2000).
97. Trapnel, *Legacy*, p. 2.
98. Trapnel, *Strange and Wonderful Newes from White-Hall*.
99. Hinds, introduction to *Cry of a Stone*, pp. xvii–xviii.
100. *Calendar of State Papers: Domestic*; Marchamont Needham to the Protector, 7 February 1654.
101. Habermas, *Structural Transformation*, p. 51.
102. Backscheider, "Introduction," p. 7.
103. Trapnel, *Report and Plea*, Appendix entitled, "A Defiance to all Reproachfull, scandalous, base, horrid, defaming speeches," pp. 49–59.
104. Matchinske, "Holy Hatred," pp. 349–50. Matchinske's more recent book-length study, *Writing, Gender and State in Early Modern England* (Cambridge: Cambridge University Press, 1998), pp. 127–155, develops an argument about "gender formation in English apocalyptic writing" through Lady Eleanor Davies's writings rather than those of Trapnel.
105. Trapnel, *Cry*, pp. 35–38.
106. Anne Phillips, "Dealing with Difference: A Politics of Ideas or a Politics of Presence?," in Landes, *Feminism*, pp. 475–495.

3

Cure for a diseased head: divorce and contract in the prophecies of Elizabeth Poole

> We cannot free the Lady that sits here
> In stony fetters fixt, and motionless;
> Yet stay, be not disturb'd, now I bethink me,
> Some other means I have which may be us'd,
> ...
> There is a gentle Nymph not farr from hence,
> That with a moist curb sways the smooth Severn stream,
> Sabrina is her name, a Virgin pure
> > The Attendant Spirit, *Comus* (The Scene changes to a Stately Palace)

> I having the gift of faith upon me for her cure, was thus to appeal to the person on the other hand, that he should improve his faithfulnesse to the Kingdome, by using diligence for the cure of this woman, as I by the gift of faith on me should direct him.
> > Elizabeth Poole, *A Vision Wherein is Manifested the Disease and Cure of the Kingdome*

> I cannot deny my hand, said she, to him that hath my heart.
> > Lady Deletia in *The Contract* by Margaret Cavendish (1656)

> when he forgot his subordination to divine Fatherhood and headship; thinking he had begotten you a generation to his own pleasure and taking you a wife for his own lust, thereby is the yoak taken from your necks
> > Elizabeth Poole, *A Vision Wherein is Manifested the Disease and Cure of the Kingdome*

As in *Comus*, our scene shifts now to a stately palace – in this case, the palace of Whitehall. Here two stories about contract theory may be told. Both revolve around a Lady who, like Milton's Lady, is faced with the contractee's dilemma of whether or not to "trust" a would-be guardian's ostensibly "honest" and "courteous" claim to offer protection and security, and whether or not to insist upon a separation of sorts in the event that this claim turns out to be fraudulent.[1] One, a young romance heroine featured in Margaret Cavendish's story, *The Contract* (1656), learns in the masquing hall to love the man who had earlier violated his agreement to marry her. A product of the "engagement controversy" of 1649–52 when Cavendish, like many royalists, refused to rescind loyalty to the Stuart heir despite the fact that the crown had failed to meet what Thomas Hobbes identified as its most basic obligation – protecting its subjects from harm and death – and despite the fact that shifting loyalties to Cromwell would have meant the return of her confiscated estate, Cavendish directs her heroine to remain bound to her "Comus."[2] She does, after all, love him.

The other Lady, Elizabeth Poole, a seamstress turned prophetess in a Particular Baptist congregation in Abingdon, entered Whitehall in 1648/49 to advise the victorious General Council of the New Model Army on the fate of the captured Charles I. Soon after, Poole published three tracts reporting on the "visions" she had presented to the council: *A Vision: Wherein is Manifested the Disease and Cure of the Kingdome* (1648), *An Alarum of War Given to the Army* (1649), and *An(other) Alarum of War* (1649).[3] In these pamphlets, Poole introduces a bit of sectarian theatre into the King's former masquing hall by representing herself as a veritable Sabrina to the nation's imperiled Lady, a healer so powerful that she is capable of leading the "Attendant Spirit" of the Army in its bid to "cure" the "disease" that plagues the entire kingdom in this critical moment of political uncertainty. Her prescription? The sick body politic must exercise its right to break contract with the monarch so that it can purge itself of its gangrenous "member" – and that would be the King himself. But the body should not kill this tyrannical Comus, rather "she" should divorce him as fast as a sectarian wife would an unregenerate husband. He has, after all, abused her.

Contract theory, like the separation of spheres, holds a highly disputed place within postmodern feminist theory. Leading thinkers grant, of course, the basic premise of liberalism's critique of patriarchalism. As Gordon Schochet describes it, the household in Filmer's patriarchalist theory

> was not an analogical or metaphorical claim that the family *suggests* or *implies* things about the state, which can be seen as somehow *like* the household. Rather his theory was based upon identity, not *similarity*. Thus, the family was a polity, and the polity was a household, and the patriarchal, biblical family was not a prototype, but was the very wellspring of politics.[4]

On this idea of "identity" between marriage and government, a theory of patriarchal "designation" was founded.[5] As royalists such as Richard Mocket and Dudley Digges argued, the wife and the political subject occupied parallel positions.[6] Their initial "consent . . . [wa]s necessary"; however, because the husband-king's privilege to rule stemmed not from this consent but from his very status as a patriarch whose authority was designated as his by God and God alone, then "once [the contract is] made the dissent of the inferior party, let it be not upon fancied, but real discontents, cannot dissolve the compact."[7] Even when the ruling party proved to be "dishonest," "he doth not thereby lose his right to govern [his children], nor are they excused from their duty of honour and obedience; so there is a contract between Husband and Wife, the violation of which on the man's part doth not bereave him of his dominion over the woman."[8] Any kind of "divorce" then – either marital or political – was out of the question. As Henry Ferne wrote in *Conscience Satisfied: That there is no warrant for the Armes now taken up by Subjects* (1643), because the king was a *"sponsus Regni"* and "wedded to the kingdom by a ring at his Coronation," then "what our Saviour said of their light and unlawfull occasions of Divorse, *non suit ob initio*, it was not so from the beginning, may be said of such a reserved power of resistance, it was not so from the beginning."[9]

As Victoria Kahn writes, "precisely because marriage in the seventeenth century was understood to be a natural political relationship involving the sovereignty of husband over wife, the [inviolable] marriage contract was an important ideological weapon in Stuart propaganda for absolute monarchy."[10] However, Carole Pateman argues, women did not fare much better in the republican critique of this absolutist understanding of the "identity" between marriage and hence political obligation.[11] Republicans did, of course, object to the fact that subordinate men were relegated to the role of the king's "wife" and hence said to be stripped of any right to divorce, no matter how abusive a situation they might find themselves in. They insisted that "Mankind is naturally endowed and born with freedom from all subjection and at liberty to choose what form of government it pleases."[12] As a founding principle, this radically transformed the terms upon which the authority of the ruler was predicated from a force that was commensurate with a higher, more preeminent law to one that was limited by that higher law because it flowed upward from the consent of the governed, each of whom was naturally empowered by their own status as an adult individual endowed with certain rights directly by God, rather than downward from God through a totem of patriarchal heads. Because of this, one might assume that there would be potential for women to be liberated as well as men from the biblical dictates of obedience. After all, the phrase "all subjection" would appear to include the patriarchal marriage contract. And women would appear to be among those members of "mankind" whose natural rights were bestowed prior to their entry into political obligation and thus remained available to them as a means of exit if and when the other party proved unworthy. However, Pateman argues, republicans such as Locke and Hobbes preserved the "sexual contract" that secured "men's political right over women" and guaranteed "orderly access by men to women's bodies" by contending that women lacked the rational powers of judgment and emotional maturity needed to "freely" grant and withhold political consent (7). By dismantling the analogy between private and public forms of obligation, and indeed driving a wedge between them, republicans trapped women in a powerless private domestic sphere and hence feminists today must grant the "incongruous character of an alliance between feminism and contract" (184) since contract theory has been defined in opposition to all that women's bodies are said to represent.

A number of scholars have argued that male contract theorists such as Hobbes and Locke still paved the way for female political equality. As Gordon Schochet notes, Hobbes actually accepted Filmer's equation of marriage with the political contract but insisted that both sets of relations – political and marital – were based on convention rather than nature, thus obedience in both realms was chosen through calculation rather than ingrained by nature (although still expected).[13] And Locke held that the very concept of civil society should be viewed as a conventional one not only so that "man" could exist coequally "with man," but also in order to recognize the degree to which "women had a level of interest that permitted them to engage in the contractual relationship of marriage" (221). This equalized women by suggesting that they, too, possessed the capacity for rationally assessing their interests and so while Locke did not enfranchise women into full citizenship, he did enact a crucial "shift in the focus of politics from the patriarchal father to the rational, rights-bearing individual" that "created the theoretical possibility of full political membership for women" (221). Likewise, Susan Amussen adds, Locke's interest in doing away with the analogy between marriage and state was incomplete. To satisfy those of his contemporaries who continued to insist on an "identity" between the home and the state, Locke radically reconfigured marriage as a voluntary contract and the family as an entity defined by "parental" rather than "paternal" authority.[14] Thus, as Mary Lyndon Shanley insists, "Nothing inherent in [Locke's] contracting of marriage dictated woman's subordination to man. Women, like men, were free beings able to define their relationship to others by their own wills and consent."[15] Like Schochet, Amussen and Shanley assert that "the theoretical arguments which emerged from these debates over political sovereignty eventually – although very slowly – became the bases for Liberal arguments about female equality and marriage."[16] In fact, Amussen implies, reactions against Locke's radical doctrine often resulted in the continued subordination of women rather than the doctrine itself (64–65).

What is more, as Shanley points out, the roots of Locke's "conceptual revolution" lay within "the political debates of both the Civil War and the Restoration" (79). Whereas Pateman detects the germs of continued female subordination within the wedge that republicans such as Locke and Hobbes drove between a public political sphere defined by egalitarian political relations among men, and a private domestic realm constituted through hierarchical gender relations, Shanley reveals a body of pre-Lockean republican thought that founded the basis for dissent from the state upon an analogous set of "inherent limitations" placed on "husbandly power" (83). As she writes, "The Civil War political debate therefore generated a secondary debate on the nature of the marriage bond. Apologists for resistance to Charles I were forced to take more liberal positions with regard to marriage and divorce than were generally acceptable" (85). Divorce was the pivot upon which this more "liberal position with regard to marriage" turned. This may have been made possible by the fact that seventeenth-century Englishwomen were recognized as having certain rights long before Locke came along, and these rights were used as a precedent upon which to build a demand for an enlarged sphere of agency for both men and women (even though, as Shanley points out, this sphere was slow in materializing). As Amussen observes, women, at least aristocratic women, were "increasingly protected by settlements defended in Chancery" (61) and women in general received protection from neighbors and family members as well as courts against abusive husbands. Also, while actual divorce was officially forbidden by the Church of England, separations were granted under certain conditions and in actuality most petitions were initiated by wives and "men obtained separations from their wives on more limited grounds than women obtained them from their husbands" (57).

In fact, it may well have been the marriage analogy's demonstrated capacity to comprehend the wife's prerogative for separation which pressured royalists such as Ferne to declare, in the face of civil war, that divorcing the King was an impossibility. What is more, the presence of the material precedent of divorce is discernible within republican contract theory. While Henry Parker claimed in *Observations upon some of his Majesties late Answers and Expresses* (1642) that "the wife is inferiour in nature and was created for the assistance of man . . . but it is otherwise in the State betwixt man and man," he also a year later in *Jus Populi* (1643) preserved the analogy between the marital contract and the social one in order to argue that the political prerogative to disobey a ruler was akin to the rights that a woman held in marriage:

> In Matrimony there is something divine ... but is this any ground to infer that there is no humane consent or concurrence in it? Does the divine institution of marriage take away freedome of choice before, or conclude either party under an absolute formalization? And if men, for whose sake women were created, shall not lay hold upon the divine right of wedlock, to the disadvantage of women: much less shall Princes, who were created for the people's sake, challenge any thing from the sanctity of their offices, that may derogate from the people?[17]

As Amussen argues, "Parker stressed the lack of arbitrary or unlimited power in marriage, and by implication, the state" and "his vision was transferred to government" (58). Herbert Palmer and the other authors of *Scripture and Reason Pleaded for Defensive Arms* (1643) even went so far as to insist that the right to rebel from a tyrannical sovereign was and should be analogous to the right that women enjoyed to self-preservation from physical abuse. Because "a Wife is tyed to her Husband by a 'Covenant of God'" which is "more ancient, and no lesse strong then that of Politik Government," then "she may by the Law of God and Conscience ... secure her Person from his violence by absence ... or any other meanes of necessary defence."[18] Likewise, Milton found grounds upon which to simultaneously advocate divorce and contractual political relations. In his preface to the revised edition of *The Doctrine and Discipline of Divorce* (1645), Milton lectured Parliament that forbidding a man from divorcing an uncompanionable woman was akin to forcing a political subject to submit to a tyrannical government: "He who marries, intends as little to conspire his own ruine, as he that swears Allegiance: and as a whole people is in proportion to an ill Government, so is one man to an ill marriage."[19] It appears as though Milton confirms Pateman's thesis by insisting that a man's ability to maintain a functional and equal public identity was dependent on his status as head of his own household:

> it cannot avoid to be concluded that if the woman be naturally so of disposition as will not help to remove, but help to increase that same discomfort and dejection of mind not beseeming either Christian profession or moral conversion, unprofitable and dangerous to the commonwealth, when the household estate, out of which must flourish forth the vigor and spirit of all public enterprises, is so ill-contented and procured at home, and cannot be supported; such a marriage can be no marriage, whereto the most honest end is wanting ... (938)

However, Milton's advocacy of divorce does not slight women altogether, suggesting at one point that "if divorce were granted as he [Theodore Beza, biblical commentator] says, not for men, but to release afflicted wives, certainly it is not only a dispensation, but a most merciful law; and why it should not yet be in force, being wholly as needful, I know not what can be in cause but senseless cruelty" (964). Additionally, if we take Milton's *Comus* as a dramatization of the right to withdraw consent, which I have done here, we see a recognition early on that women constituted a "natural" test subject for a critique of the designation theory, since it was their plight as wives that was used to undergird a patriarchalist system in which it was said that, in theory, a woman's consent, once given in marriage, was, like her chastity, irredeemable.

Shanley does contend that the "shift to contract theory" was only fully enabled when "arguments from natural law began to replace those based upon Scripture" in the thought of Locke, because "Scripture had been adequate to prove that God had intended subjects to be subordinate to the prince and wives to be subject to their husbands" (85). Because patriarchalists claimed that this scriptural emphasis on female subordination was natural, Locke contended that "all beings were free and equal in the state of nature" (90). This condition was not nullified by marriage, rather it dictated that "when they agreed to marry," both men and women "were free to set whatever terms to their relationship they wished" (90). However, both Milton's advocacy for divorce (and its ability to function as a marker for the right of exit from various forms of political obligation) and Locke's antiscriptural search for gender equality were belated compared to what was taking place within Separatism. Here arguments for divorce as well as dissent from the established church were predicated on female *spiritual* equality. As early as the sixteenth century, both the male and the female members of the Familist church had divorced by "simple declaration" before the congregation.[20] In Milton's own time, one of six women preachers, Joan Bauford, was discovered by the author of *The Discovery of Six Women Preachers* to have been preaching to a group in Feversham "that husbands being such as crossed their wives wills might lawfully be forsaken."[21] In *A Dissuasive from the Errours of the Time*, Robert Baille derisively reported that followers of Samuel Gordon in New England contended that "it is lawful for a woman who sees into the mystery of Christ, in case her husband will not go with her, to leave her husband and follow the Lords house; for the Church of God is a Christian home, where she must dwell."[22] And members of sects such as the Baptists campaigned openly for marriage to be redefined as a voluntary contract so that divorce could be legitimated in cases where either husband or wife proved to be "dishonest." Another famous episode in Edwards's endless catalogue was the story of the Baptist radical and lace-maker known simply as Mrs. Attaway, who both preached freedom of divorce for women and practiced it by, in 1648, openly divorcing her "unsanctified" husband and taking up residence with her fellow Baptist, William Jenney. She justified it by citing Milton's infamous tract of three years earlier, *The Doctrine and Discipline of Divorce*. In the *Second Part of Gangraena*, Thomas Edwards tells the story:

> There are two Gentlemen of the Inns of Court, civil and well disposed men, who out of novelty went to hear the women preach, and after Mistris Attaway the Lace Woman had finished her exercise, these two Gentlemen had some discourse with her, and among other passages she spake to them of Master *Miltons* Doctrine of Divorce, and asked them what they thought of it, saying it was a point to be considered of; and that she for her part would look more into it, for she had an unsanctified husband, that did not walk in the way of Sion, nor speak the language of Canaan; and how accordingly she hath practised it in running away with another womans husband.[23]

As part of a campaign against Mrs. Attaway, Edwards published letters that Attaway and her husband, William Jenney, wrote to one another as declarations of divorce. In his letter, Jenney, "divorced" his wife in vaguely Miltonic terms: "because you have been to me rather a disturber of my body and soule, then to be a meet help for me (but I silence). And for looking for me to come to you again, I shall never come to you againe any more" (123). But in her letter, Mrs. Attaway claimed the right to divorce for herself as a woman on the grounds that it liberated the unhappily married couple from slavery. She prayed that the Lord would be "pleased" to set her husband "at liberty" and compared his position to Jehosaphat, who "knew not what to doe" after he and the other "people of Israel" were delivered from their "bondage." "Let us looke to [the Lord]," Mrs. Attaway advised her "ex," in order to know what to do. She pledged that she would always give her "heart and affection" to him "in the Lord." And she closed, "So Committing thee into the bosome of that loving kindnesse that hath redeemed thee I rest" (123). The basic idea was that because women had souls and were therefore spiritually equal to men, then ridding one's self of an undesirable spouse was just as much a female prerogative as it was a male one. Because the destructive behaviors of an unregenerate spouse meant that he had already forsaken the original contract, the wife was entitled to "rest" her marital case.

These declarations were felt to have political as well as social ramifications, since they were so often articulated within a context of viewing religious Separatism as itself a kind of "divorce" from the established church. In *Reasons against the Independent Government of Particular Congregations* (1641), Edwards railed against sectarians' *ad hoc* divorce practices on the grounds that they damaged the family and threatened the philosophical foundations of political rule by conceding the underlying claim that the wife maintained a spiritual interest that was separate from her husband's and, by implication, that of the church. To deem a husband unregenerate was to claim that his spiritual condition differed from hers and could therefore be redeemed or damned independently of hers. These two competing interests, he insisted, would inevitably clash and lead to the subversion of patriarchal rule. Katherine Chidley addressed this claim in *The Justification of the Independent Churches of Christ*. In 1 Corinthians, she pointed out, St. Paul granted that the wife could be sanctified and the husband unsanctified and that, because their spiritual interests were separate from one another, the "authority [that] this unbeleeving husband hath over the conscience of his beleeving wife" could be challenged."[24] The very assertion of spiritual equality, then, while not an assertion of political equality *per se*, did undermine the husband's ability to "enforce" the marriage contract against a woman's will and it led, of course, to Chidley's claim that it was a woman's independent spiritual interest which underwrote her right of exit from the established church. Preventing her from exercising this right would represent an even more pernicious source of domestic and social strife. Edwards recognized this as a slippery slope that would lead to the idea that "all women at once were exempt from being under government."

As the example of Chidley suggests, the idea that contract theory is irreconcilable with female equality is undermined by the project of recovering and analyzing early modern women's texts. As I will discuss next, Margaret Cavendish and Elizabeth Poole – two seventeenth-century women from competing social and political milieus – were able to exploit the radical potential for women that each saw in contract theory as it was heatedly debated during the civil war decades. Even as they drew different conclusions about if and when to exercise the right of exit, both authors found room for innovation *within* the traditional analogy between the marriage contract and the social contract, in order to constitute women as "representative political subjects" and, by inversion, as "representative dissenters."[25] What is more, Poole's formulations provide scriptural rationales for the female equality deemed necessary for both marital and political consent as well as dissent.

If we recall, Pateman claimed that feminism and contract theory were hostile to one another because male contract theorists held that women's emotional constitutions rendered them incapable of rational calculation. While Schochet argues that the creation of the abstract individual nonetheless "paved the way" for women to be "comprehended within voluntarism," Victoria Kahn argues that Margaret Cavendish's "The Contract" overcomes Pateman's objection by grounding the decision to contract one's self to a political order within the "instability of the passions, the necessarily figurative dimension of any so-called 'binding contract'" rather than within the male republican commitment to a "calculating and calculable" self interest.[26] The story goes something like this. While yet a girl, a "Lady" is betrothed by her father to an eligible young Duke who quickly and scandalously breaks his engagement, both because he had not agreed to his own father's original decision to wed him to a child and because he now burns instead with a debauched lust for a beautiful rich widow, who he soon marries. The young Lady he betrayed eventually grows up and, now orphaned, travels to London under the guardianship of her protective uncle. He introduces the reluctant beauty to court in order to find her another husband. At her initial appearance, she and the still young, still handsome, and still married Duke come face to face for the first time and fall in love without either knowing who the other is. One would imagine that the young Lady would fall quickly out of love upon learning of the Duke's true identity. However, even when she is told that her handsome suitor is the man who had broken his contract with her, and even when presented with the alternative choice of a socially prominent and wealthy, albeit aged Viceroy, she is determined to (re)marry her first love, thus the rest of the plot revolves around the couple's conjoined efforts to have their original agreement honored.

As Kahn points out, their success in this endeavor demonstrates Cavendish's postrevolution commitment to updating both the royalist claim that consent, once given (although always assumed), could never be withdrawn and the larger "royalist fantasy that the relation between sovereign and subject could never be one of simple coercion, but will always – also – be one of affection and consent" ("Cavendish," 295). While Cavendish ultimately agrees with Hobbes's illiberal proposition that absolute monarchy is the superior form of government, she departs from his more liberal position that it is the subject's base desire for self-preservation and the fear of violent death rather than any more lofty or "romantic" sentiment that motivates him to remain loyal to his royal protector, and that the failure to provide that protection releases him from obedience.[27] By conveying her contract theory through the genre of prose romance, the very mode used by Charles and Henrietta Maria in their court masques to proselytize on behalf of "irrevocable consent," Cavendish can, Kahn writes, "reform" romance from within" (297). And she can revise Hobbes by imagining a female subject who consents to be coerced not because she is compelled to by fear and not because she is forced to by the state's monopoly over the use of violence, but because she *loves* her ruler even when he subjects her to danger rather than protecting her from it. Thus, for Kahn, while Cavendish might mystify the coercive aspects of patriarchalist obligation by cloaking it within the rhetoric of love, she also exposes the "fictional" quality of contract theory in general by "simultaneously cancell[ing] and preserving" the "illusion of self-determination" for characters who believe that they have come to love each other "of their own free will" (293).

Of course, if we accept Cavendish's story as a possible "feminist" critique of contract theory (a suggestion that Kahn, to be fair, makes primarily in the form of an aside), then one could, of course, draw the conclusion that the only option truly available for women (or anyone) within a contractual order is one of "consenting to be coerced" (even if they are under the "illusion" that they have chosen to do so "of their own free will"), and that the only fully developed "feminist" approach to contract theory is one which either rejects it altogether as a romantic fiction or which, at the very least, "exposes" its "suppression" of the role that the contingent nature of subjectivity plays within the "fiction" of self-determination (312, n. 44). Thus, it is important to add to this discussion the strong likelihood that, because Cavendish's "revisionary romance" returns us to an age when, as Kahn herself asserts, "self-ownership is apparently not a permanent option," its "feminist critique" may be seen as a reactionary and reconstructed royalist response not only to Hobbes and the Parliamentarians but also to the Lady's refutation of the logic of "irrevocable consent" in *Comus* and to the insistence upon female dissent practiced and theorized by sects such as the Baptists, including Elizabeth Poole (306). Through a brief reconsideration of *Comus* and then a discussion of the Baptists and Poole, I will argue that Milton and the Separatists actually grounded their rationale for a contractual model of social and political relations within the individual (even female) propensity for contingency, miscalculation, and the consequential need for reassessment and revision. They generated a space for religious choice by exposing the "illusion" of absolute self-determination which willful magistrates and kings demonstrated themselves to be laboring under through their prohibiting religious freedom and by creating a "counterfiction" that narrated the irresistible romance that everyone ultimately experienced with God alone.

A comparison of the stories of Cavendish and Milton suggests that Cavendish actually mutes the affective dimensions of calculation and hence any real need for the doctrine of virginity's provision for exit and repurification by constructing a plot in which the heroine faces a terrain ultimately devoid of the possibility that one can remain eternally "separate" from actual marital and political obligation – even when one is married and politically bound – by virtue of one's "marriage" to God. In Milton's subversive masque, Comus's original address to the Lady was composed of the requisite Petrarchan appeal to her feminine vanity: "Hail forren wonder / Whom certain these rough shades did never breed / Unlesse the Goddess that in rurall shrine / Dwell'st here with Pan, or Silvan" (135). Milton's Lady responded by displaying an imperviousness to flattery and by denying that her compelling appearance and her "singing" were designed to signal her interest in attracting the kind of sexual attention that he offered. "Ill is lost that praise that is addrest to unattending Ears," she states flatly to the wooing Comus, it was only "extreme shift how to regain my sever'd company" that "compelled me to awake the courteous Echo" (135–136). However, she did eventually, albeit reluctantly, agree to take Comus up on his offer to conduct her to a safe place, revealing herself to be as vulnerable as the next person to the fictive fancies of romance. Fortunately, however, she conceded to Comus while also reminding him of the presence of that "severed company" from which she was separated and with whom she hoped eventually to be reunited. The existence of this other realm suggested that there was a "gap" between the protector (the sovereign) and the protected (the subject) which provided her with a backup if and when the original decision proved fallible, which, in her case, it most certainly did. Therefore, on learning that she had been duped, Milton's Lady was able to free her mouth from Comus's masque-induced mesmerism in order to denounce what she had come to recognize as a courtier's manipulating and bedazzling machinations to seduce and control her in the name of guarding her purity, and to perform her part in the masque's final "revelation" that, when all was said and done, the only claim to "protection" which a Lady could trust and to which she was therefore obliged was the one that emanated from the virtual but inviolable and "sun-clad" chastity belt with which she was girded from within. This insurance policy was there precisely *because*, not in spite, of the fact that the individual was all too capable of falling prey to the jaws of wolves in sheep's clothing. Hence, while we assume that the Lady's return to her father's house meant that she was still eligible for marriage somewhere down the line, Milton, as I mentioned earlier, took advantage of the temporarily empowering stage of virginal maidenhood to dramatize the potential that every individual harbored, not only to give and withhold consent, but also to reclaim and cleanse it through the rebaptizing capabilities of the doctrine of virginity (and, if need be the abortifacient of St. John's wort) once it was revealed that it had been solicited in bad faith (151).[28]

Cavendish invokes Milton by endowing her Lady with the same traits of possessive individualism that had characterized his: Cavendish's Lady also sports "naturally a majestical presence" (14); after her abandonment by the Duke and the death of her father, she too experiences a diminished circle of protection; she is allied with bachelorhood through her early declaration that her experience of rejection has left her permanently averse to matrimony; and when she does begin to reconsider the possibility of marriage, she seems to own the ability to choose her own suitor as well as to harbor that Eve-like tendency to choose the good-looking bad guy rather than the nice man. However, while Cavendish's Lady appears to possess the ability to either hoard or spend her own "coin" when and where she pleases, she ultimately comes to valorize rather than refute Comus's philosophy that female beauty must be exchanged within the planned patriarchal economy of marriage that considers prospective buyers only at "courts, at feasts, and high solemnities" (156). As her uncle insists before she departs for her second entertainment, "thy beauty shall make thy way" (16) and the siren-like "invitation" sent out by the carefully staged entrances of Cavendish's young Lady into the masquing hall yield their intended results as she comes quickly to be courted by two would-be, equally aristocratic suitors, the Duke and the Viceroy. As Kahn says, in Cavendish's court-centered tale, it is the royal seat of Whitehall rather than any "somewhere else" that is held to be the true home of romance and obligation, and the Lady is there precisely to be flattered and (re)bound ("Cavendish," 298).

Furthermore, while Cavendish does give the Lady a choice between the Duke and the Viceroy, she does so by eliminating the alternative of self-sovereignty mapped out by Milton and religious separatism. Rather than remaining loyal to a man who had revealed himself to be a rake, Milton's Lady invokes the separatist "doctrine of virginity" and puts marriage on hold for another day. Cavendish's Lady, however, comes to subscribe to her uncle's "doctrine," an accommodationist creed that insists upon marriage and allows her a highly circumscribed choice between following her "heart" by succumbing to the Duke's pretty-boy "appearance," or as her uncle prefers, more "virtuously" opting for the "riches and honor" she would accrue by marrying the old Viceroy (19–20). As the uncle says to his despairing young niece, why waste your life on "some young, fantastical, prodigal fellow, who will give you only diseases, and spend your estate, and his own too, amongst his whores, bawds, and sycophants" (23). But as she had earlier decried, the

Viceroy is wizened and "worn out of fashion" (19). Neither doctrine – the niece's that favors contracting for a potentially destructive but irresistible love or the uncle's that favors contracting for wealth and security – comes close to functioning as a refrain of Milton's dissenting declaration of independence – "you can't touch the freedom of my mind" – but, in this story, they exhaust the polemical spectrum. This may be because royalists such as Cavendish understood the idea of rational, calculating self-interest to equal the grubby pursuit of aristocratic wealth by relative underlings (the Lady is, after all, a member of the gentry and so choosing the Viceroy would represent a calculated step up) rather than the "right" to engage in principle-driven consent – that is remaining politically "single" (at least for the time being) instead of marrying, honoring, and obeying as a matter of course or returning to a nonconformist state of "bachelorhood" once the marriage goes south. But it may also stem from the fact that, for royalists who opposed Cromwell, principled dissent took place within an economy of political marriage – that is, within the context of their prior commitment to the crown. This would explain why the alternative sectarian message of separatism that had proven so appealing to a number of actual young English women searching for a right of exit from the established church has been craftily neutralized within the pages of Cavendish's text.

In Cavendish's court-centered rendition, the socially competing romance hero of the Attendant Spirit – the young, handsome, hip-swinging, and doctrine-of-virginity spouting "mechanic" sectarian minister – has been manageably reduced to the figure of the Duke's "servant," a pathetic figure whose "prophecy" of an independent future of antimatrimony-for-all leaves him in a permanent and literal state of unromantic and isolated bachelorhood which the marriage-centered logic of Cavendish's plot is expressly designed to repudiate (27). The frequency with which this "separatist" buffoon is cuffed on the ear by his young master is clearly meant to elicit a cathartic laugh from a royalist readership sick of the sight of the independent preacher, as is the fact that his role as Attendant Spirit is subordinated to that of an errand boy who secretly delivers the letters exchanged between the Duke and the Lady, letters which reactivate their original and allegedly defunct marital agreement. In other words, the servant is ordered to reestablish a contractual obligation from which he himself actively dissented – a wry moment of revenge for Cavendish against those rebellious sectarians who had opposed the crown in the civil war and who, in 1656, continued to inhabit Whitehall. And in spite of the fact that the servant "spruces [him]self up" (27) at one point before entering into the gentlewoman's home – trimming his beard, washing his face – we are meant to understand that there is no danger whatsoever that he possesses the charisma necessary to spirit this or any other Cavalier-loving Lady – or her maid – out of the window and down to the river. Through this "minor character" then, the sectarian threat is comically overcome. Cavendish recoups the claim made by Thomas Edwards and other antisectarians that women's interest in religious independency was a product of sexual whim rather than a genuine attraction to his separatist "doctrine": if the autonomy-spouting servant can be rendered sexually unappealing, then his creed becomes more repugnant and laughable as well and the option he appears to offer turns out to be no real option at all.

This stacked emotional deck leaves only the Viceroy as an alternative and hence sways Cavendish's readers to further comprehend and sympathize with the "logic" behind the young maiden's attraction to the sexy young man who had humiliated her: all the power of enchantment, as well as the means by which to become not her own but "his" queen, rest with the Duke as the story culminates in a successful conclusion to his insistence that his Lady help him make their case in court: she must do this, he tells her, because "you are mine and not your uncle's . . . and I will plead my right" (30). It turns out that, violated agreement notwithstanding, the Lady had always been and would always be married to the Duke. In the end, then, there is no need to purge her of a bad choice since there was, in essence, no choice to be made. The story's objective, then, is to both invoke and erase the virginal self-sovereignty and separateness of Milton's Lady, as well as the process of revision and the preference for exit that she allegorized; not for nothing does Cavendish dub her heroine "*Deletia*" (31).

And yet, as Kahn reminds us, Cavendish reiterates a commitment to absolutism by conceding and incorporating some of the more radical ideas about political obligation wagered by Parliamentarians ("Cavendish," 295). Cavendish's is, after all, a "contract theory" and constituting romantic love rather than obedience or fear as the guiding emotion prompts her to argue that the relationship between sovereign and subject is at its most generically coherent when it is at least surrounded with the patina of choice, mutuality, and consent. Also, because the story allegorizes Cavendish's own dissent from the Protectorate in the name of her prior and binding agreement to the crown, the Duke appears as a *viable* and *legitimate* husband only after he has been injected into a matrix of possible alternatives. Thus we see the Lady engaged in a rational and calculating defense of her love for the unstable rake: as a younger man, she tells her uncle, he would be less jealous of his beautiful wife and thus less likely to keep her "in restraint, like a prisoner" (22). The fact that the Lady and the Duke also had to lie in court to persuade the magistrates to honor their voided contract likewise suggests that, in this period, it was not simply the case that the fiction of self-determination suppressed the ostensibly more authentic and enslaving operations of emotion that were allegedly at work in the calculations of political affiliation, but that the fiction of obligation was used to conceal the subversive operations of a quixotic female agency engaged in the risky but liberating act of choice. Not surprisingly, then, while Cavendish's Lady obeyed her uncle's injunction to attend her first masque, she did so begrudgingly and clad in Puritan black, another sign that the "somewhere" else implied by the doctrine of virginity had become internalized within the royal seat of Whitehall to the point that the commitment to the crown had to be dressed within the separatist rhetoric of the overdetermining "obligation" that the dissenter owed to God. This would also explain the climactic scene in which the Lady is shown in a court of law claiming, Anna Trapnel-like, to embody a "truth" that is "undecked with eloquence," pleading for her "right" to retrieve her husband as one would a confiscated estate, and insisting that the original contract be honored because it now comes complete with an element that it had earlier been lacking due to the Lady's young age – her consent, which she "with her approvement" now sets as her "handwriting" (38). Through such plot devices, Cavendish endorses the idea that female desire is an important component of stable social formations. As Kahn says, she illustrates "almost in spite of herself that true romance is as much a justification of personal and political divorce as it is of marriage" (305).

But as I also mentioned earlier, this does not give Cavendish the only "feminist" word on the subject of women and contract theory. Instead, the subject of divorce leads us to consider the contract theory proffered by Elizabeth Poole just a few years before Cavendish's romance was published, in 1656. Like Cavendish's, Poole's theory is predicated on the idea that, because the woman is the potential "wife," it is she who segues most seamlessly into the role of contractee. Like Cavendish's, Poole's allows for feelings to be taken into account. And like Cavendish's, Poole's revolves around a marriage contract that is ultimately irrevocable. However, because Poole insists on preserving a place for the "self-interested" desire for protection from harm and death that an abused wife might rationally expect, she draws upon her Baptist background to argue that the only irrevocable contract is the one that has already been drawn up between the subject and her ultimate husband, God. This is the "true romance," therefore Poole's theory explicitly allows righteous anger and "justice" to prevail over love in order to affectively underwrite a "divorce" for those seeking one from the tyrannical kings and/or abusive husbands with whom they have the misfortune to align themselves in the first place. By beginning her story at a point well after the romance has ended, and by founding her theory upon the predilection for error, Poole departs from both Milton and Cavendish to demonstrate that, for women, the logic of possessive selfhood could and did extend beyond the temporarily empowering stages of virginal maidenhood and espousal and into the submerged era of wifehood: self-ownership *is* a permanent option and can be translated into a political right of exit.[29]

Because Poole's contract theory is rooted in the philosophies and practices of the sectarian religious sphere, I will, in "The House of Spirit," begin by discussing the counterromance model envisioned by Poole's minister, William Kiffin. In "Curing the Body" I will look at the specific ways in which Poole's tracts draw upon these alternative sectarian beliefs and practices to appropriate certain powers traditionally granted to the King alone, namely, the power to critique and alter (or "cure") the very form of the body politic. In "Divorcing the King" I will continue this line of thought by looking at the ways in which Poole's sectarian emphasis on "divorce" endows the "wife" with the same rational powers of choice and exit that Milton, Locke, and Hobbes imagined for men within a free political order, even as it makes inroads into the "domestic patriarchal authoritarianism" that their works retained. And in "The Lady's Doctrine of Virginity" I will discuss the way in which the controversies that followed Poole's public appearances led her to reiterate her own right to disassociate herself from every community but one – that of her inviolable self.

THE HOUSE OF SPIRIT

According to Habermas, "the dimension of the polemic within which the public sphere assumed political importance during the eighteenth century was, in the course of the two preceding centuries, developed in the context of the controversy in constitutional law over the principle of absolute sovereignty."[30] The story of Elizabeth Poole specifies a different source for the controversy over the principle of absolute sovereignty – that of the sectarian conventicle and the alternative or "counterromance" that it offered to women and servants. Poole was christened at St. Gregory near St. Paul on December 20, 1622; her mother's identity is unknown but, as I mention in the introduction, it is assumed that her father was Robert Poole, for at around the age of 16 her life took a turn that bears an uncanny resemblance to the scene in *Comus* when the Lady escapes from her captor's grip by following the advice of her father's shepherd. Except that, in Poole's case, the story would have delighted what I interpret to be Milton's wicked sense of irony because Poole's father's servant shepherded her away from her father's house and into a church headed by a controversial separatist minister, William Kiffin.[31]

Kiffin's Particular Baptist congregation was one of the London-centered Calvinist offshoots of the larger sect of Baptists whose roots reached all the way back to Luther's nemesis, John Leiden, and the infamous Anabaptists of 1530s Munster.[32] With their ability to draw individuals away from domestic (and state) ties through their opposition to a parent's ability to make the choice of baptism on behalf of their children, their subsequent empowerment of older children – and servants – to make the choice of baptism for themselves, their rejection of an ordained clergy as well as state tithes, and their commitment to a more egalitarian style of membership organization, Baptists were said to challenge the "romantic" authority of fathers and masters to oversee the seamless transfer of subordinates from one man's house to another.[33] To endow servants and women with the power to renegotiate their spiritual state was to suggest that they had a spiritual "interest" that was separate from that of their masters, fathers, or husbands. This individualized them by giving them choices and thereby established precedents that might be used to claim further forms of self-sovereignty.[34] To try and debunk this claim, Thomas Edwards in *Gangraena* represented the Baptist practice of sending men out on the road to "gather" as an antiromantic and Digger-like "gathering" of other men's enclosed human properties.[35] As one of several examples, he tells the story of a man named Nichols who lived in Moor-Fields but who often traveled to Stepney Parish, "sometimes to draw away people and hath drawn some away" by "corrupting people and venting his opinions" (78–79). The aghast parishioners of Stepney held a meeting in which it was said, "what a sad thing it would be to have our children and wives drawn away; and it was propounded whether in such a case a man ought not to keep his wife and children from such a one; and it was answered, a man was a king in his owne family to rule and govern" (79).

English Baptists tried to reassure nervous contemporaries that, in spite of their creed's controversial history on the Continent and their own ongoing practice of rebaptizing adults, they did not present a threat to the sociopolitical order. To counter the inflammatory term *Anabaptist*, they referred to themselves as "the Baptized churches" or "the true church."[36] In 1644 they published *The Confession of Faith*, which pledged allegiance to the "civil Magistracie" and the "King and Parliament freely chosen by the

Kingdome," which were, they insisted, to be obeyed "in the Lord."[37] In 1646 the Baptist leader Benjamin Cox published *An Appendix to a Confession of Faith* to try and further calm those "who have imagined a dissent in fundamentals where there is none."[38] And as late as 1650 the Baptists' "Petition" sought once and for all to distance their church from the Leveller assertion that "the people" should run the state by asserting that Baptists, despite their history, "are not at all to intermeddle with the ordering or altering civil government . . . but solely for the advancement of the Gospel."[39] That said, it was the undeniable and provocative ambiguity of the qualifying phrases "King and Parliament *freely chosen*," "obeyed *in the Lord*," and "not at all to intermeddle . . . *but solely for the advancement of the Gospel*" (emphasis added) that was cause for concern in the first place; this ambiguity was not helped by the fact that those who had signed *The Confession* continued to hint at the idea that there was a higher government to be obeyed than that of the King and Parliament. The authors sign the very document meant to pledge their allegiance with the following words: "we doe therefore here subscribe it, some of each body in the name and by the appointment of seven congregations . . . holding Jesus Christ to be our head and Lord; under whose government *we desire alone to walk*" (emphasis added).[40] In other words, given a conflict between their religious beliefs and their rulers, the Baptists hold out the possibility of following the former rather than the latter.

What is more, William Kiffin performed a similar sleight-of-hand with the romance narrative when he was thrown into the White-Lyon prison in 1642 for "keeping conventicles." Like Nichols and other male sectarian preachers, Kiffin was characterized as a rake who violated the rights of fathers to their enclosed human properties. As Edwards claimed, Kiffin had "become a pretended preacher, and to that end hath, by his enticing words, seduced and gathered a schismatical rabble of deluded children, servants and people, without either parents' or masters' consent."[41] However, to prove that what he had done was no crime, Kiffin published *Certain Observations Upon Hosea The Second the 7. & 8. Verses*, a transcript of a sermon he had delivered "at a friends House" and for which he had been arrested.[42] In this sermon, Kiffin couches the right to independent church formation within the socially conservative genre of romance. He feminizes his romance heroine in order to describe her relationship to Christ in terms of marriage, adultery, reconciliation, and reenclosure. This allows him to dramatize his subject's Eve-like vulnerability to immature calculation and to rationalize her need for a revisionary right of exit from her *faux* contract with the state church.

As his title stipulates, Kiffin takes his text from the seventh and eighth verses of the second chapter of Hosea. This passage reads:

And she shall follow after her lovers, but she shall not overtake them; and she shall seek them, but shall not find them; then shall she say, I will go and return to my first husband; for then was it better with me than now.
For she did not know that I gave her corn, and wine, and oil, and multiplied her silver and gold, which they prepared for Ba-al. (1)

By quoting Hosea, Kiffin explains, he simply meant that God's chosen people would be redeemed by him even after they had fallen away from and rejected him. Just as the bad wife in Hosea yearned for other lovers – those material things of the earth that turn a soul's attention away from the pure things of God – but returned ultimately to her "first husband" because he was the better provider, so too would every stumbled believer return to God once he or she realized that "then was it better with me than now." All appears to be straightforward enough at this point in Kiffin's sermon; after all, as Evelyn Fox Keller has argued, the metaphor of marriage was often used during this period to restore order.[43] However, upon further reading, one quickly comes to realize that Kiffin's use of Hosea is intended as a defense of religious separatism that necessarily rebuts the patriarchalist doctrine of "irrevocable consent" to King, Parliament, and church by revealing the existence of a prior and more binding marriage contract, the one that every person has with God and that entitles one to religious autonomy. Like the Duke in Cavendish's *The Contract*, God is, as Kiffin says, a "first husband" who is "intending to set forth His owne Majesty and greatness" by "claiming a special interest" in his wife in order to call her back from another lover (4–5). While God's wife might be drawn to "leape through" the "hedge and ditch" with which her husband had surrounded her and to run into the arms of a wealthy and powerful man who promises to clothe her in "blue silke" and let her sip from a "Cup of Gold," God will "stop her way, he will hedge up her paths" in order to "reclaim her" (4–5, 3). But in this case, God stands for the right that every individual possesses to free him/herself from their obligation to attend the national church. The wife stands for "the people" who possess those rights. And that other lover (the idolatrous and divisive King Jeroboam) stands for those English magistrates who "imprison, reproach, disgrace, [and] count a sectious person" as one that "troubleth the State" (5–6).

Through this rhetoric of female adultery and domestic reenclosure, Kiffin dresses choice in the logic of coercion, thereby preserving and subverting the national romance narrative that detractors claimed was ruptured by

Baptism. He merges the male (God) and the female (the wayward wifely subject) within the same individual, thereby upholding marriage and the "social order" while simultaneously providing the women and servants who attended "conventicles" with what Fox Keller defines as a "dynamic autonomy" (148–149), a "mean between the traditional male/female images of self offered by the ideology of the couple," as Maggie Kilgour sums it up.[44] He constitutes God as the owner of the individual, thereby protecting property while dissolving the entitlement that elite men claimed to hold over the spiritual "interests" of their households. He characterizes God as a tempting Comus, who holds out "the cup" from which his fickle wife once again desires to drink, thereby retaining the patriarchalist conceit that it is the "father" who provides "true provision and protection" (8), even as he uses it to "protect" the unlicensed individual's right to serve as God's ministerial "voice" within an independent church or "Kingdom of Priests" (16–17). Finally, he depicts God as a husband who insists that his spouse's submission to him must be "free, that is it must be raised from within us from the consideration of that excellency that is Christ and his lawes," rather than predicated on calculating self-interest, or, as Kiffin puts it, her own "by-ends and respects" (14). This allows him to imply that the true violators of property, contract, and romance are those who would spirit the people away from the father's house that reside within each of them. By forbidding "conventicles," it is the Surrey judges who force their adherents to "leave home" and "whore" (2) with the established church. Like Jeroboam, the usurping magistrates have "gotten a Kingdom [and] thought to keepe it by [their] own policy, rather than going in a way of truth" (2).

Kiffin soon had the opportunity to elaborate upon his subversive romance by sketching in the details of the "home-coming" experienced by an actual lady in the wilderness, Elizabeth Poole. In *Gangraena*, Thomas Edwards claimed to know about Kiffin's illicit gatherings from a source he, Edwards, identified only as "J. R."; in turn, "J. R." received his information from "a near relation" "whose giddy headed children and servants" became Kiffin's "poor slavish prosylitites" in 1644.[45] This "near relation" may possibly have been Robert Poole, for Elizabeth joined Kiffin's London congregation around this time. As Manfred Brod speculates, Robert Poole's subsequent outrage over this challenge to his parental authority appears to have been such that either he or his daughter set up a meeting with Kiffin to discuss whether or not Poole's household had joined Kiffin's group because they had chosen to (as Kiffin maintained) or because they had been bewitched into it, as Mr. Poole charged (397). When Kiffin arrived at the meeting, he found that Robert Poole had brought in a number of known

Anglican polemicists to debate the unschooled itinerant. Kiffin backed down but Elizabeth remained a Baptist and a year later Kiffin published a pamphlet that responded to the "queries" with which he had earlier been plied by the ministers.

In *A Briefe Remonstrance of the Reasons and Grounds of those People commonly Called Anabaptists, for their Separation, etc. Or Certaine Queries Concerning their Faith and Practice, propounded by Mr. Robert Poole; Answered and Resolved By William Kiffin*, Kiffin once again denies that he was a mere "Seducer, a blasphemer, and such like termes."[46] It was, he insisted, according to Poole's "Daughters and Servants desires" that he was "willing to give a meeting to any friends [Robert Poole] should bring, that wee might fairly and lovingly declare our thoughts from the Scripture, concerning the subjects of Baptisme, as desiring that you might thereby, hearing, try all things, and hold fast that which is good" (1). And, he asked, didn't this exercise of their independent will in and of itself suggest that infant baptism could fail to insure a child's fealty to her parents' religion? What is more, he, Kiffin, could call them "home" to a "domestic" arrangement that differed significantly from the traditional one that claimed, "Every Mans proper Mansion House and Home, being the Theater of his Hospitality, the Seate of his own Life, the noblest of his sons Inheritance, a kind of private Princedom. Nay to the Possessors thereof, an Epitomie of the whole world."[47] In Kiffin's vision, as in Chidley's and Trapnel's, there is an alternative domesticity. As opposed to the romance narrative that confines women to a domestic sphere wherein choices are made for them by their fathers and husbands, the Baptist love story provides daughters and other former domestic subordinates with the means to marry into a new domestic arrangement, in which they function equally alongside their male counterparts as reckoning agents within and constituent parts of a "habitation to the Lord."

In *Gangraena*, Edwards represented the act of baptism as one of the most pernicious means of invading the sacrosanct space of the home and usurping the father's authority. As has been shown, he consistently described it as a mere prelude to – or pretext for – illicit entry of the female body spirited loose from its sexual sanctuary in the father's house. In Kiffin's vision, however, baptism was the ritualistic means of membership into the "community of believers"; therefore it conferred egalitarian membership into the body spiritual: "being by one spirit baptized into one body." As part of his answer to Robert Poole's query, Kiffin assembled a miscellany of Bible verses that painted for the forsaken father a picture of this "house of spirit":

and first know this, that infinite Love which hath redeemed a people to God, out of all Nations, tongues, and kindred, hath also made them Kings and priests unto God, to reigne with him in his spirituall Kingdome here on the earth . . . and that all those which are begotten by the immortall seed . . . even those new-borne babes that have tasted of the Lords bountie, and come to that living and precious stone, the Lord Jesus, being themselves living stones, are built up a spirituall house, being made a holy Priesthood, to offer up spirituall sacrifices, acceptable to God by Jesus Christ . . . and being quickened by Christ, are raised with him, to sit together in heavenly places . . . being by one spirit Baptized into one body . . . The old man being . . . with him . . . and the New man put on . . . thus having an entrance to the Father, the building being thus coupled together, by the same spirit, groweth to an holy Temple, and so becomes a habitation to the Lord . . . which assemblie wee are not to forsake . . . but to exhort one another daily . . . having received gifts in some measure by the same spirit, we are accordingly to dispense them for edification. (11)

Here, the house of the actual father may be vacated so that the "spirituall house" may be built by "*all* those begotten by the immortal seed," that is, even "sillie seduced servants, children, *or people*" (emphasis mine). (The "new man," it seemed, might just as well be a woman.) If the woman became subordinate flesh to her husband's head upon her entrance into the traditional household of marriage – to the point where she was often-times equated with the house in many conduct manuals while the husband was designated her indwelling spirit – the promise of the latter was that she would become *equally material and spiritual* with her brethren: all are "stones," all house the indwelling spirit of God. Furthermore, she would become equally sovereign: *all* are "kings and priests" in the "spirituall house." In other words, like the Ladies in both Cavendish's and Milton's fictions, wandering women are reenclosed within the spaces of patriarchy. But because this alternative patriarchal space is here comprised of the "spiritual house" of God, its inhabitants are in essence released into free agency.

As a result, membership in the "spiritual house" provided several other new options for a "seeker" such as Elizabeth Poole, all of which will come to play an important role in her contract theory. The first was access to "public" discourse. As Brown argues:

The organization of the [General and Particular] churches was thoroughly democratic. All male members, and in the case of a large number of churches, female members also, were allowed "liberty of prophesying," that is, of saying during the services whatever they believed themselves inspired of God to say.[48]

Article 95 of the Baptists' *Confession of Faith* enshrined this into a quasi-constitutional form: "Also such to whom God hath given gifts being tryed in the church, may and ought by the appointment of the congregation to prophesie, according to the proportion of faith."⁴⁹ This declaration so mortified Thomas Edwards that he classified it under Errour 124 in his catalogue of sectarian errors and accompanied it with a sarcastic rehearsal of its underlying logic: "That 'tis lawfull for women to preach, and why should they not, having gifts as well as men? and some of them do actually preach, having great resort to them."⁵⁰

Second, membership within the Baptist "house of spirit" opened up the possibility that one could be elected to represent the congregation before an official gathering of an entire Particular Baptist organization. Each Particular Baptist congregation elected delegates that it sent to periodic gatherings or "General Meetings." These delegates were entitled "messenger."⁵¹ According to Patricia Crawford, "no women were ever sent as messengers when the church wanted to resolve vital policy."⁵² However, it is noteworthy that Poole consistently referred to the prophecies she delivered to the Army's General Council as her "Message" and the title page to *An Alarum of War Given to the Army* states that the tract's contents had been "by the will of God; revealed in Elizabeth Pooll, Sometimes a Messenger of the Lord to the Generall Councell, concerning the Cure of the Land, and the manner thereof." By claiming this status within the virtual spheres of print and prophesying, Poole could identify herself as a legitimate representative of her church, a member of an "elect" who, because of the cultural capital she had accrued within the house of spirit, could exercise influence within the public political sphere.

The third privilege accrued through Baptist membership was, of course, the power to effect a spiritual "cure" through rebaptism and the related ritual of "laying on of hands." In many circles, all those considered to have the gift of purgation, including women, reportedly participated in these healing rituals. In the letter from J. R. that Edwards included in *Gangraena*, he recounts an incident when Kiffin and members of his Church "laid hands" upon a woman and:

did also Anoint her with Oyle; the woman recovering came into their Conventicle house, and there before many people said, That Physitians left her as they found her, but Brother Kiffin and Patience anointing her, she suddenly recovered; for which in that place, she desired thanks might be put up; which Kiffin did also relate, and according to the womans desire (return thanks:) . . .⁵³

Because healing was akin to "saving," there was a fine line between a woman's assisting a male minister in his practice and herself assuming the ministerial function of serving as a vehicle for another's salvation. What is more, because curing was synonymous with altering and transforming, it was easily translatable into the idea that one could shift one's affiliation or "obligation" from a rotten to a pure head, as Poole would advocate for postrevolutionary England, without being tainted in the process.

A final power that was conferred through Baptist affiliation – and one that, as has already been shown, was also related to the principle of revision – was the ability to divorce an "unregenerate" spouse. The idea was that, if one could choose to be rebaptized, then one could also choose not to. If a person preferred the latter, the regenerate spouse was entitled to acknowledge his original error and to leave her – even when that "spouse" was the King. The wife, too, could seek that dissolution because, again, "in the Lord," men and women were equals.

As stated, each of these four components of Baptist thought and practice play a major role in Poole's own visions. They allow her to become a "public person" capable of serving as a "legitimate representative of the people, a legitimate administrator of justice" even as they represent a set of "rights" that one may exercise within a contractual order by virtue of the private property one holds within one's self as an individual.[54] One can express or deny consent to a particular political regime by virtue of the rights to speak, represent, cure, and divorce that one gains through grace as it is received upon crossing the threshold of the private "house of spirit."

CURING THE BODY

On December 29, 1648, and January 5, 1649, respectively, Poole delivered prophecies *viva voce* to plenary sessions of the Army's Council of Officers. In his minutes of the General Council sessions at which she appeared, Secretary William Clarke briefly introduced her as "Elizabeth Poole of Abington" and went on to refer to her only as "Woman" in the rest of his notes.[55] And in a pamphlet entitled *The Manner of the Deposition of Charles Stewart*, she was described merely as "a woman of great wisedom and gravity" who came "of Hertfordshire" with a "message to the [General Council] from God."[56] Four days later, she published her own account of that "message," a small but sensational tract entitled *A Vision, wherein is manifested the disease and cure of the Kingdome, being the summe of what was delivered to the Generall Councell of the Army Decemb. 29, 1648. Together with a true copy of what was delivered in writing (the fifth of the present January) to the said Generall Councell of divine pleasure concerning the King in reference to his being brought to triall, what they are therein to do, and what not, both concerning his office and person. By E. Poole herein a servant to the most High God. London 1648.* As its descriptive title suggests, Poole's text consists of the two visions she delivered to the Army's higher-ups, each of which helps to construct one of the postwar era's most dominant themes, as Mark Kishlansky describes it: "The limited claims of Parliament to act on behalf of the people in bringing a recalcitrant monarch to heel were extended [during this time] into contractual arguments about the nature of government and democratic arguments about the liberties of the people."[57] The Whitehall debates helped dramatize differences of opinion on these critical issues among members of Parliament, the military grandees, the rank and file soldiery, religious Separatists, and Levellers.[58] By the time Elizabeth Poole entered the scene, in December 1648, the Army had assumed control over London and purged Parliament of those who wanted to negotiate with the King. Political authority rested in the hands of the military leadership, who held daily discussions about the fate of both the King and the kingdom.[59] The Levellers leaned towards a more inclusive republican commonwealth, while Oliver Cromwell and Henry Ireton tended towards a limited monarchy. In November, Ireton had laid out his plan in a document called *A Remonstrance of Fairfax and the Council of Officers.*[60] In its compromised form, the *Remonstrance* contained some elements from the Leveller's democratic platform, *The Agreement of the People* – it proposed to establish a "Covenant" which "foremost fulfills the preservation of religion and liberties" – but it also promised to protect "the king's person and authority." A number of Baptists supported this position. At a General Council meeting in November 1647, the Baptist Army "agitator" William Allen had also argued that the best "cure" for the dying nation consisted of the army generals retaining power and not handing it fully over to either the King or "the people," as the Levellers wished. And just before Poole's appearance, William Kiffin petitioned for a rejection of the proffered Leveller settlement of the government and even visited the King that September to express his support for Cromwell's plan to reach a settlement with the monarch as opposed to the Levellers' insistence that "no address" be made to the tyrant. Perhaps, these men reasoned in 1649, if one of those new Sabrinas were to come and address the General Council, her anti-Leveller insistence upon the army's retaining power would sway opinion their way. There was a woman that everyone knew of who could be asked to appear at the next meeting, a seer who had apparently gained something of a reputation within Baptist circles. Maybe she would come.

This attempt to trigger a certain type of recognition among those members of the Council who were members of or sympathetic to separatist sects may explain why Poole opened her *Vision* by adopting the riverside scene of a Baptist ceremony and applying it to the moment at hand. After reading the *Remonstrance*, she began, she assumed that England was finished and that she, as a "member in her body" was so "sensible" of her "dying state" that she could feel the "pangs of death oft-times panging" her. However, after "many dayes mourning" a "vision" was "set before" her, to "shew her the cure, and the manner of it" by this "similitude":

> A man who is a member of the Army, having sometimes much bewailed her state, saying He could gladly be a sacrifice for her, . . . was set before me, presenting the body of the Army; and on the other hand, a woman crooked, sick, weak and imperfect in body, to present unto me, the weak and imperfect state of the Kingdom. (1)

England, like the Lady, was in need of a cleansing cure. The army was her rescuing Attendant Spirit and she, Poole, was to play the part of Sabrina. Together, they would cure the comatose woman which in this case meant calling upon the army to perform its "duty" and retain the "kingly power" in its own "godly" hands rather than "betray[ing] its trust" by "giving it up" to the people.

The possibility that Poole's message was intended to oppose Leveller demands receives support from contemporary press accounts of Poole's appearance in Whitehall. An anonymous royalist pamphlet entitled *A Brief Narrative of the Mysteries of State carried on by the Spanish Faction in England* claimed, soon after news of her talks in Whitehall spread, that Poole's role had been part of a plot by Cromwell to find divine sanction for his power struggles against the Levellers. The author described Poole as a

> monstrous Witch full of all deceiptfull crafts, who being put into brave cloaths pretended she was a Lady that was come from a far Countrey, being sent by God to the Army with a Revelation, which she must make known to the Army, for necessity was laid upon her; this Witch had a fair lodging prepared for her in White-Hall where she was very retired.[61]

A pro-Leveller pamphlet published in 1660 upholds this perspective. Called *The English Devil, or Cromwell and his Monstrous Witch Discover'd at Whitehall*, it portrays Cromwell and Poole as a demonic variation on the theme of the Attending Spirit and his Sabrina, colluding to "cleanse" the body politic of the victimized Levellers rather than of the true disease – themselves.[62] At the same time, Poole's insistence on army rule may, at this point, have coincided with Leveller interests. As Brod argues, one newspaper, *Mercurius Pragmaticus*, claimed that Poole was "one of [John] Lilburne's doxies" ("Politics and Prophecy," 403) whose departure from the Leveller line was a mere symptom of her confusion as a pathetic female orator. However a possible Levellerism can also be found within Poole's own message, as she next instructs the army leaders to prepare themselves to eventually "resign [the people] up to the will of the eternall pleasure," their true ruler, and to continue debating the issue of their "lives, liberties, freedoms, or whatever" (2–3). Otherwise, she insists, the army "shall surely lose them" (2–3). As opposed to a proclamation authorizing the army to retain permanent control over the country, this appears to be a commitment to the possible establishment of a more Leveller-like commonwealth somewhere down the line. What is more, as Brod explains, Lilburne's opposition to a military "dictatorship" (402) was not as strenuous at this point as one might suppose. Lilburne himself presented a petition immediately after Poole, which also advocated the transfer of power from the King to the army, the hope being that the army would evolve into a more representative and democratic organization than would a Parliament full of "mediocrities" and placemen, as the Leveller, Thomas Harrison, put it.[63] Finally, and perhaps most importantly, while Cromwell had at first favored implementing a limited monarchy with Charles I still at the helm, he and many Baptist leaders soon came to support regicide while the Levellers and other Baptist leaders, as well as some rank-and-file Baptist members of the army, began to argue that the King should be granted the same access to due process to which, in their estimation, all free-born Englishmen were entitled.[64] This comports more with the position that Poole takes in the final section of her first message. Although she may be counted among those "religious Independents" who believed that the army was the "tool" by which the "reign of the saints" would come about as a necessary prelude to the "imminent, earthly reign of Christ," she was not among those who used this belief to "create a logic in which the King's death became necessary."[65] When asked point blank what exactly it was that she was recommending the Council do with the King, Poole surprised the room by insisting that he be "tried in his conscience" and his life spared.

While less extreme than regicide, Poole's call for a trial nonetheless bespeaks a contractual interest in a limited rather than an absolutist monarchy, one that preserves the King's life while also managing to infuse his "wife" with new powers. As stated above, she implies that each individual is ultimately entitled to "plead" with the government for liberties and freedoms and to appropriate a measure of "sovereign" self-rule for themselves, since they are ultimately "resigned" to "God's pleasure"; in fact, Poole's own claim to "direct" this legal "cure" encroaches on the Stuart king's stated divine right to serve as "'physician' of the nation" and establishes the philosophical foundation for a contractual right of exit.[66] In 1608, when religious dissenters (in this case Scottish Presbyterians) became more and more of a problem for Charles's father, James, he delivered a speech entitled "The Trew Law of Free Monarchies."[67] This monologue was structured around an epic simile borrowed from the early modern model of the body's physiological need to maintain a harmony among its various humors. The underlying principle was that it was the King's duty to "preserve a balanced constitution" by eliminating that which was diagnosed as having upset that balance.[68] In his treatise, James first restated the founding principle of patriarchalism: "The king towards his people is rightly compared to a father of children, and to a head of a body composed of divers members, for as fathers, the good princes and magistrates of the people of God acknowledge themselves to their subjects" (99). He then argued that

> As the judgement coming from the head may not only employ the members, every one in their own office, as long as they are able for it, but likewise, in case any of them be affected with any infirmity, must care and provide for their remedy, in case it be curable, and, if otherwyse, gar cut them off for fear of infecting the rest, even so is it between the prince and his people. And as there is ever hope of curing any diseased member by the direction of the head, as long as it is whole; but by the contrary, if it be troubled all the members are partakers of that pain: so is it betwixt the prince and his people. (99)

While the language is medicinally correct, it obscures a brutal reality. If citizens are giving their ruler trouble, the ruler is entitled to "gar cut them off" as one would a gangrenous limb. In the particular case of those who challenged government control over preaching, cutting them off might mean jailing them, torturing them, or fining them; all were part of the ruler's "prerogative" to balance his constitution, to "cure" himself so to speak. As Christopher Hill writes, "By precept and punishment, through bishops or immediately, governments went far to determine what was said in most pulpits" and this policy was "underlined in 1614 by the trial, torture and death sentence imposed on Edmund Peacham for having in his possession a sermon ... which the Government thought seditious."[69] As James I himself wrote in a letter to the Archbishop of Canterbury in 1622, "the abuses and extravagances of preachers in the pulpit have been in all times suppressed in this realm by some act of council or state."[70] "Curing" then was a metaphor for divesting one's self of *un*ruly elements and this amputation of the body politic was a power wielded by the head physician alone.

Poole, however, warned the council that "the cure" for the ailing nation was to be effected "not according to the former rule by men prescribed for cure," that is, not according to the traditional royalist allegory in which the King acted as physician to his own body politic. Rather, the cure was to be implemented in a new way, "according to the gift of faith in me," Elizabeth Poole, "as I by the gift of faith on me should direct him" (1). This is in effect a demand that she, a "member" of the body, now be allowed to participate in governing the nation; the basis for this claim impinges upon both the foundation of patriarchalism and its republican critique. Whereas Filmer claimed that kings received their authority from Adam's "original grant" of paternal rule, Locke countered that such a formulation would result in "as many Monarchs as there are Husbands."[71] Instead, he argued, that women were subject to their husband's "conjugal" power to serve as "proprietor of the [family's] Goods and Lands" by virtue of the law of "nature." This did not, however, give the husband the "political power of life and death over her, much less over any body else" (210). Poole chooses a different route. She preserves the idea that Adam and Eve provide a precedent for marital relations but she implies that female equality resides within Eve's ability to overcome the curse of subordination through the bestowal of grace.

This was a controversial issue in Poole's time. Traditionally, the church had relied on the Pauline epistles as their main authority for subordinating women to men because, as Paul wrote in 1 Corinthians, "But I would have you know, that the head of the woman is the man; and the head of Christ is God."[72] Early reformers, however, had to contend with the fact that the Pauline epistles were more complicated on the issue than might have been desired. Most troubling was when Paul asserted in Galatians that "There is neither Jew nor Greek, there is neither bond nor free, there is neither male nor female: for ye are all one in Christ Jesus." This language suggested that, in a state of grace, all boundaries were dissolved, especially those that pertained to hierarchically structured sociopolitical distinctions between the rationality of man (housed within his head) and the inferior irrationality of women (and servants) (housed within the body). If this were the case, then couldn't women say that their entry into the state of grace relieved them of the curse of subordination placed upon them through Eve? The Anabaptists answered yes; in reaction, Calvin penned his sermon on the Epistle of St. Paul to the Ephesians.[73] God, Calvin insisted, had ordered Eve to submit to Adam *even before* she ate the apple. Thus, her subjection was "double" and the bestowal of grace, while it might guarantee her salvation in the afterlife, could not and did not undo God's original and everlasting command for woman to obey man.

Whereas (Paul) saith, concerning wives, that they owe subjection to their husbands: *we* have to mark that this subjection is double. For man was already the head of woman even before the sin and fall of Eve and Adam [1 Timothy 2.13]. And St. Paul alleging the same reason, to show that it is not meet that the wife should reign in equal degree with her husband, saith that the man came not out of the woman, but the woman of the man ... [And] now although god's blessings shine forth everywhere both above and beneath, yet are there always tokens of cursing imprinted in them. (277–283)

Similar attempts to undo the potential that the small verse in Galatians appeared to hold for female equality under the new covenant of grace continued into seventeenth-century England. Cotton Mather, for example, insisted that the injunction to obey was to hold sway on earth, while the impulse towards the implied dissolution of hierarchy within grace was to come in the afterlife.[74]

However, the logic of "double subjection" and dueling time frames was openly rejected by at least one Englishwoman during this period. In 1617, Rachel Speght, a participant in the seventeenth-century's *querrelles des femmes*, wrote her own commentary upon Galatians. In *A Mouzell for Melastomus: Of Woman's excellency, with the causes of her creation and of the sympathy which ought to be in man and wife each toward other*, she insisted that there was only one curse of subordination placed upon Eve by God, and that was the one he levied upon Eve *after* her sin.[75] Paul's teachings, she proclaimed, actually say that the combination of Christ's assumption of human form through Mary and his promise of grace to all results in the expiration of God's injunction and the return of, as Barbara Kiefer Lewalski describes it, "women's essential equality."[76] Speght writes:

The first promise that was made in paradise, God makes to a woman: that by her seed should the serpent's head be broken: whereupon Adam calls her *Eve*, life, that as the woman had been an occasion of his sin, so should woman bring forth the saviour from sin, which was in fullness of time accomplished. By which was manifested that he is a saviour of believing women, no less than of men ... and ... by Christ's assuming the shape of man was it declared that his mercy was equivalent to both sexes, so that by Hevahs blessed seed (as St. Paul affirms) it is brought to pass, that male and female are all one in Christ Jesus [Gal. 3.28]. (272)

Poole's declaration that the "gift of faith was upon" her should be read within this context. In essence, Poole was remodeling the body politic after the egalitarian body of the Baptist church's house of spirit, in which all were in a state of grace so that an "Eve" could claim the same gifts as an "Adam," including the sovereign power of "directing the cure." By arguing that this "cure" should include a trial for the King, Poole implied that one of Eve's prerogatives was the power to judge the sovereign and to recalibrate her political obligation to him on the basis of that judgment. In her next vision, Poole fleshes out her contract theory by insisting that, if the King is judged to be a tyrant, then he is eligible to serve as the diseased limb which "gar cut off" the ailing body politic. However, for Poole, this amputation must take place through divorce, not decapitation.

DIVORCING THE KING

Poole's first vision was largely well received, perhaps because it had walked a fine line between on the one hand alluding to a universal political enfranchisement along the lines of Leveller ideas, and on the other insisting that the army retain control for the time being. In a document entitled *Summary of the Debates on the Agreement, in the Council of Officers, 16th December–6th January; and of the Examination of Elizabeth Poole on 29th December and 5th January*, the army council signaled its approval of Poole's first message by granting its divine origins. Ireton is reported to have said that he "could see nothing in her but those [things] that are the fruits of the Spirit of God ... because it comes with such a spirit that does ... hold forth humiliation." Her second appearance before the general council took place on January 5th, 1649, a mere twenty-five days before Charles I was beheaded. If she was in fact there as part of Ireton's behest to preserve the King's life, then, as Brod claims, she failed because by January 5th, the ordinance to establish the High Court of Justice for the purpose of trying the King had already passed through Commons and would be enacted (over the protest of the House of Lords) the very next day (399). This vision also appears to have earned her the opprobrium of those who may have served as her initial sponsors, perhaps because it sought to forge a lasting rationale for a nonviolent form of king removal that differed from both patriarchalist and male republican visions of rule and gender hierarchy.

At first, Poole is "on message" with the advice she delivers at the previous meeting. She begins her talk by stating that, this time, her "pretext" for speaking is her reading of *A Second Agreement of the People*, a revised version of the democratic constitution that the Levellers and other army radicals hoped would form the blueprint for monarchy's ultimate replacement.[77] Less equivocally than before, she reiterates her request that the army not follow this Leveller agenda. However, she then states that the "free admission" with which she had been met on her first outing has emboldened her to return with a follow-up plea that the council refrain from regicide. In doing so, she sets herself against those religious Independents who believed that killing Charles fulfilled "key prophecies from the Bible."[78] To make her own case, Poole states:

> The king is your Father and Husband, which you were and are to obey in the Lord, and no other way, for when he forgot his subordination to divine Fatherhood and headship; thinking he had begotten you a generation to his own pleasure and taking you a wife for his own lust, thereby is the yoak taken from your necks (I mean the neck of the spirit and law, which is the bond of your union, that the holy life in it might not be prophaned, it being free and can not be bound.) (4–5)

While Poole, like Cavendish and Hobbes, retains the "romance" of the conservative patriarchalist marriage metaphor in her comparison of the situation of the army to that of an abused wife, she does not merely rehearse the status quo in which wives are expected to "obey" their husbands. Instead, she finds a way of initiating several key revisions within the original analogy.

Poole applies the Baptist counterromance and doctrine of virginity to the situation of the body politic by calling for the "wife" to obey the husband "in the Lord, and no other way," just as the Baptist *Articles* did after they implored their members to "obey the king." The suggestion is that to obey the King in and of itself is an insufficient injunction and that there is another, more just way of obeying him – when he, himself, is acting in accordance with God's higher law. Because one enjoys a prior and more binding agreement with God that both structures and trumps any obligation that one is said to have to an earthly ruler, then if the earthly king forgets his own "subordination to divine Fatherhood and headship" by "prophaning" the ultimately "free" and unbindable spirit of his subjects, he is revealed to be a tyrant and his subjects are relieved of their "yoak." The term *yoke* is, of course, another word that links Poole's patriarchalist metaphor to contract theory. It is a reference to the yoke of matrimony as well as to the much invoked "Norman Yoke" which English civil war radicals associated with the imposition of French-style absolutism upon England by William the Conqueror in 1066.[79] By employing this term within the context of her radical appropriation of the marriage analogy, Poole implies that the wife might experience a bad marriage in as constrictive a manner as Englishmen did tyrannical monarchy, and that she is, therefore, entitled to invoke a right of exit.

But what constitutes a tyrannical transgression? As Poole describes it above, it appears to consist of "marital rape." The King "forgot" his "subordination" to God by "thinking he had begotten" his wife for nothing else but as a "generation to his own pleasure." As did the act of baptism, the invocation of marital rape suggests that the wife has an interest and a body that is separate from her husband's and that, as a result, she cannot be forced into a sexual relationship. The metaphor implies that the body of the people, too, possesses a "chastity" or "consent" which is theirs, even after they have contracted to another. If and when the sovereign tries to violate that purity (which he never ultimately can), obligation is dissolved. Poole elaborates by drawing on laws governing wife abuse, on the one hand, and the sectarian practice of divorce on the other. She writes:

You never heard that a wife might put away her husband, as he is the head of her body; but for the Lords sake suffering his terrour to her flesh, though she be free in the spirit to the Lord; and he being uncapable to act as her husband, she acteth in his stead; and having the spirit of Union abiding in her, shee considereth him in his temptations, as tempted with him: And if he will usurpe over her, she appealeth to the Fatherhood for offence, which is the spirit of Justice, and is in you; For I know no power in England to whom it is committed, save yourselves (and the present Parliament) which are to act in the Church of Christ, as shee by the gift of faith upon her, shall be your guide for the cure of her body, that you might therefore commit an unsound member to Sathan (though the head) as it is flesh; that the spirit might be saved in the day of the Lord (I believe). (5)

In one sense, this is a troubling echo of Filmer's patriarchalist claim that wives, must "patiently suffer whatever their rulers imposed while awaiting providential deliverance."[80] The army, as a wife, was resigned by law to endure her husband's physical abuse, with only the assurance that God would take care of him in the afterlife, because under common law husbands had a legal right to beat their wives although (generously) not to kill them. One could argue that Poole at least took a certain pleasure in reminding this group of men that the logic of patriarchalism required that they endure the King's tyranny as patiently as wives were told by the law to endure their husband's blows. Still, it must be granted that Poole's opposition to regicide meant that she had to refrain from radically reworking the codes upon which the defense of domestic abuse was predicated. In the next breath, she even asks her "brethren" to "play the part of Abigail" from 1 Samuel, an antityrannicide scripture in which Abigail successfully discourages David from killing her husband, Nabal, the tyrant, on the grounds that revenge belongs to God and thus David should not despoil his own new government with a founding act of usurping violence. Pushing the analogy, she intones, "Onely consider, that as she lifted not her hand against her husband to take his life, no more do ye against yours" (5). In other words, much as they might like to, they cannot kill their husband for being a tyrant. They must follow the dictates of the biblical patriarchal precedent.

However, it is also significant that Poole goes on to construct a scenario in which Abigail is at least licensed to defend herself against the abuse that threatens her life. While the King's life was to be preserved, his wife is nonetheless entitled to "hold the hands of your husband, that he pierce not your bowels with a knife or sword to take your life. Neither may you take his . . . You are to walk by this Rule. Whatsoever you would that men should doe unto you, doe yee the same unto them"(6). There is a right to self-defense, as well as an admonition based on the "golden rule" that one should not abuse another if one does not want to be abused. More importantly, while the King's use of excessive force against his wife does not provide her with a license to use force back against her assailant, it does give her the right to withdraw from a contract that was already torn asunder by his violence. Thus, Poole raises new questions about the parameters of patriarchal authority, both at state level as well as within the home, and she does so by avoiding the disorderly stereotype of the transgressive wife as one whose "consciousness of [her] conflict with and separateness from her husband" and her subsequent "articulation of herself as a speaking subject" are "interrelated" with the "plotting and execution" of her husband's murder.[81]

Conduct literatures often urged men to regulate themselves on the grounds that, while abuse was legal, it inevitably provoked troubling speculation about the terms of the marriage contract. William Gouge contended that beating one's wife exposed the paucity of the claim that, upon marriage, husband and wife became "one flesh."[82] Presumably one would not beat one's own body. Abuse therefore gave the lie to the claim that women ceased to be separate entities, physically and legally, upon entering into matrimony and paved the way for the wife to retaliate. Gouge writes: "Now a wife having no ground to be perswaded that her husband hath authority to beat her, what hope is there that she will patiently beare it, and be bettered by it? Or rather is it not likely that she will if she can, rise against him, over-master him (as many do) and never doe any duty aright?" (396–397). If the wife suspects that a husband's right to beat her is arbitrary and unwarranted, then she might logically take matters into her own hands. Abuse, intended as the philosophical embodiment of a husband's dominion over his wife, actually becomes the vehicle for exposing the fragile metaphors upon which that dominion is established. Wives who retaliated by murdering their husbands did an especially efficient job of calling "into question the legal conception of a wife as subsumed by her husband and largely incapable of legal or moral agency."[83] However, Poole's formulations also suggest that the King's abuse has exposed a seam in the conjoined flesh.

The King does not have the right to pierce his *wife's* bowels; if he does, she may hold back *his* hands. They are, in effect, two bodies. And Poole's insistence that one can, in fact, remove the yoke represents an act of resistance that both forms an alternative to murdering the King and subverts republicanism's alleged dependency on the "sexual contract."

As Pateman has pointed out, Filmer based the patriarch's right to rule on Adam's status as a father, and his ability to become a father rested upon marriage. Thus, the actual rock-bottom foundation of patriarchalism consisted of Adam's sexual or conjugal right to his wife. Because this necessarily preceded fatherhood and made it possible, then sexual dominance not fatherhood was the "original grant of government" (*Sexual Contract*, 38). And because, Pateman argues, this conjugal right was preserved by republican contract theorists, women were rendered incapable of either forming or breaking contracts. By definition, then, a contract-based society is as destructive for women as patriarchalist monarchy was for men. Poole, however, states that it is the wife's right to consent that forms the original grant of a contract theory. As punishment for taking his wife as his object of lust, the King is, after all, to undergo criminal proceedings. This anticipates Locke's concept of trust. Locke did not argue that "consent" was the vehicle through which citizens could disobey. To do so risked promoting the assumption that the lack of dissent alone served to legitimize government. Instead, he argued that it was incumbent upon citizens to obey the laws of their land as long as those laws were being adjudicated fairly and legitimately by the state. If, however, the people formed the "judgment" that government was acting illegitimately, that is "contrary to their trust," then they were "absolved from any further Obedience" (396–397). Poole also contends that the wifely half of the body politic is relieved of her obligation and freed to exercise her judgment once the head violates her trust.

What is more, while Pateman contends that feminism must stand in opposition to contract theory because of contract theory's maintenance of the conventional stereotypes of gender identity, Poole redefines the body politic even as she preserves it. The council, she writes, is entitled to "commit an unsound member to Sathan (though the head) as it is flesh; that the spirit might be saved in the day of the Lord" (5). In other words, to preserve the "body," the "head" might be sacrificed. This is a strategic reversal of James's old formulation. The head, the patriarchal seat of reason, is here termed *flesh*. As just another part of the body, it is as subject to corruption or disease as the limbs and must undergo the same treatment. This echoes a larger Parliamentarian critique of the King as a "glutted head" whose tyrannical irrational appetites must be reigned in (a train of thought also found in the Lady's scorn for her captor's feasting in *Comus*) as well as a sectarian emphasis on the "fleshiness" of earthly heads and their requisite subordination to God as a higher power.[84] As William Dell wrote, "But Christ in each assembly of the faithful is their head, and this head they dare not leave, and set up a fleshly head to themselves whether it consist of one or many men, seeing Antichrist doth as strongly invade Christ's headship in many as in one man, in a council, as in a pope."[85] By designating the King's head as "flesh," Poole includes him in this list of "fleshly heads" who supersede their bounds when they attempt to establish themselves in the throne that belongs rightfully only to God. And while the King might terrorize her flesh, Poole echoes the Lady's "doctrine of virginity" by insisting that there is still something about her that he cannot touch nor violate for it is indisputably hers, and that is her spirit. The inviolability of this spirit functions as her ability to reasonably assess her need to withdraw consent in the face of tyranny; it thus compels her to "commit" the King's unregenerate flesh to Satan. As an injunction, this language of committing the King's head to Satan is strange; modern ears might almost miss its significance. On the surface, it suggests that Poole is saying that the army should merely pray that, in the afterlife, the King will receive his just desserts – the same logic that Filmer used to argue that the subject owed an absolute obedience to the King regardless of how he was treated. However, Poole's contemporary audiences might also have very well recognized this phrase as a call for divorce. As Rachel Trubowitz and Brian Patton have argued, Poole's rhetoric points to a sectarian culture in which separatist wives were "justified in repudiating and even abandoning" their husbands if they felt themselves to be enmeshed within an "anti-Christian yoke."[86] Poole echos the language used by Mrs. Attaway when she divorced her husband by "committing" him to "the loving bosome of Jesus Christ," although, of course, Poole chooses to commit her "spouse" to Satan instead. Nonetheless, the underlying principle is the same: marriage, like the individual's relationship to government, should be a contract whose terms are consented to by both parties. And if either party violates the trust underwriting those terms, then the other, regardless of whether it is the husband or the wife, can activate his/her right to termination. As someone who claimed the ability to "see into the mystery of Christ," Poole was able to direct the army's "wife" to abandon its spouse because he "would not follow her" into that mystery, that Lord's house in which she was spiritually equal to him. And this was so from the beginning.

Interestingly, Poole's divorce metaphor may be an attempt to trump a Stuart conceit in much the same way that her appropriation of the language of curing did. There is some evidence to suggest that the rhetoric of divorce was appropriated by royalists to argue that the King would eventually prevail over his rebellious body. In 1643, William Stampe, the vicar of Stepney, delivered a sermon to his Majesty at Christ-Church in Oxford.[87] Published less than a month later, Stampe's text assures the King that God would make visible the "withdrawal" of his support from the King's enemies in several ways. One, he opines, "includes all the rest" and this was the one in which:

God withdrawes, by divorcing himselfe from his people; the phrase ye have *Jer. 3.8. I gave her a bill of Divorcement* (saith God of *rebellious Israell)* an expression borrowed from those, who by matrimoniall contract, have lived a long time together, with mutuall joy and comfort, till some high misdemeanour breakes out, which hath noe other remedy but a divorcement. (19)

Stampe's notion is, as he says, "borrowed" from those who have grounds upon which to break the contract of marriage. However, while he celebrates the possibility that God will find reasons for divorcing England's unregenerate subjects, he also dreads the "terror and amazement" that would accompany the dissolution of this "covenant": a divorce would be a "scandal," one that would "cashier" the one divorced "of all relations to God" (19). However, he then triangulates to argue that, if "we" the earthly husband do not obtain this divorce from the "whorish woman" (22), then God will effect an eternal separation between himself and us, his wife. His salvation will manifest itself quite literally when the "husband" leaves behind the whore in his quarters and goes out into the field with his army, but is not harmed or killed. In other words, winning the military war against the Roundheads is a visible sign that God has divorced the revolutionaries and retained his marriage contract with the Royalists.

Poole's divorce model represents a revengeful variation on this metaphoric scheme. If monarchy, like marriage, is a contract, then the wife may also find grounds for a divorce. However, because it is the husband who has behaved badly, the body must preserve herself from eternal ruin by giving to Satan what is Satan's, which, in this case, is the husband rather than the wife, a woman who has been wrongfully whored by her own spouse. If she is to save herself "in the Lord," then God must be shown to be separating himself from her husband and to be placing the kingly powers within the hands of a more reliable guide, the army, whose triumph over the King signifies that he, the "wife," is the one who makes visible God's choice. And the army is, in turn, guided by the "gift of faith" that God has lovingly placed within a sanctified member of the people's body.

As can be seen, Poole joins Milton and other radicals in arguing that the contract between sovereign and subject was by nature a "metaphorical" one, meaning that the "ability to transfer power to the sovereign" was only a "metaphorical transfer since power remains fundamentally with the people" and was thus "evidence of the power to revoke allegiance."[88] However, when it comes to the symbolism of gender, Poole's brief but pregnant prescriptions also offer a significant alternative to other models for king removal popularized by both Milton and Edward Sexby. In *The Tenure of Kings and Magistrates*, the defense of regicide that Milton wrote just two months after Charles I was executed in 1649, Milton contradicts the argument he made to Parliament in his preface to *Doctrine and Discipline of Divorce* by grounding the right to exit within the authority that fathers and husbands wielded over the private sphere of the household. This formula provided for the natural rights of the "individual" not by defining the wife as the perennially virginal subordinate, but by defining the husband as the sexually dominant head of the household. He writes:

And surely they that shall boast, as we do, to be a free nation, and not have in themselves the power to remove or to abolish any governor supreme or subordinate, with the government itself upon urgent causes, may please their fancy with a ridiculous and painted freedom fit to cozen babies, which is the root and source of all liberty, to dispose and *oeconomize* in the land which God hath given them as Masters of Family in their own house and free inheritance. Without which natural and essential power of a free nation, though bearing high their heads, they can in due esteem be thought no better than slaves and vassals born, in the tenure and occupation of another inheriting Lord.[89]

The single head of the monarch may be lopped off and its authority distributed to multiple heads of households. The citizen's public identity (equal to that of all other public men) is constructed through his mastery of those who reside in his household, including, we assume, his wife and children. The wife's subordination within the home guarantees his freedom. Without the authority to decapitate a tyrant that is derived through a kind of *recapitation* of every male citizen, the "individual" is no greater than a slave or vassal or, one might add, a wife. In *Killing Noe Murder*, Edward Sexby puts it in even more explicit terms, contending that

We shall sufficiently demonstrate who they are that have not a right to govern if we show who they are that have, and what it is that makes the power just which those that rule have over the natural liberty of other men. To fathers within their private families nature has given a supreme power. Every man, says Aristotle, of right governs his wife and children, and this power was necessarily exercised everywhere whilst families lived dispersed, before the constitutions of commonwealth . . .[90]

When several families join together to form commonwealths, then these heads of families are each entitled to engender consent by "mak[ing] the election" (367). Thus, as was the case with Milton, the right to remove a tyrant who violates the terms of his contract with the people, resides within "natural" rights of the fathers.

These arguments link Milton and Sexby with the contract theorists and lend support to Pateman's claim that masculinist republican contract theory failed to enfranchise women into the right to enter into contract voluntarily because it did not discard what Pateman calls the old "patriarchal claim that there is a 'foundation in nature' for women's subjection to men" (*Sexual Contract*, 45). Because this is in essence "a claim that women's bodies must therefore be governed by men's reason," then, even as the male heads of households gain new powers of consent and of making the government, women enter into the marriage contract involuntarily and are there further deprived of any notion of political rights. The "separation of civil society from the familial sphere is a division between men's reasons and women's bodies," between a public sphere in which "justice is the first virtue" and a private sphere characterized by family, sentiment, and "love" (20). Since justice does not apply to the private sphere, women are deprived of their rights. Since love does not apply to the public sphere, women are deprived of their capacity for care.

Poole, however, foregrounds the degree to which the wife's contract with the husband is also "metaphoric," that is, one in which "consent is not meaningful without the possibility of dissent."[91] Thus, like Chidley and Trapnel, Poole redraws the contours that shaped the private and public spheres even as she upholds a crucial distinction between them. Although the wife, she insists, derives her rights from her husband (and thus should not kill him), the public head does forfeit its claims to wield kingly power if it violates the wife's preexisting right to sexual consent. This she enjoys apart from him and "in the Lord." The domestic and conjugal "love" that characterized the private sphere for Milton and the contract theorists, and that constituted voluntary obedience in Cavendish's royal romance, formed, in Poole's alternative sectarian love story, the basis for public political action and dissent. Speaking as a representative of her "church," the house of spirit in which all souls were entitled to claim new forms of self-sovereignty, she says to the council: "I beseech you in the bowels of love, for there it is I plead with you [to] look upon the patience of God towards you, and see if it will not constrain you to forbearance for his sake" (6). Her "love" for the sovereign prevents her from endorsing his execution. But it does not prevent her from leaving him. Instead, she insists, she is equally constituted as a subject through her ability to seek the justice of separation. In fact it is she, a "member of the body," who must pursue it because her husband, the King, has been disqualified from doing so on the grounds that he overruled his wife's right to consent.

Poole's formulations suggest that contract theory need not be received as the equivalent of a new form of slavery for women. It was, in fact, quite rational to posit, as both she and Cavendish did, that the "wife" makes the best model for the object of contractual wooing, since it was her fallible sense of judgment that was at times in need of reevaluation, not because she was naturally inferior in her faculties but because would-be protectors were too often revealed to be wolfish violators of their innocent charges' trust. And although "the wife" was, in this equation, a literal reference to the male members of the army, Poole continually fudged the distinction between them as the imperiled Lady and her own role as Sabrina in order to suggest that she too was a member of this spiritualized and hence egalitarian body. Their interest was her interest but it was an interest that diverged from that of the King (and, as I shall show, Poole soon came to insist upon a gap between even these two allied parties of the body politic and herself). Thus, while Locke is credited with having "shifted" the focus from the prerogatives of fathers to those of the "rational, rights-bearing individual" in such a way as to anticipate "the theoretical possibility of full political membership for women," Poole's investment in the wife demonstrates that she enacted a similar type of shift several decades before Locke did. As did Cavendish's, Poole's "true romance" "threatened to undo the hierarchical, inequitable relationship between the contract parties – not only husband and wife, but also sovereign and subject," but it did so while remaining faithful to "contemporary arguments for the voluntary nature of political obligation."[92] In fact, in the next section I will argue that Poole's ultimate interest was in a possessive individual who was, in the end, "abstracted" from every marker of social identity, including that of the separatist church.

THE LADY'S DOCTRINE OF VIRGINITY

After the Levellers and antiregicides such as Poole lost the debate over execution, a "mopping-up exercise" ensued to rid the army of any remaining trace of their influence. As Brod argues, "Elizabeth Poole must be seen as part of this" ("Politics and Prophecy," 406), albeit a minor one. For reasons that remain unknown but that are trailed by a whiff of scandal, Poole had left William Kiffin's London congregation to join John Pendarves's Baptist congregation in Abingdon even before she appeared in Whitehall. Attempts were made (by whom exactly is not clear, but Kiffin, her former ally, is strongly suspected of having been involved) to jeopardize her standing in her new Abingdon congregation by implying that she had earlier been kicked out of the London branch for sexual promiscuity. According to Pendarves's wife, Thomasina, who became a particularly loyal ally of Poole during these troubled times, Poole was ousted from Kiffin's congregation for her "errors," but Pendarves does not mention whether those errors were doctrinal or political, or as it was later scandalously rumored, sexual in nature.[93] As a woman who had dared to take on powerful men, Poole, it seems, was always vulnerable to the age-old charge of being a whore, and sure enough, she soon had to contend with rumors that she had "gone about seducing." This sequence of events captures the complications that the association with a group, even a voluntary one, held for women. A woman could always face expulsion (if that is in fact what happened to Poole) if her "spiritual equality" was taken too far. The rhetoric of home and whoredom could easily be used to expel a woman on the grounds that any worldly business she might have engaged in meant that she had strayed from God, her first husband. Thus it is plausible, as has been done, to read Poole's fate at the hands of male detractors as an example of both the "serious attention given to women acting in the prototypically 'male' roles of preacher and prophet" and the extent to which they nonetheless remained "conventionally 'female,' the subject of 'male' authority, containment and appropriation."[94]

At the same time, it is also the case that, under the auspices of the freedom to choose that her spiritual equality entitled her to, a woman could join another congregation that would allow her to pursue her agenda, as Poole did when she left the London group and joined the Abingdon church. Or she could simply declare herself to be a "voluntary association" of one, which is in essence the option that Poole pursues. Thus it is also arguable that the most interesting aspect of Elizabeth Poole's short career is the fact that she actually did not go away after she failed to, as she hoped, "direct the cure" and preserve the King's life while handing him over to be tried and divested of his kingly powers. Instead, she remained in the Abingdon congregation and, on May 17, 1649, just four months after the King was beheaded (in the flesh and not just in the spirit), she published two new pamphlets. And in these texts, she declares that the house of the spirit resides not within the King, not within the state church, not within the separatist conventicle, not within the male mechanic minister, and not within the army, but within her, Elizabeth Poole, alone. Entitled *An Alarum of War*

Given to the Army and to their High Court of Justice (so called) revealed by the will of God in a Vision to E. Poole . . . Foretelling the Judgements of God ready to fall upon them for disobeying the word of the Lord in taking away the life of the King, and *Another Alarum of War*, respectively, these tracts recount a "true romance" of the single individual.

Poole's last tract, *Another Alarum of War*, is especially compelling. It consists of two pieces. The first is a copy of the letter written by Thomasina Pendarves to defend Poole against the sexual profligacy charges by comparing her to "Mary out of whom seven Devils had been formerly cast" and who was made the first messenger of Christ's Resurrection." The second is a statement of Poole's *own*, one that resolutely defends her reputation, reiterates her earlier antiregicide prophecy, and prophesies anew the dire consequences that will befall those who ignore her original messages.[95] In sum, this document delineates and embodies Poole's very own "doctrine of virginity," her persistent claim that, despite all attempts to sully her reputation, she remained in essence a virginalized spiritual self, capable of regeneration and of voicing her dissent. It was this indivisible essence, she insisted, and not the corruptions to which her socialized flesh was subject, real or attributed, which would – and should – form her lasting legacy. Poole's first step in this process is to shift from prophetess to preacher. In spite of the fact that, as she says, she had "shame cast in the face of [her] Message by many," she feels empowered to argue the following: "When I was with the Council, it was in a Vision, or Revelation, and now I am come with a word of Interpretation; the which I commit to thee deare Reader, in the spirit and bowels of love to judge" (3). Here Poole creates herself as a minister by positioning herself as the direct amanuensis of God's table talk within the house of spirit. She prefaces her title page with quotes from Isaiah, the evangelical prophet of four Judean kings who sought to save Judeah from moral, political, and social corruption. Specifically, she quotes Isaiah 30.1–18, the passages in which the prophet addresses the "rebellious children" of Judah who will not "take counsel of the Lord." "Therefore have I cried concerning this," writes Isaiah, "Their strength is to sit still." Isaiah's message of sitting still refers to the idea that the people should always "wait for God" to judge before carrying out rash actions. But before Isaiah will continue with this message, he commands his listeners to "go, write before them in a table, and note it in a book, that it may be the time to come for ever and ever." He then provides the text for them to write down in their "tables." By quoting these passages, Poole takes up the call to perform as a scribe and "write down" what God commands. She is still the speaker of truth – even if the moment of her vindication lies within a time yet to come – while the General Council members are the "rebellious children" who did not "wait" for God's judgment.

Poole continues to turn the Baptist argument for separation against her former allies by next predicting that the same destructive fate which the army's High Court of Justice had enacted upon the King's rule would eventually be visited upon theirs: "Nevertheless know that as ye have served him, so shall ye be served, ye said ye must have no respect of persons with God. It is done saith the Lord, neither will I have respect of your persons" (4). She chastises the High Court for not having recognized a woman as God's divine messenger: "Forsake not your Lord, though he change his garment and take up a forme which you have not knowne, least that scripture be fulfilled in you, They shall not believe though one should tell them" (5). She quotes from Isaiah to predict the destruction of the new regime and its "so-called" High Court of Justice, whom she likens to the Romans who "have not known what [they] did in executing Justice (as you call it) on the King" (6–7). And she returns her readers to the separatist counterromance by calling for them to reenclose themselves within the house of their true husband, God. Because they were a "rebellious People" who "say to the seers, See not; and to the prophets, Prophesy not unto us right things, speak unto us smooth things, prophesy deceits," then, the Holy One tells them, "this iniquity shall be to you as a breach ready to fall, swelling out in a high wall, whose breaking cometh suddenly at an instant." The people can avoid this punishment by "returning" for "In returning and rest shall ye be saved." Then she quotes from the Song of David in Psalms: "Kings of Armies did flee apace: and shee that tarreyed at home divided the spoyle. Wherefore separate the precious from the vile, and return yee." In other words, Poole positions herself as one of the "precious" who "tarrys at home," the seat of God's judgment, while the "rebellious children" are those who "flee apace." By calling for the General Council to "return," she implies that they are the wandering "whores" who have separated themselves from God by killing the King, while she is the virgin whose message emanated from God's house of truth.

Even more significant is the fact that she completes this radical domestic work by divorcing herself from all that may be termed corrupted flesh, including the army's General Council, her old church, and her former socially defamed self. As she wrote to the Council: "I commit you to God the onely wise and infinite Father, who is all things, and all things are God, he is all things, subsisting, all things are God, in whom subsisting." The line between God and "herself" is provocatively blurred here, to the point where Poole is God and God is "herself." What is more, Poole angrily addresses the Baptist congregation who have betrayed her as "the *pretended* Church, and Fellowship of Saints, in London: Who pursued me with their weapons of Warre, to shoot me to death at the Generall Councell of the Army, not regarding the Babe Jesus in mee Greeting" (emphasis added). In this formulation, *she* is now the true church, impregnated like Mary through divine intervention with Christ's spirit. Unlike the father's house, the house of spirit was not physical: one could not actually be confined to it or banished from it. While Kiffin could articulate it, he did not own it. Instead, the spirit was itself housed within whomever claimed to possess it.

Poole again turns the tables on her male detractors by saying that, while they had accused her "of sinne," it was they who were kept "in bonds" by the "flesh." She, on the other hand, was spirit. As she writes:

Deare Reader, thou mayst marvell that I – having had so reproachful a pursuit by them that are called Saints when I was last at the generall Councell – should hold up my head any more, to speak to them; as also having shame cast in the face of my Message by many . . . the which the Lord will judge: wherefore I shall certifie thee, deare Reader that these things came to passe according to divine pleasure for two reasons: The first is, to staine the pride and glory of all flesh in me: The second, to blinde the eyes of the wise, that they seeing might not perceive; and if thou considerest these reasons . . . in that I am come to prostrate my neck, and all the glory of my flesh to the wrath and malice of men, knowing that that which *can* be shaken in me, and all men, must be done away, that that which *cannot* be shaken may be established . . . for flesh must be consumed, that we might live in the spirit. (1; emphasis added)

Whereas the Council reduced Poole to the status of body, to "render" her, as she claimed, "the more odious," she represents herself as a pure unshakable spirit, a God-like essence that transcends all contingencies of the vessel and that defines her essential self. Finally, she closes with an explicit rehearsal of the doctrine of virginity: "Deare Brethren, I have learned this judgement, that that spirit in man . . . is the Virgin which cryeth out, and though shee have no helpe, the Law quits, saying, Shee hath done none evill, she is free . . . Farewell, Your friend in the Kingdome of the patience of Christ. Elizabeth Poole." Even after she had been slandered and violated, she was an inhabitant of the house of spirit and the legitimized womb of its word. In fact, the point at which the "spirit" and her "freedom" begins is the point at which the reach of the law ends.

The rhetorical nature of Poole's tract is in and of itself an especially appropriate vehicle – quasilegal in its implications – through which a slandered woman could recover the degradation of her body and reclaim it for herself within a rubric of self-ownership. She employs the vindication mode, a genre of redemption that she uses to revise, clarify, and reclaim the past for present and future purposes. The term *vindication* comes from *Vim* or "free" and *dicere* or "to say" and means, "To make or set free; to deliver or rescue; to claim as properly belonging to oneself or to another; to assert or establish possession of something for oneself or another. property of estates given away and become mere notions; and not vindicable, or perishable by law."[96] As this definition suggests, the vindication is simultaneously bound up with the freedom of saying, with making and setting free, with the recovery of property, and with the claim of something properly belonging to one's self or to another. Patricia Parker has written about how women who were outside of the home, especially for the purposes of speaking publicly, generated anxiety about "wandering," and "errancy."[97] These were code words for the way in which sexual promiscuity threatened to transform both the straying woman's body and the private, patriarchal spaces of the home from which she had strayed into "common" places. As Parker writes, "the relation between a potentially uncontrollable female sexuality, a woman speaking in public, and a woman usurping her proper place is made even more explicit . . . in the complex of misogynist double entendres surrounding the figure of the woman who takes upon herself the traditional male role of the public orator pleading a 'cause' or 'case' in court" (106). A "case" or "cause" is related to a woman's sexuality, as in jewel case or casket, which, as a husband's property right, "is to remain closed to those who might break in and steal" it (106). To silence Poole, her critics sought to repatriate her to the status of a piece of sexual property, an errant whore who had wandered from her proper place beside God, her husband. To redeem herself, Poole, like Cavendish's Lady, was forced to plead her case. Because doing so exposed her to the same degree of publicness that had resulted in her original humiliation, she turned to the form of the vindication. Doing so allowed her to reappropriate the "prospect" or "inventorying" of "property . . . controlled through its display to the beholder's eye" (127) by revealing the wrongs perpetrated by men against the "property" that she, as a woman, held in herself. This "first being," as Milton referred to it in *Comus* (144), resides beyond representation and thus beyond any informal or institutional structures that seek to define and possess it within a social matrix.

This is, I suggest, a claim on behalf of what can only be termed radical individualism. In the next chapter, I will argue that Poole's claims were not anomalous ones. Women were always subject to charges that they had been corrupted from within and without, that they were overdetermined by forces in such a way that rendered their speaking subjectivity multivaried and hence suspect. Thus such religious "deviants" as Poole found it to be much more within their interest to argue, as Sarah Wight and Anne Wentworth will also do in the next chapter, on behalf of something fixed and immutable, something that they alone possessed: a sense of selfhood modeled on and determined solely by the true sovereignty of God. Men such as Locke are credited with widening "the category of the political person even though it restricted that status to males." Catherine MacKinnon has argued that a "feminist" theory of the state would recognize the fact that "Individualism involves one of liberalism's deepest yet also superficially most apparent notions: what it is to be a person is to be a unique individual, which defines itself against, as distinct from, as not reducible to, any group."[98] However writings by separatist women suggest that contract theory and its interest in the individual has forgotten roots in their attempts to define the "political person" as one whose feminine vulnerability not only to being hoodwinked by rakes but also to being *wrongly accused* of such necessitates an order which makes room for the individual to vindicate herself against the bad choice itself, or against the unjust accusation that she has made a bad choice (or as in the case of Cavendish, in favor of her right to make that "bad" choice), through the contractual exits and reentries made manifest by the house of spirit's equalizing powers of grace.

NOTES

1. John Milton, "Comus," in Roy Flannagan, ed., *The Riverside Milton* (Boston: Houghton Mifflin, 1998), pp. 109–171, with reference to p. 137.
2. Margaret Cavendish, "The Contract," in Kate Lilley, ed., *The Blazing World and Other Writings* (Harmondsworth: Penguin, 1994), pp. 3–43; Victoria Kahn, "Margaret Cavendish and the Romance of Contract," in Lorna Hutson, ed., *Feminism and Renaissance Studies* (Oxford: Oxford University Press, 1999), pp. 286–316.
3. Elizabeth Poole, *A Vision: Wherein is Manifested the Disease and Cure of the Kingdome* (London, 1648); *An Alarum of War Given to the Army* (London, 1649), and *An other Alarum of War* (London, 1649).
4. Gordon Schochet, "The Significant Sounds of Silence: The Absence of Women from the Political Thought of Sir Robert Filmer and John Locke (or, 'Why can't a woman be more like a man?')," in Hilda Smith, ed., *Women Writers and the Early Modern British Political Tradition* (Cambridge: Cambridge University Press, 1998), pp. 220–242.
5. See J. P. Somerville, *Politics and Ideology in England, 1603–1640* (London: Longman, 1986), p. 25, and Susan Dwyer Amussen, *An Ordered Society: Gender and Class in Early Modern England* (Oxford: Basil Blackwell, 1988), pp. 55–56.

6. Richard Mocket, *God and the King: or A Dialogue shewing that our soveraign Lord King James, being immediate under God within his Dominions, Doth rightfully claime whatsoever is required by the Oath of Allegiance* (London, 1615), and Dudley Digges, *The Unlawfulnesse of Subjects taking up Armes against their Soveraigne, in what case soever, Together with an Answer to all Objections scattered in their severall Books* (Oxford, 1643).
7. Digges, *Unlawfulnesse of Subjects*, pp. 112–113.
8. Ibid., pp. 113–114.
9. Henry Ferne, *Conscience Satisfied: That there is no warrant for the Armes now taken up by Subjects* (Oxford, 1643), p. 81.
10. Kahn, "Cavendish," pp. 286–316, quote from p. 290.
11. Carole Pateman, *The Sexual Contract* (Cambridge: Polity Press, 1988).
12. Sir Robert Filmer, *Patriarcha and other Political Works*, ed. Peter Laslett (Oxford: Basil Blackwell, 1949), p. 53.
13. Schochet, "Significant Sounds of Silence," p. 221.
14. Amussen, *Ordered Society*, pp. 64–65.
15. Mary Lyndon Shanley, "Marriage Contract and the Social Contract in Seventeenth-Century English Political Thought," *Western Political Quarterly*, 321 (1949), 79–91, quote from p. 79.
16. Ibid., p. 80.
17. Parker, *Observations upon some of his Majesties late Answers and Expresses* (London, 1642), p. 185; Parker, *Jus Populi* (London, 1643), pp. 4–5.
18. Herbert Palmer, *Scripture and Reason Pleaded for Defensive Armes* (London, 1643), pp. 35–36.
19. John Milton, "Doctrine and Discipline of Divorce," in Flannagan, ed., *Riverside Milton*, pp. 926–976, quote from p. 932.
20. Christopher Hill, *The World Turned Upside Down* (Harmondsworth: Penguin, 1972), p. 311.
21. Anon., *The Discovery of Six Women Preachers* (London, 1641), p. 4.
22. Robert Baille, *A Dissuasive from the Errours of the Time* (London, 1645), p. 118.
23. Thomas Edwards, *A Second Part of Gangraena* (London, 1646), p. 9.
24. Katherine Chidley, *The Justification of the Independent Churches of Christ* (London, 1641), p. 26.
25. Kahn, "Cavendish," p. 305.
26. Ibid., pp. 288, 308.
27. Thomas Hobbes, *Leviathan* (Indianapolis: Bobbs-Merill, 1958), p. 112.
28. For a discussion of the advantages of the premarital stage for women, see Susan B. Iwanisziw, "The Place of Women in Early Modern English Closet Drama," Ph.D. dissertation, University of Pennsylvania, 1994.
29. Ibid.
30. Jürgen Habermas, *The Structural Transformation of the Public Sphere* (Cambridge, MA: MIT Press, 1991), p. 52.
31. Maureen Bell, George Parfitt, and Simon Shepherd, *The Biographical Dictionary of English Women Writers, 1580–1720* (Boston: G. K. Hall, 1990), p. 159;

Manfred Brod, "Politics and Prophecy in Seventeenth-Century England: The Case of Elizabeth Poole," *Albion* 31, 3 (fall 1999), 395–412.
32. Louise Fargo Brown, *The Political Activities of the Baptists and Fifth Monarchy Men* (Washington, DC: American Historical Association, 1913), p. 3.
33. Patricia Crawford, *Women and Religion in England 1500–1720* (London: Routledge, 1993), pp. 119–130.
34. Ibid., p. 149.
35. Thomas Edwards, *Gangraena* (London, 1644).
36. B. R. White, *The English Baptists of the Seventeenth Century* (London: Baptist Historical Society, 1983), p. 63.
37. William Kiffin, *The Confession of Faith of those Churches which are commonly (though falseley) called Anabaptists* (London, 1644), p. 17.
38. Benjamin Cox, *An Appendix to a Confession of Faith, or A More full Declaration of the Faith and Judgement of Baptized Beleevers* (London, 1646).
39. Murray Tolmie, *The Triumph of the Saints: The Separate Churches of London 1616–1649* (Cambridge: Cambridge University Press, 1977), p. 182.
40. Kiffin, *Confession of Faith*, p. A3.
41. Edwards, *Gangraena*, p. 6.
42. William Kiffin, *Certain Observations Upon Hosea The Second the 7. & 8. Verses* (London, 1642).
43. Evelyn Fox Keller, *Reflections on Gender and Science* (New Haven: Yale University Press, 1985), p. 88.
44. Maggie Kilgour, "Comus's Wood of Allusion," *University of Toronto Quarterly* 61, 3 (spring 1992), 316–333, quote from p. 328.
45. Edwards, *Gangraena*, p. 6.
46. William Kiffin, *A Briefe Remonstrance of the Reasons and Grounds of those People commonly Called Anabaptists* (London, 1645), p. 1.
47. Henry K. Wotton, *The Elements of Architecture* (London, 1651), p. 271.
48. Fargo Brown, *Political Activities*, p. 5.
49. Kiffin, *Confession of Faith*, p. 26.
50. Edwards, *Gangraena.*, p. 30.
51. White, *English Baptists*, p. 67.
52. Crawford, *Women and Religion in England*, p. 144.
53. Edwards, *Gangraena*, p. 56.
54. Victoria Kahn, "The Metaphorical Contract," in David Armitage, Armand Himy, and Quentin Skinner, eds., *Milton and Republicanism* (Cambridge: Cambridge University Press, 1995), pp. 82–105, quote from p. 86.
55. C. H. Firth, ed., *The Clarke Papers: Selections from the Papers of William Clarke* (London: Offices of the Royal Historical Society, 1992), pp. 150–169.
56. Anon., *The Manner of the Deposition of Charles Stewart* (London, 1649), p. 6.
57. Mark Kishlansky, *A Monarchy Transformed: Britain 1603–1714* (Harmondsworth: Penguin, 1996), p. 161.
58. Ibid., pp. 158–186. See also A. S. P. Woodhouse, *Puritanism and Liberty* (London: J. M. Dent, 1992), pp. [14]–[35] and Tolmie, *Triumph of the Saints*, pp. 144–191.

59. See D. E. Kennedy, *The English Revolution 1642–1649* (London: Macmillan, 2000) for a history of these debates that focuses on "the growth of Puritan and Leveller sentiment within the Army" (p. 6).
60. Henry Ireton, *A Remonstrance of Fairfax and the Council of Officers* (London, 1648).
61. Anon., *A Brief Narrative of the Mysteries of State carried on by the Spanish Faction in England* (The Hague, 1651), p. 69.
62. Anon., *The English Devil, or Cromwell and his Monstrous Witch Discover'd at Whitehall* (London, 1660).
63. Brod, "Politics and Prophecy," p. 404.
64. Kennedy, *English Revolution*, pp. 116–134.
65. Ibid., pp. 116, 122.
66. Margaret Healy, *Fictions of Disease in Early Modern England: Bodies, Plagues and Politics* (London: Macmillan, 2001), p. 214.
67. James VI and I, "The Trew Law of Free Monarchies," in David Wootton, ed., *Divine Right and Democracy* (Harmondsworth: Penguin, 1986), pp. 99–106.
68. Kevin Sharp, "A Commonwealth of Meanings," in Kevin Sharp, *Remapping Early Modern England: The Culture of Seventeenth-Century Politics* (Cambridge: Cambridge University Press, 2000), p. 52.
69. Christopher Hill, *Society and Puritanism in Pre-Revolutionary England* (New York: St. Martin's Press, 1997), pp. 19 and 23.
70. Ibid., p. 22.
71. John Locke, *Two Treatises of Government*, rev. edn, ed. Peter Laslett (New York: Mentor, 1965), p. 210.
72. 1 Corinthians 11.3 (King James Bible; New York: Meridian, 1974), p. 153.
73. John Calvin, *The Sermons of M. John Calvin upon the Epistle of S. Paul to the Ephesians, translated by Arthur Golding* (1577), pp. 277–283.
74. William J. Scheick, "Logonomic Conflict in Anne Bradstreet's 'A Letter to her Husband,'" *Essays in Literature* 21, 2 (fall 1994), 166–183, quote from p. 167.
75. Rachel Speght, "A Mouzell for Melastomus" (1617), in Kate Aughterson, ed., *Renaissance Woman: Constructions of Femininity in England* (London: Routledge, 1995), pp. 270–277.
76. Barbara Kiefer Lewalski, *Writing Women in Jacobean England* (Cambridge, MA: Harvard University Press, 1993), pp. 153–175.
77. Kennedy, *English Revolution*, p. 117.
78. Ibid., p. 122.
79. J. G. A. Pocock, *The Ancient Constitution and Feudal Law* (Cambridge: Cambridge University Press, 1987); Christopher Hill, *Puritanism and Revolution* (New York: St. Martin's Press, 1997), pp. 46–111; Kahn, "Metaphorical Contract," pp. 101–102.
80. Filmer, *Patriarcha*, p. 236.
81. Frances Dolan, *Dangerous Familiars* (Ithaca: Cornell University Press, 1994), p. 26.
82. William Gouge, *Of Domesticall Duties* (London, 1622), pp. 396–397.
83. Dolan, *Dangerous Familiars*, p. 26.

84. Healy, *Fictions of Disease*, p. 224.
85. William Dell, *The Way of True Peace and Unity* (1649) in Woodhouse, *Puritanism and Liberty*, pp. 302–316, quote from p. 305.
86. Rachel Trubowitz, "Female Preachers and Male Wives," in James Holstun, ed., *Pamphlet Wars: Prose in the English Revolution* (London; Frank Cass, 1992), pp. 112–133, quotes from pp. 112 and 118 respectively, and Brian Patton, "Revolution, Regicide, and Divorce: Elizabeth Poole's Advice to the Army," in Alvin Vos, ed., *Place and Displacement in the Renaissance* (Binghamton, NY: Medieval and Renaissance Texts and Studies, 1995), pp. 133–145.
87. William Stampe, *A Sermon Preached Before His Majestie at Christ-Church in Oxford* (Oxford, 1643).
88. Kahn, "Metaphorical Contract," p. 98.
89. John Milton, "Tenure of Kings and Magistrates," in Flannagan, ed., *Riverside Milton*, pp. 1057–1075, quote from p. 1069.
90. Edward Sexby, "Killing Noe Murder," in Wootton, *Divine Right and Democracy*, p. 367.
91. Kahn, "Metaphorical Contract," p. 98.
92. Kahn, "Cavendish," pp. 288 and 290.
93. In "Arise and be doing: English Preaching Women, 1640–1660," (unpublished dissertation, Indiana University, 1978), Dorothy Ludlow maintains that Poole was excommunicated because her "theological stance, insofar as it is voiced in her tracts, expressed the views of a General Baptist rather than the Particular Baptist orientation of Kiffin's group (p. 230). Ludlow does not elaborate upon her reasons for drawing this conclusion. However, as I shall show later, it appears more likely that it was an apparent act of sexual slander against Poole that most outraged her.
94. Trubowitz, "Female Preachers and Male Wives," p. 114.
95. Poole, *Another Alarum of War*, p. 9.
96. *Webster's New Universal Unabridged Dictionary* (New York: Barnes & Noble, 1996), p. 2123.
97. Patricia Parker, *Literary Fat Ladies: Rhetoric, Gender, Property* (London and New York: Methuen, 1987), pp. 106 and 127.
98. Catherine MacKinnon, *Toward a Feminist Theory of the State* (Cambridge, MA: Harvard University Press, 1989), pp. 45–46.

4

The unquenchable smoking flax: Sarah Wight, Anne Wentworth, and the "rise" of the sovereign individual

> Fool do not boast, Thou canst not touch the freedom of my minde
> The Lady in *Comus* ("Comus appears with his rabble, and the Lady set in an inchanted Chair, to whom he offers his Glass, which she puts by, and goes about *to rise*" – emphasis added)

> one grain of that precious faith, and one dram of love which the Lord gives his hidden ones, is far beyond all other things, that we can act or do; it's all of God, without our mixtures . . . My soul shouts forth with the true spiritualized Christian, this voice
> Sarah Wight, *A Wonderful, Pleasant and Profitable Letter*

> for obeying the Word of the Lord, and his Commandments, I am reproached as a proud, wicked, deceived, deluded, lying Woman; a mad, melancholy, crackbrained, self-willed, conceited Fool, and black sinner, led by whimsies, notions, and knick-knacks of my own head; one that speaks blasphemy, not fit to take the Name of God in her mouth; an Heathen and Publican, a Foretune-teller, an Enthusiast, and the like much more, whereof I appeal to God, to judge: And then let all slanderers challenge their own words.
> Anne Wentworth, *The Revelation of Jesus Christ*

The deification of King Charles and Henrietta Maria at the climax of Carew's masque, *Coelum Britannicum*, was punctuated by special effects.[1] Whereas Charles's father, King James, had years before presided over *Pleasure Reconciled to Virtue*, a masque written late in James's reign that exhorted the then young *Prince* Charles to strive to achieve the heavenly pinnacle of Atlas's steep and rocky mountain of virtue, *Coelum Britannicum* tells us that the more complacent *King* Charles preferred to have his elite access to celestial virtue served to him on the rocks, as a sovereign privilege handed down by the large stooping Atlas drawn for the occasion by the court's chief architect, Inigo Jones.[2] This approach however, harbored a catch. If heaven had literally landed on British soil, then what other earthly creature in the realm could claim that it had been crowned with sovereign subjectivity?

Roughly nine years later, in 1647, at the height of the English civil war, when Charles struggled to quite literally retain his crown, one answer to that question emerged. A well-known dissenting minister by the name of Henry Jessey published a pamphlet entitled *The Exceeding Riches of Grace Advanced by the spirit of Grace in an Empty Nothing Creature, Mistress Sarah Wight.*[3] In this tract, Jessey recounted the story of Sarah Wight, a mere 15-year-old girl, who was so convinced that she was doomed to hell for some minor wrongs she had committed that she was plunged into months of spiritual turmoil which consigned her to bed and compelled her to undertake a number of punishing fasts, which sent her into a series of sustained trances. Never believing that she, an "empty nothing creature," as she was described by Jessey, was worthy enough to earn God's favor, Wight was shown to be humbly ecstatic when she was nonetheless chosen to serve as a holy vessel for "the exceeding riches of [God's] grace." Wight's redemption was the perfect symbol for Henry Jessey's radical religious agenda in that she exemplified his commitment to the idea that every individual – no matter how lowly – was a candidate for election, thus his tract dedicated itself to further publicizing a case that, according to him, had already become a *cause celebre* throughout London as citizens came from near and far to behold the young saint in the "contemptible manger" (16) she occupied within her modest house on Lawrence Pountney Lane by Caning Street. According to Jessey, Sarah's fans were particularly enthralled by the visionary messages she was enabled to deliver upon receiving grace, messages which were recorded by Jessey and other amanuenses as carefully as Christ's disciples took down his gospel truths and which bore the authenticating markers of italics within the pages of Jessey's hagiography. For example, in an especially dramatic moment in Jessey's account, Sarah is reported to have awakened and to have issued the following proclamation as a paraphrase from the First Book of Kings. As she stated: "God hath two Thrones, one is in the highest Heavens, the other is in the lowest hearts. He dwells as truly in the lowest hearts, as in the highest Heavens, in the poorest contemptible hearts ... Do not you know that God hath two Thrones? The highest Heavens and the lowest hearts!" (23). Sarah's message was all too clear – and all too subversive: God's grace extended so far down that even a disruptive young girl could dramatize his sovereignty. The King and his court need no longer perform this task on behalf of their subjects; rather, their subjects were now empowered to perform it for themselves. Thus, in Sarah's case, the powerful message she was meant to deliver consisted not of the Carolinian claim that only the actual monarch and his chosen few were fit enough to function as earthly representatives of God's word, but of the Puritan doctrine which contended that everyone – even an "empty nothing creature" – could serve as a vehicle for revealed truth.

Male liberal political theorists are credited with having "invented" the concept of the sovereign or possessive self, the idea that the basic unit of a political order is or should be an individual who possesses a God-given right to a sphere of sovereign dominion and self-determination. However, in this chapter I will argue that sectarian women also envisioned a sovereign subject in the seventeenth century. This is worth considering because antiliberal postfeminist scholars tend to regard this construct with particularly keen suspicion, if not outright hostility. They contend that the traits assigned to this "abstract" definition of the individual actually conceal and encode a masculine character that disenfranchises women. As Linda Kerber asserts, "the classic statements of American individualism are best understood as guides to masculine conduct."[4] Alison Jagger elaborates, contending that liberalism is predicated on the faulty assumption that "the essential human characteristics are properties of individuals and are given independently of any particular social context."[5] This is problematic because it fails to recognize the fact that, as Jaggar maintains, "it is a conceptual as well as an empirical truth that human interests are acquired only in a social context" and that this renders those "interests" a function of "social constitution" rather than "individual will" (43). To assimilate this "truth" into law, we must, according to Jaggar, dismantle the very idea of the abstract, self-possessive individual and instead embrace a more feminist model of "embodiment," one in which the individual is defined not by the sovereign dominion that he/she enjoys over him/herself, but by the degree to which he/she is protectively enmeshed within the operations of "political determinism." For Naomi Scheman, women already embody this alternative model of the self because of the inherent "interconnectedness" that their "penetrable" bodies represent, and because they are "less likely," as a result, "to speak naturally in voices at once abstractly disembodied and autonomously self-defining."[6] Carole Pateman agrees, arguing that while there have been "many famous critiques of the abstract character of liberal individualism," none have challenged "the most fundamental abstraction of all: the abstraction of the 'individual' from the body. In order for the individual to appear in liberal theory as a universal figure who represents anyone and everyone, the individual must be disembodied."[7] However, as she says, this idea of "disembodiment" is once again the product of a masculine bias for it is an inherently male trait. Thus, if we are to "take embodied identity seriously," we must pursue the "abandonment of the masculine, unitary individual to open up space for two figures; one masculine, one feminine."[8]

As these comments imply, the abandonment of the "masculine, unitary individual" and the attendant embrace of a female principle of "embodiment" are often predicated upon a rejection of the following principle: that the individual possesses a degree of autonomy which allows him/her to escape or dissent from communal norms, standards, and judgments. As Scheman argues, it is false to assume that people "exist essentially as separate individuals – with wants, preferences, needs, abilities, pleasures and pains" of their own, because this assumption detracts from our ability to recognize – and institutionalize – the more feminine principle of "interrelatedness" (231). This principle consists of the "fact" that, because individuals are by no means "expert in identifying their own 'interests,'" they must be brought to "recognize" that they are both subject to and indebted to the "other." As Catharine MacKinnon writes:

The voluntarism of liberalism consists in its notion that social life is comprised of autonomous, intentional, and self-willed actions, with exceptional constraints or qualifications by society *or the state*. This aggregation of freely acting persons as the descriptive and prescriptive model of social action is replaced, in radical feminism, with a complex political determinism. Women and women's actions are complex responses to conditions they did not make or control; they are contextualized and situated. (Emphasis added)[9]

A number of scholars working specifically in seventeenth-century studies participate in this project by arguing that, because dissenting prophetesses represented a more embodied, multivocal, and fluid definition of the speaking subject, they provided a more fragmented and partial alternative to the sovereign self at the very point at which this "masculinist" idea was emerging. Rachel Trubowitz, Diane Purkiss, and Hilary Hinds have offered possible explanations for why dissenting women dropped out of literary history and why it has taken so much longer to bring their voices back to critical attention than it has aristocratic women writers.[10] In addressing this important question, they reason that the prophetesses' own social strategies for gaining a public voice ultimately backfired against them. Prophetesses represented themselves as traditionally female "empty vessels" whose voices were not their own but God's. However, while they were able to exploit this conventional identification of women with their bodies for the unconventional purpose of gaining masculine forms of social authority, they inadvertently paved the way for their detractors to silence them by reappropriating the figure of the woman as vessel – or body – and using it to paint prophetesses as whores whose bodies (like their mouths) had been too open, too publicly accessible. So, after Elizabeth Poole delivered her second message, she was slanderously charged with having gone "about seducing." Examples of "backlash" such as this prompt the conclusion that, in the end, the social and literary legacy of seventeenth-century female sectarian writers is an aborted one, ending in silenced disgrace and making sectarian women a kind of dead end on the evolutionary road to the Enlightenment. Postmodern feminism benefits from this, however, because dissenting women's texts may now be put to the latter-day task of deconstructing liberal individualism – from which women were excluded anyway – and replacing it with a more multiple, dialogic, and "embodied" conception of the self.

This new – or newly recognized – model of alternative subjectivity furthers the project undertaken by Catherine Belsey in 1988, when she called for feminists to be more observant of Louis Althusser's Marxist theory of interpellation.[11] *Interpellation* is Althusser's term for describing the process by which he believes individuals are constructed as subjects, that is, not by acts of self-determination but in and through ideological state apparatuses that serve a ruling class. For Althusser, the ideology of religion in particular benefits those in power because it manufactures deluded subjects, who, while they may believe themselves free in their subjection to the "Unique, Absolute Other Subject, i.e. God," are in fact creatures of a whole host of authorities, including, as Althusser says, "[the] conscience, the priest, de Gaulle, the boss, the engineer," and so on.[12] He finds irony, or what he terms "ambiguity," in the false assumption perpetuated by possessive individualism, that is that "the individual is interpellated as a (free) subject in order that he shall submit freely to the commandments of the Subject, i.e. in order that he shall (freely) accept his subjection, i.e. in order that he shall make the gestures and actions of his subjection 'all by himself.'" What people do not realize, he contends, is that "Their concrete, material behavior" is "simply the inscription in life" of what feminists call the "social context," and what he describes as the capitulating and "admirable words of the prayer: 'Amen-So be it'" (181).

But, as stated, it will be my argument here that sectarian women writers actually forged the model of the subject that feminists actively seek to displace – that of the "sovereign" or "abstract" individual. Identifying them as early articulators rather than victims of this principle should challenge us to reconsider its status as a masculine construct invented solely to further rather than ameliorate patriarchal domination. As the previous chapter has shown, the unstable self was precisely the definition of womanhood that Poole was trying to escape by imagining and insisting on an abstract notion of herself as a "spirit" or "soul" whose innate essence ultimately transcended all attempts by the community to define and silence her. Many sectarian women did, by all means, foreground the ways in which they were "subject to" external forces. But, so their logic went, it was precisely *because* individuals (especially women) were constantly told that they were and/or should be "riven" or interpellated by various collective overdeterminations, including those of the state, that they had to be reminded that there was a secure and stable sense of self that acted as a counter to those pressures – and that was the God-within. This internalized sovereignty often manifested itself most fully when dissenting women are represented as being in a state of crisis – just as the Lady had been when under Comus's thrall – and it took the form of "rising" through grace. Given the contexts in which they wrote, it is difficult to read their "essentialism" as dictating behavioral norms that served the interests of *the* or *a* "ruling class." Rather, by laying claim to the selfhood with which the individual was bestowed through salvation, separatist women transgressed codes governing female agency in general and lower-order female agency in particular, and criticized attempts by "others" to, as they saw it, illegitimately delimit their behavior to a particular "social context," whether those "others" consisted of their rulers or their husbands. In the next section I will argue that dissenting women writers did not deconstruct the idea that the individual was interpellated as a (free) subject in order that he "shall submit freely to the commandments of the Subject, i.e. in order that he shall (freely) accept his subjection, i.e. in order that he shall make the gestures and actions of his subjection 'all by himself.' " Instead, as I will discuss in the section entitled "A Tradition of Popular Sovereignty," they drew upon a separatist concept of the sovereign self to counter an ideological tradition defined by the very idea that female subjectivity was embodied and hence discontinuous and fragmented. In the sections "Sarah Wight: New Sovereign Woman" and "Anne Wentworth: Possessive Individual" I will discuss two women's pioneering articulations of the subject as an end unto herself.

INTERPELLATED WOMEN IN HISTORY

Early modern husbands, fathers, and sons were defined as subjects through their subordination to the King (who was in turn subject to God only), while women, as daughters of Eve, were further subordinated to their fathers, husbands, and paternalistic magistrates of all sorts, because their allegedly fragile natures were said to make them more vulnerable to being designated the repository of Satan's machinations (menstruating women were believed to be especially prone to hysteria and extremes of emotion because of the instabilities circulating fluids introduced into their systems).[13] As Janet Biehl has written (in a decidedly anticelebratory fashion), women have been "marginalized for millennia, passive and receptive for millennia, 'connected' to the point of self-effacement for millennia."[14] This collocation of the female self as partial and fragmentary and hence as subject to a process of imbrication with evil was, of course, the basis of laws against witchcraft. As William Perkins wrote in 1608, "the woman being the weaker sex, is sooner entangled by the devils illusions with this damnable art than the man."[15] But it also underwrote the numerous other ways in which women were controlled and disciplined by millennia of male authorities. Because women were deemed to be more constructed as subjects by their own passions than were men (because, in other words, they were said to have "fruitful wombs [but] barren brains"), their access to education and literacy was restricted.[16] The debate over whether or not women were stable enough to have souls also resulted in the claim that women's religious training, upon which their salvation clearly rested, had to be supervised by their husbands as well as by the high church ministers assigned to their home parishes.[17] Their supposed lack of rationality and self-control formed the philosophical underpinning of the state of English Common Law at the accession of James I, an underpinning that transferred women from the guardianship of their fathers to that of their husbands upon marriage (a relation likened to that of feudal lords and vassals), which denied them the same access to rights and property enjoyed by elite men, which required them to undergo "churching" in order to rid them of the extra pollutants their systems were infused with through birth, which prosecuted them for "petty treason" if they killed their husbands, even in self-defense, and so on.[18] Material histories of women have found that, at times, women were able to exploit various loopholes within these laws in order to enact some forms of agency, however circumscribed.[19] Nonetheless, to keep women from undergoing the processes of interpellation to which they were said to be imminently vulnerable, authorities were always poised to subject them to community-sanctioned forms of corrective reinterpellative surveillance and control, including confinement to the house, the use of bridal cages and tongue suppressers, and physical abuse.[20] As the *Lawes*

Resolution of 1632 read, a man might beat "an outlaw, a traitor, a Pagan, his villein, or his wife because by the Law Common these persons can have no action."[21]

Given our increasing understanding of the ways in which this patriarchal "social context" has, for "millennia," as Biehl says, dictated the lives of women by defining them as interpellated selves, it must be asked why it is that surprisingly similar ideas about women's "difference" continue to undergird much of postmodern feminism's endorsement of social construction theory. Scheman, for example, bases her belief in the idea that individualistic self-determination is a "male myth" on the fact that "a girl's sense of self is typically weaker than a boy's; the ego-boundaries are less strong" ("Individualism," 242). This makes the girl, Scheman argues, the ideal prototype for an embodied notion of the interconnected self. Rather than endorsing the possibility that women, too, have interests that allow them to dissent from the social whole, Scheman and other antiliberal feminists envision a world in which both men and women must capitulate to the "truth" of the self by following women's lead and subordinating their own desires (which are socially constructed anyway) to the collective scrutiny of "the community."

Interestingly, such pronouncements come at a time when feminist literary scholars have actually uncovered the surprisingly broad investment that early modern women made in the idea of the sovereign subject. Naomi Miller writes of the obvious advantages that Elizabeth I accrued by quite literally assuming the mantle of the "sovereign subject," but she also finds "emerging notions of sovereignty in the works of women writers ranging from Anne Clifford and Aemilia Lanyer to Elizabeth Cary and Mary Wroth."[22] In this chapter I hope to contribute to this project by identifying the advantages that nonelite sectarian women claim for themselves in the oppositional assumption of an exclusively omnipotent overdetermination of the construction of subjectivity. As stated earlier, critics who have studied dissenting women writers have often associated them with an alternative, more "feminine" model of the individual, seeing them as beacons that will guide us into a new era of recognizing the true "fragmentary" nature of all subjectivity. But the historical accuracy as well as the liberatory efficacy of this statement receives a real challenge from two texts pertaining to the prophetess Sarah Wight, as well as pamphlets by Baptist visionary Anne Wentworth. Speaking in voices that they represent as "at once abstractly disembodied and autonomously self-defining," Wight's and Wentworth's texts echo Milton's *Comus* by associating the essential features (and benefits) of the sovereign or abstract subject with a female protagonist who challenges and appropriates various forms of state-backed and community-sanctioned power.

In the first Wight text (published under the name of her congregationalist fellow, Henry Jessey), the young virgin is held up as a grace-filled "sovereign self," capable of anchoring an alternative "court" that competed with and decentered the monarch's traditional monopoly over exemplary sovereign selfhood. In the second, Wight herself pens eighty-one pages anatomizing (and ironically metaphorizing) the abstract fixity, which, she insists, allows all individuals to transcend the limitations of socially and politically determined embodiment. Writing later in the century, Wentworth developed an explicit rationale for abstract and even possessive individualism in order to attack marital abuse and defend divorce. In essence, her publications tell us that, when a powerless woman is faced with the powerful forces of the "social constitution" and "determinism," her one recourse is to assert the abstract doctrine of sovereign virginity and to repeat, along with the Lady, "Fool, do not boast; thou can not touch the freedom of my mind."

A TRADITION OF POPULAR SOVEREIGNTY

Dissenting women's voices formed an important, though largely unacknowledged, contribution to a grass-roots early modern movement for abstract individualism. Contrary to Althusser's tendency to see all state apparatuses as operating in tandem with one another to constitute and control subjects, the early modern religious dissent movement suggested that it was possible to fracture the ISA's monolith by pitting one component against another. Sectarians consistently cited a "higher" obedience to God the Subject, also known as "freedom of conscience," as grounds for undermining the state apparatus of the church. To do so, they drew upon what David Wootton calls a Baptist theory of popular sovereignty derived from Galatians.[23] This Pauline epistle contains such provocative statements as "For if righteousness come by the Law, then Christ died in vain" (2.21) and "Stand fast therefore in the liberty wherewith Christ hath made us free" (5.2). Sixteenth-century German Anabaptists read such proclamations as a license for bypassing earthly governors in favor of following their own consciences, which, they claimed, were directed by God. All individuals were entitled to dissent from the state church by virtue of the God-given "spirit" that each of them possessed, no matter how lowly their position was within the hierarchical "social context" of their day. Luther's *Commentary upon Galatians* was intended to thwart the potential for subversion unleashed by

Anabaptist exegesis. He tried to convince dissenters that such ideas were not meant to impinge upon the civil realm of the law. As he wrote, "In what liberty? Not in that wherewith the Emperor hath made us free, but in that wherewith Christ hath made us free . . . not from earthly bondage . . . but from God's everlasting wrath. And where is this done? In the conscience. There resteth our liberty and goeth no farther."[24] Calvin betrayed the same concerns in his *Institution of Christian Religion*. As he wrote:

> when they hear that liberty is promised by the Gospel, which acknowledgeth among men no kin and no magistrate but hath regard to Christ alone, they think that they can take no fruit of their liberty so long as they see any power to have pre-eminence over them . . . But whosoever can put difference between the body and the soul, between this present and transitory life and that life to come and eternal, he shall not hardly understand that the spiritual kingdom of Christ and the civil government are things far asunder . . . [and that] spiritual liberty may very well agree with civil bondage.[25]

The translations of these texts into English coincided with the Baptists's emergence in England in the early decades of the seventeenth century. In the face of Baptist claims that they owed allegiance to the one true King only – Christ, the son of God – James drew firmer and firmer lines between the rights of the sovereign and those of everyone else. While dissenters claimed that their direct line to God's grace gave them the contractual right to resist a tyrannical and unregenerate king on earth, James retorted by rearticulating a notion of the sovereign subject over which he was to retain a monopoly: "Now in this contract (I say) betwixt the king and his people, God is doubtless the only judge . . . because to him only, the king must make count of his administration."[26] The sovereign individual, in other words, was defined quite literally as the King alone who, as a subject was "accountable" only to God. Everyone else was to be socially constructed as a subject by him and hence quite literally "subjected" to his will. Because the people were "interpellated" as subjects by the King, they were denied any spiritual "interest" outside of his and forced to submit to his judgment.

As the previous chapter showed, English dissenters opposed this formulation with articles 68 and 69 of *The Confession*. These asserted the contractual right of political dissent by pledging allegiance to the "civil Magistracie" and the "King and Parliament *freely chosen* by the Kingdome" (emphasis added). They promised to obey earthly authorities, "in the Lord," implying that they could withhold obedience if the ruler proved himself to be outside the bounds of acceptable governance. *The Confession* ended by even more explicitly insisting that there was a higher government to be obeyed than that of the King and Parliament. The authors signed the very document intended to guarantee their allegiance with the words: "we doe therefore here subscribe it, some of each body in the name and by the appointment of seven congregations . . . holding Jesus Christ to be our head and Lord; under whose government we desire alone to walk." All, they insisted, possessed the sovereign right of judgment and this ability to "walk alone" with God.[27]

During the revolution, the Levellers based their political models for possessive individualism and rights on this religious foundation of self-sovereignty forged by Independents. A lengthy quote from John Lilburne's *The Free-man's Freedome Vindicated* encapsulates the ways in which they translated the philosophy of popular sovereignty into political terms:

God the absolute sovereign Lord and King of all things in heaven and earth, the original fountain and cause of all causes, who is circumscribed, governed, and limited by no rules, but doth all things merely and only by his sovereign will and unlimited good pleasure, who made the world and all things therein for his own glory, by his own will and pleasure gave man, his mere creature, the sovereignty (under himself) over all the rest of his creatures (Gen. 1.26, 28, 29) and endued him with a rational soul or understanding, and thereby created him after his own image (Gen. 1.26–27, and 9.6). The first of which was Adam . . . made out of the dust or clay, out of whose side was taken a rib, which by the sovereign and absolute mighty creating power of God was made a female . . . called Eve. Which two are the earthly original fountain . . . of all and every particular and individual man and woman . . . in the world since, who are, and were, by nature all equal and alike in power, dignity, authority, dominion, or magisterial power one over or above another; neither have they, or can they exercise any, but merely by institution or donation, that is to say, by mutual agreement or consent, given, derived, or assumed by mutual consent and agreement, for the good benefit and comfort each of other, and not for the mischief, hurt, or damage of any; it being unnatural, irrational . . . wicked, and unjust, for any man or men whatsoever to part with so much of their power as shall enable any of their Parliament-men, commissioners, trustees, deputies . . . or servants, to destroy and undo them therewith. And unnatural, irrational, sinful, wicked, unjust, devilish, and tyrannical, it is for any man whatsoever, spiritual or temporal, clergyman or layman, to appropriate and assume unto himself a power, authority, and jurisdiction, to rule, govern, or reign over any sort of men in the world without their free consent.[28]

Lilburne's emphasis is, of course, on the imprimatur that every individual – not just the King – receives from God to have "dominion" over him *and herself*. Because this original grant of self-government derives from God, it is immutable and inviolable; no earthly power may "appropriate and assume" it "unto himself" in order to wield it over any other. Every self is a sovereign self and should be recognized as possessing a will and a set of interests that cannot be dictated by the state. At the same time, unlike the King's version of sovereignty, the popular sovereign subject was not allowed to impinge upon the sovereignty of others.

Another Leveller writer, Richard Overton, was concerned that the idea of everyman as a sovereign simply reified the concept of sovereignty which, in his mind, should be done away with altogether rather than dispersed into all members of the body politic. He wished to replace an "absolute" understanding of sovereignty with a model of possessive individualism in which nature acted as a mediating force between God and the subject. As he wrote in *An Arrow against all Tyrants* (1646):

> To every Individuall in nature is given an individual property by nature, not to be invaded or usurped by any: for every one as he is himself, so he hath a selfe propriety, else could he not be himselfe, and on this no second may presume to deprive any of, without manifest violation and affront to the very principles of nature, and of the Rules of equity and justice between man and man; mine and thine cannot be except this be; No man hath power over my rights and liberties, and I over no mans; I may be but an Individuall, enjoy my selfe, and my selfe propriety, and may write my selfe no more then my selfe or presume any further; if I doe, I am an encroacher & an invader upon an other mans Right, to which I have no Right. For my naturall birth, all men are equally and alike borne to like propriety, liberty, and freedome, and as we are delivered of God by the hand of nature into this world, every one with a naturall, innate freedom and propriety (as it were writ in the table of every mans heart, never to be obliterated) even so are we to live, every one equally and alike to enjoy his Birth-right and priviledge; even all whereof God by nature hath made him free.
>
> And this by nature every one desires, aimes at, and requires for no man naturally would be befooled of his liberty by his neighbours craft, or inslaved by his neighbours might, for it is natures instinct to preserve it selfe, from all things hurtfull and obnoctious, and this in nature is granted of all to be most reasonable, equall and just, not to be rooted out of the kind, even of equall duration with the creature: And from this fountain or root, all just humain powers take their original; not immediately from God (as Kings usually plead their prerogative) but mediately by the hand of nature, as from the represented to the representors . . .[29]

As stated, Overton wished to dispense altogether with a model of rights acquisition predicated on a sovereign who pleads the "prerogative" of deriving his power "immediately from God." Overton appears to fear that granting this "prerogative" to everyone would result in the dissolution of all property rights, including the right to claim property-in-self, for, presumably, God could empower an individual to transgress upon rights which others hold by "nature" and "reason" rather than divine (and hence unverifiable) attribution. By inserting nature into the mix, Overton is able to argue even more forcefully that, while all individuals enjoy freedoms traditionally reserved for the sovereign, this does not mean that they enjoy a blank check to encroach upon the rights of others, as sovereigns claimed they could do. However, having said this, it is also necessary to observe that Overton still buttresses his argument with the Scripture that underwrote so many sectarian claims to sovereign selfhood. As he goes on to state, "Every man by nature being a King, Priest and Prophet in his owne naturall circuite and compasse, whereof no second may partake, but by deputation, commission, and free consent from him, whose naturall right and freedome it is" (3–4). In other words, although he tempers it, Overton's logic is as informed by the logic of popular sovereignty as it is by a concept of natural rights. Or rather, his argument demonstrates the symbiotic relationship between the two assertions – the one that says the individual receives liberties directly from God versus the one that reroutes those liberties through nature and reason. His concern was the same as that expressed later by Locke, that a popular sovereign subject, radically understood, threatened to unleash an individual whose claims to answer to God would only result in a nation of tyrants. To avoid this, both Overton and Locke constitute nature and man's rational powers as a means by which to argue that each man enjoyed a "natural" circuit and compass, one which could be breached neither by the encroachment of others, nor by the owner's own desire to impinge upon another's sphere.

In contrast to feminist claims that the "abstract" individual inevitably encoded a masculine set of characteristics and qualifications, both of these early formulations of the sovereign subject had positive ramifications for women. Lilburne's invocation of Eve demonstrates the degree to which, in his mind, the sovereign subject could be either a man or a woman. As he says, Eve as well as Adam was "the fountain" from which sprang the template for the subject. God "endued *him*" or "man" with "a rational soul or understanding," but, as Lilburne says, the first to be created in God's own image was Adam and the "second" was Eve who, despite being created immediately from Adam's rib, was nonetheless to be viewed as a direct byproduct of "the sovereign and absolute mighty creating power of God." These two are "by nature all equal and alike in power, dignity, authority, dominion, or magisterial power one over or above another." Lilburne's opposition is not between a rational (read masculine) and autonomous sovereign self on the one hand versus an "irrational" (read feminine) or "interconnnected" self on the other. Rather, it is between two equally rational and sovereign selves (male and female) on the one hand versus all "unnatural, irrational ... wicked, and unjust" attempts by members of the state (Parliament men, commissioners, trustees, deputies) or the church to "destroy and undo" either of them "therewith." Because all individuals, whether male or female, inhabit a sphere in which they are free to define their own interests and to assert their own will, then all must give their "free consent" to any government order before it can assume jurisdiction over them. One could argue, of course, that by describing Eve as rational, Lilburne was masculinizing her and distancing her from a set of characteristics traditionally defined as feminine. But, of course, that was precisely his point. Contrary to the conventional wisdom of his age, femininity was not antithetical to reason.

Overton's nature-based argument is, albeit more indirectly, also capable of comprehending women. By making nature a necessary component in the composition of the free subject, he offset a tendency within some sectarian thought to argue that the sovereign subject was, by necessity, predicated on the denigration of "female nature." For example, the Quaker Edward Burrough wrote that the internalization of the spirit of grace which ultimately underwrote the politically and religiously free subject meant abjecting any femaleness that might dwell within.[30] As he wrote, "Let ... [the Word] dwell richly in you, which will cut down, and wholly root out the whorish wo-man within your selves ... O male and female-man, wherefore keep thine to within thy head, and the head of every man is Christ Jesus" (7–8). If sovereignty entails the excision of femininity, then it might appear from this that women could not in fact function as sovereign subjects. However, even Burrough's formulation is more complex than at first appears. On the one hand, he defines the ideal subject as that which represses the female. Women are referred to as female men and the subjective, mutable, and degenerative part of man is the "whorish wo-man" within. On the other hand, Burrough levels differences conventionally posited between men and women. Both men and women are capable of "rooting out" that which subjects them to corruption and of "keeping themselves within their own heads." The implication is that women have their own heads; thus, when Burrough ends by quoting one of the premier Scriptures used to undergird patriarchalism – Paul's injunction that "the head of every man is Christ Jesus" – we understand that he intends for the term *man* to now refer both to "male" and "female men." Burrough's interest lies in defining individualism abstractly not in order to deny women access to religious freedom but to grant it to them by redefining them as creatures who contain an immutable self that is not, as it was traditionally asserted, imminently or *by its very nature* vulnerable to Satanic infection.

Like Lilburne, his effort is aimed not at denying womanhood but at redefining it.

What is more, just as constituting Eve as a rational being allowed women to escape traditional definitions of femininity as "nature" and hence as antithetical to reason, the use of nature as a medium between God and the individual made it possible for women to claim that, as nature, they were the very ground of liberty, as well as its object. As the introduction to this chapter shows, one way in which women registered this argument was by performing the role of a maternal nature capable of birthing the autonomous religiously free subject, of exercising the religious prerogative of choice for themselves, and of channeling God's word through the pure nature of their bodily vessels. In other words, women argued overtly for a "doctrine of virginity," a definition of the sovereign self that was both "abstract" and explicitly gendered in such a way as to highlight its inclusion of women. Because they were "embodied" as "penetrable" subjects, they were the vehicle for and repository of sovereignty. Katherine Chidley's first act of religious dissent from the Anglican church was to refuse to attend her churching ritual after the birth of a child, claiming that the fundamental fact of her body was not its dissolute disarray but its elemental purity, a purity guaranteed by her centered subjectivity as a mutable body that was "fixed" by the indwelling spirit of grace. As the previous chapter has shown, Poole countered in her *Alarum* that she was *not* the whore who had been rooted out from the congregation; instead, she was the virgin, immaculately impregnated with Christ's imprimatur by God alone. This idea that one is defined by a virginalized spirit or essence also forms the basis for Anna Trapnel's claim to a public voice. Like Poole, Trapnel returned to print to "vindicate" her reputation in the face of her opponents' attempts to smear her name and silence her as a prophetess. In *Report and Plea*, Trapnel wrote that she was writing to vindicate not her "self" but the "Truth" which, she argued, "stands in no need of mine or any one's vindication; but I would shew love and respect to it, in opposition to those, who with spades and shovels dig up mire and rubbish to throw upon it."[31] In keeping with her exploration of a self that lies both within and beyond her natural self, Trapnel wrote: "But the Lord knows, I would not reach out tongue, hand nor pen, to right my self, or to seek restauration of my loss, I wave that, as such a thing is below my spirit" (A3). Instead, she concluded, it is "through grace [that] I am what I am; and I live, yet not I, but Christ lives in me" (A3). In other words, the self is ultimately beyond any attempt to constitute it as a fallen subject because the "spirit" that resides within endows "her grace" with the sovereign privilege of self-determination, with "Truth," and with a set of interests that remain outside of and impervious to the declarations of the community of man. As she wrote:

> O what am I, O what am I,
> But a poor silly one;
> A bruised reed thou mak'st abide,
> That cannot stand alone.
> But O my strength is from above,
> It doth come from thee;
> Which makes me so inflam'd with love,
> And so in singing be.   (A3)

She may by "nature" be a "poor silly one" or a "bruised reed" who "cannot stand alone." However, this does not make her a subject of the "political determinism" of others. Rather, the "strength" that her natural self is given "from above" provides her, quite literally, with a voice that can be used to assert that she is something other than what society says she is.

SARAH WIGHT: NEW SOVEREIGN WOMAN

The overall point is that, contemporaneously with male Levellers, and years before Locke did so for men, both sectarian men and women writers can be found "dislodg[ing] patriarchalism's belief in the radical difference of women," and instituting a "kind of *individualism* that would give them identities that were not inherently distinct from those of men."[32] There is as much evidence to suggest that sectarian men (as Milton divined) both formulated definitions of popular sovereignty that would include women and even posited the female as the exemplary sovereign subject as there is to suggest that this concept was forged for the express purpose of excluding women. The implication was that, if a young woman – powerless in general but especially so if it was suspected that she had been "corrupted" in any way – could nonetheless be redeemed into "kingship" by God, then *anybody* could look forward to the same. Not surprisingly then, two texts published as part of this popular movement to delineate the paradigmatic sovereign subject pertain to the young Fifth Monarchist prophetess, Sarah Wight. The first, mentioned in the introduction to this chapter, is Henry Jessey's account of Wight's emergence as a cultural phenomenon, *The Exceeding Riches of Grace Advanced by the Spirit of Grace, in an Empty Nothing Creature, viz. Mrs. Sarah Wight*. The second is Wight's own tract, *A Wonderful Pleasant and Profitable Letter Written by Mrs. Sarah Wight, To a Friend, Expressing the Joy that is to be had in God in Great, Deep, Long, and Sore*

Afflictions. As stated earlier, in the former, Wight is made a "pattern" for popular sovereignty, while in the latter she herself delineates and defends an abstract and autonomous model for the individual.

Published in 1647, Jessey's text establishes Wight's brief life story. She was the daughter of Mr. Thomas Wight of the Auditors and Exchequers Offices, and Mary Wight. Her mother had been previously married to a Mr. Edward Vaughan, the King's Receiver and Surveyor for Northamptonshire and Rutlandshire. This first marriage produced a son, Jonathan Vaughan. At the time of Jessey's account, Mary Wight's second husband, Thomas Wight, was also deceased and thus she lived as a widow near London-stone. Her second husband's death may have precipitated the seven-year period of "terror and distraction of Spirit" she was said to have experienced in the not too distant past. During this difficult time, her daughter, Sarah, was "well trained up in the Scriptures, by her godly faithfull Grand-mother, Mris Wight of Daintree" (7). (When Sarah's mother emerged from her crisis period, Sarah was 9 and had begun to "read and study the Scriptures" with an intensity all her own.) Also part of the household was Mrs. Wight's maid, Hannah Gay, the daughter of dissenter Eli Jabu Gay, who tended Mary during her years of suffering. Both Sarah Wight's mother and Hannah Gay provide the two most sufficient pieces of eye-witness testimony to the despair that Wight herself subsequently experienced, starting at the age of 12 and continuing for about four years.

This period of spiritual (and adolescent) crisis was reportedly brought on by two discrete incidents. The first was one in which a "superior bid her doe a small thing, judging it meet and lawfull." Wight carried out this request, which appears to have involved taking something under dubious circumstances, but she did so "doubtingly," fearing that it was in fact "unlawful." She was seized immediately afterwards with "a great Trembling in her hands and body" and felt "condemned in her selfe" (7). About a month later, another incident occurred in which she lied to her mother, telling her erroneously that her missing hood was at her grandmother's house. Feeling that she was both a "Thiefe, and a lyar," Wight reported a feeling of guilt and despair which in turn precipitated a series of fits and fainting spells, as well as a general sense of doom and damnation. She attempted suicide several times, starved herself, and even, at one point, went into some sort of catatonic state in which she appeared to be dead. Her half-brother, Jonathan Vaughan, a student at Oxford's All Souls, appears to have played a pivotal role in his sister's spiritual development, because, as part of his lengthy and complicated narrative, Jessey reprints a "Consolatory Letter" that Vaughan wrote to his sister during her depression. In this letter, Vaughan wrote:

Doest thou despaire, because thy Tempter is a Lyon for his strength? Behold the Lyon of the Tribe of Judah, Christ the mighty God: who can and will deliver thee out of his paw. A fountain laid open for sinne, and for uncleannesse. I verily beleeve, that although for the present, you lie among the pots, of no use: yet thy God will make thee a Vessel of Honour, an instrument fit for thy Masters use; whereby he will square sinners, to his own glory. (5)

This is a noteworthy echo, again, of the brother–sister relationship imagined in *Comus*, wherein the brother offers hope that an imperiled sister, who might easily be written off as an unclean "pot of no use," may nonetheless be purified by the ministrations of grace and even transformed into a ministerial vehicle for perpetuating hope and grace to others. Jessey's text dedicates itself to narrating the ways in which the various stages of Wight's subsequent redemption fulfilled Vaughan's prophesy. As his lengthy text discloses, the nadir of her suffering became the turning point in her spiritual life. After "dying," she was reborn. After having lived as an "empty nothing creature," she was blessed with an infusion of God's saving grace: "She that was born of flesh and bloud, borne in sinne; and that was by Nature a childe of wrath: is now borne from above, borne of God, having given to her Faith and Love: and hath Jesus Christ to her a Brother, and God to her Father, and her dwelling place: he dwelling in her, and shee in him" (5–6).

According to Jessey's text, Wight's story held great potential to serve as a morality tale for others because she was a *cause celebre* from the beginning. During her months of despair, a series of doctors attended her at her bedside, including, as Barbara Dailey demonstrates, those who had been trained to investigate connections between physical and spiritual illness.[33] However, Wight, like the Lady, also received the more overtly spiritual and sympathetic ministrations of Jessey and his fellow sectarian healers. These, we are told, met with greater success. When Wight lost her sight and hearing, her neighbor, Mrs. Dupper, ritualistically bathed her eyes and held them open so that "she saw and knew her mother" (25). After Jessey and John Simpson prayed over her, she began to hear again. Jessey's text is structured in such a way as to invite the reader into this healing community. In the preface he asks his readers to pray "for the more exhaling of Jesus Christ, in the powring out of his Spirit . . . by stretching out his hand to heal (soules and bodies) that signes and wonders may be done in his Name" (A4).

But like Milton's aim in *Comus*, Jessey's ultimate aim is to enunciate the birth of the popular sovereign individual within an overtly political context. His account was published during the ferment of late 1640s London. At this time, the defeat of the Royalists had precipitated new rounds of ideological and theological conflict between the centrist Presbyterians and more radical religious Independents over the issue of toleration. Rank- and-file members of the New Model Army, enraged over their inability to collect back pay for their service in the first civil wars, had begun to agitate and to contemplate the possibility of retaining political power in their own hands. In 1647 several regiments resisted Parliament's order for the army to disband and marched on London. Violence erupted in both July and August. Wight's "public" life as a soul in crisis occurred between April and July, and many of those demonstrating in the streets were among the crowds who visited her bedside. According to Jessey, they drew assurance from her plight that God would, as promised, usher in the rule of the Saints and "pour out more of the Spirit upon his Sons and Daughters." As Dailey argues, Wight functioned as "an allegory of 'anglia rediviva' "; as Jessey puts it, she served as a lasting "*Monument* of the exceeding riches of Gods Grace" (A6). She, like all the "redeemed of the Lord," is enunciated as a member of the "Royall Priesthood, a Chosen Generation" for "He hath made us Kings and Priests unto God" (33).

A protagonist who resides even lower down the social scale than Milton's aristocratic Lady, Wight possesses a sovereignty that does not lock her into a particular identity or social position; rather, it releases her from such and allows her to "rise." This is dramatized by the fact that, as Jessey's text progresses, Wight's chamber comes to resemble many things and, within it, she assumes various sorts of powers traditionally reserved for authorized institutions and denied "empty" young maidens. Like a Shakespearean hero combined with a sectarian minister, Wight was said to have spoken "ex tempore, in Soliloquies." Thus, given the fact that visitors often crowded around her to hear her speak, her chamber resembles a sectarian congregation or "gathered" church in which attendance and participation is voluntary and moved by the spirit, rather than dictated by the law of parish membership. As Dailey has noted, the scene is also reminiscent of the *ars moriendi* tradition, in which Puritans "reenacted" the death-bed scene in order to stage a "new birth as preparatory to the soul's marriage to Christ in heaven."[34] And when others arrive to seek her advice, Wight's chamber takes on the feel of a confessional, with Wight acting as a group-certified member of the "priesthood of all believers." Finally, all of these roles may be contained under one rubric, for as the high priest, the physician, and the ultimate theological subject, Wight functions as an emissary of the "true King," Christ, as he competes with and decenters the earthly King's traditional claim to monopolize these roles.

Elevated to supreme sovereign status within her bedchamber, Wight comes to resemble a king holding court within the private–public spaces of his "Privy Chamber" or "Council." Mark Kishlansky writes that in the seventeenth century "government was not yet divided between the private life of the king and the public life of the monarchy. Nowhere was the blending of these two elements more apparent than at court."[35] While Charles I increasingly sought to separate off his "Privy Chamber" from the more public spaces of court, the latter tended to act as an extension of the former, thus the court was made up of all those who "attended the monarch, either by duty or by design" (41). This included thousands of officials and servants (from the Master of Wards to the Mistress of Wardrobe) as well as visitors who came "in search of favour" (in other words, "cutting a figure"; 41). In the Privy Chamber the King was "on display" and his duties involved collecting and discharging monies, regulating social and economic spheres of activity, and dispensing justice (41). Wight's more humble, plain-style court most certainly did not include thousands of officials or servants, but it did include a few individuals – her mother, Jessey, her doctors, her fellow congregationalists, and some actual servants – who served her needs and recorded her words. And within her own "Privy Chamber," while she did not, of course, dispense monies or regulate commerce, she did "hold court" by receiving "dignitaries" as well as those who had come "in search of favour" – in this case, the favour of spiritual hope and perhaps even redemption that came adorned with the patina of divine wisdom. In short, Jessey touted the "figures" that were "cut" by Wight's "esteemed" visitors as well as the fact that Wight, like a king, was "on display."

What is more, by making Wight's power "visible within a theatrical space devoted to mythologizing the divine origins and authority of God the sovereign and his chosen emissary on earth," Jessey's text performs a strategic appropriation of the court masque, with Wight serving as his royal actor.[36] As David Norbrook has demonstrated, masque studies benefit from looking beyond the court to find ways in which the genre was used or "reformed" for purposes other than the celebration of court power.[37] James Holstun has made a similar claim about the way in which Anna Trapnel's prophetic practice turned her room into "the site of a millennarian counter-masque of the holy spirit."[38] Likewise, Henry Jessey's use of what we might term a popular masque anatomizes the specific process by which an ordinary young girl could be turned into a heavenly form capable of loosening the court's hold over the dispensation of influence and the exemplification of virtue and wisdom within the public sphere of religious Separatism.

In seventeenth-century England, court masques were a primary means by which the Stuarts were established as what Habermas terms the "carriers of representative publicity," that is, those who were entitled to display themselves as the embodiment of some sort of "higher power."[39] The degree to which this was, as Habermas contends, a privilege reserved for the prince, the church, and the nobility is illustrated by the fact that, as Jerzy Limon writes, masques were "staged by the court for the court; no one else, with the exception of honored guests, was admitted."[40] The masque could be "'experienced' only by those who were literally seated closest to the monarch" because they were deemed the elite few in possession of a "miraculous insight into the metaphysical sphere" of the "perspective" one needed to see "the entire celestial world that is said to govern the universe" (69). The masque's dramatic action typically began with a comical "antimasque," that is, when a so-called "petitioner" entered the stage and pleaded for that "visibility" and vision that one's presence in the theatre simultaneously signified and provided.[41] Conventionally, petitioners were denied their request because, by definition *as the antimasque*, they embodied a threat to the court's exclusive claim to discern and represent truth. *Coelum Britannicum*, for example, identified Puritans as one especially disruptive group of antimasquers whose stormy claims to religious independence threatened the King's sole headship over the national church. As a result, their petition to be recognized as legitimate purveyors of divine wisdom was laughingly denied and, *vis-à-vis* the conventional banishment device of the "lecture," they were scolded off the stage and consigned to the same invisibility and oblivion that their Pilgrim predecessors were said to labor under in New England. As their lecturers scoffed, "They cannot breathe this pure and temperate air where virtue lives, but will with hasty flight 'mongst fogs and vapours seek unsound abodes. Fly after them from your usurped seats, You foul remainders of that viperous brood" (175). This fumigation then sets the stage for the masque's revelatory climax, in which the King and Queen are exalted as the rarified creatures most able to inhale and inspire virtue, and for the succeeding revels that propagate and celebrate that fact. As Habermas argues,

Something [that had] no life, that [wa]s inferior, worthless or mean, [wa]s not [traditionally] representable. It lack[ed] the exalted sort of being suitable to be elevated into public status, that is, into existence. Words like excellence, highness, majesty, fame, dignity, and honor s[ought] to characterize this peculiarity of a being that wa[s] capable of representation. (7–8)[42]

However, the masque-like composition of Henry Jessey's text dramatizes the degree to which England's empty nothing creatures were beginning to claim the elevated status necessary for legitimating themselves as vehicles for authoritative speech by democratizing the very royalist rituals used at the time to consolidate the court's grip on representative publicity.

Jessey's narrative moves through the masque's conventional stages of petition and antimasque, lecture and banishment, revelation and revels, all the while emulating what Kevin Sharp describes as the masque's "Neoplatonic philosophy" and its "ascent of cognition from the plane of senses and material objects to a loftier stratum of knowledge of forms and ideas" while rejecting its elitist investment in aligning that ascent with a class-based movement from subordinate to sovereign.[43] As did court masques, Jessey's popular masque defines the parameters of inclusion versus exclusion by listing the names and social status of those who came to witness Sarah Wight's ordeal. However, while Jessey proudly states that many of these witnesses were "persons of note, and of much esteem in London" (10), he qualifies that last statement by observing that those individuals were famous "amongst them that fear the Lord" (1–2), that is, among radical religious circles rather than at the court. What is more, his larger project is to drop these esteemed names in order to convince those of his readers who "like [doubting] Thomas will not believe" (19) the seemingly unrepresentable truth that his text has to offer – that a nobody such as Sarah Wight could be chosen to "publish to the World" the "Glad tidings uttered of the Righteousness of God, of his Faithfulness and Salvation, and of his benign Kindness and Truth" (19).

When the dramatic action of Jessey's text begins, it, like *Coelum Britannicum*, features an antimasque played by an unvirtuous and stormy Puritan, that is Sarah Wight herself. Her bouts of guilt and atheism, her sense of inadequacy and sinfulness, and her endless fasting and weeping festoon her with the antimasque's conventional props of grotesque physicality and riotous disorder. Not surprisingly, then, she is in the position of having to petition for grace and mercy. Early on she delivers a religious variation upon the petitioner's plea, saying, "Come Lord Jesus; Come Lord Jesus" (19). However, because her intended audience is not any earthly king, rather Christ, the king of all kings, she immediately understands her petition to have been answered rather than denied. As she says, "But why say I, Come? He is come, he is come, he is come" (19). This surprise twist on masque convention is underscored by the fact that, rather than experiencing the undeserving petitioner's typical fate of lecture and banishment, Wight is next empowered to play the role of lecturer to her own antimasque. But rather than exorcizing herself as the antimasque, she banishes the spiritual and even political disorder within her soul that had theretofore rendered her worthless and mean. As she exclaims upon receiving grace, "[Christ] hath dispossessed the strong man, and hath taken possession of my soul, and will dwell with me for ever, for ever, for ever" (19). This figure of the "strong man" refers, of course, to Satan, but it also functions as a thinly veiled allusion to such earthly pretenders to God's heavenly throne as the King and his bishops, whose customary claim to act as God's representatives is here both denied and appropriated. Thus, as was the case with *Coelum Britannicum*, the revelatory climax of Jessey's scene shows heaven descending on a small plot of English soil. Here, however, an "empty nothing creature" is made the *deus ex machina* through which the reestablishment of celestial order is made manifest, while the banished party consists of the instititutions that had formerly denied her vision and presence even as they compelled her blindly loyal gaze.

Through this device, Jessey's text banishes not the pretentious social subordinate *per se*, but rather the conditions which were said to render social subordinates unrepresentable, and he replaces those conditions with the grace and virtue that license the public demonstration of an everywoman's heightened perspective and authoritative pronouncements. Jessey's Arminianism and its subversion of the royal masque's emphasis on exclusion is also at work in the sections where Wight receives visitors who come to her for spiritual counseling. Sarah's visitors consist of women from different social backgrounds who now came to "petition" *her* for the "favors" of *spiritual* wealth and *redemptive* justice that she was said to have acquired through grace. But unlike the monarch's monopolistic hold over the sovereign authority that his lofty status was said to guarantee, Wight's elevation is meant to serve as a conduit through which the right to claim the sovereign privileges of grace is circulated to all. Jessey achieves this effect both by printing his masque and by depicting Sarah within the text itself as responding to every despairing woman's petition with a lecture that individuates and coronates her into a lofty knowledge of the cosmos rather than banishing her from the theatre. As Carola Scott-Luckens observes, Wight dispenses customized advice to each of her listeners in language that is "uniquely fitted to each individual."[44] For example, to one Gentlewoman who seeks her aid (because, as she says, "The Devil Rules in me"), Wight speaks in metaphors of property and possessive individualism, saying, "Christ will fetch you from [Satan], he will dispossess him, and possess himself" (65). To a woman who appears to have been of a lower class, she speaks the language of labor: "Who doth Christ work upon, but on stony hearts? His word is a fire and a hammer, to break and to melt it: and he will make them one heart, to fear him, and they shall not depart from him for ever" (83). To a widow who speaks of herself as being in "continuall horror," Wight offers Christ's substitute courtship and marriage: "He saith, Ile allure her, and bring her into the wilderness, and then speak peace to her. Thats Gods time to doe it; and then he saith to them, I will betroth thee to me for ever" (80). To a woman whose pregnancy is so far advanced that her "condition is very dangerous and hopeless," Wight speaks the language of safe delivery: "The Lord will deliver you of two Burthens at once; the burthen of sin, and your other Burthen also. Your extremity, is Gods opportunity. In him, Judah shall be saved" (103).

Finally, to a woman who appears to be a member of another race because she is "tempted" into suicide by the fact that, as she says, "I am not as others are: I do not look so, as others doe," Wight speaks the language of racial equality. "When Christ comes and manifests himselfe to the soule, it is black in it selfe, and uncomely: but He is fair and ruddy, and he cloathes the soule with his comeliness that he puts on it, and makes it comely therein: and in him the soule is all faire, and there is no spot nor wrinkle" (123). Dailey is right to point out how troubling it is that Wight racializes Christ's goodness as whiteness (449–450). However, we should not overlook the impulse that Wight displays towards equality among all individuals, regardless of such "external" factors as race, class, gender, ethnicity, and nationality. It is especially worth remembering that she was speaking at a time when those with dark skin were said by the "social context" to be destined for servitude because of the curse placed upon them by God after Ham (from whom they were said to descend) disobediently viewed his father, Noah, naked. In Wight's formulations, all souls are, by nature, equally "black," but Christ's goodness arrives to bestow cleansing salvation – and abstract sovereignty – upon everyone, regardless of who they are. As she says,

He doth not this to one onely, nor to one Nation onely, for many Nations must be blessed in him. He came to give his life for a ransome for many, to give himselfe for the life of the world. He is a free agent; and why should you exclude your selfe? . . . Did he bear and carry the Israelites, that had been bond-slaves in Egypt through the Wilderness, into Canaan . . . and will not he bear you and carry you, out of your selfe, into himselfe, though you be a bondslave to sin and Satan. (124)

In short, Wight speaks the language of sovereign enfranchisement to women who were said to be disenfranchised by virtue of their penetrable bodies, especially when those bodies were in the unpredictable "states" of widowhood, servitude, childbirth, and even radical or national difference. Conventionally, these extraneous factors were understood as making women less adept at owning and managing property, at functioning as a "head" when they were intended to serve as "hands" or laborers, and at achieving full personhood when their race and/or nationality consigned them to subordination. But Wight dismisses the "social context" which viewed such things as salient, and instead points each and every one of her "petitioners" towards the crown of abstract and disembodied selfhood that the God-within bestows. As she said to the pregnant woman "for a farewell," "Go, and Beleeve, the Lord Jesus makes you whole" (105). Wholeness, not fragmentation, is the ontological condition at which she aims. And this movement from decentered petitioner to sovereign self quite literally bestows an abstract and universally available subjectivity – or an "I" – upon her petitioners' fallen "nature." As Wight preaches, "Where the Lord doth any great thing," such as inhabiting the meek individual, "he puts his I to it. I, even I am he. I'le make a New Covenant: I'le write my Law in their heart. I'le pardon your sinnes. I'le doe them away as a thick cloud. *I change not, therefore are you not consumed*" (20; emphasis added).

The transference of this inclusive sovereignty comprises the climactic "revelation" of Jessey's popular masque: like a king, every individual is a medium for power as it is mythologized within a theatrical space. Like a king, every individual functions as a potential *coelum* who, through grace, can gain the perspective needed to act as the generalized other – to question, in this case, the legitimacy of old norms governing abject femininity and women's unlicensed access to interpretation and commentary. As Wight tells one visitor, quoting Romans, "Its our Fathers good pleasure, to give [each of us] a Kingdom . . . neither Principalities nor powers, nor any other Creature . . . shall separate the soul, it's in union with him" (49). Finally, the exaltation with which this revelation is uttered leads to the popular masque's conventional close in the form of the "revels." As Jessey says, "the Lord having thus far carried on his own glorious work in an Earthen Vessel, and brought things to such a sweet period; we may conclude with joy in the Lord" (150). Not surprisingly, however, Jessey's revel consists of an invitation for everyone to take their turn in the celebration: "And now, is this nothing to you, O yee that pass by, that read, or that stand, or sit by? Is there nothing that the Lord hereby speaks to *your* heart?" (150).

The juxtaposition of a court masque such as *Coelum Britannicum* with Henry Jessey's pamphlet narrative of Sarah Wight represents, I suggest, a shift from one Whitehall to another – from the King's Whitehall as an exclusive court sphere in which the sovereign staged his "personal rule" through the elite theatre of court masques, to Sarah Wight's own private "Wighthall," a self-declared autonomous zone in which the most ordinary of individuals – a wight – could perform sovereign subjectivity through the popular media of private churches and cheap print. This shift from the King's Whitehall to the individual's Wighthall helps to explain how the public sphere proper began to emerge, as Habermas claims, "under absolutism"

(11). It provides us with a more precise understanding of the literary and even theatrical means by which common people, including women, began to try and transcend their socially prescribed particularities and to assume what Habermas describes elsewhere as the "role of the generalized other," that is, the elevated and enlightened subject position needed to distance one's self from assigned roles by recognizing them as being structured by inherited and customary and therefore malleable social norms, rather than by nature.[45] And it suggests that the "feminine" need not be understood as inherently antithetical to the "individual." Jessey's masque suggests that the movement for religious freedom was secured by the construction of the sovereign individual, a private, rights-bearing subject position which, as Jessey tells us, God makes particularly available to those whose social inferiority renders them all the more emblematic of God's ability to reach down to the lowest of the low and to elevate them to the stratosphere of personhood and perspective.

At the same time, it addresses the concern raised by Habermas himself about grounding the democratic potential of the public sphere in what he sees as the "illusion of autonomy" perpetuated by the idea of "possessive-individualis[m] as self-ownership" rather than in what he terms a more desirable understanding of the "intersubjective constitution of freedom."[46] In other words, Habermas is averse to grounding the public sphere in property rather than in, as he says, a "network of associations" that is too diffused and disembodied to "occupy the vacant seat of the sovereign." But I would suggest that Henry Jessey's construction of Sarah Wight as a girl-king insists that we look at the complex way in which an early concept of the self-owning popular sovereign individual was constituted intersubjectively by the movement for religious separatism as the necessary and foundational unit for its political right to even form an autonomous and private sphere through the collectivizing mechanism of voluntary association.

Jessey's text ends by endorsing Wight not simply as a prophetic vessel but also as one who was licensed to assume the more traditionally masculine role of minister. He does so again by applying the more democratizing principles of Arminianism to a "high" cultural form. As Reid Barbour argues, the Anglican minister John Donne staged a "theatre of the person" in a sermon he delivered before James I by "beginning with a paen for the 'inthronization' of ministers who – as royal priests in their pulpits, clothed in the ordinance 'as with a Cloud' – are divested of inadequacies, no matter how 'so poor a man . . . stands here."[47] Subversively, Jessey predicates Wight's "inthronization" not on what Barbour describes as Locke's "smooth, progressive matriculation . . . from parental nurture through grammar school on to university and a vocation" (169) but on the instruction she reportedly received directly from Christ. In the throes of prayer, Wight asked, "Lord, What wilt thou have me to do?" and Christ's answer was, "as he said to Paul, (Acts 26.16.) *Rise, and stand upon thy feet; for I have appeared to thee for this purpose, to be a Minister and a witness, both of the things thou hast seen, and in which I appeare unto thee*" (135). Jessey repeats this injunction with approval, seconding it with, "So God had bid her *Arise*, and he had raised her soul from the lowest hell; and now he perswaded her, that he will raise up her body also: that she might be a Witness of the Grace of God, to *minister* to others, what he had administered unto her" (135). One could use Althusser to argue, of course, that Wight may have thought she was a subject who "shall submit freely to the commandments of the Subject, i.e. in order that [s]he shall (freely) accept h[er] subjection," but that she is, in reality, the unwitting creature of Henry Jessey, quite literally a construct of his own literary, religious, and political ambitions. His conclusion contains a kind of injunction that could be construed as an attempt to thwart or manipulate her own authority. He writes that "she must not count her life dear to her selfe, no not her being with Christ, which is far better then this life" (135); instead, she must dedicate herself to ministering to others. And as the case of the religious Independent Susanna Parr in 1659 illustrates, while some dissenting women agitated for the right to preach, others such as Parr felt forced to "witness" publicly in order to fully satisfy the theological requirements of their congregations.[48]

At the same time, the thrust of Jessey's text suggests strongly that Wight may have staged the entire episode in order to maneuver others into convincing her to do something that she wanted to do all along – become a preacher. Her months-long episodes of despair are reported to have ended only with her declaration that, ultimately, God had told her to be a minister. The weary ones around her appear to have been all too happy to grant her this wish if doing so would only end her long bouts of nearly lethal fasting. In fact, the narrative suggests that she manipulated them to the point where, to alleviate her suffering, they began offering *her* a biblical foundation upon which to justify her preaching. Some of their examples, unlike her own citation of Paul, even featured women. These included Peter's wife's mother who, in Mark, began to minister after being cured of a fever by Jesus, as well as a place in Luke where "Christ said, *Maid arise*" (137). Wight evinces skepticism and demands more and more examples until, finally, her attendants (like weary courtiers) hit upon the one that appeared to her "more full, more particular, and more familiar," that is, the moment in Mark 5 that reads, "Damsell, I saw to thee, Arise; and straight way shee arose, and walked. And he commanded that somewhat should be given her to eate" (137). Sure enough, she is next seen sitting up, eating, and demanding that her Maid "turn [back] to the Scriptures" (that were quoted to her earlier) and reread them to her "one by one" because, as Wight crows, "they never had been given in to her in all her life before" (138). One could conclude that Wight had refused to eat until doing so was scripturally coupled with a call to the ministry. Why, she wants to know, had she never been shown these parts of the Bible before? She even has the satisfaction of learning that her long fought for example has been emulated, for not long after there are reports of one "H. T." (Hannah or Anna Trapnel) who "then had great enjoyments of God, and could not take in a crumme or sip of the creatures, for full six dayes together" (139). In other words, one might gather that Wight got what she hoped for all along and, in doing so, scored a victory for wanna-be girl preachers everywhere.

The Lady does "arise" to speak. In the very next scene, an entire "Party" composed of several ministers, along with "many Christian friends," comes to "wait on her" in her "middle-roome," which has been "prepared for the dutie" (143). There Wight sits "veiled" and, when all are seated, she issues "instructions" for "some direction and furtherance herein, both to the Party, her selfe, and to her Mother, and to all present" (144). Afterwards, "the Assembly in convenient time was dismissed; many being greatly refreshed in the Lord, who had thus exalted his great and Glorious Name, in causing Light, thus to shine out of Darkness, restoring her soul from so deep despair" (146). Wight is veiled but she is no *feme covert*. Instead, the formal church-like atmosphere that is evident in Jessey's rhetoric (instructions, assembly, etc.) conveys the idea that Wight has achieved speaking authority within and before her community. This scene in fact actually recalls us to one of the original sins, which, if we recall, first sent Wight into her state of despair: the loss of her "hood." An otherwise inexplicable moment in the text might be explained through recourse to this veiling scene and its embedded allusion to Paul's injunction in 1 Corinthians 11.3–13 that women could pray or prophesy in church as long as their heads were covered. By veiling Wight, Jessey actually unveils her as a preacher. Her legitimizing "hood," once lost, is now found. The veil, like a heavenly cloud, hovers about her like a crowning halo. Subsequently, Jessey recounts a scene in which Wight attends a regular church only to find that a series of male ministers have been mysteriously impeded from preaching. Outside, however, she takes matters into her own hands by initiating a series of consultations with women "in deep despaire" (147). This time, she does not confine her ministry to her chamber but, like a pilgrim sovereign, makes a progress of sorts through the countryside so that she may counsel individual women in their own homes.

Another sign that Jessey's Sabrina progressed beyond her "helper" role is the fact that three years later, in 1650, Wight herself published a text entitled *A Wonderful Pleasant and Profitable Letter Written by Mris. Sarah Wight, To a Friend, Expressing the Joy that is to be had in God in Great, Deep, Long, and Sore Afflictions*.[49] This text functions explicitly as a popular sermon or theological treatise that celebrates and repeatedly enacts the move from decentered to centered selfhood that she performed in Jessey's account. Time and time again throughout her text, Wight expounds her doctrine of abstract sovereignty as a counter to notions of the individual as inevitably embodied and interrelated and hence subject to the dictates of others. She begins by telling the "Sir" to whom she is writing that they are *both* in a "winter-season of affliction," a period of "storms and tempestes" that all souls experience when they are "silently waiting upon God." During these times, she advises, she finds it a "Christian crown of rejoycing, to retire in the Spirit, to hear what God speaks: for none speaks or teaches like him; never man spake like Christ" (2). At first glance, this appears to be a rather formulaic statement about salvation; however, it contains a quite radical claim: that, during times of contention and strife, she removes herself from earthly teachers and retires into herself, her spiritual "crown," "to hear what God speaks." It is here that she finds, as the Prophet David did, "that *God is good of a truth, to his purified, sincere, single-hearted Israelites, in the midst of all troubles*" (2). For Wight, in other words, there is something that acts as a counter to the pressures of interpellating apparatuses, of "Pharaohs bondage, at the Red-sea, in the wilderness, in the firy furnace" and that something consists of the fact that, "at all times, he is a present help to us, and an Ark or hiding place for us, from all storms and tempests" (2).

Wight is insistent that this one-woman "Ark" is omnipresent and infallible: "there is no condition so sad, but there is balm enough in Gilead, suitable comforts of supplies in Israels God, to revive and raise up a fainting spirit. The depths of misery we find, are never beyond the depthless depths of mercies" (2). In fact, the more one is plunged into a state of misery, the more one is assured that he/she will thereby "learn to make the Lord alone our stay and trust" (3). Again, Wight's Baptist-like insistence on the "Lord alone" represents her "doctrine of virginity" as one in which earthly teachers and authorities might be displaced through recourse to the abstractions bestowed by grace. It is a call to the transgression of bounds and to the transfer of authority to the bounded but "free spirit" (5). Wight acknowledges the subject's "interrelatedness" but she objects to any claim that says that the material conditions under which subjectivity is forged should subordinate individuals socially and legally to others' efforts to dictate their place and identity. First, she conventionally insists that the bestowal of grace is a recipe for selflessness – "A Christian's happiness lies in being emptied of all self, self refined, as well as gross self; and in being filled with a full God" (5). However, as she says, "Certainly, that soul that denies it self most, seeks it self most: for the more it endeavors to advance the Lord in all, above all enjoyments, experiences, gifts, graces, relations, or any creature, or creature comforts; the more we exalt our condition in him" (5–6). In other words, the effacement of the self is equal to the ultimate recovery of that self, because the self that is formed in relation to God alone is freed from all "relations" with others. The self-in-society is entangled within a "web woven with interminglings of wants and favors, crosses and blessings, standings and fallings, combats and victories, and the like, which hath and doth accompany a poor soul in its pilgrimage; as it did the Israelites of old in theirs." There are "seasons, varieties, & changes in the outward world of mankinde" that are "true to *Solomon's* description" which she "daily behold[s]": "living, and dying; coming into the world, and going out of it; planting, and plucking up; killing, and quickening; wounding, and healing, breaking down, and building up; weeping, & laughing; mourning, and rejoycing" (7). The world is defined by "mutability" and it is "written in everything of the first man Adams state, even in the height of his first glory" (8). However, she knows that all the "precious *sons and daughters* of Sion" can "experimentally witness the truth of this, not only outwardly, but inwardly" and that "When this glory shall be abolished, then will a more pure and lasting glory disclose it self: the decreasing of the one, makes clear way for the increasing of the other" (7, 8; emphasis added).

Wight's inclusion of "daughters" as well as "sons" in her address is significant. She is preaching the doctrine of virginity not only to men but to women as well, insisting to them that, in spite of all the forces that preside over them in the world, there is a core self that transcends those forces – a "more pure and lasting" self that precedes even the "first glory" of Adam. While she does not mention Eve, the implication is the same as Lilburne's or Rachel Speght's when they claimed that there was a state of freedom that existed prior to the fall that comprehended both men and women once they reentered into a state of grace. God, Wight writes, is the "Potter" who may do with his children "at his dispose" for they are "more his then our own," yet the implication is that, whatever self the saint presents to the world is the one that the world must accept, for the saint may claim that it was God who molded him as such. This was a powerful claim for a woman to make on behalf of other women, who, as traditionally understood, were most certainly putty in the hands of their fathers and husbands.

Again Wight's formulation of the fixed self is in fact one that allows for changes of all sorts to occur: "The great Jehovah may put what paint he will upon things, and what Day he pleaseth into us: and we with beholding the present colour subject to change, with the present eye, may be confident in what we see, both in judging it, and other things by it, not rightly knowing him that judges it, nor considering what various changes both the eye and colour are subject to undergo" (10). In other words, there may be a gap between the self that appears to the world and the intentions of its creator. This gap is where the sovereign subject rests. It is not a space that enforces uniformity and homogeneity; rather, it provides for, indeed is dependent upon, an ethos of indeterminacy through which one could legitimately disobey earthly authorities and conventions by refashioning both the self as well as conceptions of others (however powerful) in conjunction with what one determines "God's will" to be. Within this space of configuration and reconfiguration, the low can be brought high and the high low. In terms of the former, while "all things are at first brought forth in weakness in the inward world, as well as in the outward world . . . whatever [the Lord] doth shall be for ever; nothing can be added to it, or taken from it" (11). An individual cannot be manipulated from without because of the assurance he/she enjoys from the Lord within. Likewise, a powerful man "may seem to be wonderous wise, to have notions of great weight, even of eternity upon him; & yet he cannot reach eternity as man; being but a vain empty nothing, the purposes he hath in him, are but poor low, shallow things" and when he is "stripped of all, of inside and outside . . . and so made naked to divine purpose," his soul will be "dissolved to nothing, as the Sun doth wax" (11). "Riches, honours, parts, and abilities" will not matter any longer. As Wight says, she "cannot do" these things – that is, she possesses none of them – and yet she is "not troubled at it" because, ultimately, "it's all of God, without our mixtures" (12). As this passage shows, it is precisely a notion of an uninterpellated subject that Wight seeks, for it is this formulation that allows her to escape the contingencies of class, rank, social standing ("honours"), and even of perceived abilities, something that women in particular had to be concerned with. She has had enough of being told that her subjectivity – her ability to attain personhood – was contingent on external factors. Instead, in her formulation, all externalities are stripped away in and by grace – all individuals are equal to one another; all stand "naked to divine purpose" and hence to self-determination.

Wight next provides an incredibly literal and concrete description of the sovereign self. As she writes, "the sensible and full enjoyment of thy Spirit, will cause my soul to return satisfied to her rest, praising the God of all our mercies; not caring what others boast of, when thou art become the Crown of my glory, the top of all Royalties to me" (12). Here, she quite literally crowns herself. Everything else – all other contingencies that impinge upon her – she will "abhor, & cast away, as filthy raggs of no value," so that she may dwell solely upon that which is conveyed into her by "his Spirit alone." He alone is "the Author of every good and perfect gift we enjoy" (14). Locke's rejection of this model of absolute sovereign selfhood stemmed from his fear that it licensed unlimited disobedience and anarchy. However, Wight seeks to demonstrate that the idea of popular individual sovereignty is not antithetical to – but rather necessary for – the placement of strict limits on the power that any one individual, especially someone who claims to derive authority from God, might claim to exercise over any other. Indeed, self-sovereignty is dependent on delineating the limits of the sphere in which any given individual enjoys his/her liberty. As she writes:

The outward and inward man hath but a poor, lowe, dark, shallow knowledge of the things of God, whatever they may pretend to have. There is no soul able of it self to reach these things; they are only spiritually discerned and known by the sight of the Spirit: it's by this Spirit only, that the soul comes to know, observe, and understand the ways and wonders of God in the deeps, and his various motions and operations in things which he doth. (15)

Even as she elevates each individual "spirit" to a level of new knowledge, she tempers that elevation by contending that the soul needs some affirmation from the Spirit in order to achieve understanding. Even then, as one looks around at "things, times, places and persons," one sees only a "present appearance of this or that"; one does not know "what it is, whence it came, what it means, or whither it tends" (16). If one "judges according to a present outward appearance," then one "shews himself to be what he is, and what God will have him to be, A fool in himself" (16). God will see to it "that the pride of his glory may be stained, and God alone exalted" (16). Wight's words appear to suggest that the self is incapable of judgment and determination in general. However, she goes out of her way to suggest that what she really means is that the self is incapable of determining the status of another. If one attempts to judge another "according to a present outward appearance," then one will make a fool of him/herself. This statement liberates any given individual from being determined by the always potentially mistaken judgments of others, especially when those judgments are predicated on conventional stereotypes governing "outward appearances." In short, one can judge or determine one's own fate, but not that of another. This interpretation is underscored by the fact that Wight's words are directed specifically at those who perceive themselves to be in positions of social or political authority, for she at pointed times makes reference to a wider social context in which she intends for her words to be read. As she says, her argument is that "the holy seed appear[s]!" in every individual. This abstraction works as a hedge against the "varieties or changes in the inward or outward world running through them" from which "they are not exempted," but by which they are not determined: "What ever their cloathes, their appearances be, yet their life and substance is still the same" (17). For every person – both the inward and the outward man – knows nothing and relies upon the "spiritual man that shall grow up to perfection, and live and flourish" (18); all enjoy "the coming of this full enjoyment of all blessedness & happiness" (18).

In the next section of her letter, Wight describes several personal losses, each of which serves as a prelude to reiterating her key narrative journey from an interpellated self who is subject to multiple contingencies to one that is unified and sovereign through her identification with God alone. One sense of loss she describes is, ironically, the composition of Jessey's pamphlet, *The Exceeding Riches of Grace Advanced*. "Since that little unknown book was made," she writes, "of Gods glorious Displayings of light and love upon a poor, dark, forlorn nothing-creature in an unexpected time, I was not then capable of the publishing of it: if I had, I could not be free, fearing how it might be with me afterwards" (24). Interestingly, the publication of the very text that "crowned" Wight with selfhood appears to have been the cause of her second bout of depression. "Truly, since then, I have had a sharp Winter-season, mourning for the loss of all that comfort: I have been stripp'd so bare of seeming comfort since, that I cannot boast of that, nor of any comforts" (24). However, again, this process of being stripped in the winter season results, not in any sort of recognition that she is, after all, a dissolute and multiple subject, but that, in essence, she is a nothing who is simultaneously – and only – God's: "I cannot boast . . . of any comforts, but of the God of comforts; nor of any enjoyments, or experiences; not of any gifts or graces; but of the giver alone, and of my infirmities, and in that Power of Christ which hereby is made more manifest in us: the Lord alone is the boast and glory of his people" (23–24). Wight continually repeats this investment in that which is fixed and immutable, not in that which is mutable, including the fixed immutability of her own printed text. She hopes that her own "poor stammerings," once fixed in print on paper, will also serve as that rock which, like Peter's water, "miraculously became a solid path to lead him to his Lord" (50).

Soon after, her language becomes especially impassioned and infused with the desire to convey the absolute absoluteness of what she refers to as the "unquenchable smoking flax" of the spirit. She writes:

> for whom he loved once, he loved for ever, to the end, and in the end, endless, ever, out of sin into grace, and out of grace into glory: neither should any of the water which I had cast upon the smoking flax, quench it, by disowning and doubting of the realities of my state, and the truth of those precious appearances I had enjoyed from the Lord: this smoking flax, was God beginning a good work in my soul, who would perfect it for his praise. (63–64)

And again: "what is of God shall and will stand, all winds and weather, against all the many tempests and violent stormes of all principalities and powers of spirituall wickednes in High places; all this hath been in vain for this fire, though a little while it did but Smoak; Yet it will Blaze, and that with fervent heat: it will never go out; it's God Everlasting" (63). This "smoking flax," Wight's vivid emblem of the essential self, is so inviolable and inalienable that "it overcomes all, and can be overcome of nothing" (65). This reference is drawn from Matthew 20, a scripture that legitimizes breaking human laws (in this case, that of the Sabbath) in the name of Christ's overarching rule. In the face of Philistine objections to the transgressions committed by Jesus's disciples in the temple on the Sabbath (including eating), Matthew reports that Jesus was only fulfilling the prophesies of Isaiah, who, he says, commanded all to behold God's servant, his chosen and beloved in whom the spirit of judgment had been placed. However, in carrying out his responsibilities of judging the Gentiles, it was ordained that "He shall not strive, nor cry; neither shall any man hear his voice in the streets. A bruised reed shall he not break, and smoking flax shall he not quench, till he send forth judgement unto victory" (Matthew 12.19–20). The idea that a "smoking flax" shall not, under Christ's new order, be quenched until the final judgment day is an interesting one, for it revolves around the understanding that something vulnerable is, under Christ's new law, made invulnerable. Flax is, by its nature, highly combustible, however, here, it cannot be quenched because it is protected by God.

Wight's use of the image of the "smoking flax" also draws on the rhetoric of improvement and innovation that was prominent within agricultural discourses of the time, discourses which often conveyed the injunction that everyone, not just the sovereign, possessed the right and duty to advance the nation through agricultural improvement. As a hot new commodity in the seventeenth century, flax was often featured in these discussions; thus its history reveals it to be an apt egalitarian symbol for Wight, in her quest to open up sovereignty to everyone. In the late sixteenth century, Elizabeth I had issued a series of proclamations upholding Henry VIII's statutes on the cultivation of hemp and flax seed and penalizing any who violated this statute.[50] However, by the middle of the seventeenth century the crown had lost the ability (and perhaps also the will) to regulate this crop. As Leonard Cantor recounts, because flax, along with hemp, was a staple in the production of linen, rope, netting and canvas, it was one of the commercial and industrial crops whose cultivation skyrocketed during this time of enclosure and rapid development of new agricultural techniques for production and field management.[51] New ideas in husbandry were in part gaining support due to the food shortages that punctuated the period. Many blamed the shortages on state-imposed impediments to enclosure and improvement, thus deregulating crops such as hemp was seen as a boon to both individual and national advancement. It was labor intensive and thus helped to reduce the unemployment brought about by famine and economic recession; also, producing more domestically reduced the dependency on more expensive flax that was being imported from abroad. Soon, flax was grown both by permanent farmers, predominantly in the corn-growing areas, as well as by itinerant "flaxmen" who would contract with landowners to grow a single crop before moving on to do so again elsewhere (52). This, along with the fact that flax was often cultivated by small farmers, meant that it became known as a poor-man's crop, albeit one that was also associated with the more modest forms of upward mobility that agricultural improvement and enclosure represented, as much for agricultural servants and small-time farmers as for wealthier yeomen.

Wight's use of this metaphor in *Letter To a Friend* points again to her interest in positing the individual as one who, because s/he is so vulnerable to outside forces, is in especial need of God's agency and in arguing that through that agency the self gains new forms of power and mobility. As stated, in its raw unprocessed form of "tow," flax is weak and vulnerable to fire. Because of this, the mighty Samson is able to break the bonds or "withes" the Philistines use to bind him as easily as if they were a "thread of tow" that "is broken when it toucheth the fire" (Judges 16.9). And, as Isaiah states in another passage, "And the strong shall be as tow, and the maker of it as a spark, and they shall both burn together, and none shall quench them." The idea is that because tow is highly flammable, it is vulnerable to destruction (interpellation) by forces over which it has no control. However, if God, as its maker, performs as the igniting spark and sets fire to it, then the tow burns bright and cannot be quenched by others. Wight places God in the role of an improving farmer who "perfects" his crop to the point at which it becomes hardy and capable of withstanding all sorts of weather, as well as all attempts by others to burn it out, even as *he alone* may ignite it without destroying it.

Wight's citation of a scriptural reference that also has analogues in nature and in agricultural technologies actually mediates between the sovereign subject posited by religious sectarians on the one hand, and the one imbued with rights by "nature" by Overton on the other. While she most certainly locates sovereignty within God, she also, like Overton, introduces the element of nature into the equation. God works through the individual by way of nature and natural analogies. And just as the Levellers argued that one accrued rights through nature in the form of passing through the mother at birth, Wight also imagines a mediating force through which the individual receives sovereignty from a "mother." In the opening letter to Lady Fleetwood, R. B. had written that he hoped Wight's text would speak to her "inward Man," a figure that, as stated, echoes Burrough's anatomy of the sovereign self as one that subordinates the feminine to the masculine. In the body of her letter, Wight too employs this rhetoric, stating at one point that "this veile of darkness I find also to be that vile woman which Solomon speaks of: her specious pretenses to man in his lost condition, to bewitch us from the true knowledge of our dear God and his ways and spirituall Worship" (68). However, souls who are infused with Christ also appear in a more positive female form, as "fit Brides for the Marriage of the Lambe," and she draws her tract to a close with a much more androgynous image of the sovereign self. She ends by praising "God our Father, and Wisdom our Mother, which is Christ" (67). This internalized parental team of God the father and Christ the mother allows the individual to be "free and joyfull in himself, from the bondage of corruption, by awaking and arising from under the black dark veils of Ignorance and Unbeliefe, saving us from our enemies which are too strong for us, and so redeeming and gathering us to himselfe" (67). Grace reveils that which has been unveiled; it allows those who are said by others to be tainted to instead claim that they are purified and restored to full subjecthood. Christ, "the overtopping mountain," provides the means by which those enemies may be resisted, but, as Wight states, Christ is "our mother" and resides in human's fleshly natures. Thus, while she does not invoke the language of rights *per se*, she does invoke a larger social and even political context within and against which the individual is ultimately defined as autonomously "free and joyfull in himself."

ANNE WENTWORTH: POSSESSIVE INDIVIDUAL

As Vera Camden notes, the late seventeenth-century writings by Anne Wentworth serve as an "exposé of the very suppression of the radical spirit" that female prophetesses underwent, as well as a record of Wentworth's own attempts to construct an "autonomous authorial self" as a defense.[52] In fact, in this section I will argue that Wentworth used the early modern feminist theory of popular sovereignty to articulate a highly developed concept of possessive individualism. Like Poole's formulations in particular, Wentworth's insistence on self-sovereignty was forged under fire: her writings describe a years-long campaign by her husband, her family, and even her fellow Baptists to frighten her into submission after she decided to leave the church. Once again, while postmodern feminists today search for alternatives to the "bounded self" which, they argue, will give rise to a more "constructive relationship" with "the other," Wentworth illustrates an early modern woman's articulation of and commitment to the idea that, because she is one of God's chosen who is filled with grace, she possesses a highly bounded property-in-self that allows her to "escape," as she says, any attempt by the social context to construct her relationships with abusive "others."[53]

Like Poole, Wentworth was a member of the Particular Baptist church, and, like Poole, she both laid claim to certain freedoms under the auspices of its principles and experienced oppression at the hands of its members. Wentworth's troubles may have been exacerbated by the fact that the persecution suffered by dissenting sects after the Restoration often led them to become more conservative, especially where the behavior of women was concerned.[54] Wentworth writes during the politically volatile late 1670s, a period that felt the full brunt of the repressive antisectarian Clarendon Codes and that saw the Popish Plot and the Exclusion Crisis as well as the execution of Catholics and Whigs. These crises are present in Wentworth's writings: she continually invokes scenarios of doom and apocalyptic threats that, she warns, England faces in the seemingly immediate future. She describes England as a Babylon in which the King's life is threatened and "unjust laws" are implemented (presumably a reference to the Clarendon Codes). And yet, Wentworth reserves the bulk of her wrath for her husband and for the couple's fellow Baptists, because of the scourge they visit upon her personally after she dares to criticize a powerful man. Her texts are structured so that she, alone, occupies the position reserved for the collective space of "the saints" or of "England" in millennial writings such as Mary Cary's. All the persecution in the world comes down to her, and according to her, God is willing to go to great lengths to punish her detractors for inflicting wrongs upon her. In short, her first two publications are unfailingly dedicated to defining the limits of community and to privileging the individual as a sovereign end unto *her*self.

In her earlier work, *A True account of Anne Wentworths being cruelly, unjustly and unchristianly dealt with* (1676), Wentworth recounts – somewhat vaguely – the ways in which she was rejected by her London Baptist congregation after she experienced a period of illness followed by a miraculous recovery and religious epiphany.[55] Almost cryptically (to posterity anyway), she hints that part of her recovery had to do with her decision to expose the true character of her husband, a man who was obviously regarded as an upstanding member both of his business community and his congregation (he was even a "saint" in his church's eyes) but who Wentworth reveals as a cruel man at home. Her long period of illness just happened to coincide with the eighteen years in which she had been her "Husbands wife." By the end, she was, she said, "consumed to skin and bone, a forlorn sad spectacle to be seen, unlike a woman; for my days had been spent with sighing, and my years with crying, for day and night the hand of the Lord was heavy upon me, and my moisture was turned into the drought of Summer" (9). All the while, she says, she kept her silence, even though her "bones waxed old through [her inward] roaring all the day long" (9). She finally lapsed into a fever that "grew so hot, and burnt so strong" that she was "past all cure of man, and given over by them, and lay at the point of death" (9). At that moment, however, she was saved in the "nick of time" by "the great Physitian of value," the "good *Samaritan* passing by, and seeing me lye wounded, and bleeding to death." This saviour "spake as he did to the woman, Luke 13.11. And said unto her, Woman, thou art loosed from thine infirmity; and he laid his hands on her, and immediately she was made straight and glorified God" (9).

This cure not only bestowed health upon her but also lent her the sense of self she needed to bypass earthly Attendant Spirits and speak publicly about her troubles. Her language suggests that her years-long illness had been a function of her husband's abuse, and that her revelation of his true nature may have exposed him as a wife beater. Regardless of whether or not this was her specific allegation, her decision to speak out against him was met with immediate opprobrium and denunciation by members of their church, especially by such male leaders as Thomas Hicks and William Dix, who reportedly drew up some sort of "Bill," as she describes it, charging her with "misbehaviour in life and conversation, or neglecting of [her] duty to their Brother, in not obeying him from the first day of [her] Marriage unto the day of [her] healing, complete 18 years the third of January, 1670" (16). Wentworth even implies that, for criticizing and exposing him, her husband, on February, 13, 1673, sent "three men" to his wife at home to "fright and amaze" her by "speaking things so false, and laying things to [her] charge" (17). Just as soon as she was "commanded of God so to" speak, "they persecute me for it and wound and pierce me again for making mention of his name, and oft and many a time since by their violent Charge misusing and abusing of me, brought me to the gates of death . . . for bearing my witness for him" (17). However, rather than "embrace and accept" the ways in which she was "contextualized and situated" by her community, Wentworth warns, "but now at their door will it lye for stopping my mouth and quenching of the spirit," because

there is a greater witness in Heaven, the Father, Son, and Holy Ghost, and these three are one, who knows how all that weakness came, and why it could not be cured by man, and I was not raised up for naught by such a powerful hand, nor for this end, that my Husband and his Brethren should always afflict and oppress me, and abuse me at their pleasure, and not suffer me to speak of the things of God. (9–10)

And so she does speak as she determines that God has taken the side of "the weak Woman that could hardly Live, only strong in the Lord," rather than that of a man who would be such a "terrible and oppressing King to rule so over a Wife, and bow her so low down" (17).

Wentworth again explicitly denies the power of the community to determine her status when she says, "since February 73" the community has claimed that God "Charges [them] with Labouring with all [their] might and strength to force my Conscience, and would make a rape of my Soul, to have it bow down to you" (18). But, she insists, echoing the Lady, while it may be possible to rape the body, it is not possible to rape the "true self," for it resides elsewhere. As she says: "no hurt my Soul got, for the Son of God hath been with me all this while" (18). In other words, even as the community invokes its God-given, sovereign right to "force" her, she can counter with a God-given, sovereign right to resist that force. To make this claim, she elaborates on the distinction she wishes to draw between body and soul:

as I find some not to be satisfied, with all my yielding my Body, to lay that as the ground, and as the street for them to go over; yet that will not satisfie nor content them, as now they have proved it themselves, unless my Soul bow down also unto them, which can never be done to satisfie man, I am contented to yield up my Life, but the Life of my Soul, that pretious Jewel is kept in my Father's Hand, and it is not possible to pluck it out of my Father's hand, that to struggle and wrastle with me, to spend my Life out is in vain, when my Soul is set upon the Rock, and that they can never gain; but Soul oppression is far greater than Bodily oppression, that it can be no longer born to bind the Spirit of God too hard and long, makes it at last break out into a flame . . . (5)

Like Poole and Wight, Wentworth articulates a doctrine of virginity, an abstract definition of selfhood as one that transcends all embodied contingencies. While as a weak woman she is more vulnerable to force, she has at her disposal a powerful counterforce – the claims that the soul has to transcend identities that the collective wishes to impose on the body. The more pressure that others exert, the more volatile the abstract spiritual self may become in its defense.

Wentworth finds power in offering woman up as the paradigmatic sovereign self, as Jessey had done. In fact, the low esteem in which she (a woman who is forever in peril of being ruined by rape) is held by her community, is in turn precisely that which allows for the "rise" of her ascent into selfhood to be all the more dramatically staged. She writes:

for though they could not bare truth, yet the Lord would have me speak truth, and the more they dashed at it, and beat the poor weak instrument for it, the more the Lord of Life, who was the Agent, confirms it, and in the close now gives his reasons why he would have this work done, and chose such a weak, foolish, despised Woman as I, and to satisie all strangers that may read this, why it was so great a sore to professing men, in speaking the way as the Lord led me, and declaring my experience as he taught me, and required to have recorded by me for the honour and glory of his own name . . . (6)

Abused by her husband, rejected by her community, Wentworth renounces all forms of social "interrelatedness." While (all too) cognizant of the degree to which others attempt to and often succeed at constituting and contextualizing her identity for her, Wentworth insists that she possesses a God-given agency with which to resist such efforts and to define for herself who and what she is.

At the end, Wentworth signs off as an author who is both literally and figuratively alone in the world, with only the small modicum of self to rely on when all else fails. It is a simultaneously grandiose and modest gesture, this aspiration towards an inviolability that can be claimed through this small but, as Wight would call it, "unquenchable smoking flax." Wentworth writes:

I am not a woman spending my time in the pleasures and vanities of the World, and what my manner of life and conversation is, that is seen and known; and if the Lord spare my life a little longer, he will enable me to give sufficient proof to the world, that all and every word these my persecutors hath spoken against me since the beginning of this work, it all sprung from that evil spirit which is the Father of lies . . . (11)

She ends by inscribing her name and the spatially as well as ontologically solitary location from which she writes: "From the house of my abode, this ten years in Kings-Head-Court in White Cross-street neer Cripple Gate. Writ and ended in my retirements between God and my self all alone, June 26, 1676." When the community utterly fails the individual, even the socially weakest soul still possesses a self and an identity – a "my" or a "home" (especially one so aptly named "Kings-Head-Court") from which to proclaim an enduring "I."

We know that the Lord did spare Anne Wentworth's life a "little longer," because she went on to publish a second pamphlet entitled *A Vindication of Anne Wentworth, Tending to the better preparing of all People for her Larger Testimony, which is making ready for Publick View. Publishd According to the Will of God.*[56] In this work she once again insists on providing "sufficient proof to the world" that she spoke the truth about her husband's character and that, in spite of his attempts to thwart her, she was entitled to prophesy and to write (as the tract itself proves). In the course of her argument Wentworth takes the dynamic she developed in her first work to an even greater extreme. In *True Account* she contended that she was entitled to speak out even if it alienated her body from her soul, and her individual self from the world. In this tract she wants to erect an even more unassailable defense for this move by contending that her prophecies and writings have been undertaken even against her own will because God has called her to him, even threatening to kill her if she disobeys. Such an extreme declaration may have been her attempt to short-circuit what she implies was her actual husband's threat to kill her if she obeyed God's injunctions to write. At the same time, it most clearly divests her of a sense of self at the very moment when she is claiming it. Again, however, Wentworth argues from within rather than outside of the logic of the sovereign self. Positing God as a possessive tyrant who owns all rights to her allows her, as it did Locke, to provide a foundation upon which to resist the tyrannical claims of would-be earthly rulers. What is more, she denies the assertion that says that, because she is God's creature, she therefore has no claim to a self outside that which is constructed by others. Or as she puts it, just because she is subject to

God's dictates does not mean that her "enemies" are right to say that she is "distracted, and beside [her] self" (8).

First of all, she contends, if she appears mad, it is because, "as the *Preacher* says, *Eccles. 72., Oppression makes a Wise man Mad*" (8). Second, it is her enemies who will ultimately be found to be mad for denying that she is in her "right mind," and third, because God's Messengers have, "throughout all ages been blasphemed in his Prophets," she takes their criticism of her as a "further measure of [her] conformity to [her] Saviour" (8). Again, Wentworth's logic is directed not towards constituting the self as multiple and fragmented, but towards insisting that God's sovereignty runs through her and provides her with a subversive continuity. As she puts it, it is "my *just* and *necessary* liberty to attend a more then ordinary call and command of God to publish the things which concern the *peace of my own Soul, and of the whole Nation*" (6). She, like Wight, is an example for the community to follow because she is a sovereign individual capable of opposing the dictates of that or any community: her "self" and "the Truth" are coterminous.

Wentworth, like Poole, chooses the vindication mode because, as mentioned, her arguments rest upon a definition of the individual as one who possesses a property in her self that anticipates and rivals the formulation forged by Locke more than twenty years later in his *Two Treatises* (1698). Whereas Locke was inspired by the belated publication of Filmer's *Patriarcha*, Wentworth's articulation of the possessive self emerged out of her experience as a woman who reports nothing but abuse at the hands of her husband and her community. Her interest is not in capitulating to the dictates of the group, but in insisting on a core of self that lies beyond the social matrix. Locke claimed that weaker men should not be subjected to the tyrannical abuse of stronger ones on the grounds that all were the work of their maker, God. Because they were his property alone, they each deserved equal protection under the law. In her work, Wentworth anticipates this move by transferring the deed of ownership from her husband to God in order to defend herself against her husband's abuse. It is God, she states, "whose I am in Spirit, Soul, and Body." She writes:

I do therefore . . . in the fear of my husband who can kill both Soul and Body, further declare, That I was forced to fly to preserve a life more pretious than this natural one; and that it was necessary to the peace of my Soul, to absent my self from my earthly Husband, in obedience to my Heavenly Bridegroom, who call'd and commanded me (in a way too terrible, too powerful to be denied) to undertake and finish a work, which my earthly husband in a most cruel manner, hindered me from performing, seizing and running away with my Writings. (4)

By positing God as a more supremely patriarchal ruler or sovereign husband than man is, Wentworth is able to argue that divorcing her "natural" husband is merely a form of obedience to her divine one, God, who commanded her to perform the work denied her by her earthly spouse – that of writing religious tracts.

In accordance with Baptist precepts, Wentworth, like Poole, insists that she will submit to "every rule given forth by the Spirit of God, to govern the relation of Man and Wife" but only if those rules are given forth "*in the Lord*" (5). In other words, those laws must conform to her standards of what constitutes a just law, otherwise she is entitled to disobey them. However, Wentworth extends this argument in the same radical direction that Poole took (and that Wentworth herself rejected in her earlier work where she resigned herself to the fact that she might have to lose her actual life, even if her soul was ultimately immune to rape). Poole's arguments indirectly redefine the actual marriage contract as one that the wife could extricate herself from once its original terms were violated. Wentworth, of course, applies the language of consent and contract to her own, quite literal marriage, arguing that she is absolutely justified in removing herself from the "unspeakable Tyrannies of an Hard-hearted Yoak-Fellow" (1). She writes:

it would be very easie for me, from the great Law of *self-preservation* to justifie my present absence from my Earthly Husband to all persons who have learn'd to judge of *Good* and *Evil*, not only according to the *outward Act*, but the *inward Spirit* and *Principle*; . . . For as much as the Natural constitution of my mind and Body, being both considered, *He* has in his barbarous actions towards me, a many times over done such things, as not only in the *Spirit* of them will be one day judged a murdering of, but had long since *really* proved so, if God had not wonderfully supported, and preserved me. But my natural life, through the springing up of a *better*, not being otherwise considerable, then as it is my duty to preserve it in a subserviency to the will and service of that God, whose I am in *Spirit, Soul,* and *Body*. (4)

Here, Wentworth explicitly states that both her spirit (and soul) and her body belong to God, and hence she is, without ambiguity, entitled to divorce her husband in order to preserve her body against any form of abuse *before* it becomes life-threatening. Although she certainly implies that her husband nearly killed her, it is unclear if she means that he nearly beat her to death or if she was (no less simply) made miserable by his refusal to allow her to write. Either way, it is her duty to *not* endure her husband's abuse, for to do so would be to allow him to damage a property that does not belong to him but to God (and hence her) alone.

Again, Wentworth argues that she retains the indisputable right to perform this transfer of power from her "earthly husband" to "her Heavenly Bridegroom" not because she is a subject multiply interpellated by earthly powers, but because she is singly interpellated by God alone. The "spirit" with which he infused her "Soul" trumps any claims to power that one might have over her "natural life." It is this fixed quality of the sovereign individual that permits her to transgress conventional mores and roles while retaining an ability to resist both the laws that govern them and the hegemonic customs and conventions that unofficially perpetuate them. As she writes quite explicitly in the language of performance:

And however man judges me in this action, yet I am satisfied, that I have been obedient to the Heavenly Vision herein, not consulting with flesh and blood . . . *And I am enabled in his power to role my self upon him*; and my heart is fixed, trusting in him; and comforted with his word, in which he has caused me to hope, having no confidence in the Arm of Flesh, knowing that the Earth is the Lords, and the fulnes thereof; and that he knows all my weaknesses, and wants, and my willingness to work, so far as he inables me, that my own hands may administer to my necessity . . . (5; emphasis added)

Wentworth is able to mutably "role herself upon" God because her "heart is fixed." In other words, because she is a sovereign self, she enjoys a freedom to alter her situation. Positing an essential self that is endowed by her maker with the sovereign right to self-determination does not preclude but rather creates the conditions for the process by which that self may justify change and transformation. Claiming a fixed sovereign subjectivity provides her, as it did Poole and Wight, with the ability to define for herself what her role as a woman will be. What is more, like Poole, Wentworth is able to construct a subjectivity and a voice that is separate from her husband's but which does not entail her murdering him.

To be sure, the seventeenth-century religious Independency movement created a set of conditions that were highly conducive to the rise of new forms of female agency. However, writings by Wight, and even more so, by Wentworth, demonstrate the interest that women had in ironically using congregationalist precepts of sovereignty to position the individual, not the congregation or any other community, as the ultimate repository of self-determination and empowerment. As women, they were imminently vulnerable to charges of whoredom and mental instability, even by members of their own religious communities, thus as women, they were interested in presenting themselves as exemplary models for a sovereign subjectivity said to be available even (or especially) to the lowliest of the low. As

L. Susan Brown has written, liberal ideas do not "deny the social, they simply acknowledge that individuals can and do question and challenge the social situations in which they find themselves."[57] This idea was especially useful for sectarian women who criticized prominent male leaders. When controversy arose, the congregations that individuals relied upon to bestow a recognition of sovereignty could also claim to take it away, thus weaker women invested a large amount of time and energy in pointing out that the source of abstract and possessive individualism lay outside the community. The bestowal of inalienable sovereignty did not require the group's approval, thus it could be (and was) quite frequently laid claim to in open defiance of the group's collective imperative. When an Attending Spirit revealed himself to be just another Comus, the Lady still said her piece.

NOTES

1. Thomas Carew, "Coelum Britannicum," in David Lindley, ed., *Court Masques* (Oxford: Oxford University Press, 1995), pp. 166–193.
2. Ben Jonson, "Pleasure Reconciled to Virtue," in Lindley, ed., *Court Masques*, pp. 117–125. See Lindley's introduction to court masques, p. ix; Stephen Kogan, *The Hieroglyphic King: Wisdom and Idolatry in the Seventeenth-Century Masque* (Rutherford, NJ: Fairleigh Dickinson University Press, 1986), p. 191.
3. Henry Jessey, *The Exceeding Riches of Grace Advanced by the Spirit of Grace in an Empty Nothing Creature, viz. Mrs. Sarah Wight Lately Hopeless and Restless* (London, 1652).
4. Linda K. Kerber, "Can a Woman be an Individual?: The Discourse of Self-Reliance," in Richard O. Curry and Lawrence B. Goodheart, eds., *American Chameleon: Individualism in a Trans-National Context* (Kent, OH: Kent State University Press, 1991), pp. 151–166.
5. Alison M. Jagger, *Feminist Politics and Human Nature* (Brighton: Harvester Press, 1983), p. 42.
6. Naomi Scheman, "Individualism and the Objects of Psychology," in Sandra Harding and Merrill B. Hintikka, eds., *Discovering Reality* (Dordrecht: D. Reidel, 1983), p. 231.
7. Carole Pateman, "Introduction: The Theoretical Subversiveness of Feminism," in Carole Pateman and Elizabeth Gross, eds., *Feminist Challenges: Social and Political Theory* (Boston: Northeastern University Press, 1987), p. 8.
8. Carole Pateman, *The Sexual Contract* (Stanford: Stanford University Press, 1988), p. 224.
9. Catharine MacKinnon, *Toward A Feminist Theory of the State* (Cambridge, MA: Harvard University Press, 1989), pp. 45–46.
10. Rachel Trubowitz, "Female Preachers and Male Wives," in James Holstun, ed., *Pamphlet Wars: Prose in the English Revolution* (London: Frank Cass, 1992), pp. 112–133; Diane Purkiss, "Producing the Voice, Consuming the Body:

Women Prophets of the Seventeenth Century," in Isobel Grundy and Susan Wiseman, eds., *Women, Writing, History: 1640–1740* (Athens, GA: University of Georgia Press, 1992), pp. 139–158; Hilary Hinds, *God's Englishwomen: Seventeenth-Century Radical Sectarian Writing and Feminist Criticism* (Manchester: Manchester University Press, 1996).

11. Catherine Belsey, *Critical Practice* (London: Routledge, 1988).
12. Louis Althusser, "Ideology and Ideological State Apparatuses," in *Lenin and Philosophy and Other Essays* (New York and London: Monthly Review Press, 1971), pp. 127–188, quote from pp. 180–181.
13. My thinking about the status of women and the feminine in medieval and early modern England has been influenced by a number of studies, including Sara Menelson and Patricia Crawford, *Women in Early Modern England* (Oxford: Clarendon Press, 1998); Patricia Crawford, "Attitudes to Menstruation in Seventeenth-Century England," *Past and Present* 91 (1981), 47–73; Patricia Crawford, "The Construction and Experience of Maternity in Seventeenth-Century England," in V. Fildes, ed., *Women as Mothers in Pre-Industrial England* (London: Routledge, 1990), pp. 3–38; Patricia Crawford, "Sexual Knowledge in England: 1500–1700," in Roy Porter and Mikulas Teich, eds., *Sexual Knowledge, Sexual Science: The History of Attitudes to Sexuality* (Cambridge: Cambridge University Press, 1994), pp. 82–106; Susan Amussen, *An Ordered Society: Gender and Class in Early Modern England* (Oxford: Basil Blackwell, 1988); Kate Aughterson, ed., *Renaissance Woman: Constructions of Femininity in England* (London; Routledge, 1995); Audrey Eccles, *Obstetrics and Gynecology in Tudor and Stuart England* (London: Croom Helm, 1982); Antonia Fraser, *The Weaker Vessel: Woman's Lot in Seventeenth-Century England* (London: Weidenfeld & Nicolson, 1984); Katherine Usher Henderson and Barbara McManus, *Half Humankind: Contexts and Texts of the Controversy about Women in England, 1540–1640* (Urbana: University of Illinois Press, 1985); Susanna Hull, *Chaste, Silent and Obedient: English Books for Women, 1475–1640* (San Marino: Huntington Library, 1982); Nancy Armstrong and Leonard Tennenhouse, eds., *The Ideology of Conduct: Essays on Literature and the History of Sexuality* (New York: Methuen, 1987); Ruth Kelso, *Doctrine for the Lady of the Renaissance* (Urbana: University of Illinois Press, 1956); J. Larson Klein, *Daughters, Wives and Widows: Writings by Men about Women and Marriage in England, 1500–1640* (Chicago: University of Chicago Press, 1992); Alan Macfarlane, *Marriage and Love in England. Modes of Reproduction, 1300–1800* (Oxford: Basil Blackwell, 1982); Mary Prior, *Women in English Society, 1500–1800* (London: Methuen, 1985); Hilda Smith, "Gynecology and Ideology in Seventeenth-Century England," in Berenice Carroll, ed., *Liberating Women's History: Theoretical and Critical Essays* (Urbana: University of Illinois Press), pp. 97–114; Lawrence Stone, *The Family, Sex and Marriage in England, 1500–1800* (London: Weidenfeld & Nicolson, 1977); Merry Wiesner, *Women and Gender in Early Modern Europe* (Cambridge: Cambridge University Press, 1993); Linda Woodbridge, *Women and the English Renaissance* (Chicago: University of Chicago Press, 1984).

14. Janet Biehl, "Ecofeminism and Deep Ecology," *Our Generation* 19, 2 (spring/summer 1988), p. 24.
15. William Perkins, *Discourse of the Damned Art of Witchcraft* (1608), p. 168.
16. *Letters in Honour of the Duchess of Newcastle*, p. 166, cited in Fraser, *Weaker Vessel*, p. 4.
17. W. R. Prest, "The Law and Women's Rights in Early Modern England," *Seventeenth Century* (6), 169–87, and C. Stopes, *British Freewomen: Their Historical Privileges* (London: Swan Sonnenschein, 1894).
18. See A. L. Erickson, *Women and Property in Early Modern England* (London: Routledge, 1994); W. Coster, "Purity and Puritanism: The Churching of Women 1500–1700," in W. Sheils *et al.*, eds., *Women in the Church*, Studies in Church History 27 (Oxford: Basil Blackwell, 1990), pp. 377–87; Martin Ingram, *Church Courts, Sex and Marriage in England 1570–1640* (Cambridge: Cambridge University Press, 1987); and Frances E. Dolan, *Dangerous Familiars* (Ithaca: Cornell University Press, 1994).
19. Naomi Miller, *Changing the Subject: Mary Wroth and the Figuration of Gender in Early Modern England* (Lexington: University Press of Kentucky, 1996). Miller quotes David Simpson who, she notes, "urges the importance of moving the ongoing debate about agency and subjectivity beyond the polarities of either 'self-empowerment' or 'total determination,' to engage increasingly with the 'difficult and perhaps indecisive registers of the middle range' " (p. 6).
20. See A. R. Jones, " 'Nets and Bridles': Early Modern Conduct Books and Sixteenth-Century Women's Lyrics," in Armstrong and Tennenhouse, *Ideology of Conduct*, pp. 39–72.
21. Anon., *The Lawes Resolution of Woman's Rights* (London, 1632), p. 144.
22. Naomi J. Miller, "Sovereign Subversions: Ruling Women in Jacobean England," in Amy Boesky and Mary Thomas Crane, eds., *Form and Reform in Renaissance England* (Newark: University of Delaware Press, 2000), pp. 247–267, quote from p. 247.
23. David Wootton, *Divine Right and Democracy* (Harmondsworth: Penguin, 1988), intro., pp. 41–77.
24. Martin Luther, *A Commentarie of Master Doctor Martin Luther upon the Epistle of St. Paul to the Galatians* (London: George Miller, 1644), p. 8.
25. John Calvin, *The Institution of Christian Religion*, trans. Thomas Norton (London, 1634), pp. 4–20.
26. James VI and I, "The Trew Law of Free Monarchies (1598)," in Wootton, *Divine Right and Democracy*, pp. 99–106.
27. William Kiffin, *The Confession of Faith of those Churches which are commonly (though falsely) called Anabaptists* (London, 1644).
28. John Lilburne, *The Free-mans Freedome Vindicated* (London, 1646), pp. 11–12.
29. Richard Overton, *An Arrow against all Tyrants* (London, 1646), pp. 3–4.
30. John Perrot, *A Wren and the Burning Bush* (London, 1660), p. 10. Edward Burrough, *An Alarm to All Flesh with an Invitation to the True Seeker, Forthwith to Flye . . . into the Life etc.* (London, 1660), pp. 7–8.
31. Anna Trapnel, *Report and Plea* (London, 1654), pp. A2–A3.

32. Gordon Schochet, "The Significant Sounds of Silence: The Absence of Women from the Political Thought of Sir Robert Filmer and John Locke (or, 'Why can't a woman be more like a man?')," in Hilda Smith, ed., *Women Writers and the Early Modern British Political Tradition* (Cambridge: Cambridge University Press, 1998), pp. 220–242, quote from p. 238.
33. Barbara Ritter Dailey, "The Visitation of Sarah Wight: Holy Carnival and the Revolution of the Saints in Civil War London," *Church History* 55, 4 (December 1986), 438–455.
34. Ibid., p. 439.
35. Mark Kishlansky, *A Monarchy Transformed: Britain 1603–1714* (Harmondsworth: Penguin, 1986), p. 41.
36. David Bevington and Peter Holbrook (eds.), introduction to *The Politics of the Stuart Court Masque* (Cambridge: Cambridge University Press, 1998), p. 5.
37. David Norbrook, *The Reformation of the Masque* (Manchester: Manchester University Press, 1984).
38. James Holstun, *Ehud's Dagger: Class Struggle in the English Revolution* (London: Verso, 2000), p. 285.
39. Jürgen Habermas, *The Structural Transformation of the Public Sphere*, trans. Thomas Burger and Frederick Lawrence (Cambridge, MA: MIT Press, 1991), p. 16.
40. Jerzy Limon, *The Masque of Stuart Culture* (Newark: University of Delaware Press, 1990), p. 71.
41. Lindley, *Court Masques*, pp. xi–xiv; Kogan, *Hieroglyphic King*, p. 196.
42. Habermas takes this quote from Carl Schmitt's *Verfassungslehre*, 3rd edn (Berlin, 1957), page number not cited.
43. Kevin Sharp, *Criticism and Compliment: The Politics of Literature in the England of Charles I* (Cambridge: Cambridge University Press, 1987), p. 199.
44. Carola Scott-Luckens, "The Broken Tabernacle: Bodily and Cosmic Paradigms in Henry Jessey's 1647 Soul-Narrative of Sarah Wight," unpublished essay, p. 10.
45. Jürgen Habermas, *Communication and the Evolution of Society* (Boston: Beacon, 1979). For a feminist critique of Habermas's formulation of the "generalized other," see Seyla Benhabib, "The Generalized and the Concrete Other: The Kohlberg–Gilligan Controversy and Feminist Theory," *Praxis International* 5, 4 (January 1986), 402 ff.
46. Jürgen Habermas, "Popular Sovereignty as Procedure," in James Bohman and William Rehg, eds., *Deliberative Democracy: Essays on Reason and Politics* (Cambridge, MA: MIT Press, 1997), pp. 35–68.
47. Reid Barbour, *Literature and Religious Culture in Seventeenth-Century England* (Cambridge University Press, 2002), p. 169.
48. Susanna Parr, "The Case of Susanna Parr," in Elspeth Graham, Hilary Hinds, Elaine Hobby, and Helen Wilcox, eds., *Her Own Life: Autobiographical Writings by Seventeenth-Century Englishwomen* (London: Routledge, 1989), pp. 101–115.

49. Sarah Wight, *A Wonderful Pleasant and Profitable Letter Written by Mrs. Sarah Wight, To a Friend, Expressing the Joy that is to be had in God in Great, Deep, Long, and Sore Afflictions* (London, 1650).
50. See, for example, Elizabeth I's proclamation, *Where in the Parliament holden at Westminster in the xxiiii. Yeere of the reigne of the late... King Henry the eight and By the Queene. A proclamation, inhibiting the execution of any exemplification of her Maiesties graunt of the penaltie of the statute for sowing of hempe and flaxe seed* (London: Christopher Barker, 1579).
51. Leonard Cantor, *The Changing English Countryside, 1400–1700* (London: Routledge & Kegan Paul, 1987), pp. 49–50.
52. Vera Camden, "Prophetic Discourse and the Voice of Protest: The Vindication of Anne Wentworth," *Man and Nature* (1989), 29–38, quotes from pp. 32 and 35.
53. Jennifer Nedelsky, "Law, Boundaries, and the Bounded Self," *Representations* 30 (spring 1990), quote from p. 168.
54. See the introductory notes to Anne Wentworth in Graham *et al.*, eds., *Her Own Life*, pp. 180–183.
55. Anne Wentworth, *A True account of Anne Wentworths being cruelly, unjustly and unchristianly dealt with* (London, 1676), p. 9.
56. Anne Wentworth, *A Vindication of Anne Wentworth, Tending to the better preparing of all People for her Larger Testimony, which is making ready for Publick View. Publishd According to the Will of God* (London, 1677).
57. L. Susan Brown, *The Politics of Individualism* (Montreal: Black Rose Books, 1993), p. 18.

5

Improving God's estate: pastoral servitude and the free market in the writings of Mary Cary

> Alas good ventrous youth,
> I love thy courage yet, and bold Empris,
> But here thy sword can do thee little stead,
> Farr other arms, and weapons must
> Be those that quell the might of hellish charms,
> He with his bare wand can unthred thy joints,
> And crumble all thy sinews.
>
> Comus (The Attendant Spirit habited like a Shepherd)

> And thus by their praiers, and by the word of their Testimony, Saints doe smite the earth
>
> Mary Cary, *Resurrection of the Witness*

> And as the winde bloweth where it listeth, though we see it not, so doth the spirit and God hath not tyed himself to give out his spirit to such particular men, and to no others, but to whom he pleases. He did not tie up the spirit of Prophesie in Law, neither to the Priests and Levites, nor the Prophets, nor the sons of the Prophets; but gave out of that spirit to Amos a Heards-man, and to others
>
> Mary Cary, *A Word in Season to the Kingdome of England*

The issue of toleration impinged upon the economic sphere of seventeenth-century England. Because the established church was underwritten by tithes, those who favored the separation of church from state often waged their battles through the language of property rights, asking such questions as who was and was not "entitled" by God to engage in the "labor" of ministering, and who was and was not obligated to pay for this service? In this chapter I argue that the writings of the Fifth Monarchist pamphleteer Mary Cary participated in efforts to articulate an "economy" of toleration that would permit "mechanic" men and women to preach.[1] Thus far, the two critics who have discussed Cary's writings in detail have tended to ally her with a "utopian socialist" practice and perspective on government and economic affairs. The first, Alfred Cohen, has criticized her for this, labeling her a "totalitarian."² The second and more recent, Jane Baston, is more celebratory of Cary's progressiveness.³ My discussion, however, while granting the presence of such "socialistic" elements in Cary's publications, will maintain that the rhetorics through which she opposed tithes and advocated the disestablishment of the state church may be just as accurately described as "protocapitalistic." For Cary, loosening the national church's monopoly on preaching and replacing it with a "free market" in ministerial labor offered the firmest guarantee of sustained access to the franchise for those traditionally forbidden to preach.

I suggest that, contrary to those who call Cary a socialist and hence a totalitarian, her writings insist that various forms of grass-roots communication, voluntary association, and persuasion through free preaching should supercede statism as the means by which revolutionary change was to come about. Ultimately, Cary's works imagined the "rule" or "ministry" of "militant saints" to be the sort of "warfare" that one wages with a pen, an Independent pulpit, and a printing press rather than with the regulation and centralization of a socialist state. Next, I will contend that Cary's arguments in favor of privatizing the ministry are couched in metaphors that only at times gesture towards the "radical socialist" idea that the franchise of preaching is a "commons" to which all should have access. Just as, if not more often, she represents preaching as a proto-Lockean form of the labor theory of property and of property-in-self to which all God's "servants" are entitled within a capitalist economy of enclosure, improvement, and ministerial wage labor. Overall, Cary's works reinforce the vision put forth by *Certain Quaeres*, the Fifth Monarchist petition of 1649, which imagined that Christ's kingdom would be established through voluntary association and nonviolence, that is, "by the spirit of Christ, calling and gathering people into families, churches and corporations, till they thus multiply exceedingly."⁴

THE SUBORDINATE'S PLOT

Cary, like the other women I have discussed, fashioned her speaking persona – and her political agenda – by carving out an alternative narrative from within a conservative discourse about a conventional domestic subordinate. Cary undertakes a surprisingly systematic and Sabrina-like revision of early modern discourses governing the figure of the "trusty servant." As a seamstress, Cary fell into this broadly defined category, but her motivation for this typological identification appears to be more political than autobiographical, for it is put to work on behalf of her calls for religious toleration. And because her enactment of servitude is intended to function as an "obedient" assertion of political power, it opens up new possibilities for the status of agency within the "servant's plot" which permeated a great number of early modern social, legal, and literary scripts.

As Fran Dolan has revealed, the early modern figure of the "trusty servant" was understood to be both a seemingly benign domestic figure as well as a "monstrous anomaly," part beast, part man, because he/she was both a stranger and a "familiar" within the household.[5] Depended upon yet subordinate, the servant straddled social categories and hence generated an enormous amount of anxiety. Both early modern literary texts and the transcripts of actual trials sought to enforce a certain plot which, as Dolan puts it, "articulates the fear that the other and the enemy might be the person who makes your fire, prepares your food, and lodges in your own [house]" (67). To curb this anxiety, a literary work such as Shakespeare's *The Tempest* stages a "plot" of "petty treason," that is, a social and legal narrative which likened a servant's disregard for his master's orders to an act of treason against the sovereign. *The Tempest*, writes Dolan, "represents [servants such as] Caliban and his fellow conspirators in order to trivialize and overmaster them; it grants them their own plot in order to subordinate it to a plot structure and a larger cultural narrative that diminish their significance and locate power and prestige elsewhere – in the master and his story" (69). As Dolan continues, actual trials such as that of the Earl of Castlehaven reinforce this plot. Castlehaven was tried for numerous sexual offenses, including sodomizing several of his servants and forcing one of them to rape his wife. While the court acknowledged the fact that the servants were the earl's victims, it also punished them for failing to disobey their master. Dolan writes: "[the] legal process resubordinates them [the servants] by interpreting them as agents rather than victims and punishing them for their complicity in their master's social and sexual inversions" (85). Thus, servants are granted the power of agency but only in a form that renders that agency subversive and even dangerous because it necessarily takes the form of disobedience.

Dolan notes that one act of resistance against the "subordinate's plot" of petty treason can be found in the play, *Arden of Faversham*. This text represents the narrative of petty treason as less containable and more problematic than does *The Tempest*, because in it "the subordinate plot does not know its place" (72). The play refuses to be the master's play and "instead plays out the multiple plots of the subordinates" (74). It "*acts out* petty treason," but it can only do so by scrambling the dramatic structure – and the social order it represents – which in "master plots" was maintained by the subordination of the subordinate's plot to the level of subplot. In *Arden* "the subordinates' plots are thus *the* plot." Dolan writes:

> As the lower-class characters and their numerous plots surge out of the substructure to take over the main structure (when they refuse to be subordinated), the play inherits from them an uneasily comic feel. The play moves outside of the genres that give shape to experience in its attempts to tell a true story about a local event, to represent life as confusing and generically mixed, and to describe the operations of Providence as disorganized and obscure. It questions the social order and dramatic forms that achieve cohesion by excluding or subordinating the story of petty treason. (77)

The play succeeds in granting to servants their own form of agency, a form different from that generated by and on behalf of the masters' interests. However, it achieves this goal by staging the very spectacle that champions of order feared: chaos and anarchy. The exercise of any sort of autonomy by underlings, so this argument went, inevitably resulted in social (and artistic) disorder.

The writings of Mary Cary offer another subversive appropriation and reinterpretation of the subordinate's plot. In fact, it is possible to suggest that early modern Protestants in general were understood by their contemporaries to have staged petty treason on a large scale. Early on in the Reformation, thinkers such as Calvin were forced to address the implicit threat that claims on behalf of a freedom of conscience were said to pose to traditional forms of "mastery." In his *Institution of Christian Religion*, Calvin tried to reassure his readers that "spiritual liberty may very well agree with civil bondage."[6] However, he also asserts that when magistrates overstep their legal bounds and encroach on the subject's religious freedom, then God "sometimes of his servants . . . raiseth up open avengers and furnisheth them with his commandment to take vengeance of their unjust government, and to deliver his people, many ways oppressed, out of miserable distress." He tries to blunt the impact of this undeniably subversive claim by adding that "though the correcting of unbridled government be the revengement of the Lord, let us not by and by think that it is committed to us to whom there is given no other commandment but to obey and suffer." However, he has also, however intentionally or unintentionally, provided a logic through which subsequent acts of disobedience could be defended as forms of servitude to God's higher law, as calls to "obey and suffer" God's commandments above those of earthly rulers. In this way, Protestantism opens up a form of resistance to the subordinate's plot that both differs from and, at points, overlaps with that performed by *Arden of Faversham*. Its emphasis upon direct, unmediated access to God's truths most certainly threatened certain forms of hierarchy and order. The individual's ability to interpret Scripture for him/herself and even to "preach" it to others was a form of agency that went beyond "obeying and suffering." However, by working within the discursive construct of a servant's obedience to God, the most lordly and superior of all masters, religious dissenters could represent their disordering of social conventions as a higher form of duty and bondage. They were simply obeying God's master plot and suffering his command to speak on his behalf. This unsettling rhetoric created an alternative version of the "subordinate's plot," one which reversed convention by casting ministers and magistrates in the role of unruly servants who refused to obey their master's demands that his other, truer servants be allowed to propagate his word. Intolerance on the part of England's church masters was made to function as the root of the violence and chaos that often accompanied calls for religious and political reform.

In mid-seventeenth-century England, John Saltmarsh's *Smoke in the Temple* enacts this third variation on the master–servant drama. In what might be described as an early "bill of rights," Saltmarsh states that "The liberty of the subject is that of soul as well as body, and that of soul more dear, precious, glorious: *the liberty wherein Christ hath made us free. Be not ye then the servants of men in the things of God.*"[7] For Saltmarsh, quite a lot of things fell within the rubric of "the things of God," including the liberties of speech, the press, and of course preaching. However, he contextualizes access to these traditionally denied privileges within the economy of order by exploiting the potential for religious freedom within biblical inscriptions of servitude. The exercise of these new forms of agency posed no threat to "order" because they were a product of God's will and mastery. Similarly, the author of *The Ancient Bounds* invoked the distinction drawn in Romans between social and political servitude on the one hand and religious servitude on the other, in order to demand freedom of conscience:

Who art thou, says the Apostle, *that judgest another man's servant?* (Rom. 14.4). Man in a natural or politic consideration, is the servant of men, of his prince, and the republic; but man in a religious consideration, is only the servant of God, and he stands or falls to his own master. He is the servant of men to their edification by holding forth his light and conscience before them; but he receives neither his law nor his judgement from man. God accepts perhaps whom man rejects.[8]

This passage both redefines the forms of servitude it wishes to retain and dispenses with those it does not. While conceding the claim that men are still to serve other men as well as their prince, it nonetheless moves to the conclusion that adherence to God's law – the true master – liberates believers, or God's servants, from the religious law of earthly masters. Yet it does so by redefining the liberty of preaching as devotional servitude, as meeting the needs of others by leading them to religious truth through "holding forth [one's] own light and conscience before them." As Michael Walzer argues, disobedience was ironically "reinforced by piety."[9] This formulation is at the root of later liberal models of individual liberty. As Locke would argue several decades later, individuals were free because they are "the servants of one sovereign master, sent into the world by his order and about his business."[10]

As a Fifth Monarchist, Mary Cary was in a particularly good position to represent toleration as a "greater servitude" to the true monarch, Christ, rather than to the flesh and blood pretenders to his throne. As B. S. Capp argues, while a group such as the Quakers contained a "high proportion of gentry, prosperous yeomen and rich tradesmen," the Fifth Monarchists attracted "the very bottom strata of society (excluding paupers), the labourers and servants, that is, apprentices and journeymen."[11] What is more, surviving church lists show that Fifth Monarchist groups, like sectarian churches in general, contained a large number of women. Not surprisingly, then, contemporaries claimed Fifth Monarchists were "the worst of men, the Scum, and very froth of baseness." Even the Fifth Monarchist leader Christopher Feake claimed that his "saints" were "a company of illiterate men and silly women"; likewise, Venner's Fifth Monarchist manifesto of 1661 refers to them as a "poor, obscure, illiterate group" (82). Members of the common classes saw millenarianism as a tool by which to typologically empower themselves through various figures from the Book of the Revelation, and to gain a voice for effecting social change by "looke[ing] for a temporal Kingdome" (43). Fifth Monarchists believed that Christ's return was imminent and that, as chosen saints, they would dispossess standing powers, take the reigns of authority into their own more capable hands, and await the return of the fifth and only true monarch, Christ. To be sure, as Capp says, such millenarian beliefs were not confined to Fifth Monarchists, rather, they were a surprisingly widespread phenomenon in this period, encompassing royalist thinkers as well as forming the "most striking and fundamental characteristic of the formal preaching [of the Presbyterians] before the Long Parliament" (38). However millenarian ideas were more apt to be deemed a threat to social and political order when they "passed down to the common people and were reshaped in accordance with the people's own and different hopes" (42). At times, Fifth Monarchists proclaimed that they would have an actual role to play in bringing about the fifth monarchy, a role that may have involved the taking up of arms. Their writings often exploited the one form of agency that the master's plot granted to "servants" – that of violence – by rehearsing disturbing scenarios from Revelations in their texts, and several Fifth Monarchists were also, of course, involved in actual political events that included public disturbances or threats thereof.[12] As a result, Fifth Monarchists gained a reputation for being an extreme fringe group that wished to violently overthrow any existing regime, be it Charles I's hereditary privilege or Cromwell's quasi-republican Protectorate, in order to willfully induce Christ to return to earth. They threatened, in other words, to undertake the subordinate's plot of petty treason against England, "God's estate." Capp concludes: "It becomes clear that the furore produced by the Fifth Monarchists in the seventeenth century sprang not from the fact that they held millenarian ideas, but that they developed a potent and dangerous synthesis in which these ideas became the justification for violent political action and sweeping social changes" (20). As Cohen argues, "That the ideas of the Fifth Monarchy Men add substance to the assertion that there is an ideological affinity between revolutionary chiliastic thinking and modern authoritarianism can be best seen from a study of the works of one of the popular writers of the movement, Mary Cary."[13]

Other scholars, however, speculate that seventeenth-century reports of subversive activities by Fifth Monarchists may have been exaggerated by authorities seeking their own rationale for using violence to suppress groups who questioned state authority. While praising Capp's groundbreaking history of the Fifth Monarchists, B. R. White contends that Capp's claim that an essential characteristic of the Fifth Monarchists was "the right and indeed the duty of taking arms to overthrow existing regimes and establish the millennium" must be tempered by the complicating fact that, as White writes, "the Fifth Monarchists were divided about when to use violence. Some of them were far from clear on the crucial point as to whether they should take any such initiative before the return of Christ."[14] In a study of the writings and religious associations of John Pendarves, the minister of the Baptist church that Elizabeth Poole joined after her excommunication from William Kiffin's congregation, White concludes that Pendarves cannot be found to have committed himself "to any programme of violence aimed at bringing in the Kingdom but rather to a summons to repentance and preparation for the coming of the Spirit in judgement and power to cleanse and invigorate the true people of God" (263). As Jane Baston has argued, Mary Cary deserves a similar second look. As I will detail here, Cary's arguments unquestionably at times exploit the menace and disruption embodied by transgressive servants. However, it is also important to observe that, in her writings, Cary is scrupulous about conveying a sense of order, both aesthetically and politically. She composes her texts according to the strictest plain-style emphasis upon argumentation through enumeration of reasons and points. And her visions propagate a different form of oppositional agency for the servant than the pathologized subversion staged by *Arden of Faversham* or even the other-worldly quietism offered by Pendarves. Most often, this agency involves calling for and enacting the forms of liberty that allowed her and other social subordinates to promulgate religious teachings. Saints should act, she insists, not through the use of force, because this is a form of agency that she herself actually associates with the need to protect and maintain state religion. Instead, saints should act through various forms of information dissemination within a free market of independent preaching and publication, including "preaching" through the very sort of voluntary and independent exegetical interpretation and argumentation that Cary strategically models through her own market-circulated texts. In fact, I suggest Cary's writings are meant to signal the aesthetic coherence and logical unity that, she contends, results from the agency deployed by the servant who, while subverting earthly prohibitions against something like female preaching, is in fact acting in accordance with God's command to propagate the word.

To represent the servant's agency that she both describes and performs as being necessary rather than antithetical to social order, Cary places her subversion of institutional hierarchies within the discursive economy of conventional master–servant relations. In *A Word in Season to the Kingdom of England. Or, A Precious Cordiall for a distempered Kingdom. Wherein are laid down things profitable and usefull for all, and offensive to none that love the Truth and Peace*, Cary, like the author of *The Ancient Bounds*, makes the following demand upon the men who "sit at the Sterne" of government:

Make no Laws for the consciences of [God's] people, nor suffer any to do it by any authority derived from you; for that were to take the Crown off the head of Jesus Christ, and put it on your own head; and those people that shall subject their consciences to those Lawes, Christ Jesus will say unto them, *In vain do you worship me observing for Doctrines the commandments of men*. O therefore beware how you subject your selves, or your people in spiritual worship to any rules, but those that Jesus Christ hath appointed.[15]

As stated, the servants who actually comprised membership of dissenting sects were often cast into the traditional role of the treasonous servant, seeking to violently overthrow the state. Cary, however, authorizes herself as a writer by casting herself in the role of a "mean servant" to Christ, one whose words are meant to bring peace to a land that is disordered (or, in her metaphor, violently ill) because *its leaders* are using violence to repress God's servants.

Cary builds upon the idea that England is an ailing society that needs to be cured of its violent "distemper" by advising her readers that her own published tract of political advice should be imbibed and digested as a restorative and medicinal "cordiall." She directs this cordial even more specifically to "those that are in highest Authority" in the hope that "the sweet and comfortable effects of it shall descend to all the members, the whole body, to the strengthening and heightening of it, & making of it famous among all the nations" (12). Through this device, she imagines a new form of agency for the servant, one that does two things simultaneously. It transforms servility into the more socially authoritative roles of physician, administering a cure to the head, and ultimately of head minister, counseling the head of the body politic on what political course to pursue on behalf of its citizens. And conversely, it converts the authoritative role of minister and counselor into the role of servant. The literary genre, if we may call it as such, of the cordial is a servant's discourse, one that fulfill's *The Ancient Bound's* claim that "in a religious consideration" servitude involves "edification by holding forth [one's] light and conscience" before others.[16] Serving a cordial to the "head" preserves the hierarchy of the body politic even as it represents a peaceful means by which an underling alters the social order in order to accrue new forms of authority. Cary retains a master plot by attributing mastery to God and inserting herself into that narrative as a Sabrina-like figure who administers a cure to others. But by emphasizing the primacy that Jesus's monarchical decrees for spiritual freedom are to have over any earthly king's desire for religious regulation, she can gesture towards a notion of providential order and design while claiming the right to preach and prophesy for herself and all other "mechanics."

In her next tract, *The Resurrection of the Witnesses*, published the next year, in 1648, Cary continues to rhetorically transform transgressive forms of religious agency into orderly forms of obedience to God, who, she argues, is the true agent of change.[17] In her preface, "To the Reader," she defines her own rhetorical purpose as strengthening "the faith of Saints" for believing that the return of Christ to earth and his installation of the fifth monarchy was truly at hand. As she adds, "the Lord hath already lifted up his Saints from under the vassalage of their enemies, and hath begunne to put the cup of trembling into the hands of them that afflicted them" (A7). In other words, the servants have already been freed by Christ, who comes to serve in their place. And the service that Christ performs is, of course, that of disestablishing the authorities. It might appear from the phrase "the cup of trembling" that Christ makes for a rather volatile, unpredictable, and even threatening servant, one who places a shaking and splashing cup into the nervous hands of the master. This "trembling" could signify a kind of menacing palsy that threatens to overturn the cup, spill its contents, and undo the orderly exchange. And yet it is also intelligible as a sign of the servant's conventional modes of humility, deference, and respect. Thus even as Cary appears to invoke the idea that a servant's agency is comprehensible only when it is equated with disorder, she also suggests that, when the humble Christ is doing the serving, political disestablishment is reconcilable with meekness. This is evident by the fact that Cary is visible here as a writer of this independent text, one which symbolizes her own humble attempt at serving through persuasion rather than violence. Cary continues this strategic play in a subsequent passage. Here, she addresses those

> who, look for farther judgements to come upon this Kingdome (wherein outwardly the Saints may suffer also), because of the great provoking sins of this Kingdom, as drunkenness, and adulteries, and oaths, and their entering into so many Covenants concerning religious things, for which they have no sufficient warrant, now in the times of the Gospel, and the oppressions of the poor, and meaner sorts of people, and the great neglect of doing justice generally, &c. (A6)

In this formulation, Cary appears again to threaten, implying that Christ – by way of his servants – will take his punishment out on everybody, including Fifth Monarchists, if they fail to obey his injunctions. She acknowledges that death and destruction would be warranted under the circumstances, saying "That it is true that if God should deal with this Nation, according to its demerits; then in deed no other could be expected, but an utter desolation of it, that it might either swim in bloud, or burn with fire untill it were consumed" (A6). At the same time, she follows this statement up with a declarative "But" and then lists the reasons why the odds against violence are slim, albeit not nil. God will hardly reign down terror upon his "Kingdom" since there are "thousands of righteous persons in London, and in all England a very great number" (A6–A7). What is more, it is the persecuting governors who are "wicked" rather than the servants themselves, thus it is the "masterplots" that God seeks to "contain." As she says, "And how many plots of wicked men, wherein they endeavoured the ruine of this Kingdome, hath God blasted? Having such a great number of his precious jewels in it."

Second, she writes that God would never destroy his enemies when he "can by his Covenant of Grace, bring many of them in to the obedience of Christ, and make them of persecutors to become eminent Saints, and call those his people that were not his people" (A7). In other words, the implementation of the Fifth Monarchy, rather than resulting in the violent destruction of the nonsaint, in actuality represents the time in which God will be most actively saving people through Grace. She herself writes, she says, in order to provide her needy readers with "encouragement, consolation, information, or quickening." She is, as she says, "Thy friend to serve thee – M. Cary" (A10). And indeed, in "The Preamble" she links herself to God's "angel" and "servant," John, who penned Revelation after "God gave it unto him, to shew unto his servants things which must shortly come to passe" (13). God chose such instruments as "Apostles, and Prophets, and Evangelists, and Pastors, and Teachers" not only because it was his "will" to do so but also "to shew his sovereignty over all his people; therefore he sends them about his work, they being all at his royall command" (14–15). The servant's duties of working and following commands are observed; however, the ends to which they are put may serve to displace the royal commands of earthly masters. That disobedience, however, is to take the specific form of preaching and printing and Cary's tract, again, enacts the kind of agency that she here describes. The main body of *The Resurrection of the Witness* is structured like a sermon and consists of two parts: "An Exposition upon Part of the Eleventh Chapter of the Revelation" and "An Application" of this chapter and verse. Cary has already exhorted her readers to understand this section of Revelation as an actual prophecy that is to be taken literally, and she repeats several times to them that they should understand truly that "The time is at hand" (30–31). At the same time, whenever the literal interpretation of this chapter implies that actual violence or destruction is to ensue, Cary goes out of her way to state that the Scripture is actually "mystically" rather than "materially spoken" (75).

For example, in her reading of Revelation chapter 11, verse 5, "And if any man will hurt them, fire proceedeth out of their mouth, and devourest their enemies," Cary claims that while it is indeed true that "The Saints in a sense, are the Judges and Executioners of their enemies" and that, as Revelation states, any man who hurts them will be devoured by fire, it is also the case that this fire actually symbolizes "that breath of the spirit that proceedeth out of their mouth, in their praiers" which "both pronounce the sentence and bring down the fire of wrath upon their enemies" (73). Prayer rather than arms is named as the weapon of choice. Thus she begins the next section with the caveat: "As the fire mentioned in the former verse, was not material fire, but it was mystically spoken," so the rain mentioned in chapter 11, verse 6 is not "materiall rain," but rather the "waters of the Spirit" that the wicked would lack "in the daies of their prophesie" (76–77). And the water that the enemies turned to blood is symbolically fulfilled by the "Spirit of prophesie" which the saints used to "hold forth the Testimony of Jesus Christ, in the purity of it all" and to overcome the corrupted waters of the "Romish Doctrines, and Popish Canons" (79). These Anglicans and Presbyters "gave forth, as equivalent unto the very dictates of the Spirit it self: and they declared them to be of as great authority, and of these waters they made all that did adhere to them to drinke: and with these waters they contented themselves, never caring for the waters of the Spirit" (79). However, this use of force is to be countered by nonviolent means: "And thus by their praiers, and by the word of their Testimony, Saints doe smite the earth" (81).

Prayer and testimony define active intervention on the part of those who would call themselves saints. This is true even when Cary appears to be calling for bloody warfare. As she next writes, according to Jesus's order, saints should "prophesie in a despicable, sad, and low condition, cloathed in sackcloth" for the dictated period of "a thousand two hundred and threescore years" (81). When one does the math, this means that "1664 should be the year wherein the Witnesses should finish giving Testimony, cloathed in sackcloth" (82). However, she notes that the Holy Ghost, having forgotten to add in leap year days, actually intended for the year 1645 to represent the expiration date for the sackcloth phase. And while 1645 marked the end of the days of prophesying and the beginning of the war between "the Beast" and "the Saints of Jesus Christ," this war is here denominated as "the late warre that hath been by him made in Ireland and England." The first round of civil war in England, in other words, had *already* fulfilled John's prophecies. These violent events, she claims, are the "earthquake" predicted by the Book of the Revelation (118). Thus they complete the vision of *The Resurrection of the Witness*, wherein the Roundhead army, thought to be dead and defeated in 1645, came back to life to claim victory for God's elect. The war was, of course, no "mystical" war and Cary here clearly sanctions the literal fire that emerged from the mouths of Roundhead guns and cannons. Interestingly, however, she does so after the fact in the same way that she withheld *The Little Horn's Doom and Downfall* from publication until after 1645 (the year when it most certainly could have

Pastoral servitude and the free market in Cary's writings 227

been read as an actual call to arms). By doing so, her tracts may be read as a call for peace. She writes:

For after the Army, which was for the Witnesses, stood upon their feet, in 1645, they so cast that power that men had over their consciences, and over their persons and estates for their conscience sake; as it was not possible for the Beast, nor any of his Adherents to recover that power again, over the consciences of the Saints in this Kingdome (though they did with all their strength, and greatest industry endeavour it afterwards) for the Witnesses then standing upon their feet; there was such an earth-quake, great Babylon was so shaken, as England fell from it; the yoke of bondage which was upon the conscience of Saints in England, was then cast off: And this was one effect of the great earth-quake, which there was in mysticall Babylon, at the resurrection of the Witnesses: that England fell from it. (107)

She does claim that there is still a "farre greater earth-quake" to come (113). This, she notes, will be the third of the "three woes" predicted in Revelation and, in the final section of her tract, she uses Scripture to predict the future of this conflict. Once again, however, she employs the "servant's logic" of both invoking the specter of actual petty treason and then displacing it onto God and calling for nonviolent methods of historical change.

In "The Application," Cary identifies a series of "Deductions" that, she argues, follow from her explication of Revelation. The first deduction is that the saints must expect to experience the "sufferings of saints worke" during the last phase of the implementation of the fifth monarchy in England. However, quoting Phillippians 1.28, Cary bids them "To be in nothing terrified by their adversaries; which is to them (saith he) an evident token of perdition, but to you of salvation, and that of God" (116). They have nothing to fear, she adds, because, as 2 Thessalonians 1.6 says, "It is (saith he) a righteous thing with God, to recompense tribulation unto them which trouble his Saints" (116). In the second deduction she writes that this recompense comes in the form, ironically, of God empowering "wicked men" so that they might afflict his saints and induce the apocalypse. She writes: "So that no enemy can rise up against the people of God; but it is of God, and God usually doth it, that he may pour out the fuller viols of wrath upon them" (116). Interestingly, however, she adds: "I say usually, it is so, but it is not alwaies so: for some enemies of Saints are sometimes chosen vessels, as Paul was: but ordinarily it is so, and so it shall be with the Beast: for both Babylon of old, and this mystical Babylon, after they had afflicted, and oppressed the people of God, so much as was before ordained, were appointed to take off the dregs of that cup of trembling, which they put into the hands of the people of God" (117). Here, Cary both annuls the specter of a violent overthrow of rulers by the saints and performs an interesting role reversal between master and servant. Whereas in the second phase of the fulfillment of the prophesy of Revelation, Christ had put the "cup of trembling" into the hands of those who had "afflicted" his saints, the third phase demands that the "cup of trembling" be put into the hands of the saints themselves, as they must now suffer at the hands of the wicked men assigned by God to afflict them as a sign of the impending fifth monarchy. But now the "wicked men," in afflicting the saints, have been cast into the role of "serving" them. The oppressors must not only place the cup into the hands of the saints, they must also "take off the dregs," the final step in the process of pouring and serving someone a cup of ale. Persecution, Cary argues, rather than being a sign that the servant is being put back into his/her "low" station, signifies instead the fact that the servant has been elevated to his/her proper high station, and that the punishment of petty treason signifies the end of the existing social order rather than its restoration.

At the same time, God will serve his afflicted saints by taking the cup from them and putting it back once again into the hands of those who have said to his saints, "Bowe down, that we may goe over." As God acknowledges (speaking through Cary's text in this section, Isaiah 51.21, 22, 23), "and thou hast laid thy body as the ground, and as the street to them that went over" (117). Whereas God had for "so long" allowed the saints to be walked over by their earthly masters, he now comes to "reward" the oppressors "double" for all the "cruelties" they have done to "the Saints." In the subordinate's plot, masters who subordinate unruly servants are said to have done God's bidding; here Cary envisions the "hellish reward" that awaits those masters who disobeyed *their master*, God, by illegitimately subordinating his true servants. In fact, while in the eighth deduction Cary warns of the "coals of fire" that will fall upon the heads of those who "wrong the Saints," her overall purpose in this section is to warn those in power to "beware how they offer any violence to any one of the Saints of God, either to their lives or liberties" (152). She presents political oppression as a subversive variation on the master's plot. In this narrative, it is the master's attempt at quelling the agency of the saints that results in social upheaval and in a kind of spiritual vacuity that she lists as the ninth deduction. She calls upon Parliament to renounce its power over the free exercise of religious conscience, saying:

O therefore, that in the consideration hereof you might at last lay down that imposing power, although thereby you may seem to lose, that honour that you seek from men, and to lose much of these outward things, the things of the world, which at best are but vanity: for it is far better to be without these, and have a good conscience, than to enjoy much of these, either with a troubled, or feared conscience, and a hardened heart. It is better to be at enmity with the Beast herein, and lose much of the world, then to enjoy abundance of the world, and soon after to perish with the Beast. (168)

In other words, rather than call on the army to institute a new religious hierarchy atop which the chosen saints of the Fifth Monarchists would sit alone, Cary calls upon members of the new Parliament to refrain from repeating the prescriptions that earlier had resulted in their own persecution:

Consider you what your condition was about seven or eight year ago; at what time you were trampled upon by the Bishops (which was a treading underfoot of the Beast). Call to mind how some of you were pilloried, and had your eares cropt and many of you imprisoned, and fined, and by severall other waies were persecuted, and troubled by the members of the Beast your adversaries. (169)

Instead, she exhorts them to remember that "you are all children of the same Father, and have all one Lord Jesus Christ, and have all one Spirit, and have all drank of one cup of affliction" and hence to "Unite, unite, unite!" (172).

She even asks them to love their "weak brethren" who "doe not know so much of the minde of God, in some circumstantial things as you (whether you be Presbyterians, Independents, or Anabaptists) conceive you do" (172). For though there may be "differences" in the "circumstances" of worship, she "could wish, that these distinctions of difference might be all laid aside, and that all that belong to Jesus Christ might only be called Saints, and the servants of Jesus Christ, and by such generall expressions as include them all" (173). And she ends by once again calling for the saints to commence with their "work": "Let them sing praises unto the most High in the morning, and shew forth his loving kindness and faithfulnesse in the nights" (194). In Cary's vision, God does work through his servants; however, while these servants are granted new forms of speaking and writing authority, their "agency" is also circumscribed at moments when we would expect it to be otherwise, especially when it comes to enacting social change through violence and new forms of domination. The servant's agency is construed in precise opposition to disorder. The subordinate's plot is both refuted and recuperated in her tracts, almost always in the name of limiting the ability of anyone to rule another. Undue mastery, not disobedient servitude, threatens providential design.

IMPROVING GOD'S ESTATE

Modern critics tend to equate servants' discourses with the subversion of emergent capitalism rather than with its perpetuation. Clement Hawes, for example, valorizes Cary as a practitioner of rhetorical "mania," which he defines not in psychological terms but rather as a class-based "discursive construct – a product indeed, not only of language, but of rhetoric, and, hence, of politics and ideology."[18] He defines this ideology as one that combined a working-class critique of hierarchy with a call for the disestablishment of all forms of property. However, while large portions of Cary's tracts simply call upon "servants" to preach in order to pave the way for (and enact) the advent of the fifth monarchy, she also, in *A Word in Season*, establishes the philosophical and protocapitalist economic foundations upon which subordinate classes may claim preaching as a "right" or "property" of which they cannot be deprived by England's magistrates.

As Laura Brace observes, one of the primary motivations for envisaging property in the mid-century was its relationship to the question of who "owned" religious faith, that is, who was, as a result, entitled to preach.[19] This was an economic as well as a political issue, because subjects were required to pay tithes to support the Anglican clergy and this tithe represented the economic "fact" that the clergy enjoyed a guaranteed monopoly over religious discourse. As a result, those who defended the idea of a state church and the tithes collected to maintain it did so within a complex matrix of both private and public property. Their major premise was that God was the supreme title-holder to the earth and that he was therefore entitled to all its increase. Subjects could never be proprietors themselves, but were understood to be simply "stewards" of or tenants upon his estate: "The earth being the Lords, and the fulnesse thereof, and the corn, Wine, Cattel, fruits and earthly creatures we possess, not really ours, but Gods own."[20] Everyone who worked did so with the understanding that they always owed God "rent" in the form of a tenth – or tithe – of all that they produced. Practically speaking, of course, tithes were turned over not to God but to the church, primarily as a maintenance fee for ministers. Thus, while tithes were in theory a rent owed to God, they were in practice a concrete embodiment of the idea that ministers were landlords with an indisputable claim upon a tenth of all that others produced. As Richard Culmer insisted, tithes represented his right as a minister to the "free peculiar estate" established by God for the maintenance of his estate.[21] They were, he insisted, "my Free-hold, my Propriety" (14).

Because tithes were "owned" by ministers in the same way that land was owned by landlords, they conferred upon their owners an established or permanent "interest" in the workings of the nation (which in their case meant the established church). In exchange, ministers, through preaching were said to turn this "freehold" into a kind of "commons" that was available to all their parishioners. One had only to attend the parish to which one was assigned geographically to sow and reap the benefits of this "gift." The interesting result of this complicated logic was that supporters of the state church could employ both a property-based defense of tithes as well as one that argued tithes had the force of law through custom. Tithes were a function of tradition, a part of the public life of the community; as one commentator claimed, they did *not* "rise out of any private mans Estate, but out of a publike patrimony, to which God is proprietor, and his Ministers are his pensioners."[22] As Brace argues, this was a delicate formula. "Tithes seemed to have become public property payable to a private landlord who was bound to take into account the public interests of his rent payers" (90). This meant that protithers could paint antitithers as threatening both property and the commons. For his part, Culmer argued that the abolition of tithes would lead to the extinction of property and the onset of "a Community."[23] At the same time, it was argued that those who refused to pay tithes were, for private gain, withholding something that customarily belonged to the community. To combat this latter argument, John Crook argued that tithes were *not* property and therefore ministers could not claim access to them by recourse to custom, because "Property is that which a man hath a just right to and interest in, without injury to another, and is derived to him, either by descent, purchase, or gift, *and not by custome onely*."[24]

Because debates over tithes were so intertwined with the institutions of land ownership, they were, during this period. increasingly infused with the language of enclosure and improvement that accompanied debates over property. Christopher Hill observes that Presbyterians such as William Prynne and other, more "bourgeois" Puritan groups adopted old Anglican defenses of tithes by drawing upon conservative analogies of property to authorize themselves as an elite ministry whose privileged access to the pulpit was protected by the state and perpetuated through the licensing mechanism of ordination. As Hill notes, the clergy signified their right to ministerial property through the figure of the hedge which, at the time, marked the enclosure and improvement of property. As a result, for Hill, "the struggle against . . . impropriated tithes, runs parallel to the struggle against enclosures, an attempt to recover communal wealth privately appropriated."[25] Hill's own analysis of the analogy of enclosure and the enforcement of a state religion culminates in a discussion of the Diggers' primitive communist critique of property. Their leader, Gerard Winstanley, saw tithes as a feature of the Norman yoke and foresaw a day when Christ, the "head Leveller," would cut all the hedges down.[26] However, as stated above, it was just as often ordained ministers and conservative commentators who put forth, as Brace says, "a much more trammeled and conditional vision of the ownership of faith related to a wider vision of community and order" while many religious radicals, including those of the ostensibly less "severer sects" as the Quakers, claimed recourse to their freedom of conscience as "a part of themselves, and as something which they owned absolutely and individually" (5). In other words, tithes were viewed by many religious Independents as a forcibly confiscated form of possessive individualism; thus, their interest in repealing them was done in order to protect a particular definition of property rather than to subvert property *per se*. As Robert Winter argued, tithes represented the theft of "the laws, liberties, and properties of the people of England."[27]

This shift in the understanding of tithes was accompanied by a transformation in the concept of property. Tithes were no longer a form of rent to which ministers were entitled by virtue of their inherited attachment to a freehold; rather, they derived from what Locke would later refer to as the labor theory of property. Locke wrote: "Though the Earth, and all inferior Creatures be common to all Men, yet every Man has a Property in his own Person. This no body has any Right to but himself. The Labour of his Body, and the Work of his Hands, we must say, are properly his."[28] Well in advance of Locke's formulation, antitithers often represented the collection of tithes as an unfair form of "engrossing" or stealing of the fruits that they owned through having "appropriated" them to himself through labor. Ministers, "like other Plunderers preserve [their] ill-got Goods by Force."[29] As stated, many tithe-payers were actual husbandmen who, within the current system, were quite literally forced to turn over a tenth of their produce to the state-sponsored clergy, whether or not they attended a state church. The 1644 act made it possible for clergymen to have their parishioners arrested or to confiscate some of their goods – often at several times their original rate – if tithes were withheld. Thus the "metaphor" of tithes as the fruits of one's labor was quite literally played out simultaneously within the church "economy" as well as within the actual market of agricultural work. However, all parishioners owed a tithe whether or not they were landholders, plus opponents of tithes often opposed this tax because they wanted workers of all trades to be able to serve as ministers in their own right, whether or not they were properly licensed to do so. As a result, the debate over tithes also had implications for other spheres of work, even though the metaphors used were drawn primarily from the traditional discourses of husbandry and the market in agricultural produce.

Religious independents who opposed tithes had hoped that Cromwell's new government would abolish them once and for all. However, while the Protectorate's Rump Parliament conceded the presence of the antitithe movement and granted that there was a debate to be had over whether or not, as Brace says, "property in impropriate tithes belonged by law to individuals or to the state," it ultimately concluded that "in principle . . . incumbents, rectors and impropriators 'had a legal property in tithes'" (29). Whereas the Protectorate government succeeded in reforming land taxes so as to deny the ability of landlords to shift their tax burden on to their tenants, the reassembled Rump "demonstrated their inability to agree upon an alternative form of maintenance by passing a stringent measure enabling vicars to recover their predial tithes" (29). They too did so within the discursive paradigm that positioned God as the owner of England's estate and they did so as part of the "Grand Instauration" movement which, throughout the 1650s, transferred the agriculture-based discourses of enclosure and improvement from practical discussions over land management to debates over a broad array of public policies. Grand Instaurationists took the high Puritan position that improvement was necessary for fulfilling God's intentions for man and earth. Linked to Genesis and the creation, God appeared as the husbandman who, as Brace says, "created the pattern for all subsequent improvement of chaos. He made all creatures, plants, fruits, trees and herbs serviceable to mankind who was expressly created to 'husbandize the fruits of the earth'" (68). Puritans who were newly enfranchised by Cromwell into such institutions as the ministry, the universities, and the government itself began to accompany these visions with actual plans – some carried out – for large-scale projects designed to convert wastelands and woods into fields and homes. These included such state-financed works programs as massive fen drainage as well as the implementation of universal education and a government-sponsored "Society for the Propagation of the Gospel." In this context, it is easy to see how the "private" discourse of improvement could be used to enforce and exact financing for large "public" ventures, both in terms of land use as well as various forms of social and religious policies, including resolving the "problem" of the poor by installing them in workhouses.

It is primarily these socialistic (Grand Instaurationist) schemes of wealth redistribution and poor relief with which critics such as Cohen (negatively) and Hawes and Baston (positively) associate Mary Cary. However, in *A Word in Season*, Cary actually attacks the ideological pillar upholding what she views as the already "socialized" state church and the economic system of tithes that financed it. And she does so by appropriating and revising one of the central tenets – and tropes – upon which that system was based – that of England as God's estate or vineyard – and putting it to work on behalf of a more free-market vision of the (ministerial) franchise. Cary wrote in 1647, years before most of the Quaker writings that Brace cites were published and at a time when there was still hope that Parliament would abolish tithes and the clergy that they sustained. While encased in the Grand Instaurationist rhetoric of national improvement, Cary's tract suggests that the proimprovement discourses of independent improvers could also be used to critique the nation-based improvement agendas of both the crown-supported Anglicans and the emerging Puritan Commonwealth, and to imagine an economy predicated more upon "private enterprise" and individual contracts.

Cary begins by subverting the equation that other seventeenth-century texts drew – and that Hill continues to draw – between the dissolution of the state church and the dissolution of enclosed and improved property. She takes her text from the fifth chapter of Isaiah, the original of which says:

Now will I sing to my well beloved a song of my beloved touching his vineyard. My well beloved hath a vineyard in a very fruitful hill: And he fenced it, and gathered out the stones thereof, and planted it with the choicest vine, and built a tower in the midst of it, and also made a wine-press therein: and he looked that it should bring forth grapes, and it brought forth wild grapes. (5.1–2)

In her own adapted version, Cary applies the vineyard metaphor from Isaiah to England's political situation by placing God in the role of the master of England's estate. She writes:

The great God, having wrought by his owne arme, great deliverance for this Kingdome of England, doth doubtless now expect that England should bring forth answerable fruit, when he had hedged and fenced his vineyard (Isa. 5) And bestowed choyce favours upon it, he looked (saith the text ver. 4) that it should bring forth grapes and it brought forth wilde grapes. (1)

As can be seen, Cary uses this Scripture to say that, while God is still the supreme title-holder to England's estate, his estate has failed to flourish under the regime of stewardship embodied in the national ministry. Again, while opponents of religious Independency argued that religious freedom wrought social disorder, Cary counters that it was, in fact, the intolerance practiced against religious Independent preachers by the ordained clergy and the magistrates that "brought forth wilde grapes" from God's "hedged and fenced" vineyard.

In terms of the metaphor of property, however, Cary departs from the social agenda often ascribed to a servant's script by critics such as Hill and Hawes. Even though God's original plans failed to materialize, Cary does not, as one might expect, voice the idea that property itself had failed as an institution. Had she followed Scripture, this *could* have, in fact, been her argument. In Isaiah 5.3–6, the enclosed estate's failure to bring forth cultivated as opposed to wild grapes leads the prophet to call for the leveling of hedges:

And now, O inhabitants of Jerusalem and men of Judah judge, I pray you, betwixt me and my vineyard . . . And now go to; I will tell you what I will do to my vineyard: I will take away the hedge thereof, and it shall be eaten up; and break down the wall thereof, and it shall be trodden down: And I will lay it waste: it shall not be pruned, nor digged; but there shall come up briers and thorns: I will also command the clouds that they rain no more upon it . . .

With this in mind, it is worth noting that 1647, the year in which Cary published this tract, was a year of harvest failure and this fact could have also lent itself well to the idea that enclosures should be razed rather than extended. However, Cary stops just short of drawing such a conclusion from Isaiah. Instead of arguing that the walls of God's failed vineyard should be destroyed and, presumably, replaced with a commons, she insists upon the continued viability of enclosure and improvement. Instead of giving God "just cause" to complain of his estate's demise, she counters:

But that it may not be so, let all the people, from the highest to the lowest, from the King that sits upon the Throne to him that sits upon the Dunghill; let Parliament, and Synod, Citie and Country, attend to the insuing discourse (and let it sinke deep into their spirits) which doth contain a Narration (wholly drawne from the Scriptures) of those paths which (a nation walking in them) will be the readiest way, and shortest cut to a happie and flourishing estate. (1)

In other words, the leveling of the hedges is out and further improvement is in: there are still paths to be cut if the estate is to flourish.

Cary blames the estate's deteriorated condition not on the institution of property itself, but on its mismanagement by the clergy, those corrupt stewards and "violent" men who participate in "the troubling, wronging, and oppressing the Saints of Jesus Christ" (1). The solution, however, is not, as Puritan Grand Instaurationists would have it, to replace one set of stewards (Anglicans) with another (Presbyterians). Rather, the path that must be cut consists of eradicating state-supported middle men altogether. To be sure, Cary asks the "public men" to whom she directs her text to act as steward figures in the stead of corrupt ministers, but unlike the expanded government powers that Grand Instaurationists and Presbyterian ministers imagined for themselves through the figure of the steward, Cary asks the rulers to use their power to first remove the corrupt stewards from the church and after that, to remove themselves as mediating stewards between God and his true "laborers."

Lastly, though there be many precious men abroad, that by your permission do preach the word, yet they are few in respect of the multitudes of people in the kingdome, that have none to preach unto them, and that cry for bread, but cannot have it: O therefore let it be far from you to stop the mouthes of any godley men, that have the gifts of speaking to edification, exhortation, and consolation! And though they have not all taken degrees in the schooles of men, yet if they have been good proficients in the schoole of Christ, if they be experienced Christians, let them be protected by your authoritie, in discharging their dutie, in improving their talents to their Masters use and the kingdomes good, for the harvest is great, but the labourers are few; therefore let not the labourers that God hath sent forth, be forbidden to worke in the Lords Vineyard, least the blood of those that perish be charged upon those that hinder these labourers. (7)

Whereas "public men" in a centralized system are empowered to "license" the trained clergy to manage the estate through preaching (and to fence it off from the untrained), Cary asks them to assume the role of deregulators and vigilant protectors of everyone's God-granted right or even "duty" to "labor" in this endeavor, regardless of whether or not they have acquired state-sanctioned qualifications. She envisions a world of independent producers and consumers, one in which each congregation would be free to employ the minister of its choice based upon its own preferences and needs. If the governors can "clear" the "paths" that obstruct this voluntarist market from developing, then a whole nation may walk in them. In other words, allowing individual churches to function independently of the government's centralized control over the religious "workplace" actually leads to the fulfillment of a "common good." A state-created worker shortage will be alleviated and the national estate allowed to prosper under the improving tutelage of its master, God.

While on the one hand it sounds as though Cary is calling for the dismantling of barriers (clearing a path so that all may labor in a commons), I suggest that she actually argues from within the logic of enclosure and improvement, not from without. She does so by predicating her argument on a labor theory of property, one in which individuals gain the right to preach because they labor to do so. By positioning God as the estate-owner and eliminating state-backed middlemen of all stripes, Cary is able to argue essentially that anyone who "labors" on God's behalf may stake out a claim to his/her own ministry. Indeed, Cary's own ministerial text is itself intended to embody both the increased effort needed to implement the improvements that she contends will finally help the estate to flourish, as well as the idea that anybody – not just officially ordained ministers – retains an "interest" in doing so through "preaching." Her title plays upon the metaphor of renewed cultivation in that it offers a word "*in season*" because the harvest of her own sustained labor is ripe and ready to be plucked. The pamphlet's main body itself consists of two lists: one of the "negative paths" which the strife-ridden, war-torn nation should abandon in its struggle to obtain "deliverance from God" if it wants to avoid "ruine," and another of the alternative "positive paths" which, she insists, the nation should carve out if it still hopes to "bring forth answerable fruit."

As I discussed earlier, Cary signs her text, "By the meanest of the Servants of Jesus Christ, M. Cary" and she imagines her work functioning as a cordial or "spirit." The spirit may be viewed as a product of God's vineyard and of her own labor therein. She "serves" it voluntarily, as an act of service or communion. And yet, she also has it in mind that she – as well as someone else – should pay for and profit from that service. As Cary's subtitle tells her readers, her cordial is one "Wherein are laid down things *profitable* and usefull for all, and offensive to none that love the Truth and Peace" (emphasis added). A discourse of "profit," as James R. Siemon argues, becomes, in this period, "synonymous with 'advancement,' that which 'nourishes every faculty' . . . and becomes thereby a proper end of property rather than a synonym for appropriation and violation of the moral economy."[30] The final line on her title page notes carefully, and in conjunction with her printer, that this tract, like the majority of penny pamphlets in circulation at the time, is "*to be sold* at the Black-spred Eagle at the West end of Pauls" (emphasis added). God gives Cary the spirit with which to write. Cary owns the fruit of her labor as a result of the effort that she put into its production; it is alienable to others through the marketplace of print; both the printer, R. W., who works for Giles Calvert, as well as the owners of the shop at the Black-spred Eagle at the West end of Pauls may expropriate its profits; and to whomever chooses to buy it, Cary might function as a self-styled prophet.

In this sense, the circulation of Cary's own text within the print market, as well as the metaphors of estate ownership and improvement that it utilizes, are analogous to two different but interrelated sets of material conditions of property and development that defined the time period in which Cary wrote. The first has to do with a dynamic that Leonard Cantor describes, one in which previously landless peasants could establish a right of occupation – or "interest" – simply by demarcating their territory through the visible signs of industry. The second has to do with the property-in-self that the wage laborer possesses and alienates within a market-based system. Cary builds her arguments around what she represents as the liberatory potential of both. In terms of the first, Cary's vision of laborers working to improve God's estate (and, by extension, their own plight) points to the gains that even some of the humblest of peasants accrued under the enclosure movement. As Joan Thirsk has argued, we need to revise the "crudest accounts" of enclosure movements that tend to define much of modern criticism. These accounts contend that, as Thirsk writes, "all over England men were enclosing their land and turning it into sheep pasture, because the wool of the sheep was more profitable to grow than any other produce on the farm. Enclosures were carried out with ruthless disregard for the rights and interests of the smaller farmers and cottagers, and were the cause of much misery and social unrest."[31] Instead, she argues, we need to understand that "enclosure took many different forms"; it was comprised of "agricultural diversity and regional specialization" and encompassed a much broader array of proponents from different classes than the bipolar model she attempts to displace. Likewise, Andrew McRae notes that the rhetoric of improvement emerged early on in the period as a "distinctive and coherent discourse" that subverted conventional socioeconomic and political hierarchies.[32] During the sixteenth century, improvement discourses touted the "house-father" landlord who was expected to supervise and enlighten estate management through his expertise in husbandry and estate improvements. Husbandry was, Brace claims, presented as "both gentlemanly and godly, and as an ideal which could also accumulate wealth" (48), however, the discourse began to shift from an emphasis on the role of the gentle husbandman exercising the authority of improvement over the individual estate and towards a "godly commonwealth" in which every individual was held to be socially responsible for (or possessive of the right to engage in) "collective" agricultural improvement. New publications argued that "even the lowliest husbandman has a duty to the commonwealth to improve the land and himself" (48), but this appeal to "duty" often concealed the aggressive pursuit of a "right" for everyone, including landless peasants, to enclose. As Leonard Cantor observes, while "prosperous merchants and farmers" did acquire land upon which to "establish parks and erect mansions," it was also the case that

During a time of growing population and land hunger, there were many landless peasants who built themselves huts and cleared pieces of land in the commons or woods, a little way away from the villages, encroachments which like those of today's squatters often attracted the opposition of the villagers. However, in the seventeenth century it seemed to be a common rule that a squatter could establish a right of occupation if he could build his cottage in the night and send out smoke from his chimney in the morning.[33]

And as Thirsk contends, in the seventeenth century, "when common pastures were enclosed, parcels were allotted to all who claimed common rights, including both cottagers and peasants holding strips in the open fields. In all cases, each man was master of his own piece of land, to hedge or fence it, and cultivate it as he pleased" (107).

One can imagine how easy it was for Grand Instaurationists to appropriate the discourse through which these material developments were propagated on behalf of the argument that, if "everyone" could become an improver, then "everyone" was obliged to contribute to institutionalized improvement projects for the benefit of all. According to Brace, Quakers were among the first to "develop" or appropriate the improver's discourse to a point where they could claim immunity from such state-backed forms of "improvement" as the continued maintenance of an ordained clergy by "cultivat[ing] a [discursive] landscape within which they could claim entitlement to their [own] faith and to their [own] property" (59). This vision accepted both the idea of God as the owner of the national estate as well as the necessity for improvement upon a national scale. However it imagined an entirely different mechanism for implementing it, one that involved the devolution of ministerial "improvement" and cultivation from the state-financed ministry to the autonomously Independent church and even to the "self." Cary, however, anticipates this argument. The physical artifact of her own pamphlet serves as the chimney smoke that signals her independent and self-proclaimed participation in the "improvement" of the nation's estate, as well as a labor-based entitlement to her own intellectual estate within the public sphere of publication and debate. Even her use of the term "paths" instead of "walls" or "hedges" may point to the more humble forms of enclosure and improvement undertaken by the emergent, self-proclaimed property owner. As Cantor writes: "Walls were sometimes used [for enclosure] but as these were costly they were mainly restricted to areas where freestone was locally available or to the gardens of richer yeomen and gentry . . . in many parts of the country, fields were bounded by earth banks, without hedge or wall" (47). (The fact that in her later tract, *Twelve Humble Proposals*, Cary quotes the counterintuitive language of Isaiah 58.12, which refers to the Lord as "The restorer of paths to dwell in," further suggests that she understands a path to be something that can demarcate and enclose rather than simply open and conjoin.[34])

By emphasizing the continued improvement of the (e)state over its dissolution, Cary's remedy for the problem of religious Independency departs even from that envisioned by other radicals, such as the "Ranter," Abiezer Coppe. Coppe also appropriated the metaphor of the vineyard on behalf of Independency, claiming that because ordained ministers trampled God's vineyard through, as Brace says, "abusing his servants and persecuting his saints and prophets" (50), then God would come to eliminate them, "the middlemen," and reclaim the vineyard for himself. As Coppe writes: "He will recover his Vineyard out of your hands, and what will you do in that day? (To dig I cannot, and to be I am ashamed)."[35] However, for Coppe, God's reclamation of the estate resulted in a vision of "improvement" through the lack thereof. In other words, God would provide all benefits without requiring anything in exchange. Laborers no longer had to engage in work itself, much less in wage labor under the tutelage of a corrupt steward. As Coppe puts it, "Here thou hast Wells which thou diggest not, houses which thou buildest not, vineyard and Olive yard which thou plantest not" (68). The goal, as Brace puts it, "was to rest and put an end to labour. Everything would be freely and directly provided by the Lord for his servants. Property relationships in the land of bondage had been straightforwardly exploitative and oppressive, and so were simply abolished in the land of the living Lord" (50).

Again, for Brace, it was the Quakers who are said to have "moved away from the Ranter ideal of rest and an end to labour" (52). They "objected to the self-interested misuse of certain sorts of power associated with property rights," but their resistance to tithes "was not, as many of their contemporaries suspected, a rejection of property itself," or, for that matter, of work (49). Rather, "they were protecting their vision of property from the vagaries of an arbitrary legal system" (49). In their writings, "the husbandman no longer appeared as an exploitative middleman but as the epitome of an honest labourer working for God to improve both his own soul and the state of the nation" (52). The Quakers saw themselves *as their own husbandmen* who "needed to rescue property from inaction and corruption and create a new vision of property as a civic virtue based on productivity and improvement" (49). But again, in advance of the Quakers, Cary articulated a version of this argument. Rather than putting an "end to labour," as Coppe envisions, Cary envisions an increase in, rather than a dissolution of the "work ethic," and whereas thinkers such as Martin Lluelling argued that "mechanic" preachers were "enclosure breakers" for the threat they posed to the clergy's customary entitlement to their parishioners' support through state-imposed tithes, Cary attacks tithes by undermining one definition of property – that which "entitles" clergy to a tenth of parishioners' earnings – while enforcing another – that which protects her and other religious Independents from having to turn over a portion of that which they own to pay tithes. In her list of the "negative paths" that the nation could take, should it choose, to "ruine," she includes the following:

In mine eares said the Lord of hosts, of a truth many houses shall be desolate, even great and faire, without inhabitant, when by unjust, and unreasonable wayes, men shall pluck away the lands, or estates, or detain the wages of the poor, and needy, or those that in comparison of themselves are in a meane condition, on purpose to feather their own nests, and to build them great and faire houses; it is the ready paths [sic] to destruction, and to leave their houses without inhabitants. (1)

While Cary defends England as the same sort of God-owned state articulated by those who defended tithes, she does not accept the idea that tithes were thereby the minister's property, nor does she call for an end of property itself. Instead, like the Quakers, she represents tithes as the appropriation of the property of others, and this includes the "lands, or estates, or . . . wages" of the poor.

This emphasis on wages as a form of property leads us to the second set of material conditions to which Cary's metaphor alludes – that of the rise of the wage laborer. As stated, antitithe narratives encompassed and perpetuated a shift in the definition of actual property rights. Prior to this period, "passive" rights were those that entitled one to a portion of the wealth produced by another's labor. Anglican clergy invoked their passive right to protect tithes but opponents rejected it and replaced it with one in which the property that one held in labor entitled one to an "interest" within the franchise of preaching.[36] Alternatively, by insisting on a "right" accrued through labor as opposed to one acquired through an a priori legal attachment to land (however indirect), Quakers could argue that anyone possessed the right to "acquire" and "sow" his own ministerial discourse. One ideological variant of – or corollary to – "enclosure," then, was the ability of everyman to hedge off the "fruits" that he himself had appropriated through work. This meant excluding them from the appropriating claims of any ministerial commons. Cary's objection also echoes the outcry that accompanied the punishment of those who withheld tithes. As stated above, the 1644 act allowed Parliament to confiscate crops and livestock from those who refused to pay tithes and even to imprison them. But, while Cary anticipates the

Quakers' property-based opposition to tithes, she differs from their agenda in a key way. Whereas the Quaker discourses of improvement center around the self-made yeoman (a reflection, perhaps, of the economic composition of their membership), Cary developed an "active" model of property which extended the land-based privilege of "interest" to those who had only the most tenuous connection to an actual piece of land – laborers. To do so, she utilizes not only metaphors that point to small-scale, independent enclosure and improvement, but also to the traditional contractual economy of the servant who negotiates directly with his/her master.

Cary spearheads this effort through the biblical herdsman, Amos. To those who wished to restrict the work of ministering to the national church's stewards, she writes:

Let it be far from you so to do, for then you do endeavour to quench the spirit: for though you do permit some to Preach Jesus Christ, yet if you do prohibit any from Preaching Jesus Christ you do quench the spirit and oppose the freeness of the spirit, who is a free Agent. And as the winde bloweth where it listeth, though we see it not, so doth the spirit and God hath not tyed himself to give out his spirit to such particular men, and to no other, but to whom he pleases. He did not tie up the spirit of Prophesie in Law, neither to the Priests and Levites, nor the Prophets, nor the sons of the Prophets; but gave out of that spirit to Amos a Heards-man, and to others ... (4–5)

As opposed to stewards whose privileges were linked to inherited land or to husbandmen whose privileges were linked to land acquired through labor, Amos is divorced from the land, a "free agent" – unmoored, like the wind. This language could harken back to the idea of Amos as a peasant who grazed his sheep upon the commons before enclosure. But the idea of free agency also links him with the agricultural servants and/or day laborers who worked for employers in exchange for wages. Shepherds especially were in great demand during this time as more and more lands were enclosed for the purpose of grazing sheep.[37]

In Amos 7.14–15, Amos recounts how, in spite of his lack of social status or official training in the school of prophecy, he was quite literally called from his rural labors in Tekoah by God to prophesy in Beth-el about Israel's fate during the oppressive and decadent reigns of Uzziah, the king of Judah, and Jeroboam, the king of Israel. As he says to his would-be oppressor, Amaziah, "I was no prophet, neither was I a prophet's son; but I was an herdsman and a gatherer of sycamore fruit: And the Lord took me as I followed the flock, and the Lord said unto me, Go, prophesy unto my people Israel." Amos's literal mobility – his role as a wandering herdsman as well as his social movement from servant to prophet – reminds us that Cary's rhetoric of "paths" might also function as a reference to the roads traveled by agricultural laborers. As Ann Kussmaul writes, "The mobility of farm servants set them apart from all others," and when the term for seasonal contracts ended, "the country roads swarmed with servants moving to new hirings."[38] Not unlike Cary herself, Amos used his newly acquired and God-given mobility to write his own book envisioning the immanent blessings of a restored Israel, the desired return of the Messiah, and the establishment of the fifth Messianic reign. And not unlike Cary's writings, Amos filled his writings with violently populist rhetoric that was spoken allegedly in the Lord's words rather than the author's and that forcefully suggested that a few changes should be made before Christ returned.

According to Cary, Amos's entitlement to preach stems not from a mediated stewardship over land or even from land acquisition through labor, but directly from that "spirit" which God has granted him and which cannot be taken away. Cary does not define "spirit" here, but soon after she links it to the monetary "talents" that, in the Book of Matthew, God grants to his laboring servants through individual contracts. This makes Amos an interesting alternative to both the idea of the steward who retains rights through his inheritance of a freehold, as well as the husbandman who retains them through acquiring land through labor. It allies him with the gardener in Shakespeare's *Richard II*, a character who for Siemon embodies this era's "'articulated combination' of feudalism and capitalism" ("Landlord not king," 17). In pursuit of the "stated aims of profit," defined elsewhere as "industry, thrift, individual discretion, efficiency and private property rights" (24), this gardener "labors rather than owns" (26). His "land-holding status is left totally undetermined" and

> [h]is authority derives specifically from "skill," from efficient management rather than from title of land or birth – the mainstays of feudalism's juridical-conditional structure ... What the gardener actually possesses is neither capitalism's absolute property in land nor feudalism's conditional right to land but the capital of skill in his occupation. (26)

This means that "his status by virtue of this possession is represented as manifestly more secure than that entailed in the inherited land" (27) and it accords with the "emergent values registered" in writings by William Perkins, an ardent Independent who argued that "an occupation is as good as land, because land may be lost; but skill and labour in a good occupation is profitable to the end, because it will help at neede, when in land all things faile" (27). Cary's Amos, as noted, is similarly imagined. Rather than doing away with property altogether, Cary locates the "interest" that it confers within the labor power that Amos the herdsman may alienate to his employer, God, through work. Doing so more strongly secures the poor's right to preach than does land ownership because it constitutes that right as a possession in and of itself. And while this is not an "absolutist" capitalist value of land ownership, it does operate in accordance with an emergent liberal notion of a "property-in-self" that is expressed through labor.

For many modern scholars, wage labor served only to further enrich the already prosperous rather than, as Cary may be suggesting, to draw upon its contractual nature to advance the "interests" of a class that was previously deemed to possess little to none. As Raymond Williams argues, agrarian texts during this period often put forth an "aristocratic version of spiritual husbandry" which achieved "the magical extraction of the curse of labour . . . by a simple extraction of the existence of labourers."[39] And while Christopher Hill describes and even celebrates the new forms of "liberation" enjoyed by the "masterless men" who roamed from job to job, he also maintains that wage labor was a "slavery" into which peasant men and women were "forced" by enclosure and the increasingly coercive power of the state.[40] Brace quotes approvingly those "opponents of enclosure" who "recognized" the fact that "the improvers' confidence that private wealth creation would automatically produce public benefits was misplaced and failed to take into account the creation of a landless proletariat" (81). And yet the "problem" with this landless proletariat was that, as one seventeenth-century nay-sayer whom she quotes put it, "it hardens mens hearts one against another: for, they make their little estate into a stock and so they get to some Market-Town, and either turn Usurers, Ale-house-keepers, or Maultsters, to no small hurt of the Commonwealth" (81). The assumption is that market towns, usury, and ale-houses were in fact repugnant because they represented new forms of class mobility. As Brace concludes, "Lack of property and a reliance on labour alone was seen as creating a lack of liberty and independence . . . Only the conjunction of land and labour could provide a basis for freedom" (75). Recently, however, Siemon observes that the very "word enclosure, like the hedges that embody it, functions during the period as an exemplary instance of the heteroglossic – an arena for the criss-crossing of disputed and competing values and orientations" (23). So, for example, an aristocratic landowner such as Sir Thomas Smith can be found defending "the common field system" against not only "the landed knight" but also against "the general will attributed to those actually working the land" (23).

Cary's rhetoric links her with those who viewed wage labor as something other than slavery. Not only does she not extract "laborers" from her discourse of improvement, she constructs them as a privileged and necessary component of improvement, a model class upon which to found her plea for a desired form of upward mobility, in this case, a universal access to preaching. What is more, as Kussmaul argues, the social and legal structures through which agricultural wage labor was more traditionally organized at this time lent themselves quite well to performing as the historical analogue for Cary's desire to forge a new "free market" in preaching. Agricultural service was by and large "a private institution, practiced within the farmer's family, defined not by law but by custom" (31). Contracts were verbal and flexible even as both sides had recourse to a public court of law set up to adjudicate complaints. And while wages had been fixed since the "de Servientibus" regulations of 1349 and the "Statute of Labourers" of 1350–51, and taxes on both parties were calculated accordingly, both sets of controls were increasingly felt to be ineffectual and unenforceable, and, as Kussmaul observes, it was not unheard of for courts to hear cases in which masters, competing for good workers, were found to be in violation of the law because they gave "wages in excess of the assessed rates" (36). Hill paints a vivid picture of the literal and class mobility that these arrangments allowed for, as "Beneath the surface stability of rural England" there moved a "seething mobility" of diverse peoples, including Separatists and itinerant preachers, moving "towards areas where labour was in demand."[41]

According to Kussmaul, the emphasis upon improvement only increased the demand for agricultural workers in the seventeenth century. While, in the first half of the century, population increases meant that landowners enjoyed a boom in cheap labor, these conditions were reversed in the second half of the century, largely because the improvement movement increased the demand for hired labor. Because enclosure led to changes in the "shape, size, and control of holdings," it was a "labour-using process" that involved the "creation and maintenance of the hedges and fences that separated newly enclosed holdings, and turned commons and waste into farms" (116). And because, as the last chapter has shown, improvement efforts spawned an interest in new crops such as flax as well as in innovative ways of raising old crops; it created more need for workers in hoeing, weeding, and harvesting. Neal Wood concurs, arguing that the fierce competition among small "capitalist farmers" led to the "growth of a rural wage-labor force and its increasing specialization, by the division between landowning and farming, and by the appearance of middlemen in the various stages of production prior to marketing."[42]

As stated, Cary appears to find value in drawing upon this already existing but still evolving narrative of master–servant market relations within the improver's discourse. In her vision, God appears to be more of a pressured yeoman whose eyes have been opened to the need for even more aggressive improvements and an increase in the labor force than he does either a genteel, aristocratic "ancient freeholder" of yore or a disillusioned encloser and would-be communitarian of Isaiah. For his part, Amos appears to be much more of a valued and compensated worker and a recognizably essential component of the forms of improvement that Cary envisions, rather than a "slave." As Cary writes, if her readers, like Amos, drive upon the positive rather than the "negative" path offered by her tract, then they, like him, will "surely reap the benefit of it, either internally, or externally, or both." The bump in the road is made out to be the interference of governors who impede the progress made, and the benefits shared, by the cooperative efforts of the would-be improver and his "laborers." Along with foregrounding rather than effacing the labor of the hired worker, Cary even alludes to the labor shortage that defined her period by proffering the idea that God's estate is failing because of the lack of pastoral laborers produced by laws protecting the clergy's monopoly over religious labor. If allowed to continue, this shortage will threaten the levels of productivity needed to feed those "that cry for bread, but cannot have it." As noted, the collective knowledge bank that Cary taps into is one wherein laboring to improve the enclosed estate was popularly associated with an increased demand for workers and for an increased production of food; the confluence of these two factors helped to decrease the numbers of periodic famines that were the result of the population boom. As Siemon argues, there is evidence to suggest that by the mid-sixteenth century enclosure and improvement were equated not simply with the oppressive displacement of those who had previously subsisted off farming the commons, but also with the increased production of "work" that allowed a whole new class of "workers" to emerge – and survive (24). While this emergence suppressed wages, it also increased food production and thus helped to increase the flow of much-needed foodstuffs throughout the entire economy. What is more, Reay argues that tithes were viewed as creating an actual "disincentive to tillage, and thus one of the causes of shortage of bread. They were a tax on yield which, it was argued, failed to take into consideration any expense or outlay involved in obtaining that yield. In real terms, in terms of profit, tithes amounted to far more than a tax of the defined one-tenth" ("Social Origins," 106).

Cary's text assumes the cultural vitality of such a perception that, if the estate is not made more efficient through continued improvements

Pastoral servitude and the free market in Cary's writings 247

enabled by the increase of more laborers in the work pool, and/or if tithes are not lifted so that husbandmen can retain more capital with which to improve the prospects for their harvests, then the country will continue to experience the periodic (spiritual and literal) hunger associated with a preimprovement subsistence economy. This may explain why, in 1647, the year of harvest failure, she calls for more rather than less improvement and for more rather than fewer wage laborers. The scriptural Amos, it must be noted here, is known for having cursed his oppressor, Amaziah, with the following prophecy: "Behold, the days come, saith the Lord God, that I will send a famine in the land, not a famine of bread, nor a thirst for water, but of hearing the words of the Lord" (8.11). If the potentially oppressing Amaziahs of her own day, Cary warns, do not refrain from obstructing their Amoses from performing their work on behalf of their church's "estate," then they too will preside over an era of continued ministerial labor shortages and hence (spiritual) famine. To prevent this, workers must be allowed to work on behalf of their improving master, "the great God, [who] . . . wrought by his owne arme great deliverance for this Kingdome of England."

Winstanley argued against wage labor because it prevented the laborer from claiming any rights to that which he appropriated from the land. Instead, he had to turn over that which he harvested to the landlord in exchange for a sum that was worth less than the market value of the produce. But rather than viewing this alienation of the worker's labor as problematic because expropriative, Cary views it as beneficial for both the "capitalist" and the "worker." While resisting the notion that the state-supported clergy retain the right to "expropriate" surplus value from the wages of workers by force, Cary does not do away with the notion of expropriation altogether. Rather, she shifts the right to expropriate to the great agrarian capitalist in the sky, God, who, it is assumed, would be embodied in the private congregation that hired the minister-servant. As I mentioned earlier, the enabling "spirit" that Amos derives from God is later linked by Cary to the "capital" that God grants to – and expropriates from – his laboring servants through individual contracts within the privatized economy of ministerial labor that takes place upon the nation's privatized and "enclosed" religious estate. In the list that comprises the positive paths to a flourishing estate, Cary's *Word* includes the following policy prescription:

Let it be far from you to hinder any, because every talent which the Lord Jesus hath given, he requires an improvement of it to his use; and it ought not to lie hid in a napkin, and therefore the Apostle saies, Every gift is given to profit withall. Now we know what the Lord said to him that did not imploy his tallent. Cast ye the unprofitable servants into utter darkness; there shall be weeping and gnashing of teeth, Math. 25.30. So fearfull is the doom of him that imployeth not his tallent: what then will become of those that shall forbid any to imploy their tallents? But, O be you wise, and as soon as you are Ordained of God to be, as for the punishment of evill doers, so for the praise of them that do well, so manifest your selves to be. (5)

Cary is referring, of course, to the Parable of the Talents from Matthew 25.14–30. As James Holstun has written, Christ's Parable of the Talents was "a favorite of Christian capitalists," thus it is interesting to explore Cary's use of it here.[43] In the parable, a lord, before departing on a journey, gives each of his three servants a custom-designed wage that corresponds "to every man according to his several ability." In the lord's absence, the servants go to work with their capital. The first parleys his five "talents" into a 100 percent windfall profit. The second does the same with his two talents but the third servant, who had received only one talent, declares it barely worth the effort. Instead of investing in trade, he withholds it from circulation by burying it. Upon the lord's return, the first two servants are declared to be "good and faithful." For the surplus they created, they are made "ruler over many things" and are granted grace: "Enter thou into the joy of the lord." The third, however, tries to reason with his lord in this way: "Lord, I knew thee that thou art an hard man, reaping where thou hast not sown, and gathering where thou hast not strawed." After delivering this critique accusing his master of the exploitation of the surplus value of his workers, the servant prepares to return the original talent to his lord. This is a fatal error. The master had, in fact, been interested both in profiting off the labor of others and in rewarding the laborer with a share in the economic gain. Thus, the lord replies,

Thou wicked and slothful servant, thou knewest that I reap where I sowed not, and gather where I have not strawed: Thou oughtest therefore to have put my money to the exchangers, and then at my coming I should have received mine own with usury. Take therefore the talent from him, and give it unto him which hath ten talents. For unto every one that hath shall be given, and he shall have abundance: but from him that hath not shall be taken away even that which he hath, And cast ye the unprofitable servant into outer darkness: there shall be weeping and gnashing of teeth.

As Brace notes, this passage was often cited by antienclosers to argue that "Men flattered themselves that their goods belonged to them absolutely, but they would find that their riches were not their unconditional property, but God's talents committed to them, to be employed to best advantage" (*Idea of Property*, 79). To show how tenuous the connection that Hill draws between support for enclosures and support for tithes actually was, this "socialistic" argument against enclosure was made on behalf of continuing support for tithes. Prophecy was, after all, a "gift" rather than a commodity and it was the ordained ministers who had been entrusted with the care of it. And yet, as the Quaker, Crook, had argued, tithes were not the "property" of the ordained clergy because one could not lay claim to something as property "by custom." Rather, property was the result of something being inherited, purchased, or received as a "gift." And Cary clearly appropriates this conceit on behalf of a different sort of economy: one in which the "gift" is given in the form of wages in exchange for labor already or still to be performed, and in which workers are then allowed to take that gift and "profit" from it themselves by parleying it through investment and usury into a greater amount than it was originally worth, both for their own benefit as well as their master's. (Locke, too, argued that, along with labor, one acquired property rights through gift, bequest, and exchange.[44]) Again, Cary finds liberatory potential within the act of expropriation, especially for those previously deemed to have been of little worth. God's expropriation of some of the surplus value of the Independent minister's labor is what allows that laborer and his/her labor to come into being as such. Without God's investment in individual laborers, the ministerial stewards would have maintained their monopolistic control over the franchise of preaching. By selling their labor to God (*vis-à-vis* one another), Cary's independents open up new markets for themselves as competing ministers within a free market of preaching.

In fact, the Parable of the Talents was also a staple feature of early modern defenses of usury. Christ, pro-usurers argued, saw in usury a working analogy for the usefulness of everyone's labor to God and hence to each other. Even those deemed to possess such little abilities that they were granted a correspondingly small sum to invest were nonetheless viewed as worthy of participating in such a way that, eventually, would increase their worth. Hence the equation seen earlier of laborers who were able to parley the small amount of capital they earned as agricultural wage laborers into a usury practice or the ownership of a tavern. As stated, Cary encases her argument for religious Independency in an "interarticulated" rhetoric of both gifts and "communion" on the one hand, and of profit and a desire for increase on the other. Also, as stated, she attacks the clergy as "middlemen" whose efforts serve only to impede rather than facilitate growth. However, this does not mean that she is against the very idea of mediation, of taking something given in exchange for something else and adding value to it by transferring it on to others in exchange for further compensation. As Wood argues, the new model of the improving yeoman was one that relied increasingly on wage labor as well as on "the appearance of middlemen in the various stages of production" (*Agrarian Capitalism*, 18). In her seventh deduction of *The Resurrection of the Witnesses*, Cary deploys another image that suggests her interest in the role of the value-adding usurer:

blessed and happy is the condition of Saints: for they have an *unction from the holy Ones*, they stand in the presence of the Lord of the whole earth. They are precious in the eies of God, and profitable to men: for they empty the golden oil, they have received from the holy one into others; the Spirit as it floweth from them, sometimes penetrates into those that are strangers, aliens to Jesus Christ, whereby they are brought home to the imbraces of Jesus Christ: and then Saints are excellent in their eyes also.[45]

Here, she positions saints as expropriators in order to prove their worth through the labor of negotiable mediation. "They are profitable to men" because they receive the "golden oil" from the estate owner/producer, God, and they then "empty it" as it "floweth from them" into "those that are strangers, aliens to Jesus Christ." The mechanic preacher adds value and gains agency through the transfer of healing balms from God to his consumers, just as the servant does through serving God's cordial to the governors.

These arguments invoke a voluntary and contractual model for religious labor that mirrors that of master–servant employment practices. Anyone might engage in this employment as long as someone else is willing to hire them for it – and expropriate from it. Nobody is forced to subsidize laborers they do not wish to have work for them, and God is not forced to manage his land according to the dictates of others. Specifically, unskilled workers shut out through the regulations of licensing *vis-à-vis* his consumers in the Independent congregations, or rather, who qualifies as "skilled" versus "unskilled," would be subject to individual determination. Finally, Amos does "appropriate" wealth from his work – the wealth of being able to preach at all rather than not. Cary defines his claim to do so as the "spirit" that God is privileged to give out to whomever he chooses but, almost tautologically, the individual laborer may also make that spirit as manifest as chimney smoke simply by laying a claim to it through the labor of preaching. Practically speaking, Cary is alluding to and attempting to legitimize a system of "itinerant preaching" that was already in place and operating just beneath the radar of government attempts to rout it out. In this system, the individual congregation served as the vehicle through which God's orders were conveyed, and those orders took the form of each congregation choosing for itself who to adhere to and who, consequently, to support out of pocket. The distinction between God and his congregation is elided so that the "middleman" ceases to be a "steward" in the conventional sense of the word, but rather serves as the unmediated conduit for God's will. These ministers could be – and sometimes were – in a very real sense wage laborers who worked on behalf of individual churches' autonomous estates, rather than as stewards of lords over a collectively held national freehold. While biased against this new freelance system of aggressive individual pursuit of new preaching opportunities, Thomas Edwards's *Gangraena* (1645) provides a glimpse into its operations when he writes that, unlike "we Ministers," Independents do not "sit still expecting a call to places," rather, "they are forward men, bestirring themselves to attain this place and that."[46] After "strongly labouring" to attain as many lecture slots in as many churches as possible (even, in the process, creating lecture nights where there previously were none, on Mondays for example), they then cast "an eye toward good pay; a Hundred pound a year for preaching once a week in one place, and Seventy pounds per annum for preaching once a fortnight at another, and a Peece for a Sermon as soon as they have done, and a good supper for another" (71). As Edwards concludes, "In a word, our Sectaries are become Pluralists, Nonresidents, and some of them Ubiquitaries, and are well paid for it" (72).

While there is no mention here of any women receiving wages for preaching, the fluidity of this system allowed women to style themselves as ministers simply by ministering to other women in childbirth or to their own children. Or, by participating in the open-ended group discussions and/or the dynamic "pros and cons" debates over particular Bible verses that, Edwards gripes, counted as a "ministry" within some congregations (93). Or by attracting crowds to their kitchens, parlors, and bedchambers to hear them preach and prophesy. As the cover illustration of *A Discovery of Six Women-Preachers* (1641) implies, opponents of Separatism mocked female dissenters for incorporating a "*company* of women preachers" (emphasis added).[47] And finally, it allowed someone like Cary who, as far as anyone can tell, was hired by exactly nobody to serve as their pastor, to nonetheless style herself as a "minister" through the print market.

The "spirit" through which she claims her right to do so may be once again linked to the idea of possessive individualism, whereby "Every man by nature being a King, Priest and Prophet in his owne naturall circuit and compasse," or as Grotius and Pufendorf would later put it, his "suum."[48] The abstract sphere of the personally embodied "suum," as opposed to the concrete sphere of a piece of land, entitled its owner to act as a priest and/or prophet within – or without – a gathered church. As Brace writes of this model: "Ownership rights were established as a result of individual action, and so could not be ordered on the basis of what others perceived society's role to be" (*Idea of Property*, 104). The many feminist critics who have consistently maintained that the interests of capitalism were antithetical to the interests of women have not yet explored the possible reasons why such a formulation as the Parable of the Talents was attractive to early modern women. This parable was utilized not only by a plebeian woman such as Cary, but also by the poet An Collins, as a way of quite literally advancing her worth as a cultural authority. Authors of conduct manuals claimed over and over, there was a fixed economy of gender values and, within that economy, women were in and of themselves worth nothing. They yielded something of value only after they had been sprinkled with a little male seed money. As Nathaniel Ward put it in his own tract decrying mechanic preaching, they were "a nothing, a nil, fitter to be kicked as to be listened to."[49] Thus, the idea that the Bible contained injunctions urging – insisting – that even those with little worth can – must – take part in a wage-based investment scheme that allowed them – *vis-à-vis* their "suum" – to parlay the "worth" bestowed upon them by the "seed money" of God into a greater sum appears to have caught women's attention. As Collins writes in her self-authorizing poem "The Discourse," those prone to "survey her works that worthlesse seem," should consider the following arguments, including one from Matthew 25.14–29:

> Next in respect of that I have receiv'd
> Is nothing to that some have, I do confesse,
> Yet he to whom one Tallent was bequeath'd,
> Was cald to strict account, nevertheless;
> As well as he that many did possess,
> From which I gather, they have no excuse,
> Which of ability will make no use.[50]

Even the seemingly "worthless" are worth something in God's market economy and must therefore be expected to "account" for themselves.

The argument that ministerial work was wage labor as opposed to the stewardship of a freehold appears to have been so effective that the clergy began to use it themselves and to argue that withholding tithes was akin to withholding their wages. However, opponents pointed out that the difference lay within the economic systems that buttressed each competing laborer's claim to garner pay. While antitithists held that ministers did not "own" tithes because husbandmen, themselves, had performed the work that produced them, they did concede that ministers owned their own ministerial labor and were entitled to the fruits thereof. Nonetheless, because ministers were part of a state-sponsored monopoly over religious work, their parishioners were akin to customers who were forced "to come to [their] Market-place and buy of [them], and none other."[51] Antitithists thus argued for a form of liberalizing the market over the fruits of God's harvest. The clergy's prices, so this argument went, were fixed rather than negotiable and customers were bound to pay, whether or not they were satisfied with – or even partook of – the produce. Were it not for government subsidies, these ministers would be less assured of business. Those who wished to hire them could do so, but they would face competition from anyone else who wished to open their own religious franchise in the oxymoronically conceptualized "appropriated commons" of God's England. What is more, antitithers implied, ministers just might have to go out and get a job to support themselves as preachers. (This as much as anything appears to have horrified the clergy. As Prynne insisted in *A Gospel Plea*, someone who had spent "sixteen or twenty years time and hard study day and night at their Books in schools, and Universities" should hardly be expected to work at a trade.[52] The antitithing Independents had supplied the nation with enough preaching cobblers and tinkers already.) The existing system controlled the available pool of workers to such a degree that there were no longer enough to go around. What is more, it was maintained through state-backed forms of coercion whereas the emerging one was sustained through the more private and multiple acts of individual negotiation between the "master" and his "laborers." To combat what she perceives to be the inadequacies and injustices of the status quo, Cary moves beyond the act of "appropriating" the existing model of wage labor for argumentative purposes. Instead, she argues that the religious labor economy itself should be even more fully shifted from a "Customary or status society" to a "possessive market" one. C. B. Macpherson identifies the four "essential properties" of a customary or status society as the following: (1) work is "authoritatively allocated to groups, ranks, classes, or persons" and this allocation is enforced by custom or law; (2) these groups or ranks of persons are confined to that type of work and are rewarded on a scale determined by the consensus of the community or by the ruling classes; (3) there is no "market" or "unconditional individual property" in land because the uses to which a given piece of land may be put are determined by the community or the state; and (4) the entire labor force is tied to the land or to the performance of assigned tasks or masters and is thus not at liberty to sell itself on an open market (because there is no such market).[53] In contrast, the possessive market society features the following eight postulates:

(1) work is not assigned "authoritatively"; (2) rewards are not allocated "authoritatively"; (3) contracts are authoritatively crafted and enforced; (4) each individual seeks "rationally to maximize their utilities"; (5) individuals own their labor and may sell or "alienate" it as they choose; (6) individuals own land and resources and may alienate them as they choose; (7) individuals often seek greater amounts or higher levels of "utilities" or power than they already possess; and (8) some individuals may possess more skills than others (54–55).

Cary's model in a *Word in Season*, while encased in the language of an estate-based status society and drawing on the customary reliance upon contracts between masters and servants, has much in common with the possessive market structure. The customary contract model still retained a number of status-like features, including the gendering of certain types of labor and the automatic rewarding of some tasks at higher rates than others. Cary, however, draws on the emergent discourse of improvement to argue that, as a landowner, God should be allowed to manage his estate according to his own design and that, as a part of this effort, he alone must be allowed to determine the number and qualifications of his workers, and workers are free to bargain for their worth on an individual or a group basis. Workers are among the prized capital of the landlord's increase and forbidding *anyone* to preach is akin to interfering with God's right to direct his worker's labor and to dispose of the agricultural products of his estate as he sees fit: "For he that toucheth them, toucheth the apple of Gods eye, and they are the props and pillars of a kingdom" (2). At the same time, workers may demonstrate worth through alternative channels to those prescribed by law. Cary attacks the very idea of status when she argues that, even though Independent "mechanic" ministers "have not all taken degrees in the schooles of men, yet if they have been good proficients in the schoole of Christ, if they be experienced Christians, O therefore let it be far from you to stop the mouthes of any godley men, that have the gifts of speaking to edification, exhortation, and consolation!" (2). And yet, as this same passage shows, she does not exclude the idea that some may be more "proficient" and "experienced" as well as endowed with greater "gifts" in the "school of Christ" than others. Nonetheless, it is important to stress that this disparity does not undermine the plea she makes to the rulers to permit and protect a relatively free ministerial market economy in which God's wishes are expressed through and within the voluntarist logic of individuals and individual congregations. To repeat her passage on Amos:

for though you do permit some to Preach Jesus Christ, yet if you do prohibit any from Preaching Jesus Christ, you do quench the spirit, and oppose the freeness of the spirit, who is a free Agent. And as the winde bloweth where it listeth, though we see it not, so doth the spirit, and God hath not himself to give out his spirit to such particular men, and to no other, but to whom he pleases. (5)

To the objection that this would mean permitting those to preach who might spread "errors," she counters with an argument that basically suggests, *caveat emptor*. "Not only learned men, but those that are learned and really Godly men, may account some circumstantial truths . . . to be errors, and some errors to be truths" (8). While she concedes that the "mouths" of those who preach in error should be "stopped," she goes on to argue at length that who is in error and who in truth is a determination that can only be decided by God on the day of judgment (7).

This formulation means that Cary actually develops a subjective theory of value. While she argues that one owns one's labor and hence can alienate it to a master, this does not lead her to contend that labor is, therefore, the factor that determines the actual value of the product. Rather, as Cary insists, there is no true "inherent" worth of something, or at least not one that is apparent to the consumer in this lifetime. Instead, the worth of a product lies within the consumer's willingness to purchase it. The consumer is the one to make this determination, not (fully) the laborer and not (fully) the capitalist expropriator. Were it otherwise, that is, were the product of ministerial discourse to be deemed to have a fixed value based on the amount of labor that went into it, then the state could step in – as it had in fact always done – and determine whose product was of greater or "true" worth and whose was not. In such a scenario, women's work would most certainly be counted among the worthless. This is why, I suggest, Cary insists that the governors not intervene to pick winners or losers but rather leave that up to the consumer to determine in the short run and for God to decide once and for all at the day of judgment.

In further keeping with an emphasis upon a possessive market economy is Cary's argument that the work of the ministry should not be apportioned "authoritatively" by official authorities. In *The Resurrection of the Witness*, she argues most strenuously against the idea of a centrally planned division of labor among ministerial workers, by calling for a deregulation of the monopolies currently granted to various church officers in the ordained clergy over specific forms of religious "work": evangelical, pastoral, and prophetical. Interestingly, she does so by first stating that God has made each of these a "common" work available to all, but this virtual commons disestablishes the government's ability to manage the market. Resisting the idea that God is a monopoly-granting governor who has "dispensed out the gift of prophesying to one, of teaching to another, of Apostleship to a third," she instead argues that he gave "all these gifts to one" so that everyone has the ability to perform any or even all of these forms of labor. At the same time, however, that she argues against a state-sanctioned division of labor, she also notes that God may grant one or more or all to any given individual based on that person's predisposition, thereby suggesting that a given person might specialize if s/he chooses. But no earthly master may determine who will exercise which gift or who has the aptitude for one or another; only God may make such determinations by way of the power he invests within individual congregations:

So that the reason why they are particularly spoken of, is, because that some Saints may be more eminently fitted for one of them, then for the rest; and not that they, that have one of these gifts, have only one of those gifts, and is utterly void of the rest, and this will be the more confirmed, and cleared by comparing this, with that passage, 1 Cor. 12.8, 9, 10. *For to one: is given by the Spirit the word of wisdom, to another the word of knowledge, by the same Spirit, to another faith, by the same Spirit, to another the gifts of healing, by the same Spirit, to another the workings of miracles, to another prophesie, to another discerning of Spirits, to another divers kinds of tongues, to another the interpretation of tongues.* Here the Apostle speaks of several gifts, and saith that one is given to one, and another to another and a third to a third, &c. And his meaning is, That one Saint is more eminent for one gift, and another for another, and not that he that had the word of wisdom, had no knowledge, nor no faith, &c . . . But now as some might be eminent in one of these gifts only; so some might be eminent for two, or three: and others might be eminent for them all. And those that were eminent for one only, could not be said to have none of the rest. (127–128)

The context in which this message is delivered is the current one in which a centralized religious economy "ordains" who is fit for what form of religious labor. In contrast, she argues, "Now for you to silence any that do preach Jesus Christ, of what rank soever, it is an endeavour to quiet the spirit: which the Lord grant you may not do" (5).

At another point, Cary synthesizes passages from 1 Peter 4.10 and 1 Corinthians 12.7 to state, "But Prophesying, and Evangelizing, and feeding, and teaching, and building up one another, was common to all in the Church, as every one had received the gifts for to minister, as good stewards of the Grace they had received! For their gifts are not given to be laid up in a napkin, *But the manifestation of the Spirit, is given to every one to profit withall*" (129). The metaphor of stewardship points again towards the language associated with the ordained clergy within the status society (that is, ministers are freeholders upon God's estate). However, Cary marshals that rhetoric here in order to enable members of the actual servant class to engage in forms of social activity and authority formerly unavailable to them and reserved only for licensed bishops, deacons, and pastors. In other words, even as she speaks the language of a commons and of preaching a gift, she alludes to a possessive market in which some individuals may "want a higher level of utilities or power than they have." As she continually states throughout this section of *Resurrection*, performing such work is not a form of disobedience but of loyal servitude. It is, she insists, "the duty of all the brethren, according to their severall abilities" (132) and allowing individuals the freedom to pursue one or more activities creates a spiritual network of multiple acts of exchange that result, as she puts it, not in anarchy or chaos, not in disobedience, but in "Communion among Saints" that "they may receive benefit from one another, as Christ hath appointed" (136).

The texts that Hill cites to support his equation of religious freedom with the destruction of enclosure are ones in which church discipline "was male, imposed by male elders. Bunyan thought that separate women's meetings would subvert male power (his word in the church). For his Bedford congregation discipline was the hedge; in *The Pilgrim's Progress* false pilgrims tried to get into the way by climbing over the wall."[54] As a female member of the lower orders, it would seem that Cary had more to gain from tearing down hedges than she did by erecting them. But Cary's *Word in Season* complicates Hill's argument as well as those of other modern critics who posit an absolute equation between the enclosure of land and the subordination of women *vis-à-vis* the trope of "husbandry." As Christina Malcomson has written in her study of Marvell, "The impulse of 'luxurious man' to enclose 'willing nature' and make it serve his interest is put in terms of the seduction and enslavement of women and the perversion of female sexuality."[55] The implication is that such early modern discourses on property and enclosure have pushed modern critics to argue that property and capitalism are, in fact, analogous to female subordination. The profusion of analogies between the enclosure of land and the sexual bondage of women within early modern discourses is certainly not to be ignored. And yet scholarship also needs to contend with a counterdiscourse such as Cary's. She appears to have been keenly interested in formulating definitions of property and markets that would protect her from what she arguably saw as a form of enclosure-breaking and property confiscation carried on by men against her. This included exacting tithes from her while at the same time stripping her of her own "right" to preach, which, she argues, she is entitled to as part of the wage-based "talents" she should receive in exchange for the labor she performs on behalf of God.

This may be one reason why Cary is so drawn to describing England as an enclosed estate in need of further improvement rather than as an estate awaiting the leveling of its hedges, and to describing preaching as a "labor" and a service rather than a "status" activity in need of a state-granted monopoly. And while the male shepherd, Amos, is her typological template, she is careful to stress the following to the governors:

Do not you enact any laws against any Saints exercising the gifts of the spirit, that are given to them in Preaching or prophesying: because the Lord hath promised in the latter dayes, to power out his spirit more abundantly upon all flesh, & your sons *and your daughters* shall prophesie: . . . Now what a sad thing would it be, if when god shall call forth some of his people to this great *worke*, any humane power should stand in opposition to it, and say, such and such men shall not do such a *work*. (6; emphasis added)

It is precisely certain formulations of ownership and exchange through the path-breaking work of labor that provide Cary with the opening she desires. England is God's, therefore no one has the right to extract the surplus of her work and to direct it to the maintenance of their own monopoly over religious labor. Instead, each servant is free to write individual contracts with God (*vis-à-vis* the congregation), to take their orders directly from him (them), and to work on behalf of anyone willing to listen. Anyone who interferes with that minister's "right to work" interferes with God's contractual relationship with his laborers. God's mastery over the estate quite literally allows for all "laborers" to retain the fruits of their labor (tithes) rather than handing them over to the "commons." For Cary, this system did not exclude women, rather it "hedged them in" and protected their right to enunciate their dissent.

Through the print market, Cary submits a counterdiscourse on enclosure, improvement, wage labor, and usury. Her metaphors reify new definitions of property even as they subvert old ones, in that they quite literally ask the governors to erect hedges between the sphere of the individual "suum" and their own power. Brace argues that writers of husbandry manuals, "like their modern commentators," viewed "the complications in moral attitudes which accompanied early modern economic change" as an opportunity to frame "explicit arguments that private ownership, self-interest and self-enrichment could be beneficial to the common good or the Commonwealth" (*Idea of Property*, 63). From Cary's perspective, arguments *against* "private ownership, self-interest, and self-enrichment" were deeply implicated within – indeed at times equivalent to – arguments against female preaching.

NOTES

1. Mary Cary's œuvre consists of *The Glorious Excellencie of the Spirit of Adoption* (London, 1645); *A Word in Season to the Kingdom of England. Or, A precious Cordiall for a distempered Kingdom* (London, 1647); *The Resurrection of the Witnesses. And England's fall from – the Mystical Babylon – Rome* (London, 1648; 2nd edn, 1653); *Little Horns Doom and Downfall; or a Scripture Prophesie of King James, and King Charles*, published with *A New and More Exact Mappe, or Description of New Jerusalem's Glory* (London, 1651); and *Twelve Humble Proposals to the Supreme Governours of the Three Nations now assembled at Westminster* (London, 1653).
2. Alfred Cohen, "The Fifth Monarchy Mind: Mary Cary," *Social Research* 31, 1 (1964), 195–213, quote from p. 205.
3. Jane Baston, "History, Prophecy, and Interpretation: Mary Cary and Fifth Monarchism," *Prose Studies* 21, 3 (December 1988), 1–18, quote from p. 6. Baston provides an extremely useful overview of Cary's life and place in mid-seventeenth-century Fifth Monarchist thought. Cary also receives substantial treatment in Kate Lilley, "Blazing Worlds: Seventeenth-Century Women's Utopian Writing," in Clare Brant and Diane Purkiss, eds., *Women, Texts and Histories 1575–1760* (London: Routledge, 1992). She is mentioned more briefly in Elaine Hobby, *Virtue of Necessity: English Women's Writing 1649–88* (London: Virago, 1988); Stevie Davies, *Unbridled Spirits: Women of the English Revolution, 1640–1660* (London: Women's Press, 1988); and Susan Wiseman, "Unsilent Instruments and the Devil's Cushions: Authority in Seventeenth-Century Women's Prophetic Discourse," in Isobel Armstrong, ed., *New Feminist Discourse: Critical Essays on Theories and Texts* (London: Routledge, 1992). She is also discussed in several different contexts in Hilary Hinds, *God's Englishwomen: Seventeenth-Century Radical Sectarian Writing and Feminist Criticism* (Manchester: Manchester University Press, 1996).
4. *Certain Quaeres* (London, 1649), p. 6.
5. Frances Dolan, *Dangerous Familiars: Representations of Domestic Crime in England 1550–1700* (Ithaca: Cornell University Press, 1994), p. 67.
6. John Calvin, *The Institution of Christian Religion* (London, 1634), p. 4:20.
7. John Saltmarsh, *Smoke in the Temple* (London, 1646), p. 68.
8. Anon., *The Ancient Bounds* (London, 1645).
9. Michael Walzer, *The Revolution of the Saints* (Cambridge, MA: Harvard University Press, 1982), p. 194.
10. John Locke, *Two Treatises of Government*, rev. edn, ed. Peter Laslett (New York: Mentor, 1965), p. 311.
11. B. S. Capp, *The Fifth Monarchy Men* (London: Faber & Faber, 1972), p. 82.
12. Louise Fargo Brown, *The Political Activities of the Baptists and Fifth Monarchy Men* (Washington, DC: American Historical Association, 1913).

13. Cohen, "Fifth Monarchy Mind," p. 199.
14. B. R. White, "John Pendarves, the Calvinistic Baptists and the Fifth Monarchy," *Baptist Quarterly* 25 (1974), 251–271, quote from p. 263.
15. Cary, *Word in Season*, p. 3.
16. Anon., *Ancient Bounds*.
17. Cary, *Resurrection of the Witnesses*.
18. Clement Hawes, *Mania and Literary Style: The Rhetoric of Enthusiasm from the Ranters to Christopher Smart* (Cambridge: Cambridge University Press, 1996), p. 28.
19. Laura Brace, *The Idea of Property in the Seventeenth-Century England* (Manchester: Manchester University Press, 1998), p. 5.
20. William Prynne, *A Gospel Plea for the Tithes and Setled Maintenance of the Ministers of the Gospel* (London, 1660), p. 109. As Brace notes in *The Idea of Property*, "the reference is probably to Leviticus 27:30–32" (p. 108).
21. Richard Culmer, *The Ministers Hue and Cry* (London, 1651), p. 10.
22. John Gauden, *The Case of Ministers Maintenance by Tithes* (London, 1653), p. 39.
23. Richard Culmer, *Lawles Tythe-Robbers Discovered* (London, 1655), p. 13.
24. John Crook. *Tithes No Property to, nor lawful Maintenance for, a Powerful Gospel Preaching Ministry* (London, 1659), p. 1.
25. Christopher Hill, *Puritanism and Revolution* (New York: St. Martin's Press, 1997), p. 175.
26. Christopher Hill, *Liberty against the Law: Some Seventeenth-Century Controversies* (Harmondsworth: Penguin, 1996), p. 292.
27. Barry Reay, "The Social Origins of Early Quakerism," *Journal of Interdisciplinary History* 2 (1980), 119.
28. Locke, *Two Treatises*, p. 329.
29. Sir Robert Howard, *The History of Religion* (1694), p. 326. See also Ambrose Rigge, *To All the Hireling Priests in England* (London, 1659).
30. James R. Siemon, "Landlord not King: Agrarian Change and Interarticulation," in Richard Burt and John Michael Archer, eds., *Enclosure Acts: Sexuality, Property, and Culture in Early Modern England* (Ithaca: Cornell University Press, 1994), pp. 17–33, quote from p. 23.
31. Joan Thirsk, "Tudor Enclosures," in Joel Hurstfield, ed., *The Tudors* (New York: St. Martin's Press, 1973), pp. 104–127, quote from p. 104.
32. Andrew McRae, "Husbandry Manuals and the Language of Agrarian Improvement," in Michael Leslie and Timothy Raylor, eds., *Culture and Cultivation in Early Modern England: Writing and the Land* (Leicester: Leicester University Press, 1992), pp. 35–62, quote from p. 37.
33. Leonard Cantor, *The Changing English Countryside, 1400–1700* (London: Routledge & Kegan Paul, 1987), p. 46.
34. Cary, *Twelve Humble Proposals*, p. 13.
35. Abiezer Coppe, "Some Sweet Sips, of Some Spirituall Wine," in Nigel Smith, ed., *A Collection of Ranter Writings* (London: Junction Books, 1983), p. 65.
36. Brace, *Idea of Property*, pp. 101–104.

37. C. B. Macpherson, *The Political Theory of Possessive Individualism* (Oxford: Oxford University Press, 1962), p. 282.
38. Ann Kussmaul, *Servants in Husbandry in Early Modern England* (Cambridge: Cambridge University Press, 1981), p. 49.
39. Raymond Williams, *The Country and the City* (St. Albans: Paladin, 1975), p. 45.
40. Christopher Hill, *The World Turned Upside Down* (Harmondsworth: Penguin, 1972), pp. 39–56.
41. Ibid., pp. 48–49.
42. Neal Wood, *John Locke and Agrarian Capitalism* (Berkeley: University of California Press, 1984), pp. 17–18.
43. James Holstun, *Ehud's Dagger: Class Struggle in the English Revolution* (London: Verso, 2000), p. 380.
44. Locke, *Two Treatises,* pp. 357–361.
45. Cary, *Resurrection of the Witnesses,* p. 150.
46. Thomas Edwards, *Gangraena* (London, 1645), p. 71.
47. Anon., *A Discovery of Six Women-Preachers, in Middlesex, Kent, Cambridge, and Salisbury* (London, 1641). The cover is a woodblock print, and depicts a woman preacher seated on a stool encircled by yet more women preachers who are performing on her the Baptist ceremony of laying on of hands. Interspersed among their heads is the sideways caption, "A company of women Preachers."
48. Hugo Grotius, *Of the Authority of the Highest Powers* (London, 1651) and Samuel Pufendorf, *On the Duties of Man as Citizen* (London, 1673).
49. Nathaniel Ward, "The Simple Cobbler of Aggawam," in Perry Miller and Thomas H. Johnson, eds., *The Puritans,* rev. edn (New York: Harper, 1963), vol. I, pp. 226–236, quote from p. 232.
50. An Collins, "The Discourse," in Sidney Gottlieb, ed., *Divine Songs and Meditacions* (Tempe: Medieval and Renaissance Texts and Studies, 1996), pp. 8–30.
51. Edward Burrough, *The Reign of the Whore Discovered* (London, 1659), p. 19.
52. Prynne, *Gospel Plea,* p. 31.
53. Macpherson, *Political Theory,* p. 49.
54. Christopher Hill, *The English Bible and the Seventeenth-Century Revolution* (Harmondsworth: Penguin, 1993), p. 149.
55. Christina Malcomson, "The Garden Enclosed/ The Woman Enclosed: Marvell and the Cavalier Poets," in Burt and Archer, *Enclosure Acts,* pp. 251–269, quote from p. 255.

Conclusion

> But now my task is smoothly done,
> I can fly, or I can run
> Quickly to the green earths end,
> Where the bow'd welkin slow doth bend,
> And from thence can soar as soon
> To the corners of the Moon.
> The Attendant Spirit, Comus

> There hath been too much despising and disdaining of me already
> Anne Wentworth, A Vindication

In a small group of sectarian women writers, liberalism finds its "mothers." Their formulation of such core liberal ideas as property-in-self, the separation of church from state, and a free marketplace devolved heteronomously from their expressed desire for liberty of conscience. Their private spheres of public performance were the kitchen, the birthing room, and the bedchamber, and the public stages upon which they performed their private selves included the prison cell, Whitehall, and Parliament, since, after all, their "suums" accompanied them wherever they went. Their ideological criticism of political domination took the "exclamatory" forms of visions of contractual relations between the subject and the body politic, pleas for freedom of religious conscience, vindications of the possessive individual, and words in season favoring a free market in preaching. Their rhetoric of reason was infused with the ostensibly competing, more literary languages of marriage, motherhood, midwifery, domestic and agricultural servitude, and religious devotion. Their protoliberal influences included the mythical – the Welsh goddess Sabrina – the biblical – Hannah, Jael, Christ, and Amos – and even the crypto-Catholic – the Virgin Mary, a penetrable self who was immaculately impregnated by the spirit alone.[1] (Even as Protestantism claimed to have purged itself of all things Catholic, the Marian precedent of effacing Joseph lurks behind the Protestant and then liberal emphasis on bypassing flesh-and-blood fathers.[2]) Their use of domestic identities and rhetorics as a language through which to articulate liberal precepts rewrote many of the scripts that were said to govern women's identities and lives, by fashioning speaking subjectivities that transcended limitations of class and gender while distancing their speakers from the stereotypes that saw "transgressive" women as criminals and murderers. Finally, as the above epigraph from Anne Wentworth suggests, their claims were often "despised" and "disdained" in their own time. Perhaps they need not be in ours.

As Jeremy Waldron has written, modern Lockian scholars, in considering the "methods and substance of the *First Treatise*," have to contend with the "strange and disconcerting" fact that they have legible "foundations" in Christianity and that, as a result, "the freedom and equality of the people of England – perhaps the freedom and equality of people everywhere – might turn on the precise meaning and accumulation of biblical verses about the kings, generals, and judges of Israel, the ancient patriarchs, the endowment of Noah, and the creation of Adam and Eve."[3] How much stranger and more disconcerting might it be to suggest that such things might also turn on the social and exegetical practices of a motley company of separatist women. Hopefully, their "Christian foundationalism" will not automatically prejudice the modern reader against at least listening to their arguments on behalf of foundationalism. Annabel Patterson has returned to John Lilburne's struggle for the right to a jury trial in order to offer the following:

what are sometimes referred to as natural or inalienable rights took a very long time to claim, and even longer to instantiate. It is even more important to remember that their successful instantiation in the United States depended on, in the causal sense, their having been claimed, and claimed unsuccessfully, in England, where for at least three centuries before the American Bill of Rights was articulated, the evidence of what new rights were necessary was painfully established by those who . . . were not agile enough to outwit the system.[4]

I find this statement to be quite plaintive, extremely relevant to the discussion at hand, and a fitting note upon which to end. While the religious dissenting women I have discussed were not always "agile" enough to outwit the system, their texts do survive somewhere in between total anonymity and recognizable "greatness" to tell alternative stories about women's relationship to a set of liberal ideas, which is increasingly believed to have developed in opposition to the interests of the female.

Thus, if I must offer any conclusive "moral" to the story of the writings I have analyzed here, it is to say simply that postmodern feminism can benefit from having recourse to a body of women's work that is as willing to interrogate such categories as "protection," "care," "the public good," and "the social context" as it is overly utopian schemes of the liberatory qualities of the private sphere and the individual. Texts by sectarian women suggest that a ruling order's bid to "protect" women from being "exploited" in a private sphere can mask a desire to discipline and punish said women for participating in traditionally forbidden activities within zones they themselves have demarcated as private so as to continue their "transgression." A recourse to "care" can take the form of forcing women to finance and/or submit to institutions that function by subordinating and pathologizing them. An insistence on *the* "public good" can be invoked to prevent women from capitalizing on a "private interest" that impinges upon the privilege that a powerful elite has accrued through state-granted monopolies and protections. Valorization of the "social context" over and above the individual can be utilized to suppress rather than foreground the fact that different women subscribe to different sets of values and desires and that these differences can define rather than defy an experience of liberation. Attempts to subvert "foundations" can erode the very base on which feminists and other minority voices rest their right to speak. In short, a feminist critique of liberalism can, however unwittingly, represent an assault on the exercise of prerogatives that were first articulated in part by women. This by no means places them beyond the reach of debate, but it does suggest that the terms on which that debate might take place could be reconfigured to address the concerns of liberalism's female avant-garde.

"A new feminism," argues Pamela Grande Jensen, "shares with contemporary feminism a desire to advocate women's interests by exploring their basis" but "departs from contemporary feminism by embracing the aims of liberal democracy" even as it "takes into account friendly modifications and ancient [liberal] alternatives" to the male liberal tradition.[5] It has been my aim in this book to demonstrate that the writings of sectarian women reveal such an agenda to be not a wholly "new feminism" but an old one to which we can also look for a not-so-ancient alternative as well as friendly modifications to and even a renewed set of rationales for liberalism. Sectarian women were invested in a sphere of privacy but did not allow that the private sphere within a liberal order consists simply of the unpaid performance of domestic drudgery and/or the serving of tea. Rather, they describe a liberal order that distinguishes between the public and the private in order to safeguard a subversive realm which teems with alternative and innovative social and economic practices. Sectarian women envision the individual as an end unto herself but do not take that to mean that the individual will never associate with other individuals or engage with them in any sort of collective enterprise. Rather, they posit possessive individualism as the philosophical ground upon which new types of voluntary associations and collective endeavors can form and function. At the same time, they maintain the individual as the base unit of society in order to protect themselves from slander and persecution when the community proves itself all too capable of marginalizing and demonizing their difference, self-proclaimed or imputed.

Paradoxically, then, a materialist feminist search for the relationship between early modern women's writing and the cultural conditions under which it was produced yields, in the case of sectarian women, materialism's allegedly "humanist" other – a transhistorical essence. While sectarian women appear to have agreed that "the subject" is produced within historically specific ideological formations that predate and therefore shape its experiences, they did not infer from this claim that there was as a result no such thing as an individual who had any claims to make other than those made on his/her behalf by something called the community. After all, "the community" is no more a "transhistorical" precept than the individual and no less a product of historically specific ideological formations which predate and therefore shape it as a category of interest. Thus, in the narrated experiences of sectarian women, denominating the communities that helped them to speak, while nonetheless preserving a gap between their selves and those same quixotic social worlds meant preserving themselves from what might have been an even greater silence.

NOTES

1. Violet O'Valle, "Milton's *Comus* and Welsh Oral Tradition," *Milton Studies* 18 (1983), 25–44.
2. See Achsah Guibbory, *Ceremony and Community from Herbert to Milton* (Cambridge: Cambridge University Press, 1998). "Though Protestantism, in its emphasis on the priesthood of all believers, could encourage spiritual equality for all men, it narrowed the possibilities for women's relation to the sacred in eliminating female models of devotion, as it prohibited adoration of the Virgin Mary and female saints and banned their images" (p. 168).
3. Jeremy Waldron, *God, Equality and Locke: Christian Foundations in Locke's Political Thought* (Cambridge: Cambridge University Press, 2002), p. 16.

4. Annabel Patterson, "Very Good Memories: Self-Defense and the Imagination of Legal Rights in Early Modern England," in Austin Sarat and Thomas R. Kearns, eds., *Legal Rights: Historical and Philosophical Perspectives* (Ann Arbor: University of Michigan Press, 1996), pp. 17–38, quote from p. 20.
5. Pamela Grande Jensen, ed., *Finding a New Feminism: Rethinking the Woman Question for Liberal Democracy* (Lanham: Rowman & Littlefield, 1996), p. 2.

Index

Abingdon church, 156
abstract individualism, 31–34 *see also* possessive individualism
Achinstein, Sharon, 7
Alarum of War Given to the Army, An (Poole), 116, 138, 156, 180
Allen, William, 140
Althusser, Louis, 170
Amos, Book of, 242–247
Amussen, Susan, 118–120
An(other) Alarum of War (Poole), 116, 157–160
Anabaptists, 4–7, 132, 144, 174
Ancient Bounds, The, 32, 38, 219, 223
Antinomian Controversy, 32, 37
Apology for Church Covenant, An (Mather), 39
Arden of Faversham, 217, 219, 222
Arrow against all Tyrants, An (Overton), 177–178
Astell, Mary, 46–47
Attaway, Mrs., 122
Avery, Elizabeth, 40, 41

Backscheider, Paula, 63, 65
Baille, Robert, 121
Baptists
  Confessions of Faith, 132, 137, 175
  Levellers' democratic platform and, 140
  Poole and counterromance of, 147
  privileges of, 137–139
  theory of popular sovereignty, 174
Barash, Carol, 46
Barbour, Reid, 191
Baston, Jane, 52, 216, 222, 233
Bauford, Joan, 121
Belsey, Catherine, 170
Benhabib, Seyla, 27
Biehl, Janet, 172, 173
Bilbrowe, Mary, 73
Boughen, Edward, 102
Brace, Laura
  on husbandry, 238, 240, 258
  on itinerant preachers, 251
  on Parable of the Talents, 248
  on Quakers, 239, 240
  on tithes, 230–233
  on wage labor, 244
Braithwaite, Richard, 67, 68
Brief Narrative of the Mysteries of State carried on by the Spanish Faction in England, A (anonymous), 141
Briefe Remonstrance, A (Kiffin), 136
Brod, Manfred, 135, 141, 155
Brothers of the Separation, 39, 70, 74–75
Brown, L. Susan, 28, 210
Brownist Haeresies Confuted, The (anonymous), 6
Brownist's Conventicle, The (anonymous), 41–43
Brownists Synagogue, The (anonymous), 41, 70, 71
Bunyan, John, 257
Burrough, Edward, 179

Calvin, John, 144, 175, 218
Camden, Vera, 50, 202
Cantor, Leonard, 200, 238, 239
Capp, B. S., 220, 221
Carew, Thomas, 62, 166, 186
Cary, Mary
  anticipates Quakers, 234, 239, 241
  enclosure and improvement and, 233–241
  Little Horn's Doom and Downfall, 226
  ministerial franchise and, 229–259
  Resurrection of Witnesses, 223–229, 250, 255
  socialism attributed to, 51, 52, 215–216
  subordinate's plot and, 222–229
  Twelve Humble Proposals, 239
  usury and, 249
  voluntary and contractual model for religious labor, 12–13, 250–258
  wage labor and, 241–249
  Word in Season to the Kingdom of England, 13, 222, 230, 233, 247, 257
Case, Thomas, 75

267

Castlehaven, Mervyn Touchet, Earl of, 217
Cavendish, Margaret, 47, 77, 123
   "The Contract," 116, 124–128, 130
Certain Observations upon Hosea (Kiffin), 133
Certain Quaeres (Fifth monarchists), 216
Chidley, Daniel, 76, 80
Chidley, Katherine, 11, 75–85
   answers Edwards, 77, 84–85
   divorce and contract theory, 123
   Good Counsell to the Petitioners for Presbyterian Government, 90
   Justification of the Independent Churches of Christ, 11, 75–85, 123
   as Leveller, 76, 81, 85
   Levellers influenced by, 86–92
   publications of, 75
   religious dissent of, 180
   use of Book of Judges, 79, 82–83
   use of Samuel 1, 78–82
Chidley, Samuel, 11, 76, 80, 81
   Cry against a Crying Sinne, 81
   Dissembling Scot set forth in his Colors, 81
   as Leveller, 76, 81, 85
   Separatists Answer to the Anabaptists Arguments Concerning Baptism, 81
   Thunder from the Throne of God against the Temple of Idols, 71
Clark, William, 139–146
Clifford, Anne, 77
Clinton, Lady Elizabeth, 38
Coelum Britannicum (Carew), 62, 166, 186
Cohen, Alfred, 51, 216, 221, 233
Cohn, Norman, 51
Coke, Sir Edward, 86
Coleman, Thomas, 74
Collins, An, 252
Confessions of Faith (Baptists), 132, 137, 175
Considerations Concerning Marriage (Reyner), 67
"Contract, The" (Cavendish), 116, 124–128, 130
contract theory
   Cavendish and, 124–130
   divorce and, 115–123
   Kiffin and counterromantics, 131–137
   as male construct, 25–31
   Poole and, 139–147
Coppe, Abiezer, 35, 240
Cox, Benjamin, 133
Crawford, Patricia
   on Baptists, 33, 138
   public versus private religion and, 68, 72, 74
   on sectarian women, 5, 35, 49
Cromwell, Oliver, 96, 100, 103–104, 140
Crook, John, 231, 249

Cry against a Crying Sinne, A (S. Chidley), 81
Cry of a Stone, The (Trapnel), 36, 93, 102–105
Culmer, Richard, 230

Dailey, Barbara Ritter, 183, 184, 189
Davies, Lady Eleanor, 4
Dell, William, 33, 151
Diggers, 231
Digges, Dudley, 117
Discovery of Six Women Preachers, A (anonymous), 72–73, 251
Discovery of Some Prodigious New Wandring Blazing Stars and Firebrands Styling Themselves as New-Lights (Prynne), 74
Dissembling Scot set forth in his Colors, The (S. Chidley), 81
divorce
   Baptists and, 139
   evolution from impossibility of
   Poole's redefinition of contract theory and, 146–155
   separatist churches and, 122–123
   Wentworth and, 207–208
Dix, William, 203
Doctrine and Discipline of Divorce, The (Milton), 120, 153
Dolan, Frances E., 45–46, 217–218
Donne, John, 191
Dykstal, Timothy, 65

Eaton, Samuel, 41
Edwards, Thomas, 6
   Baptists and, 132, 136, 138
   Chidley and, 77, 78, 84–85
   Gangraena, 74, 78, 132, 135, 136, 138, 251
   on itinerant preaching, 251
   on Kiffin, 133, 135
   Reasons against the Independent Government of Particular Congregations, 77, 83, 123
   on sectarian preaching, 5, 42, 74
   on sectarians and divorce, 122–123
Eisenstein, Zillah, 27
Elshtain, Jean Bethke, 64
enclosure and improvement
   Cary and, 233–241
   tithes and language of, 231–232
   see also wage labor
English Devil, or Cromwell and his Monstrous Witch Discover'd at Whitehall, The (Levellers), 141
English Gentlewoman, The (Braithwaite), 67, 68
Erbery, William, 44
Exceeding Riches of Grace Advanced by the Spirit of Grace, in an Empty Nothing Creature, The (Jessey), 12, 36, 167, 181–194, 198

Index 269

Feake, Christopher, 97, 220
Featley, Daniel, 7
Ferne, Henry, 117
Fiery Flying Roll, A (Coppe), 35
Fifth Monarchists, 4, 93, 220–222
    Cary's vision of, 225–229
    characteristics of, 220
    militarism attributed to, 220–222
    totalitarianism attributed to, 51–52
Filmer, Sir Robert, 26, 116, 118, 144, 150
flax, used as metaphor, 199–201
Flower of Friendship, The (Tilney), 67
Fox, Margaret Fell, 50
Fox Keller, Evelyn, 134, 135
Fraser, Nancy, 64
Free-man's Freedome Vindicated, The (Lilburne), 86, 176, 178

Galatians, Paul's Epistle to the, 144–145, 174
Gallagher, Catherine, 34, 47
Gangraena (Edwards), 74, 78, 132, 135, 136, 138, 251
Gardiner, Judith Kegan, 50
Gay, Hannah, 182
Gentles, Ian, 85, 87, 89
George, Margaret, 52
God
    as first husband, 134
    as source of self, 47–50
God and the King (Mocket), 25
God's Englishwomen (Hinds), 91
Good Counsell to the Petitioners for Presbyterian Government (K. Chidley), 90
Goodwin, John, 71
Gouge, William, 66, 149
Grand Instaurationists, 233, 235, 239

Habermas, Jürgen
    on absolute sovereignty, 131, 190
    on masque, 185–186
    on public versus private sphere, 44–45, 75, 93–95, 101
    Structural Transformation of the Public Sphere, 93
    on Trapnel, 94, 101
Hacker, Andrew, 13
Harris, Edward, 7
Harrison, Thomas, 142
Hawes, Clement, 52, 229, 233
Hempstall, Anne, 73
Hickes, Thomas, 203
Hill, Bridget, 46
Hill, Christopher, 52, 143, 231, 234, 244, 245, 257
Hinds, Hilary, 13, 91, 169

Hobbes, Thomas, 118
Hobby, Elaine, 53
Hogarde, Miles, 72
Holstun, James, 53, 63, 65, 185, 248
home-based churches
    religious independency and, 69–71
    Trapnel and, 99
    women's traditional role threatened by, 62–69
How, Samuel, 41
Hughes, Ann, 85, 86
Hutchinson, Anne, 32, 37

improvement, *see* enclosure and improvement
interpellation, 170
Ireton, Henry, 140, 146
Isaiah, Book of, 158, 234–235
itinerant preaching, 250

Jacob, Henry, 69–70, 72
Jacob Church, 5
Jacquette, Jane S., 28, 51
Jagger, Alison, 168
James I, king of England, 143, 150, 175
Jenney, William, 122
Jensen, Pamela Grande, 28, 29, 264
Jessey, Henry
    Exceeding Riches of Grace Advanced by the Spirit of Grace, in an Empty Nothing Creature, 12, 36, 167, 181–194, 198
    use of masque by, 185–191
Jones, Sarah, 9–11, 33, 39
Judges, Book of, 79, 82–83
Justification of the Independent Churches of Christ (K. Chidley), 11, 75–85, 123

Kahn, Victoria, 117, 124–125, 127, 129, 130
Kelly, Joan, 64
Kerber, Linda, 168
Kiffin, William
    Briefe Remonstrance, 136
    Certain Observations Upon Hosea, 133
    counterromantics and, 132–137
    on King and Parliament, 140
    Poole and, 8, 131–137, 155
Kilgour, Maggie, 135
Kishlansky, Mark, 140, 185
Kussmaul, Ann, 243, 245

labor theory of property, 232–233
Landes, Joan, 63
Lathrop, John, 5
Laud, Archbishop William, 4, 5
Legacy for Saints, A (Trapnel), 95

Levellers, 75
  advocate republican commonwealth, 140–142, 146
  Chidley's influence on, 86–92
  Chidleys as, 76, 81, 85
  on possessive individualism, 176–178
  right to petition and, 85–92
Lewalski, Barbara Keifer, 145
liberalism
  sectarian women writers and, 262–265
  seen as masculinist tradition, 25–31
Lilburne, John, 76
  Free-man's Freedome Vindicated, 86, 176, 178
  Poole and, 141
Limon, Jerzy, 186
Little Horn's Doom and Downfall (Cary), 226
Lluelling, Martin, 240
Locke, John, 3, 144, 150
  labor theory of property, 232, 249
  marriage and government, 118–119, 121
  Pateman on, 26–27
  possessive individualism, 178, 220
  Two Treatises of Government, 91–92, 207
Ludlow, Dorothy, 49, 71, 77, 85, 87, 91
Luther, Martin, 174

Mack, Phyllis, 34, 49, 78, 80, 82
MacKinnon, Catharine, 27, 64, 161, 169
Macpherson, C. B., 253
Malcomsen, Christina, 257
Mansell, Richard, 72
masculinist tradition, 25–31
Maske Presented at Ludlow Castle, A (Milton), 1–6, 62
masque
  Carew's *Coelum Britannicum*, 62, 166, 186
  Jessey's use of, 185–191
  Milton's *Maske Presented at Ludlow Castle*, 1–6, 62
Matchinske, Megan, 102–105
maternal agency, 32–39
Mather, Cotton, 145
Mather, Richard, 39
McEntee, Ann Marie, 85
McRae, Andrew, 238
Mendelson, Sara, 68
Miller, Naomi, 173
Milton, John
  Cavendish compared to, 125–128
  on Christian liberty, 32
  Doctrine and Discipline of Divorce, 120, 153
  Maske Presented at Ludlow Castle, 1–6, 62
  Tenure of Kings and Magistrates, 153
Mocket, Richard, 25, 116

Needham, Marchamont, 96
"New Lights," 68–69
Norbrook, David, 185

Of Domestic Duties (Gouge), 66
Overton, Richard, 177–179

Palmer, Herbert, 120
Parable of the Talents
  Cary's use of, 248–249
  usury and, 249
  women and, 252
Parker, Henry, 119
Parker, Patricia, 160
Parker, Thomas, 40, 41
Parr, Susanna, 192
Pateman, Carole, 25–27, 29–30, 65
  Jacquette on, 51
  on marriage and government, 117, 123, 150, 154
  on possessive individualism, 168
patriarchal political theory, 25–31
Patterson, Annabel, 263
Patton, Brian, 151
Pendarves, John, 155, 221
Pendarves, Thomasina, 156
Perkins, William, 172, 243
Perry, Ralph Barton, 85, 91, 92
Peter, Hugh, 11, 95
Phillips, Anne, 105
Poole, Elizabeth, 12, 123
  Alarum of War Given to the Army, 116, 138, 156, 180
  An(other) Alarum of War, 116, 157–160
  Baptist privileges and, 137–139
  contract and self-interest, 130
  Kiffin and, 8, 131–137
  possessive individualism and, 155–160, 171
  redefines contract theory, 146–155
  on the right to judge the sovereign, 139–146
  Vision Wherein is Manifested the Disease and Cure of the Kingdome, 12, 116, 139
Poole, Kristen, 31
Poole, Robert, 8, 135
Porterfield, Amanda, 32, 41
possessive individualism
  envisioned by sectarian women, 171–174, 180–181, 209, 262–265
  envisioned by sectarians, 174–180
  postfeminist scholars' interpretation of, 166–171, 173
  women denied, 171–174
  see also abstract individualism; Wentworth, Anne; Wight, Sarah
Powell, Vavasour, 95
Presbyterians, 231

Index

privacy, *see* public versus private spheres
property-in-self, *see* possessive individualism; wage labor
prophetesses, 40–43, 169
Prynne, William, 42, 74, 253
public versus private spheres, 43–45
   feminists on, 63–65
   home-based churches and, 66–75
   religious separatists and, 63, 65–66
   see also Chidley, Katherine; Levellers; Trapnel, Anna
Puritans, 102, 186, 233 *see also* Fifth Monarchists
Purkiss, Diane, 34, 36, 50, 169

Quakers
   Cary anticipates, 234, 239, 241
   improvement and, 239, 240
   on tithes, 241
   wage labor and, 241

Radzinowicz, Mary Ann, 11
Reasons against the Independent Government of Particular Congregations (Edwards), 77, 83, 123
Reay, Barry, 246
religious separatism, *see* Separatists
Report and Plea (Trapnel), 11–12, 93, 95–101, 180
Resurrection of the Witnesses, The (Cary), 223–229, 250, 255
Revelation, Book of, 225–227
Reyner, Edward, 67
Richard II (Shakespeare), 243
right of exit, 147
right to petition, 85–92
Rutherford, Samuel, 33

Saltmarsh, John, 40, 219
Samuel 1, Book of, 78–82
Sauer, Elizabeth, 50
Scheman, Naomi, 168, 169, 173
Schismatick Sifted, The (Vicars), 9, 74
Schochet, Gordon, 28, 94, 116, 118, 124
Schwoerer, Lois, 10
Scott-Luckens, Carola, 43, 188
Separatists, 3–8, 63
   abstract individualism and, 31–34
   divorce and, 122–123
   God as source of women's self, 47–50
   Kiffin and, 131–137
   maternal agency and, 32–39
   private sphere and, 43–45, 99
   prophecy and, 40–43
   public versus private spheres and, 63, 65–66
   voluntary association and, 35–40, 42
   see also home-based churches

Separatists Answer to the Anabaptists Arguments Concerning Baptism, The (S. Chidley), 81
servitude, *see* subordinate's plot
Sexby, Edward, 153
Shakespeare, William, 217, 243
Shanley, Mary Lyndon, 118, 121
Sharp, Kevin, 187
Siemon, James R., 237, 243, 244, 246
Simpson, Henry, 97
Smith, Henrie, 66, 68
Smith, Hilda, 46
Smith, Sir Thomas, 244
Smoke in the Temple (Saltmarsh), 219
socialism, 51–54
sovereign individual, *see* possessive individualism
Speght, Rachel, 145, 195
Spirit Moving in the Women Preachers, A (anonymous), 9, 69
Springborg, Patricia, 46
Stallybrass, Peter, 67
Stampe, William, 152
Structural Transformation of the Public Sphere, The (Habermas), 93
subordinate's plot
   Cary and, 222–229
   Fifth Monarchists and, 220–222
   Protestantism and, 218–220
   "trusty servant" figure, 217–218

Talmon, J. L., 51
Tempest, The (Shakespeare), 217
Tenure of Kings and Magistrates, The (Milton), 153
Thirsk, Joan, 238, 239
Thomas, Keith, 9, 33, 35, 43, 48
Thunder from the Throne of God against the Temple of Idols (S. Chidley), 71
Tilney, Edmund, 67
tithes
   Cary attacks, 241
   concept of property and, 232–233
   language of enclosure and, 231–232
   ministerial labor and, 252
   premise of, 230–231, 246
   see also Parable of the Talents
To Sions Lovers (Jones), 9–10
Tolmie, Murray, 69–70, 72
totalitarianism, 51
Trapnel, Anna, 11–12, 43, 75, 92–106
   Cry of a Stone, 36, 93, 102–105
   Habermas on, 94, 101
   Legacy for Saints, 95
   preaching of, 73, 95–101
   public versus private spheres, 101–106
   publications listed, 93
   Report and Plea, 11–12, 93, 95–101, 180

Trubowitz, Rachel, 78, 151, 169
True Account of Anne Wentworth being cruelly unjustly and unchristianly dealt with, A (Wentworth), 12, 203
Tub-preachers Overturn'd (anonymous), 68–69
Twelve Humble Proposals (Cary), 239
Two Treatises of Government (Locke), 91–92, 207

Vaughan, Edward, 182
Vaughan, Jonathan, 182
Venner, Thomas, 220
Vicars, John, 9, 74
Vindication of Anne Wentworth, A (Wentworth), 12, 206
virginity, doctrine of, 1–3
  Cavendish and, 127
  Poole and, 155–160
  Trapnel and, 96, 100
  Wentworth and, 205
  Wight and, 194
Vision Wherein is Manifested the Disease and Cure of the Kingdom, A (Poole), 12, 116, 139
voluntary association, 35–40, 42, 72

wage labor
  Cary and, 241–249
  itinerant preachers and, 250
  ministerial work as, 252
Waldron, Jeremy, 92, 263
Walzer, Michael, 37, 220
Ward, Nathaniel, 41, 252
Warnicke, Ruth, 44
Weil, Rachel, 25, 47, 93
Welde, Thomas, 37
Wendell, Susan, 28, 31

Wentworth, Anne, 37
  divorce and, 207–208
  illness and cure, 203
  persecution of, 202, 203
  possessive individualism and, 12, 31, 173, 202–210
  self-defense of, 204–210
  True Account, 12, 203
  Vindication of Anne Wentworth, 12, 206
White, B. R., 221
Wight, Mary Vaughan, 182
Wight, Sarah
  early life and crises of, 182–183
  formulation of sovereign self, 181, 183, 187, 194–202
  Jessey's portrayal of, 12, 36, 167, 181–194, 198
  possessive individualism and, 173
  preaching of, 43, 74, 184–185, 187, 192–194
  Wonderful Pleasant and Profitable Letter, 12, 181, 194–202
Wight, Thomas, 182
Williams, Edith M., 75
Williams, Raymond, 244
Wilson, Thomas, 11
Wiltenburg, Joy, 45
Winstanley, Gerard, 231, 247
Winter, Robert, 232
Wiseman, Sue, 78
Wonderful Pleasant and Profitable Letter, A (Wight), 12, 181, 194–202
Wood, Neal, 245, 249
Woodhouse, A. S. P., 75, 85
Wootton, David, 49, 174
Word in Season to the Kingdom of England, A (Cary), 13, 222, 230, 233, 247, 257

Zaret, David, 45